Exploring participation

11·95

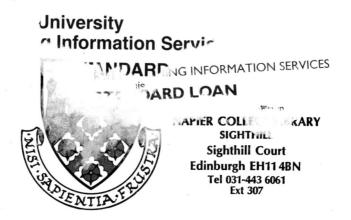

Exploring participation

Paul Bate and Iain Mangham
*Centre for the Study of Organizational
Change and Development,
University of Bath, Bath, Avon, UK*

JOHN WILEY & SONS
Chichester · New York · Brisbane · Toronto

British Library Cataloguing in Publication Data

Bate Paul
  Exploring participation.
  1. Employees' representation in management—
  Addresses, essays, lectures
  I. Title   II. Mangham, Iain Leslie
  658.31'52'08   HD5650   80-41415

  ISBN 0 471 27921 8

Typeset by Computacomp (UK) Ltd, Fort William, Scotland
Printed by The Pitman Press, Bath, Avon.

Contents

Acknowledgements

We would like to thank Addison-Wesley Publishers Limited for permission to use the extract from *Managing with People* by J. K. Fordyce and R. Weil in this book.

PROLOGUE

The hitch-hiker's guide to participation

This book covers some four years of our work with one organization which for the purposes of this record we have called Samuel Alpen Ltd. Under its real name, Alpen exists and flourishes somewhere in the British Isles, as do, under their real names, all of the characters represented in these pages. All of the events that we describe occurred, although our interpretation of them may be held to be idiosyncratic if not actually downright misleading by others who were party to them.

Our objective is to describe in some detail the day to day activities and interactions of managers, supervisors, workers, and consultants as they struggle to devise and implement participative approaches to decision-making in a large and sophisticated enterprise. We present the entire activity as a journey, a voyage of discovery, an exploration of uncharted territory, largely because the conceit appeals to us, but partly in an attempt to structure and organize our impressions.

Throughout we have attempted to avoid academic jargon; this may have resulted in some lack of precision but has, we trust, at the same time produced a much more readable account of our travels. Although not directly claiming to be in the entertainment business, we are not averse to giving others a good laugh, even if it is at our own expense. Nor are we above offering some instructions to those about to undertake a similar journey; he, or for that matter, she who also seeks the Golden City of Participation may garner many a tip, many a hint, and, occasionally, a direct injunction from these pages; we trust they will also learn a great deal about the difficulties of involving employees in decision-making. Lest we are seen to promise too much, may we hasten to add that we cannot offer the complete Michelin map of the territory; the best we can do is to mumble mystically that each must find his own path. We can, and do, offer some comments, however, on the contours of the land and the nature of the terrain likely to be encountered. It should be noted, however, that what we report is very much work in progress and that the direction of our progress remains unknown. In this respect we can offer no more than the sketchiest of maps of part of the strange country through which we have travelled.

A word about style is in order here before launching straight into the narrative. We take very seriously the point made by Johnson (1975) that: 'Idiosyncracies of person and circumstance are at the heart, not the periphery, of the scientific enterprise' and this book is an attempt to present what has actually happened to us on our journey from our position four or five years ago to the point we are at now. Our account, therefore, is messy, since the events and circumstances we found ourselves in were messy; despite massive temptation, we have eschewed the example of many in the field and have not provided a textbook case of social psychological research. Let us be clear, since experience has taught us that an enterprise such as the one we are embarking upon is liable to misunderstanding. We are not claiming that other approaches to the recording of field activities are invalid. On the contrary, many present splendidly systematic analytic accounts of how research was done and ought to be done. Such accounts, however, do not accord with our experience on this occasion (nor, to be honest, on any other occasion, but the fault may lie with us rather than the method), so we have decided to set down what we saw to be happening in the form of a narrative with occasional comment. In the final chapter, we consider the impact of the experience on our ideas and ourselves (in so far as the two are separable) in some detail, but come to few conclusions since, as we have mentioned, we consider the present volume to be an interim rather than a final statement.

By way of acknowledgement, we warmly record our thanks for assistance to a number of our colleagues; particularly to Bob Westwood, Bryan Johnson, and Tony Murphy who helped us at Alpen and whose conversations over the years inform much of what we have written; to the many employees at Alpen who have enriched our thoughts beyond measure in the months and years we have spent with them; to Dr Albert Natchkirk and Professor Edith Warmbody who read and commented upon the manuscript; and to Joan Budge who typed and retyped drafts of it, performing legendary feats of interpretation in so doing—a truly creative activity. Finally, as always, to our wives and families—Wendy, Olive, Catriona, and Alasdair—who have given us the time and space not only to make dozens of journeys to Towcester, but also to complete this record of our experiences.

SPB/ILM

Bath, June 1980

| **Scene** | A large chemical factory somewhere in the Midlands |

Scene   A large chemical factory somewhere in the Midlands

Time   1975 to the present day

Cast   (a) *At Alpen Industries*

Ken Stevenson,* Managing Director, succeeded by Tony Harris*
Eric Campbell,*†‡ Personnel Manager
Simon Teffler,*† Director of Pharmaceutical Production
Charles, Manager, Production Services
Mark, Senior Manager responsible for canteen arrangements
George and Tim, Directors

The Steering Group originally consisted of Ken Stevenson (Managing
Director), the Production Director, the Personnel Director, Eric
Campbell (Personnel Manager), Frank Anderson (Chemical Plant
Manager), and Iain and Paul from Bath

Chemical Plant	*Packaging*
Frank Anderson,* Manager	Michael,† Head of Packaging Operations
Tom Croker,* Section Head	Bert, Section Head
Ray Baker,* Supervisor	Ernie, Section Head
Huw Perrett*	Fred,† Section Head
Trevor Pascoe*	Ron Brass,† Section Supervisor
Jack Vincent*	Arthur, Section Supervisor
Al Hamilton*	Shirley† (Chargehand)
Josh	Ethel† (Chargehand)
	Mary†
Dry Products	Charlie†
Kingsley,‡ Head of Department	Maggie†
Roger,‡ Section Head	Joan†
Frank, Section Head	Margaret†
Dave,‡ Supervisor	Sheila†
Becky‡	May†
Herbert‡	Alan†
Dan‡	Dick†
Peter‡	Harry
Steve‡	
Kieron‡	
Annie	

Tom, Ray, Trevor, and Jack also acted as 'trainers' to the Packaging
Group, and later, joined by Charlie and Joan from the Packaging
department, 'trainers' to the Dry Products Group

(b) *From Bath*

Iain*†‡   'The consultants'
Paul*†‡
Bob Westwood, Research Assistant
Sally, a colleague

* Member of Chemical Plant Working Party
† Member of Dry Products Participation Group
‡ Member of Packaging Participation Group

CHAPTER 1

If I were you I wouldn't start from here

By way of introduction we would like to remind our readers of the famous if apocryphal story of the tourist who, upon realizing that he was hopelessly lost, enquired of a local the way to the large town he wished to visit. After some moments of thought, the local turned to the tourist and declared: 'Ah well, sir, if I were you and I wanted to get there, I wouldn't start from here ...'. As authors of this book, we consider ourselves to be in a somewhat similar circumstance; knowing what we now know and wishing to arrive at the Golden City of Participation, we certainly would not have started from the 'here' that we are to outline below. Nevertheless, 'here' is where we are, or, to be more precise, is where we were, and since this book is the record of a journey, it is necessary for us to set down our departure point and to bear with whatever dignity we can muster the comments of the locals (the participation experts) as they watch us stumble blindly forwards and backwards.

We began with some clearly identifiable intellectual luggage, some mental freight which we considered would be of value along the route; indeed, at the onset of our journey we believed that the baggage initially selected would not only be extremely useful but was essential for all serious travellers. Over the long haul we have modified our position, trimmed our load, as it were, not necessarily by discarding everything: indeed we have added a number of pieces. Rather we have distributed the weight somewhat differently, packed our intellectual bags in a different order and, perhaps most importantly, recognized that certain ideas were little more than fashionable encumbrances. The repacking is contained elsewhere in this volume; for the moment we want to set our intellectual baggage as it was at the beginning of our journey. To avoid the often subtle reinterpretation that goes on in the writing up of research adventures, as far as possible we have preserved the actual words and phrases we used at the time. From our present perspective, there is much that is arrogant in what we were thinking and writing then, and a little that has turned out to be misguided, but in the interests of a proper account of where we have been, it seems advisable to present our notions as they were: good, bad, and indifferent. Many of our initial ideas were contained in a paper we wrote about one year after our work with Alpen began which was itself based upon notes made during the initial weeks and months, and it is from this paper (see Appendix II) that we present extended quotations in an attempt to capture the attitudes and stances we were adopting at that time. 'Here' is where we started, although we may well have been advised, had we asked, to start 'elsewhere'.

We were, then, quite firm in our determination to set it all down:

1

The task, then, for researchers on participation should be explicitly to delineate the models that guide their work and thus open them to continual analysis and evaluation. It is with this objective in mind that we begin by describing our own value premises about organizational change and participation, followed by an account of how these were operationalized in a model of the various stages of a PDM [Participative Decision Making] experiment.

(1) Functional perspective

Our approach to both participation and planned change may be defined as 'contingentistic', 'relativistic', or 'particularistic'. It derives from what has become, during the past decade, an important strand of conventional wisdom on the subject of organizational design and behaviour, and goes by such names as open systems theory or contingency theory (e.g. Woodward, 1965; Katz and Kahn, 1966; Lawrence and Lorsch, 1967, 1969; Emery and Thorsrud, 1969; Lupton, 1971; Child, 1972, 1973; Baker, 1973; Dessler, 1976). Such theories advise a cautious, idiosyncratic, 'it-all-depends' approach to organizational design, and reject the view held by early 'classical' theorists and human relations writers that there are universal principles of good practice, and standard formulae of effectiveness which can be identified and applied in any situation. They are grounded in the assumption that people, things, events, and situations are neither independent nor constant, but interact and vary in a complexity of different ways to produce outcomes that are difficult to predict. Unlike the 'Lego-logic' (Mangham, 1974) which characterized early views on the management of organizations, the logic of contingency is 'its acknowledgement that the process of designing organization involves the selection of a configuration that will best suit that particular situation which prevails' (Child, 1973), and not the mere plugging in of standard components.

The slow transition from the universal to the particularistic perspective has also been witnessed in the participation literature during recent years, although it cannot be said with any degree of certainty that it has yet gained a wide measure of acceptance. In an analytical sense, this has been reflected in a rejection of simple cause–effect relationships between participation and satisfaction and productivity, and a focus upon such conditioning variables as personality needs and value systems (Vroom, 1960; French *et al.*, 1966; Tosi, 1970; White and Ruh, 1973; DeVries and Snyder, 1974), culture and demography (French *et al.*, 1960; Cascio, 1974; Juralewicz, 1974), technology and organizational structure (Heller and Yukl, 1969; Thorsrud and Emery, 1969; Rus, 1970; Heller, 1971, 1973), and the nature and form of the PDM system itself (Patchen, 1970; Ritchie and Miles, 1970; Lischeron and Wall, 1975b).

Our own assumptions can best be summarized in a quotation from M. P. Fogarty: 'Each manager, union leader, and government official faces a unique set of problems in his own time and place. To match it he needs a system tailor-made to fit his own case and to cover all aspects of it, each in its proper relationship to the system as a whole. It has to be a system, because joint relationships are a seamless web in which each part influences the rest and none can be safely taken in isolation from the rest. But it cannot be a system made up simply by plugging in standard components irrespective of their national and industrial environment, for the components available ... are multi-purpose, and the service to be expected from each varies according to the context in which it is used. ... All levels of the network are important; one must never depart from the concept of the seamless web or leave a foothold for the hellish words either/or ...' (Fogarty, 1972).

(2) Structural perspective

Another strand of conventional wisdom which influenced our approach has appeared in a great deal of contemporary discussion and analysis of industrial relations. This has been referred to as the pluralist framework (Cyert and March, 1959; Clegg, 1960, 1975;

Kornhauser, 1960; Polsby, 1963; Kerr, 1964; Fox, 1966, 1971, 1973). Its starting point is that organizations are, using Polsby's words, 'fractured into a congeries of hundreds of small interest groups, with incompletely overlapping memberships, widely differing power bases, and a multitude of techniques for exercising influence on decisions salient to them ...' (Polsby, 1963, p. 118). In this respect, it differs from a unitarist perspective such as that held by early human relations workers who described and prescribed a unified authority and loyalty structure for the enterprise, who assumed that managerial prerogative was willingly legitimized by its members, and asserted that common objectives and common values united and bound people together in a co-operative system. Pluralists, in contrast, stress that opposition is both natural and legitimate; that the stake-holders in the enterprise do hold divergent perspectives and aspirations; that 'management's power superiority is no longer sufficient to permit the luxury of imposed solutions' (Fox, 1973, p. 194); and, finally, that a mutually acceptable basis for collaboration—'antagonistic co-operation' (Simmel, 1955)—has to be arrived at and maintained by coalition-type bargaining and compromise. ...

(3) Process perspective

Much of the theory of pluralism reflects some of the disadvantages of beginning and ending with this perspective alone. The root of the problem lies in the pluralist assumption of bargaining parity between the parties, and a rough equality of skills between them, such that the outcome of the process is a 'golden mean' (Eldridge, 1973) or satisfactory compromise. As several writers (Pen, 1966; Miliband, 1969; Eldridge, 1973) have recently reminded us, industrial relations systems are characterized by an asymmetry of power and authority, where dominant individuals or coalitions enjoy a decisive and permanent advantage in the process of competition. To establish a pluralistic structure, such as the one described above, might be merely to institutionalize and reflect the inequalities of a situation in a process of pseudo-participation. As Allen has tersely observed, in collective bargaining 'employees with no power may get nothing. There is no automatic distribution based on a sense of fairness or equity. Shares have to be fought for, sometimes bitterly' (Allen, 1971). Furthermore, because collective bargaining is founded essentially upon power struggles, and not on these 'consensus' criteria of equity, dignity, and fairness, or even upon understanding each other's point of view, and because its agreements rarely serve as principles of precedent for subsequent negotiations, any shift in the balance of power between the parties will mean that one or other of them may mobilize to improve on its previous gains or to minimize its previous losses. In brief, the pluralistic perspective may well become a self-fulfilling prophecy since the processes it may give rise to, while containing short term conflict, may perpetuate longer term conflicts. More seriously, there is a danger that participants in these processes may begin to perceive (and thus make) them permanently oppositional and meaningless. Cole has written that 'this has led to the viewpoint that the best course is simply to mobilize for the inevitable economic struggles. Such an attitude cannot be concealed. It manifests itself plainly and is contagious; the result is that the difficult and delicate problems to which the parties must address themselves are approached in a spirit of futility and belligerence' (Cole, 1963).

In this part of the paper we would like to develop the argument that in accepting the *structural* implications of the pluralistic perspective, one does not have to embrace the inevitability of *processes* of competition, mistrust, and disjuncture. The processes that occur between parties in a pluralistic structure, we believe, are negotiated and, given certain conditions, negotiable. To illustrate this point we need to outline, very briefly, our perspective on interaction and organization.

The perspective we are proposing is derived from a number of sources but its heaviest debt is to writers in the symbolic and strategic interactionist tradition (Mead, 1964; Blumer, 1965, 1969; Goffman, 1970; Eldridge, 1973; Mangham, 1975, 1977, 1978). From this perspective, man is seen as uniquely self-aware, someone who defines, designates, evaluates, plans, and organizes his actions by way of a process of self-interaction. In other words, he is an object to himself, has conceptions of himself, and acts towards himself. As Blumer has noted, man's actions are not contingent upon the 'objective world' but determinant of it: 'The process of self-interaction puts the human being over against his world instead of merely in it, requires him to meet and handle his world through a defining process instead of merely responding to it and forces him to construct his action instead of merely releasing it' (Blumer, 1965, p. 536). Thus, put into a situation which he perceives requires some line of action from him, man will identify what he wants, establish an objective or goal, map out a prospective line of behaviour, note and interpret the actions and intentions of others, size up the situation, and so on—in short, he will construct his act.

An important point to be made here ... is that these constructions will be based upon selective perceptions and experiences, and will not be right or wrong in any absolute sense. In fact, to the observer, and sometimes even to the person himself, these constructions might appear highly prejudiced and one-sided, lacking in balanced appraisal, and highly inappropriate to the situation. In other cases the person may be unaware of the nature, origins, and consequence of his perceptions since, over a period of time, and as a consequence of replication and repetition, they may move beyond the realm of introspection to become what Mangham (1974) has called 'world-taken-for-granted-perspectives'.

From this interactionist viewpoint, 'joint action', such as one might encounter in many PDM situations, can be characterized as a series of moves 'made in the light of one's thoughts about the other's thoughts about oneself' (Goffman, 1970), which are in some way fitted together. Each participant necessarily occupies a different position, ascribes meaning by interpreting and defining a web of symbols which surrounds him, and conveys indications to other participants as to how they should act. Blumer has traced how different individual acts come to fit together: 'Their alignment does not occur through sheer mechanical juggling, as in the shaking of walnuts in a jar or through unwitting adaptation. Instead, the participants fit their acts together, first, by identifying the social act in which they are about to engage and, second, by identifying each other's acts in forming the joint act. By identifying the social act or joint action the participant is able to orient himself. But even though this identification may be made, the participants in the joint action that is being formed still find it necessary to interpret and define one another's ongoing data. They have to ascertain what the others are doing and plan to do and make indications to one another of what they do' (Blumer, 1965).

The result of such interpretations, definitions, and acts is collective structure; cycles of behaviour are established between actors (or groups of actors). In Allport's terms: 'there is a pluralistic situation in which in order for an individual (or class of individuals) to perform some act (or have some experience) that he "desires" to perform (or for which he is "set"), it is necessary that *another* person (or persons) perform certain acts (either similar or different and complementary to his own). In this we have what can be called a fact of collective structure' (Allport, 1962). A series of cycles or patterns of behaviour are built up which gradually assume an automatic, taken-for-granted nature (Weick, 1969; Mangham, 1978). In the words of Strauss (1963) this is the 'negotiated order' and, as such, it can be an order which exists between individuals, between groups, or between large collectivities. It is a tacit temporary agreement about the 'meaning' of a situation or set of circumstances and the appropriate, complementary behaviour to be enacted within that situation or circumstance.

Meaning, as we have noted above, does not reside outside the actor(s) in any situation, it is imported by the actor(s). Crucial to our model is the view that the participants in PDM will bring with them definitions and interpretations, predispositions and repertoires to create the environment to which they can respond. The PDM situation will constitute a flow of experience all of which will be *potentially* available for attention to all participants, but most of which will go unnoticed as the parties to the interaction seek to bring into play patterns, or cycles of behaviour with which they are familiar. In so doing the workforce will ascribe 'meaning' to certain management actions, and the management will ascribe 'meaning' to the actions of the workers. The range of ascribed meaning may be wide and—since ascription is retrospective and influenced by attitudes in the here and now—variable (Weick, 1969). Seen in one light, an action may be termed 'co-operative', in another 'antagonistic'. Not only therefore will the situation not be one of simple co-operation or conflict, as the unitarists and pluralists would have us believe, but it could be one marked by co-operation *and* conflict, domination, exploitation, consensus, indifference at different times. ...

That passage, written some four years ago, represents all too clearly our particular location at the beginning of our journey. We had some ideas, or to be more accurate, we had picked up some ideas; as can be seen by the way we put them on, they were not yet part of us. They represent some of the freight we had extracted from the wide range of intellectual bags and baggage available to us. As yet they did not sit too well upon us. The notions of contingency, of pluralism, and of process consultation had been part of our intellectual cargo for some time, but the idea of 'negotiated order' and the much more fundamental notion of 'symbolic interactionism' were relatively new appurtenances and, as such, somewhat uncomfortable and but loosely tied to our other goods and chattels. Nonetheless, foolhardy to the last, we went on to spell out some of the implications of the foregoing for the practice of participative decision-making as we then saw it:

Firstly, it should be noted that pluralistic structures provide an arena for the negotiation of meaning between as many different definitions-of-the-situation as there are participants, but no guarantee that these can be fitted together to form a joint act nor that such acts will be stable. Secondly, in view of the fact that PDM may involve people who have not previously been required to define and interpret each other's 'symbolic communications' in a face-to-face situation, it might be expected that there will be difficulty in achieving any joint acts in the early stages, and considerable discomfort may be felt by these people. ... The interactionist perspective highlights the different definitions and world-pictures of participants, and implies that joint change acts can only be brought about by a sharing of meaning, an understanding of (although not necessarily a sympathy for) other participants' definitions and interpretations of various people, events, acts, and situations, and the negotiation of new contingent meanings. In brief, this perspective suggests what the primary objective of the PDM change programme should be, and draws attention to the magnitude of the problem of achieving it. Furthermore, in doing these things, it also begins to define the role of the OD consultant, and to suggest how he might facilitate the process of change: 'If we want to know how order is sustained within an organization we must consider the organization as seen by its members; if we want to effect change we must influence their definitions and bring about a re-construing, a re-negotiation of the world-taken-for-granted by the actors concerned. From this perspective, Organization Development becomes less a matter of values, feelings, and styles of management and much more a process of helping individuals and groups examine their definitions and processes of interaction in order to accelerate or facilitate changes' (Mangham, 1975).
    An important feature of the perspective adopted by the authors in the present study is to create circumstances in which the parties to the joint action could not only talk about substantive issues concerning their work and decision-making but also could become aware of the nature and processes of their interlocked behaviour and, once aware, choose either to change it or persist in it. Such an approach is built upon the premise that since order is socially constructed and socially sustained, it must be capable of being socially transformed. 'Awareness is the key' (Mangham, 1970). As Berger (1963) notes: 'all revolutions begin in transformations of consciousness'. Once the social actor knows what he is doing and what is happening to him he is in a position to change things. In order to know what he is doing, to understand more fully the nature of the collective structure in which he is engaged, the actor must achieve some form of role-distance (Stebbins, 1969), disengagement (Mangham, 1977), or alienation (Mangham, 1970). Alienation in the sense that it is used theatrically by

Brechtians illustrates clearly the concept we are addressing. Brecht's purpose in the theatre was to prevent the actors and audience getting carried away on a wave of emotionalism and was expressed very simply in his rejection of the word 'einbilden' (to imagine) in favour of the term 'abbilden' (to portray). The former implies involvement and lack of consciousness, the latter relative detachment and a degree of critical appraisal. The act of alienation creates conditions for portrayal by making the familiar strange: 'We make something natural incomprehensible in a certain way, but only in order to make it all the more comprehensible afterwards. In order for something known to become perceived, it must cease to be ordinary: one must break with the habitual notion that the thing in question requires no elucidation' (Brecht, 1940). Alienation—the act of stepping or standing outside oneself—transforms one's awareness of own and other's behaviour in such a way that 'givenness becomes possibility' (Berger, 1963).

The *process* emphasis of the change programme, therefore, becomes one of helping the parties involved in the PDM situation become alienated, gain insight into the nature of their interaction—what is going on around individuals/groups, within them, and between them. In short, we sought at regular intervals to focus upon the processes of interaction, the cycles and patterns of behaviour, to enable the participants to question their own definitions, interpretations, and behaviours and to give them opportunity to re-define, consensually to validate alternative meanings and actions. In this way we sought to bring about an understanding of patterns of conflict, aggression, and co-operation, and feelings of confusion and satisfaction as they occur within the PDM arena. In short, we pay attention not only to *what* they participate in but also to *how* they participated and how they conceptualized their experiences. ...

Basically what we were arguing then was that the ideal route to participation lay along the relatively untrodden path marked 'Process Awareness'. If only the participants could become more aware of the circumstances they created for themselves and others by the way in which they defined situations and the way in which they consequently behaved, they would be able to exercise more control over their joint destiny. Amazingly we failed to note at the time that the path was relatively untrodden for good reasons; it was narrow, precipitous, and sometimes shrouded in mist—as we were soon to find out.

Such, then, was our basic baggage: notions of contingency, pluralism, process, and negotiated order. We also packed a set of ideas to do with organizational change which we wrote about, then, as follows:

There have been many attempts to define a multi-stage model of planned change. Perhaps the earliest and most succinct was that of Kurt Lewin (1946) who characterized change as occurring in three phases: unfreezing, moving, and refreezing. This three-step process, simple, clear, and bordering on the naive, has formed the basis for many subsequent models of change. Schein (1969), for example, later developed considerably many of Lewin's original ideas, examining more carefully the sub-processes involved within the three broad stages. Lippitt, Watson, and Westley (1958) also elaborated some of these ideas in a five-step process of organizational consultancy: development of a need for change, establishment of a change relationship, working towards change, generalization and stablization of change, and achieving a terminal relationship.

More recent models of planned change, whilst still clearly influenced by the Lewin criteria, use the language of organization development and action research (French and Bell, 1973; Clark, 1972). Lawrence and Lorsch (1969) suggest a four-stage model: diagnosis, action planning, action implementation, and evaluation. Schein (1969) outlines seven stages: contact with the client, defining the relationship, selecting a setting and method of work, data gathering and diagnosis, intervention, reducing involvement, and termination.

Other writers have developed both descriptive and prescriptive models of change. Greiner (1966), for example, from a survey of several case studies of planned change, arrives at a model characterized by a strong emphasis upon pressure and intervention at the top: 'Until the ground under the top managers begins to shift, it seems unlikely that they will be sufficiently concerned to see the need for change both in themselves and in the rest of the organization' (Greiner, 1966). This emphasis is present in almost all available models of planned change (Argyris, 1970; Blake and Mouton, 1969; Golembiewski, 1972; Fink, Taddeo, and Beak, 1971). Also present is an emphasis upon participation within the change process, not only between the consultant and the client—an emphasis within the literature and practice of Organization Development which stresses that the consultant will do little *to* or *for* the members of the organization but a greal deal *with* their active collaboration—but also a sharing of decision-making within the client system. In the cases studied by Greiner

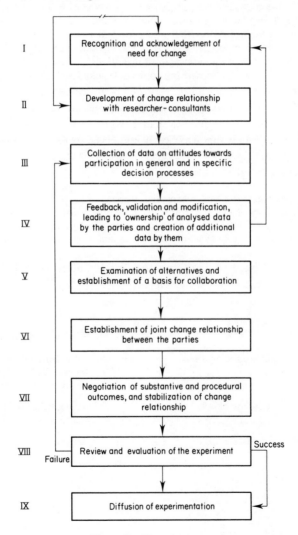

Figure 1   The change model.

(1966), successful change attempts were marked by *shared* approaches where authority figures sought the participation of subordinates in making decisions about changes. Less successful cases were characterized by either a unilateral approach—order, decree, or restructuring—or by a delegated approach.

The model we developed for use in this project draws upon the literature and the experience of the authors (see Figure 1 page 7). Like many others it was prescriptive and normative, and, of course, was originally based on our view of the change process, but unlike them it was explicitly derived from a theoretical approach to the implementation of PDM (as outlined in the first part of the paper). The contingency aspect, for instance, was explicit in the data-collection stage, which focused on issues relevant to the participants and specific to their situation. The emphasis upon a pluralistic structure was evidenced in the bringing together of several groups with different perspectives and (in contrast with many change models) in the lesser emphasis on bringing about change exclusively from the top. The process orientation is less immediately obvious since Figure 1 implies a rigidity and fixity which in practice was not the case. In fact each stage was *negotiated* with the result that the parties concerned were not only involved in the change process but also part-creators of it. The result was clearly a framework for the intervention process (i.e. implementing changes) and not one which sought to predict and explain the process of change itself.

At the last moment we crammed into our rucksacks Gene Dalton's (1969) model for induced change which we liked very much. It seemed to us, at the time, to provide us with a rudimentary instrument for measuring and monitoring our journey. Dalton's work went further than Lewin's model and was of a different order to our own (although ours was clearly influenced by it). He claimed that during periods of change there was not one process at work—as in Lewin's sequence—but several, all moving simultaneously:

Where influence was successful, changes occurred not only in the way an individual related to the influencing agent, but also to his co-workers and to himself. As interaction patterns were dissolving and reforming, changes were taking place within the individuals involved, changes in their feelings about themselves and in the objectives they sought.

He identified four major subprocesses that, in his studies, tended to characterize successful change: each reflected movement:

Away from	and	*Toward*
Generalized goals	⟶	Specific objectives
Former social ties built around previous behaviour patterns	⟶	New relationships which support the intended changes in behaviour and attitudes
Self-doubt and lowered sense of self esteem	⟶	A heightened sense of self-esteem
An external motive for change	⟶	An internalized motive for change

Dalton combined these processes as in Figure 2 below

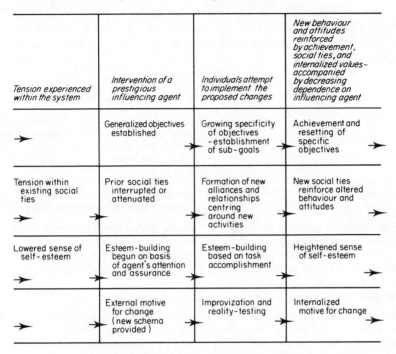

Tension experienced within the system	Intervention of a prestigious influencing agent	Individuals attempt to implement the proposed changes	New behaviour and attitudes reinforced by achievement, social ties, and internalized values-accompanied by decreasing dependence on influencing agent
→	Generalized objectives established	Growing specificity of objectives -establishment of sub-goals	Achievement and resetting of specific objectives →
Tension within existing social ties →	Prior social ties interrupted or attenuated →	Formation of new alliances and relationships centring around new activities →	New social ties reinforce altered behaviour and attitudes →
Lowered sense of self-esteem →	Esteem-building begun on basis of agent's attention and assurance →	Esteem-building based on task accomplishment →	Heightened sense of self-esteem →
→	External motive for change (new schema provided) →	Improvization and reality-testing →	Internalized motive for change →

Figure 2   A model of induced change.

Such, then, were the manifest elements of intellectual paraphernalia with which we were encumbered as we began our trek towards the Golden City of Participation. It is clear that we were also freighted down with numerous value premises most of which we did not take time to examine, and decide whether or not to discard or repack. The choice of the social scientist is between being aware of his values and making them explicit, or being unaware and letting the reader get them by inference—by indirections finding directions out. For travellers intent upon showing others the virtues of awareness, our own initial position left much to be desired; we listed some of our mental freight and wholly, perhaps even wilfully, ignored other elements of it. In retrospect, it seems necessary and it certainly seems more scientific openly to present the values than to leave them buried and implicit. The reader should note, however, that we can by no means be sure that we would have articulated our values in a similar manner had we thought and had been inclined so to do at the time. In this case, the 'here' we began with and the 'here' we seek to recapture is likely to be different in emphasis if not in kind.

The very selection of a problem or an area to work in indicates a value. The fact that we chose to work in the broad area of organizational change and the more specific one of industrial participation says something about the kind of issues which concern us and the kind of people we were. Underlying much of what we were working on then, as to a large extent now, was some vague notion of health or effectiveness deriving ultimately from biological analogies. Underlying much of the scientific work of biology is the concept that health is preferable or better than sickness. The notion is explicit, for example, in the work of Fordyce and Weil (1971), who identify organizations as either healthy or unhealthy according to an extensive set of characteristics:*

Some characteristics of unhealthy and healthy organizations

Unhealthy

Healthy (The description of an organization may appear millennialist. It is perhaps more a statement of direction than a state that has been achieved by any known organization.)

1. Little personal investment in organizational objectives except at top levels.

1. Objectives are widely shared by the members and there is a strong and consistent flow of energy towards those objectives.

2. People in the organization see things going wrong and do nothing about it. Nobody volunteers. Mistakes and problems are habitually hidden or shelved. People talk about office troubles at home or in the halls, not with those involved.

2. People feel free to signal their awareness of difficulties because they expect the problems to be dealt with and they are optimistic that they can be solved.

3. Extraneous factors complicate problem-solving. Status and boxes on the organization chart are more important than solving the problem. There is an excessive concern with management as a customer, instead of the real customer. People treat each other in a formal and polite manner that masks issues—especially with the boss. Nonconformity is frowned upon.

3. Problem-solving is highly pragmatic. In attacking problems, people work informally and are not preoccupied with status, territory or second-guessing 'what management will think'. The boss is frequently challenged. A great deal of nonconforming behaviour is tolerated.

4. People at the top try to control as many decisions as possible. They become bottlenecks, and make decisions with inadequate information and advice. People complain about managers' irrational decisions.

4. The points of decision-making are determined by such factors as ability, sense of responsibility, availability of information, work load, timing, and requirements for professional and management development. Organizational level as such is not considered a factor.

5. Managers feel alone in trying to get things done. Somehow, orders, policies, and procedures don't get carried out as intended.

5. There is a noticeable sense of team play in planning, in performance, and in discipline—in short, a sharing of responsibility.

6. The judgement of people lower down in the organization is not respected outside the narrow limits of their jobs.

6. The judgement of people lower down in the organization is respected.

7. Personal needs and feelings are side issues.

7. The range of problems tackled includes personal needs and human relationships.

*The following material is reprinted with permission from J. K. Fordyce and R. Weil, *Managing with People*, pp. 11–14. © 1971 Addison-Wesley Publishing Company, Inc.

8. People compete when they need to collaborate. They are very jealous of their area of responsibility. Seeking or accepting help is felt to be a sign of weakness. Offering help is unthought of. They distrust each other's motives and speak poorly of one another; the manager tolerates this.

8. Collaboration is freely entered into.People readily request the help of others and are willing to give in turn. Ways of helping one another are highly developed. Individuals and groups compete with one another, but they do so fairly and in the direction of a shared goal.

9. When there is a crisis, people withdraw or start blaming one another.

9. When there is a crisis, the people quickly band together in work until the crisis departs.

10. Conflict is mostly covert and managed by office politics and other games, or there are interminable and irreconcilable arguments.

10. Conflicts are considered important to decision-making and personal growth. They are dealt with effectively, in the open. People say what they want and expect others to do the same.

11. Learning is difficult. People don't approach their peers to learn from them, but have to learn by their own mistakes; they reject the experience of others. They get little feedback on performance, and much of that is unhelpful.

11. There is a great deal of on-the-job learning based on a willingness to give, seek, and use feedback and advice. People see themselves and others as capable of significant personal development and growth.

12. Feedback is avoided.

12. Joint critique of progress is routine.

13. Relationships are contaminated by maskmanship and image building. People feel alone and lack concern for one another. There is an undercurrent of fear.

13. Relationships are honest. People do care about one another and do not feel alone.

14. People feel locked into their jobs. They feel stale and bored but constrained by the need for security. Their behavior, for example, in staff meetings, is listless and docile. It's not much fun. They get their kicks elsewhere.

14. People are 'turned on' and highly involved by choice. They are optimistic. The work place is optimistic and fun (why not?).

15. The manager is a prescribing father to the organization.

15. Leadership is flexible, shifting in style and person to suit the situation.

16. The manager tightly controls small expenditures and demands excessive justification. He allows little freedom for making mistakes.

16. There is a high degree of trust among people and a sense of freedom and mutual responsibility. People generally know what is important to the organization and what isn't.

17. Minimizing risks has a very high value.

17. Risk is accepted as a condition of growth and change.

18. 'One mistake and you're out.'

18. 'What can we learn from each mistake?'

19. Poor performance is glossed over or handled arbitrarily.

19. Poor performance is confronted and a joint resolution sought.

20. Organization structure, policies and procedures encumber the organization. People take refuge in policies and procedures, and play games with organization structure.

20. Organization structure, procedures, and policies are fashioned to help people to get the job done and to protect the long-term health of the organization, not to give each bureaucrat his due. They are also readily changed.

21. Tradition!

21. There is a sense of order, and yet a high rate of innovation. Old methods are questioned and often give way.

22. Innovation is not widespread but in the hands of a few.

22. The organization itself adapts swiftly to opportunities or other changes in its marketplace because every pair of eyes is watching and every head is anticipating the future.

23. People swallow their frustrations: 'I can do nothing. It's *their* responsibility to save the ship.'

23. Frustrations are the call to action. 'It's my/our responsibility to save the ship.'

Just as we, like many others before and since, have assumed that health is better than sickness, we have also considered maturity to be better than immaturity. It is good, we assumed, to grow up psychologically as well as physiologically; organizations can develop and should be encouraged to do so. Maturity, of course, is a very large concept with a cluster of characteristics. Among them, as among the list of healthy characteristics provided by Fordyce and Weil, is the ability of people within organizations to be responsible for their actions, to make decisions, to be flexible and adaptive, and to be able to fulfil themselves. To us, a democratic organization represented a more mature, a more grown-up way of living and one more likely to encourage maturity in its members than does an authoritarian institution. Our approach was in no way as clear as this but, no doubt, we had a strong, if somewhat diffuse, notion that organizations could be 'better', more 'healthy', if involvement in decision-making was more widespread.

It seemed apparent to us at that time that at least in our terms there were not many mature organizations about. Most that we had experienced either directly as employees or indirectly as consultants and researchers appeared to be characterized by immature and unhealthy characteristics. In particular we considered that much of the immaturity centred around the control of shop floor employees. We considered that in many circumstances they were treated and responded in an unhealthy fashion and undoubtedly part of our motivation in becoming involved with participation at all was a desire to redress the balance: to release some of the energy, encourage some of the potential, but also—to be frank—to deprive the management of some of its prerogatives which we considered illegitimate. We were, we now believe, motivated in part by a somewhat inchoate set of vaguely socialist principles which went beyond ideas of maturity and health, although obviously encompassed them.

We say 'vaguely socialist' because we were certainly not Marxist in our leanings. We held clearly to the value of evolutionary rather than revolutionary approaches to change and, at that time, neither of us gave much thought to widespread changes in society or in organizations, certainly not changes which involved the workforce in the ownership of enterprises. We took the workforce (blue collar employees in our perception) to be repressed rather than oppressed and, again somewhat vaguely, held on to notions of free enterprise and the larger values of capitalist societies and the rights of individuals and organizations to make a profit and to exploit, within the vaguest of limits, the resources available.

Thus in the most general and unexamined fashion, we were for motherhood and the flag, for virtue and against vice. Wishing to accelerate 'development', willing to tinker with the socioeconomic system or have it tinkered with but not wishing *radical* changes. Middle of the road, middle-class academics, fully laden, setting out on foot for the distant peaks.

To summarize, this opening chapter has been concerned to delineate as honestly as possible our starting point, where we were intellectually and in terms of our values at the onset of this particular journey. Our movables, our goods and chattels, included ideas of contingency, of pluralism, of symbolic interactionism, and of a process orientation to working with our clients. Our model of change, perhaps more explicit than many of our other frameworks, was based upon a relatively simple and perhaps simplistic stepped approach to changing behaviour in organizations. Our values, somewhat less immediately accessible and certainly less readily inspected by us or anyone else, were based upon notions of health, maturity, development, and the fundamental rectitude of the prevailing socioeconomic system. Thus equipped, we began our long trek, not without misgiving but somewhat reassured by Bateson's maxim: 'An explorer can never know what he is exploring until it has been explored.'

CHAPTER 2

Setting off on the wrong foot

Our ideas about contingency, pluralism, and the process orientation were modified almost as soon as we had formulated them. For example, although we recognized the plethora of interest groups within the particular company with which we had undertaken to travel, we did not insist upon them all, even the majority of them, being represented on the Steering Group for the project; a decision which was to have consequences for our later actions. More of that later; for the moment, a word from our sponsor.

Alpen Industries is the UK-based arm of Samuel Alpen International, which, in turn, forms a part of the giant Samuel Alpen & Company Inc., founded and based in Cincinnati, USA. World-wide the company manufactures and sells ethical pharmaceuticals, agricultural chemicals (fertilizers, animal drugs, pesticides), and, through its subsidiary Elina Marty, cosmetics and fashion goods. The company is very successful, with sales running at well over £1.5 billion a year (1978) and profits running at record levels year after year throughout the 1970s.

Alpen Industries (UK) operates on three sites—one in Glasgow, one at Towcester, and a research centre at Lyme Regis in Dorset. Although each site has a management team, effective control is vested in a central management group operating out of London, which, in turn, clears its major decisions with 'key people' at Cincinnati. The plant at Glasgow is unionized, a circumstance viewed with a mixture of fascination, horror, and regret by visitors from the USA. Neither Towcester nor Lyme Regis is unionized and it is the expressed concern of the company (i.e. Cincinnati) that this state of affairs should continue.

One of us had a strong connection with the company both as a consultant and previously as a senior manager with one of its foreign subsidiaries (not the UK branch). Thus he was familiar with many of the senior managers both in the UK and the Cincinnati headquarters, and he was very familiar with the culture of the organization.

Immediately prior to the experiment with which we are concerned in these pages, he had been working with the senior group in London. The group had identified a number of areas in which it anticipated some problems—pricing, market shares, organization, and legislation—and had particularly considered the impact of possible government intervention around the area of worker participation. The Bullock Committee had been set up and was collecting information and the popular management journals were full of exhortations and plans for greater worker involvement. The UK Operations group (the senior group in London) considered a report drawn up by some members of its Personnel Department and, in the light of its recommendations and some gentle pressure from one of us, it decided to sponsor an experiment in 'worker involvement'; note, not 'participative decision-making', but the much grander and vaguer 'worker involvement'. The question of where the experiment was to be conducted was addressed. Glasgow was ruled out on the grounds that it was unionized and 'we already have more than enough problems with their involvement as it is.' Lyme Regis was also deemed uncongenial since 'they are mostly graduate staff and only interested in their own individual work'. Towcester was clearly the last hope and there was much debate about the risks involved in conducting the experiment there. Some argued that it was ideal because it was non-unionized, some that precisely because it was non-unionized it should be left alone: 'If you start asking people what they want, the next thing you know they'll be organizing to get it.' Others argued that the company management style would 'simply have to change. Look, let's face it, we are a paternalistic lot, pat them on the head and give them sixpence stuff. From cradle to grave with Samuel Alpen. I'm not saying that's been wrong in the past, it's clearly served us well, but it's not going to be viable in a few years time. People are better educated, more aware of what's going on; they are not going to be content to let us take the decisions for them; they'll want to know, to be involved ...'

'To be involved, yes, but only on issues that directly affect them. ... I hope we are not thinking of involvement in issues such as capital requisitions, pricing policy and so on ...'

'Good God, no ...'

'Certainly not.'

'Maybe not now, but one small step along the road and we are committed, there's no going back. We involve them in anything—and don't get me wrong, I'm not necessarily opposed to it—and we end up involving them in virtually everything.'

'What's so wrong with that?'

The question was treated as a joke to which all, including the inquirer, responded with loud laughter.

Eventually, since it was clear that the Managing Director of Alpen Industries (UK) wished to do something, it was agreed that Towcester would provide the site. The Managing Director of the site who was, like his counterparts at Glasgow and Lyme Regis, a member of the UK Operations group, 'volunteered' to find an appropriate group within his overall site. The UK Personnel Director agreed to 'touch base' with his colleagues in Cincinnati and the meeting ended with a degree of self-congratulation—'We are actually doing something about participation, not just talking about it ...'.

A degree of self-interest

We clearly had an interest in the discussion since at that time we were both beginning to look around for a research site that might offer the prospect of 'a bit of the old and a bit of the new'. One of us had been on the OD research road for nearly a decade, and was now a weather-beaten and rather lonely traveller, but, as ever, eager to add more weight to an already weighty kit-bag marked 'action research'—a compendium of experiences and skills relating to organizational change, team development, and management education. An expedition to the Golden City of Participation offered plentiful opportunity for this, while also opening up a new, interesting, and topical area of study. The chance of moving into the industrial relations field, and participation in particular, held some appeal. The other, having previously made only brief forays into the world of industry to plunder sufficient food for academic thought (the last being a three-year research project on London dockers' attitudes to participation), was eager to continue with his participation studies. Alpen of Towcester offered a site for further data accumulation and corroboration. While notions of action research and OD were still relatively new to him and were regarded with great suspicion, he was still prepared to travel with someone who espoused these notions, since he, too, wanted companionship and felt that both had a good deal in common in a wider sense with regard to social background and education, an explorer's instinct for fun and adventure, some energy and personal ambition, disdain for the routine and lazy, and, perhaps above all, a conviction that by combining forces and talents, they could possibly approach participation from a new and different perspective.

Now, returning to our role in the discussion in London, whilst taking care not to commit ourselves to notions such as the prevention of unionization, we attempted to help the group arrive at a decision. It was considered that deferrals could result in delay and eventual abandonment of the idea, thus depriving us of a potential research site. Occasionally the members of the Operations group turned to us (or to be more precise, to the one of us present) and asked for an expert opinion on some or other aspect of participation. Occasionally, although not often, this was given. 'Not often', since it was considered necessary that the commitment to 'do something' should emanate from the group and not be 'sold' to them, and 'occasionally' because it looked as though, without the desired expert input, they would not 'buy it'. The relationship was truly symbiotic in that we needed their support to acquire a site and they needed us to know what to do with the site.

From the point of view of those actually to be involved, however, the managers and employees at Towcester, they needed neither of us. In effect, although their Managing Director had volunteered their co-operation, effectively they had been instructed to participate by the London headquarters. The irony of this was not lost on any of the parties involved: 'You will participate as of eight o'clock, Monday 6th January'.

We appeared on the dot of eight o'clock complete with intellectual impedimenta and began our discussions with the senior management group at Towcester. It was soon clear that they were far from committed to any ideas of participation or involvement. As there had been in London, considerable concern was expressed about the issue of unionization: 'What bothers me is that this is likely to be a back door for the unions. They can't get in through the factory gates—we had an approach from USDAW, we let them talk to the workforce and only a dozen bothered to go—but this way, we're actually setting up trouble for ourselves. I mean, it seems like we are asking them to make demands of us which we are not going to be able to fulfil …'.

Another manager was even more explicit: 'Look, Towcester is pure, it's not been touched by unions, it's the virgin the corporation doesn't want to spoil, so what the hell are they up to in London, inviting trouble like this?'

Others argued the need for change: 'You know, we have got away with it for years. We've had no union issues here simply because we pay above the rate to keep them out. We can't go on doing that for ever and even if we could, there's other things beside money. More and more people want to be consulted, want to know what's going on ...'.

'I'm not sure that's right. Most of them come here to earn their wages and couldn't give a bugger about being involved. They don't want to know, they are quite happy to leave that to the management ...'.

'You can't say that about them all and, in any case, since we never have involved them, we've no real way of knowing what they think ...'.

'One thing we have not considered is that by setting up our own worker involvement scheme rather than helping the unions get in, it may on the contrary keep them out. ... If we consult the workforce directly, why should they look outside for someone to talk on their behalf?'

'Because they may need some muscle to get something done, that's why.'

'They haven't up to now.'

'They haven't needed to, they haven't got together to identify any issues to fight over.'

This discussion went on for some considerable time, actively encouraged by us since we wanted the members of the group to air their concerns and to identify the issues which the proposed experiment raised for them. Throughout the debate we tried to make them focus upon the implications of participative decision-making for their own management style. Throughout the debate this was resisted and the widening of the project into notions of participation and *decision*-making was strongly challenged. 'Now let's be clear what this is about, it's about sharing information, nothing more. In some circumstances, I agree, we have to be more open what it is we are about, but I don't think we want to go down the route of asking them to decide. I am paid to do that ...'.

In turn, we challenged their definitions: 'Involvement seems to me to imply much more than passively receiving information when you feel like giving it. If I'm to be involved, if I'm to participate, I want to be active, to influence something. It's no use you simply telling me something after it's been done, that's not involvement, it may not even be communication ...'.

'Communication, that's it. That's what it's all about, I'll buy that. We need to tell them more, that's clear ...'.

'I don't think even that's clear, most of them don't want to know ...'.

It would be tedious to go into further detail. Suffice it to say that the argument swayed backwards and forwards for a considerable period of time, with ourselves becoming more and more involved as advocates of participative decision-making and opponents of what we took to be exercises in communication. In one sense this partisan approach was risky—we risked expulsion. In another, it was necessary since we did not wish to begin with this group under false premises. In any event, we felt confident that the interest of the London Operations group would be sufficient to carry the day. The authority of that group was such that no one at Towcester was likely to challenge it, however indeterminate the brief it handed out. Furthermore, it was thought that, one of us had connections with the corporation at a level beyond London which might be activated in the event of local recalcitrance. In adopting the line that we took, therefore, we considered ourselves to be, correctly, in a win/win circumstance. With various degrees of reluctance, the Towcester management accepted the idea they were to play host to a pretty ill-defined experiment in worker involvement which meant going somewhat beyond 'better communication', but stopping well short of unionization and negotiation over issues such as pay and conditions. After further discussion, it was agreed that the ideal location for the experiment would be the Chemical Plant.

The Chemical Plant occupies an isolated position on the site, away from the main factory, comprising the Capsule Plant and such other departments as Filling and Finishing, Laboratory and Technical Services, Stores and Warehouses, and Administration. Within the plant, several kinds of chemical are manufactured in reaction vessels situated on each of the three floors of the modern building, and are dried, sieved, and packed on the ground floor. Although the process is automated, working conditions are unpleasant and dangerous. There were sixteen process operators working in four shift groups. Each of these had a supervisor and, during the day, three indirect service workers, a section head, and plant manager. Each group worked four consecutive daytime shifts of twelve hours, followed by four days off, and then worked four twelve-hour night shifts, and so on. Basic wages of the process operators were very high compared with other workers on the site and in the local labour market.

The selection of the Chemical Plant was based upon a number of criteria: the location for the experiment had to be relatively isolated, it was preferable that the activities of the personnel involved were relatively autonomous, the numbers had to be limited to enable us to be aware in detail of the reactions produced by the new form of working, and its pattern of work needed to be reasonably stable—we did not want spectres of redundancies or sudden upsurges in unemployment to disturb the relationships. It is to be noted that, at this stage at least, none of us raised the question of whether or not anyone in the Chemical Plant wanted to be involved in the experiment. Just as the senior management group at Towcester had been told, 'You will participate', so, apparently, the management and operatives of the experimental site itself were to be informed.

Or not quite so arbitrarily, since we suggested that a Steering Group be set up to guide and monitor the project. The idea for such a group derived from our conviction that the overall aim of the project was the negotiation of change, not the imposition of a blueprint or a formula for participation. It seemed to us then as now that, throughout the process, careful monitoring is essential to determine whether or not needs are being met and actions are being taken as agreed upon. This is best achieved by the provision of a relatively formal (in establishment, not necessarily in style) monitoring process. Furthermore, it was important that the initiation of the programme was seen to be approved of and overseen by relevant, prestigious, and authoritative figures. As Dalton (1973) puts it: 'The person being influenced needs confidence that the change can, in fact, be effected, and a large part of the confidence comes initially from this confidence in the power and the judgement of the influencing agent.' The Steering Group was charged with initiating, co-ordinating, and monitoring the programme of worker involvement in the Chemical Plant. Ideally it should have consisted of all those who had the power to defend or destroy the project. We noted in a paper we wrote prior to the experiment at Towcester (Appendix I) that:

A large part of the power and influence [to bring about change] must rest with the Steering Committee. This group charged with initiating, co-ordinating, and monitoring the change programme *must* include all who have the power to defend or destroy the project. Qvale (1973), for example, reinforces the point when he indicates that the 'choice of parties for co-operation' [in experiments in industrial democracy] should be determined by consideration of who could immediately harm the project. ...

The Steering Committee is critical to the success of the venture and considerable time should be invested in helping it work effectively ..., particularly at the process level. That the time is well spent is evident. Much of the success of the second Norwegian experiment at Hunsfor Fabrikker (a paper mill) has been attributed to the transfer of 'experimental initiative to a local action committee inside the company' (Bernhardsen, 1969; Thorsrud and Emery, 1970). And in Great Britain, the incorporation of a 'Main Joint Working Party' for initiating change at the Mitchedean plant of Rank Xerox was seen to have contributed significantly to the evolution of effective participatory systems (Peacock, 1972).

The Steering Group we set up included the Towcester Managing Director, the Production Director (within whose division the Chemical Plant lay), the Personnel Director, the Chemical Plant Departmental Manager, our good selves, and a further representative from the Personnel Department who was nominated to act as the internal change agent. Thus only managers were involved in the Steering Group meetings. In view of what has already been written in these pages about pluralism, this may appear somewhat surprising; no representatives from the direct supervision and none from the shop floor. However, the notion of managers sitting down with supervisors and employees and negotiating a programme of change was regarded by the senior managers with some hilarity. In effect, we had to accept that the level of involvement on this particular site was such that the idea of participation in planning further involvement was not simply disturbing, it was incomprehensible. It was clear to us that our starting point was a circumstance of active discouragement of discussion between the various levels of employees. Each and every manager apparently accepted this state of affairs as the 'natural' way of doing things. In this respect they behaved as any manager (or shop floor employee) in any organization; they had been socialized to accept and even approve of the Alpen way of doing things. Promotions had signalled the attributes, the values, the definitions, and the outlooks prized by more senior management, and the daily round had inexorably brought about the situation where the company's taken-for-granted perspectives had been internalized and were acted upon. The Alpen way of doing things had become second nature to them. A pervasive and subtle process as captured by Perrow (1972):

The superior has the power or tools to structure the environment and perceptions of the subordinate in such a way that he sees the proper things and in the proper light. The superior actually appears to give few orders ... instead, he sets priorities ('we had better look at this first', 'this is getting out of hand and creating problems, so let's give it more attention until the problems are cleared up') and alters the flow of input and stimuli.

Thus, over time, procedures, regulations, 'ways of behaving around here', however irksome they may have once appeared, are gradually accepted as the individual's own 'premises of thought and action, until compliance with them is no longer reluctant, or even indifferent, obedience, but an expression of personal preference and will' (Kaufman, 1972). Thus, at Towcester, it had come to pass that managers did not sit down with employees to make joint decisions on anything and it was unimaginable that there were circumstances in which such action may be appropriate. Shared decision-making about sharing decision-making is, in any event, a somewhat bizarre notion; if the management had been prepared to take this step, it could be argued that no further steps would be required. In any event, they were not prepared so to do and we—ever willing to tack in the face of prevailing winds—went along with them.

So I like being a bloody monkey

Our next step was to meet the employees and negotiate the project with them. It was agreed that the internal change agent, who was said to have a clear link to the workers in the Chemical Plant, and was, in fact, their Personnel representative, would brief the workforce.

To us, this first step appeared to be quite straightforward and unproblematic: after all, the individual in question had been responsible for their area for some time, would know the people involved, and, as a member of the Steering Group, was conversant with the proposed work, and could prepare the ground for our entry. The briefing duly took place and the Personnel representative reported back, 'No, no problems. They all seemed to accept it. Some, in fact, showed a good deal of interest and are looking forward to talking with you.' Reassured and optimistic, we made arrangements to meet the four shift groups separately one week later.

On the appointed day, we arrived armed with paper and pencil, together with a programme that would have done justice to a finely planned military campaign. At the gatehouse, we received an unexpected message from the Personnel Office: 'See the Personnel Director immediately. Do not proceed to the Chemical Plant.'

The Personnel Director was embarrassed and apologetic. 'They, or more precisely, "B" shift, have refused to see you. They don't want to know. Some of the other shifts are not too keen, either.'

'But you said they had been enthusiastic ... wanted to see us. ...'

'Yes, that's right. I can't understand it. ...'

Having mulled things over for a while, we decided to try to establish contact, to ask the shift people to see us on the understanding that there would be 'no commitment', and no strings attached. The message went out and the workers agreed to the request.

Accompanied by the Personnel representative, we met the people concerned in the Chemical Plant canteen. In the half hour that followed, they let it be known in no uncertain terms that they were not going to co-operate, and certainly were not going to participate.

'Why not?', we asked.

'Because it's a load of rubbish, that's why', they replied. 'He—him, Kojak over there (pointing to the Personnel representative who was not over-endowed with hair)—he told us that we would only be able to talk about certain things, things agreed by the managers, and that they would pick the people to go on the committee. What is the ruddy point? We've had all this in the past. Nothing's happened. It's just their way of keeping us down and keeping the unions out.'

As on the previous occasion with the management, we found ourselves once more moving quickly from advocates of 'free choice' to becoming defenders of the participation cause. It came as something of a surprise to us to discover the strength of our commitment to getting the project underway, being prepared to discard at such an early stage the hallowed notion of contingency which—to recall—should have led us to conclude that: if a change programme needed to reflect the aspirations and goals of the prospective participants, and needed to be tailor-made to their requirements, and if (as was the present case) people clearly did not want participation, or any change for that matter, the 'best-fit' solution was that we did not proceed. What we had not reckoned with was that *our* requirements would be so central to the contingency notion, and that people (in our view) could so misconstrue what was being proposed. Thus, convinced that *their* objections were founded upon misconceptions, and that they were rejecting what they saw as an imposed management programme, rather than the kind of participation we had in mind, we pushed ahead and managed to 'negotiate' a second meeting where we could discuss the proposal further.

Suitably chastened by this experience, we proceeded to meet the members of the remaining shift groups. Here the problem was different, in that this time we could not get a view one way or the other about participation. People appeared to be completely unconcerned, both about us and the programme, indifferent to the 'exciting' notions we were putting forward. The few that volunteered any comment almost apologized for not really knowing what participation was all about, while we, trying desperately to reassure them, offered a few stumbling definitions. Again, contingency had let us down badly, since we had not reckoned on people not having an attitude to participation—no goals, needs, or aspirations for involvement, no meanings on which we could hook the programme being proposed. Badly shaken, we consoled ourselves with the knowledge that they would at least be likely to go along with what we wanted, and with the belief that attitudes would begin to form once they actually began participating.

The members of the notorious 'B' shift were not as compliant when we met them again on the night shift shortly after. Harold, their self-appointed leader (physically an extremely large man) began:

'We've decided not to talk to you.'

'Can we ask why not?'

'Yes, you can.'

'Why won't you speak with us?'

'You're working for them up there.'

'We're not working for anyone other than ourselves.'

'I don't believe you. Who in their right mind would come along here at ten o'clock at night to this dump?'

'Good point. But believe us or not, we are doing this for research, not for anyone else.'

'OK, then we don't believe you.'

Still the other members of the group said nothing. Harold began to open up:

'You want to know why we don't give a damn? There's no bloody point, that's why. I've been with this company for sixteen years, I've seen the bloody directors passing through on their way to some bloody place or other. They're all the bloody same, nice as pie until you ask for something or question something. Ten years ago, something happened with me and they haven't forgotten it. And then you come along just like the rest and make out you're doing something for us. That's crap and you know it. What the hell do you think you can do? Have you ever tried changing that lot up there? Have you ever tried doing my job—same bloody thing night in night out. It's bloody boring, that's what. Do you know, even a bloody monkey could do my job!'

Ever vigilant, we saw our opportunity and took it:

'Well, that's the point. Participation might make your work more satisfying ...'

'I don't need it. I like being a bloody monkey!'

From this moment, the meeting went rapidly downhill, Harold countering everything we said, and we (becoming increasingly angry) accusing him of not listening and preventing his colleagues from speaking. Finally, he stood up, stretched himself to his six foot six inches, pointed a fist at us that bordered on the size of a ham, and shouted 'I'll take no more of this crap from you. I'm going and these men are going with me. Come on, you lot.' They, looking sheepish, did not budge. He tried again, unsuccessfully, and finally made a grand exit, slamming the door after him. The 'meeting' continued, although not for long, because the remaining people remained as passive as their colleagues had been on the other shifts. The next morning, we received an urgent telephone call from the factory—Harold had lodged a complaint of intimidation, and the directors wanted to know how and why we had upset him. After prolonged discussion, we were able to clear ourselves and suggested that the whole matter be allowed to drop.

Having secured minimal consensus from three of the four groups to proceed, we moved on to the data-collection stage of the experiment—and on to new problems.

Adventures with the boy-scientists

It will be recalled that one of us, fresh from his studies in the London docks, was keen to add to the data he had collected there on 'workers' propensities to participate'. In seeking to pursue this interest at Towcester, he was clearly and unashamedly motivated to make his way in the academic world; participation for him, then, was a matter of trends and indices, intellectual analyses in moments of quiet reflection. For the other one of us, whilst analyses of propensities to participate promised few delights, the approach had the attraction of being, superficially at least, much more systematic than his own approach to data collection. The details of the method of data collection and of the analysis may be found in Appendix II in a paper written immediately after our first few faltering steps along the road to Participation. In its format, its language, and its rigorous exclusion of anything which might be termed 'gossip', it reflects well our aspirations to be taken seriously as 'scientists'; the men in the white coats reducing all to numbers and taking care not to be seen to be emotionally involved in our data.

What follows is an attempt to provide the reader with the story behind the data collection; an attempt to move beyond the po-faced to a description of what it felt like to be taking those first steps. Careful comparison of the two accounts—that which follows and that which appears in Appendix II—will reveal some passages that are identical, some that overlap, and some that contradict. We are in no position to enter into a discussion of the 'truth'; suffice it to say that the earlier presentation reflected our aspirations to be taken seriously by those we then took as our reference group (broadly speaking, 'academics') and that this current view of our efforts reflects our desire to take ourselves not too seriously.

Why, what, and how

We have answered, at least in part, the question as to why we collected data at all. We needed it to supplement data already collected and to advance our academic respectability. Clearly we also needed it in order to move forward with the project; it did not seem reasonable at that time simply to stroll into the Chemical Plant, declare we were setting out on a journey to Participation, and invite whoever so wished to join us. We needed some way of focusing our activities, some way of placing one foot in front of the other. We chose to adopt a four-stage approach: familiarization, creation of interview schedules, checking of schedules with the Steering Group, and, finally, the interviews with each member of the Chemical Plant.

The flavour of our activities is, we believe, well caught in the following extract from the paper which appears in full in Appendix II:

(1) The derivation of items for an interview schedule

Firstly, the operators, supervisors, section head, and plant manager were given a preliminary interview and asked to describe in detail their rights and obligations with regard to what they did or could do, and what decisions they made or could make. The interviews were held with each person in turn and lasted from one to two hours. They began with an introduction along the lines: 'As you know already, we are interested in your attitudes towards your job and various aspects of it. However, before we can decide which issues to focus upon, we need to know more about the job itself. We hope that while we are familiarizing ourselves with you and your job, you will also be able to familiarize yourself with us. Before we start, may we stress that we are particularly interested in the responsibility aspects of your job—that is, the discretion, judgement, decision-making power, or influence that you do or do not have—and the more detail you can give us on this, the better it will be.' Initial discussions then took place around each person's job description, which had been made available to us by the Personnel Department. The aim was to discover whether the duties comprising the formal job description were, in fact, being performed by the designated person—if they were, then their precise nature was ascertained; if they were not, attempts were made to discover who was performing them and why. This was followed by a wider questioning on people's work rights and obligations, such as those pertaining to training, discipline and grievance procedures, remuneration, hours of work, holidays, sickness benefits, and so on.

As a result of this first stage, it was possible to build up a perceptual ('as I see it') and normative ('as it should be') map of activities and substantive and procedural decisions, reflecting various attributes of the roles of different levels of employees in the Chemical Plant. This map, as we explained later to members of the Steering Group, contained information on the potential sources, areas, and varieties of involvement. Firstly, with regard to the sources, employees might be involved in a number of duties: those which were part of their formal role description but which were, in fact, being performed by a superior or subordinate; those performed by their superiors as part of their formal roles; those which should have been but were not being carried out by anyone; and those carried out by people in other departments but which directly concerned the Chemical Plant. Secondly, this involvement might take place in three areas of decision-making: the task performance (e.g. work speeds and methods); task environment (e.g. the physical conditions of the job); and task conditions (e.g. determining the contractual aspects of employment). Thirdly, that this involvement might take two forms: enlargement, where a person's job duties were extended with regard to doing rather than deciding, and participation, where a person's job duties were not necessarily extended, but where his personal influence on determining what they should be was increased.

The language of the report adequately reflects our behaviour at that time: in our eagerness to be seen as boy-scientists by those who we took to be significant—other academics and some members of the Alpen management—we strove in earnest to promote the notion of participation as a concern for 'roles', 'activities', and 'decisions' and rigorously eschewed the language of anecdote and feeling. There is an arm's-length quality about the passage above which we now believe characterized our early stance to the work at Towcester. The workers' responses had to be programmed and fitted into a schedule, systematically and coldly.

Subsequent to these initial interviews, we drew up an interview schedule which served to distance the actual concerns of the employees; in effect we required them to respond only within the categories we provided for them. Digression—which we often found more interesting than their attempts to respond to our formal questions—was, nonetheless, seen to be unproductive in terms of what we were setting out to measure. A further extract sets out what we took to be the appropriate areas for study:

(2) The creation of data by interview

During the week that followed the familiarization period, a list of separate activity and decision items was drawn up by us and subdivided into twelve role 'zones' (mainly corresponding with the subheadings of people's job descriptions): *production and ancillary issues* included such activity items as 'drive fork-lift truck as and when required', 'check stock levels and stock records for variance', and 'take corrective action in the event of breakdown', and such decision items as 'the decision as to who shall drive fork-lift truck when required', 'the decision on procedures for handling solvents', and 'the decision on methods of labelling and coding drums and vessels'; *scheduling and manning* included both activity items (e.g. 'produce, review, and modify annual schedule in line with plant capacity'; 'prepare weekly production schedule and output targets'; 'prepare daily work schedule') and decision items (e.g. 'decision on moving men to another department'; 'decision on shift and manning levels'; 'decision on nature and extent of promotion opportunities'); *plant and equipment* referred to 'checking and identifying faulty equipment', 'raising capital requests for new or replacement items', and other activity items, and to decision items such as 'deciding on new plant or equipment'; *quality* issues included 'establishing annual re-work targets', 'carrying out in-process analytical checks', and 'liaising with quality control' (all activity items), and such decision items as 'deciding on quality levels and criteria'; with the exception of the 'decision as to where budget cuts should be made', all other items under the heading *costs* related to activities (e.g. 'draw up raw materials budget for forthcoming year' and 'take action generally to reduce waste of time, material, and plant services'); the *safety* issues were also mainly activity related (e.g. 'review plant safety procedures', 'carry out daily safety checks', and 'read, publicise, and ensure compliance with statutory safety requirements') with one or two exceptions relating to decisions such as 'decision on and implementation of new safety procedures' and 'decision to purchase safety equipment for particular jobs'; activity items subsumed under *personnel and training* included 'test and select senior operators' and 'conduct appraisals', whereas decision items referred to 'decide on implementation of disciplinary code'; *documentation* issues were all activity related (e.g. 'write manufacturing ticket' and 'keep effluent treatment log'); the remaining five areas, *remuneration* (e.g. 'decision on changes in pay methods', 'decision on pay grade for plant employees'), *hours of work* ('length of working week', 'shift starting times', 'length of rest periods', etc.), *holidays and leave*, *sickness and injury*, *pensions and life assurance benefits*, and *discipline and grievance procedures*—the personnel or contractual areas—referred exclusively to decision items.

There were, in total, sixty-three activity items and fifty-six decision items finally included in an interview schedule for the next stage, and although the distinction between them was sometimes slight, people were later asked to provide different kinds of information on each.

Thus, after some weeks of talking to operatives, supervisors, and managers, we had an impressive array of questions to ask, little boxes to tick, and Likert scales arranged for response. It remained for us to check these out with members of the Steering Group. We noted shortly afterwards that

What followed were some … constructive comments on the dangers and illegitimacy of asking certain questions. Ironically, most anxieties were expressed at this time by members of the Personnel Department who, until then, had not been directly affected by the experiment but by virtue of their now being implicated by certain items became very protective towards their own traditional prerogatives. However, by adopting a position which required them to make a rational case for *not* including the item and by relying on the pressures wilfully brought to bear on them by the production managers, we were able to keep the original list intact.

A dozen lines which more than hint at a discussion marked by considerable disagreement. Much of the comment was far from constructive. It consisted of the Personnel Director and the Managing Director declaring that certain categories of question could not be included in the schedule:

'There is no way in which we are going to encourage operatives to believe that they have a say in what they are to be paid.'

'Are you seriously suggesting that we ask them about when they should start and when they should stop? You must be out of your minds!'

'Discipline and grievance procedures are clearly laid out—they can like them or lump them. They are not going to discuss them.'

By design, we had left these categories to the end of the schedule, hoping to establish certain criteria for inclusion/exclusion of items with the Steering Group before we came to what we considered would be 'sensitive areas'. The production representatives on the Steering Group were, as it turned out, highly sensitive to certain issues: 'You can't ask that; it implies it is open to discussion, which it isn't. Management decides about shift and manning, the workforce has no say in that.' All such assertions were met with assurances from the Managing Director or the Personnel Manager to the effect that: 'That may have been the case up until now, but if we are to take involvement seriously, we have to ask ourselves whether such prerogatives are reasonable. In any case, in asking people about their attitudes to these items, we are not committing ourselves to any change, we are merely providing ourselves with some information about how they feel about the current way we decide.' Not surprisingly, such blandishments were returned once they too began to declare that other categories were not appropriate for investigation. By the end of the day they were well and truly hoist with their own petards.

Our part in this often acrimonious discussion was not only to arrange the presentation so that the more contentious items came later in the conversation but also to state firmly and unequivocally that the exclusion of such and such an item would invalidate the 'entire scale'. Throughout we adopted—perhaps we even believed in it—a posture of quasi-scientific detachment: if the work is to be done, then it is best done with these splendid scales we have constructed which, though you may doubt it, are morally and politically neutral. The boy-scientists won the day inasmuch as every category remained in the schedule and we went on to use it in interviewing each and every member of the Chemical Plant.

The Spanish Inquisition

Both of us turned up at each interview and sat, pencils at the ready, as our respondents were trundled into the office one by one. We gave a standard spiel to each of them and then went through our schedule for a couple of hours seeking, occasionally with considerable difficulty, to have our questions answered in line with the instructions we presented.

The following instruction and scale was given for the *activity* items:

'Here is a card with a one to five scale on it which corresponds to various attitudes you may have towards different aspects of your work. What I shall do is read out and describe to you a list of work activities which you may or may not be performing at present, and I would like you to choose a number on the scale which corresponds to the way you feel about either continuing with or performing each activity in the future. Your choice should be determined as far as possible by consideration of your ideal and should not be limited by feelings of inability or lack of opportunity to carry it out. Is that clear? For example, how much would you like to be able to drive or continue driving the fork-lift truck ...?

1	2	3	4	5
Would not like to at all	Would not much like to	Not bothered one way or the other	Would quite like to	Would like to very much indeed'

In some cases our interventions were more complicated still:

Three separate aspects of the *decision* items were investigated, namely the respondents' aspiration, perceived ability, and perceived opportunity for participation. For these the following instructions were given:

Here is a different card with a one to five scale on it which corresponds to differing degrees of influence that employees can have on various decisions associated with their jobs and work in general. Again what I shall do is read out and if necessary describe to you a list of decisions which you personally may or may not be making at the moment, and using the scale, I would like you for each decision to

(i) choose a number which corresponds to the amount of influence you would *ideally* like to have—regardless of your present abilities and opportunities—upon the making of this decision in future;

(ii) (having done this) choose a number which corresponds to the amount of influence you *think* your present personal abilities might limit you to with regard to the making of this decision;

(iii) (having done this) choose a number which corresponds to the amount of personal influence you are presently allowed to have on the making of this decision.

1	2	3	4	5
No influence at all	A little influence, i.e. complaining, advising, or making suggestions	As much influence as the person who makes this decision at the moment	A little more influence than the present decision-maker	Absolute personal control over making the decision'

It is all too easy to be smart after the event (or, as is the case with many critics and commentators, as a substitute for ever becoming involved in trying anything), but it is clear that in our eager pursuit of 'hard' data neither of us was sufficiently aware of what the process of enquiry was doing to our respondents. We were inviting them to come on a journey with us but we were effectively placing barriers between ourselves and themselves. Our paraphernalia of interview schedules, rating scales, and the like—and our insistence on talking the language of role, task, and decision— were undoubtedly alienating. Had it not been for the 'digressions' that some of them insisted on making about Welsh rugby football, about voluntary hospital service, about families, pets, and gardens, we would have made no real contact with our travelling companions. Indeed, more than one of them told us that the process we put them through was 'a bit like third degree torture' and some, when we came to know them better, saw the activity as designed solely for our benefit: 'thought you must be writing a thesis or something.'

The 'hard' data which emerged from the interviews may be discovered in some detail at the end of the present volume; our problem, having collected a mass of responses, was how to use it.

Negotiating the next step ...

An important question to be addressed in any programme of planned change is: 'Who's problem is this anyway?'. A secondary but important question is: 'Who wants to do anything about the issue?' (Schein, 1969; Beckhard, 1969; Bennis, 1969; Argyris, 1970; Golembiewski, 1972). Put in other terms, no change will be forthcoming if there is no ownership of the problem and no commitment to do anything about it *within* the system (Greiner, 1966; Dalton, 1969).

It will be recalled that the pressure to experiment initially came from outside the system and whatever tension occurred was a result of this pressure rather than a factor associated with participation or lack of it. Participation was not an issue in the factory, nor the plant; internal pressure to change practices and procedures was minimal. In this circumstance, our intervention by way of meetings with both the management and the men and our data collection was catalytic. We served to focus an issue which, at best, had been somewhat diffuse and ill-defined. A less generous observer could argue that our intervention created the issue. However, if change were to be effected it was necessary that we did not remain alone in the ownership of the problem and the commitment to the data. Thus the crucial stage of the process of planned change was to feed back the data and provide an opportunity for the participants to choose whether or not they wished to proceed. In Argyris' (1970) terms we were providing what we took to be valid information in order to facilitate choice and internal commitment to any change which may be agreed. We recognized that several pressures were operating against a free and informed choice. Firstly, the experiment had the blessing and interest of the London management group and, even though we had agreed that the local plant was our client and its needs were to be paramount, the pressure of attention was very real. Secondly, we noted that we, ourselves, were interested in pushing on to the next stage: our needs, as experimenters, were to learn more and not to suffer the research equivalent of arrested development. Thirdly, we recognized that our interviews and questions had produced some form of tired inevitability expressed as 'well, we can't stop now' on the part of management, and an equally tired 'it's irrelevant' or 'they won't do anything about it' on the part of the workers.

In feeding back the results of the interviews to the management we consciously attempted to maintain our boy-scientist stance: 'Here are the data, let the facts speak for themselves; the diagnosis, the attribution of meaning, the determination of action is yours.' Unfortunately the facts did *not* speak for themselves and it soon became obvious that they were not as clear to the management as they were to us. As our theory should have led us to predict, there was a great deal of questioning as to the meaning not primarily of the data but of terms such as 'deficiency scores' (see Appendix II—roughly speaking, the difference between how the workers wanted things to be and how they perceived them actually to be). To the management, 'deficient' was an evaluative term and a non-positive one at that. The ensuing discussion of the charts and figures we provided was made much more difficult by our refusal to lead the group to solutions. We appeared to be almost 'wilfully silent'. Several comments were made about 'woolly-minded academics' and 'people who don't have to work for a living'. The obvious confusion of the group and the pressure upon us to justify how we had 'been spending the last few weeks' soon led us to abandon our neutral position and to move towards a more active role of explaining and offering alternative courses of action. Even so our intervention remained slight and was qualified by drawing the attention of the management to the process dynamics of the situation; that, for example, they were pressing us into doing the diagnosis for them and making minimal effort themselves. The point was taken and the management group resolved to take the material away, decide what it may mean to them, and consider what they may do next. They also decided that we would be of no use to them in that process—thus moving rapidly from dependence to counterdependence. We pointed out to them the pressures to do something and said that these should be acknowledged and considered as overt factors rather than be allowed to operate covertly. We sought to be very clear with the group that a commitment to meet with the workforce around any of the issues was, in fact, a first step along the road to participation and as such would be difficult to go back on. No longer would there be talk about participation, but actual participation through talk about it.

At a subsequent meeting we were confronted with a number of points written on a blackboard by the management:

Objectives
1. Agree specific topics for further involvement of Chemical Plant staff
2. Agree methods and broad lines of communication
3. Agree methods of processing topics

Suggested topics
Safety; Suggestions; Allocation of holidays; Shift changeover arrangements; Immediate task enlargement; Job descriptions

Considerations
1. External (company) considerations may force you to choose some topics
2. Are we certain that supervisors' attitudes are compatible with some of the suggested topics?
3. Consider selecting a topic, carefully observe, and evaluate the changes that are occurring
4. In selecting a topic, make sure that it is one where action can be implemented fully

During the meeting that followed we assumed a process consultant's role in order to help the group members become more aware of how they perceived and arrived at their list of alternatives and plans for action; we said little, content to remain on the sidelines as the management prepared for the journey.

By the end of that meeting the following substantive and procedural conditions for collaboration had been agreed: a working party should be established to consider the issues described above; communications should take place as follows:

1. A note should be sent to the operators outlining the agreed topics and asking for nominations for their representatives; 2. The site managers should be kept informed of the progress of the project by a statement at their next meeting; 3. The employee representatives should be paid for attendance at the meetings; ...

the first meeting to be held in March 1976; we ourselves should meet separately with all the groups prior to the first full meeting of the working party; the first meeting should deal with only one or two of the agreed issues; and, finally, management representatives of the working party should give serious thought to any background information they needed to action issues, to the time that should be allocated to each item, and to the nature of the meeting itself (e.g. 'who addresses the meetings, the role of the outsider, how meetings should be recorded, how and to whom the minutes should be circulated, frequency of meetings, and evaluation criteria').

We agreed to feed back the results of the interviews, shift by shift, for the supervisors and section head individually, and to ask the workforce for their views about the issues and about the idea of sitting down with the management to discuss some of them.

The reaction to the data from the workforce was mixed, some accepting it with an apathetic attitude, some considering it irrelevant, some becoming excited and wanting to do something about it. In many of these meetings we abandoned our quasi-scientific neutral stance and explained the data; in some we presented it coldly and analytically, in many we summarized and enthused about it. We were also advocating that the workers 'sit down' with the management, although occasionally, catching ourselves in this role, we backed off and returned to our commitment to a 'free and informed choice'. There was considerable ambivalence around any move towards a joint meeting marked by a strong desire 'to get something done' and an anxiety about the consequences, expressed in references to firings and collective redundancy money. The result was a high level of anxiety.

The level of anxiety was also high amongst the plant senior management and the supervision. Although we involved the supervisors and the section head, we did not devote a great deal of effort *with them* considering the implications of a joint meeting with management. The working party, we told them, was to contain the section head and one representative of the supervisors and we considered this sufficient safeguard for their views. Additionally, the working party involved one worker from each shift, the Plant Manager, Personnel Services Manager, and the Managing Director. The worker representatives and the supervisor representatives were elected by their respective colleagues (by shift in the case of the workers). The management representatives consisted of those with a direct interest in the operation of the plant and those with the power to effect changes on a broader front should they be necessary.

Imperceptibly and unconsciously, our talks with the Steering Group and with the members of the Chemical Plant ceased to be talks about whether to have a working party and became more concerned with when it should have its first meeting and what should be on the agenda. Somewhere we had rejoined the path and now found ourselves prepared to move steadily if slowly along it with a number of companions.

All agreed to a meeting—a meeting without commitment to continue from either side, but a step forward for all that.

Some reflections

Looking back on this early stage with the benefit of hindsight which endows us all with 20/20 vision, we are inclined to give ourselves eight out of ten for effort and around five out of ten for actual achievement. We remain convinced that knowledge about desires, and opportunities for involvement, are factors which must be taken into account if we, or anyone else for that matter, are to gain a better understanding of participation. We are equally convinced that it is the prime task of *research* to determine more precisely and more comprehensively their nature, correlates, and effects. We are equally convinced that the way we approached it is the way not to do it. Imbued with a strong sense of what we took to be science—if it can't be measured, it doesn't exist (measurement precedes existence)—we effectively forced our clients to respond along lines determined by us. We had enough sense to let them suggest the areas, elaborate on them, and even extend them, but we regarded such activities at once as more interesting *and* an embarrassment to our schedules.

From the standpoint of planned change, however, the data—and particularly the way we chose to feed it back to the management and the men—proved to be of little more than entertainment value to anyone. If we are to accept Friedlander's (1966) comment that 'a mutual learning should emerge from the research situation', we clearly failed. Even on terms more acceptable to boy-scientists (notions of validity, reliability, statistical correlation), we produced nothing of value since we did not go on to add to our data. After the feedback sessions, neither the data nor the interviews which produced it were referred to by workers, supervisors, or managers. We made one or two further attempts ourselves to follow the precepts of good scientific practice and then, with remarkably little reluctance, we discarded the manual: 'Not needed on journey'. We had not realized that we had it with us as we set out, we now reckoned that our load was lighter by the ton.

CHAPTER 3

Another step along the way

The first session, the meeting without commitment from either side, was chaired by one of us and was concerned to explore possibilities and to agree the basis for future meetings—if there were to be any. The meeting was held in the office of the Managing Director, a large room with panelled walls, thick carpet, and expensive furniture; few of the operators had been in it previously and each was visibly impressed if not actually intimidated by the surroundings: 'God, it's big enough in here to have a band practice!'; 'Nice bit of furniture in here, could do with some of it for our house!'; 'Make a nice tea room for the Plant, this would, wouldn't it?'

The members of the working party sat around a large polished oak table; each had been provided with paper and pen and individual ash trays; 'Bit like Parliament, isn't it?' The operatives sat to one side of the table, the management and supervision to the other. Ken Stevenson, the Managing Director, was invited to make some introductory remarks:

'Well, I must say how very pleased I am to see you all here today. I must say there have been times when I have wondered whether or not we'd make it but now that we have, I can only say that I am delighted. I want to make it clear that both myself and the management group are wholeheartedly behind this project, we want to see it work well and we will do everything in our power to make it work. It is my intention to use this new group to help myself and the management team to do a better job wherever possible. I think that one way we can do that is by identifying problems as and when they occur, right back to the starting point, and taking the time to talk through them with you until we arrive at some kind of solution quickly rather than letting them build up and blow up. ...'

He went on to say that although some decisions might actually take longer to make as a result of the involvement of themselves, he was concerned that by making better use of their information, and themselves as resources, the decision would ultimately be more appropriate and more effective. He pointed out that the committee would seek to draw on the expertise of the various levels of employees on the site and it would be one of the responsibilities of the members to communicate the views of those whom they represented to the committee and to communicate, in turn, the views of the committee or working party back to their constituents. He further pointed out that, as far as he was concerned, he wanted no restricition on the issues to be raised for discussion and stated that if a decision could be made at the meeting, then it would be made. Wherever and whenever such a decision was inappropriate, he would be prepared to take back whatever recommendations were jointly made to the relevant decision-making bodies. In conclusion, however, he urged that the working party should give priority to issues which could be resolved locally.

'Above all' he stated finally, 'the commitment of us, each and every one of us, is essential if we are to be successful. I am fully behind this group and want every one to use it as an opportunity of raising and resolving issues. Again, welcome and let's get down to work. ...'

Tom Croker, the section head, was the first to speak, forcefully and scornfully attacking the entire concept of 'worker involvement' and 'participation':

'Well, Mr Stevenson, it's all right talking about commitment and all that but these lads here haven't got any. Most of the lads they are supposed to be representing don't care about it at all. They are not interested in participating ... they can't even be bothered to elect anyone to the committee, we had to fix it to get these lads here ... most of 'em, anyway. The rest of the workers don't care, think it will be a waste of time. You ask 'em anything and they don't want to know; last week, for example, we had a problem on a drier, so knowing this meeting was coming up, I asked the product engineers to show a plan of the proposed modifications to the lads. Get their comments. Let 'em participate. Make a few points. None of 'em wanted to know ...'

At this point, he was interrupted by Huw Perrett, one of the operatives:

'That's not true, Tom, I certainly made a comment about the drier and Josh ...'
'OK, OK, one or two of you made some minor points but let's face it, Huw, most people could not give a toss, most just wanted the bloody engineers out of the Rest Room so they could get on with their card games. Let's be honest, hardly any of 'em could care a damn about what you are up to today.'

Eric Campbell, the Personnel Manager, newly assigned to the worker involvement project, intervened to explain at some length that 'simply because some people at the time do not appreciate the possibilities of greater workforce involvement in the decision-process, the principle is not thereby invalidated'. This was received with silence on the part of the operatives and management alike, a silence only broken by Stevenson speaking again:

'Tom Tom, it's good to hear your point of view, but we are where we are. We *do* have a number of us round the table, however we got here and whatever the level of support for us being here—we've got to try and make it work.'
'Yes, well I can see that, Mr Stevenson, the only thing I wanted to point out is that no one else in the Plant is interested. As far as they are concerned, it's all a load of hot air; they don't want to be involved, like with the drier, you can ask them for their views and they haven't got any. ...'

Trevor Pascoe, another employee representative, cut in: 'Perhaps we don't give 'em even if we've got 'em because we reckon they won't be listened to.'
'What do you mean by that? We were inviting you to comment on the drier and you said nothing. You particularly, I mean, you said nothing, not a dickie bird. Never opened your mouth.'
'Perhaps I thought it would be a waste of time.'
'What do you mean? Waste of time? We were asking you for your opinion.

Seeking your involvement and you said nothing. Are you saying I wouldn't have listened to you if you'd got around to saying something ...?'

'Well, you didn't take any notice about the barrels or about the demin. plant, did you?'

'What, what, come on, what are we talking about? When didn't I take any notice. ... Come on, you can't just go around making these sorts of comments; when was this?'

Huw Perrett cut in: 'We're talking about the drier.'

'No, we're not, he's saying something about the barrels and the demin. plant, he is. He's gone off the drier.'

'Well, I'm still talking about the drier. You said none of us wants to participate and I said I made a comment, so did a couple of others. Some of 'em said nothing because they didn't understand the drawing. Technical drawings aren't something everyone understands straight off ... maybe it should have been explained instead of just stuck up and left for us to make points to the engineering blokes. They think we are idiots anyway.'

'Well, if you can't work out a simple technical drawing of a bloody drier ...'

Frank Anderson, the manager of the Chemical Plant, clearly alarmed at the direction the conversation was taking, intervened hurriedly:

'I wonder if it might be a good idea to forget about the drier for the moment. That's a bit too specific. Let's stick to what we are supposed to be here for which, as I take it, is to identify some relevant issues for communication and consultation and to work out how we are going to operate in this group ...'

'Not at all, if he's going to go around calling us all bloody idiots'—this from Jack Vincent, another shopfloor representative, in turn interrupted by the soothing tones of Ray Baker, the supervisor spokesman:

'Now, now, Jack, Tom never said that ...'

'Well, if you never heard it you must be deaf. He said if we couldn't follow the bloody drawing we must be idiots, didn't he?'

'I never heard that said and, in any case, there's no point in setting off with a fight. We are here to try and get something out of it, not squabble with each other. As I see it, we need to agree a list of topics and sort out how we are going to deal with 'em ...'

'That's how you see it, but he doesn't, Tom doesn't. He thinks we are a lot of yobs who have got nothing to contribute anyway ...'

'I never said that ...'

A chorus of dissent: 'You did! You did! Don't want to be involved. Idiots, you said!'

'Well ...'

'There you are, you see, Ray, he agrees that's what he said ...'

'I'm not agreeing. I've not said that you lot are idiots. But I don't think you'd deny that some of your mates are idiots, thicker than this table. All I said was that some of 'em don't want to know, some of 'em have got nothing to put in ... I'm not saying that about you.'

Frank Anderson, much relieved, returned to his theme:

'What I think we should do is take an issue, it doesn't matter which, though I suggest it isn't the drier, and have a preliminary chat about it, then do our homework so that we can get it sorted at the next meeting ...'

'Or before' said Tom, 'everything doesn't have to come here to be sorted, does it? We can sort things through the normal channel, don't have to wait for these meetings ...'

'Well' continued Frank, 'let's just agree a topic, get some idea of what it's all about, then see if we can actually get something done. What shall we take first? How about operator training and safety?'

'How about the annual shutdown?' enquired Trevor.

'Well, that's not the sort of issue that can be worked on here.'

'Why not?'

'Well, there's no point. The entire plant shuts down and you all take your holidays then. That's something Tom and I fix and there's nothing to be gained from getting into that here ...'

'I think there is. There's a lot of feeling around about the way that it's fixed by you and Tom. I thought we were allowed to raise any issues. If we are only going to discuss the things you want to discuss, then what's the point of us being here?'

'What is the shutdown issue, Trevor?'

'Well, Mr Stevenson, every year, as you know, we close down for a couple of weeks to allow for plant maintenance, etc. Now some of us, mostly them without school-kids, prefer that shutdown to be early summer so we can take our holidays in the less expensive time and others of us—with kids—prefer the shutdown to be in the school holidays. We seem to switch about year to year with the result that some of us are dissatisfied every year.'

'That's fair, then, isn't it?' interjected Tom, 'Quite fair, if it suits you one year and Huw another?'

'Well, in a way I suppose it is, but we want to know if it is the only way of doing things. I mean, do we all have to be off at the same time?'

'What do you mean, do you all have to be off?' demanded Tom, 'Of course you do. If the plant's closed, you can't be in doing nothing and if it's operating, you can't be clearing off to Spain on your bloody holidays.'

'Well, that's what we're asking, that's what we want to be clear about ...'

'I would have thought it was clear enough even for you, Trevor, let's face it, you can't be going off on holiday any old time. Even in these participative days, we have to have some discipline ...'

'What had you in mind, Trevor?' Eric Campbell asked, ignoring the continuing comments of Tom Croker.

'Well, I don't know if it's possible, but couldn't we allow people who don't want to take their holidays at shutdown times to come and help with the maintenance doing unskilled, cleaning or labouring jobs and letting them have their holidays at a different time?'

'Could that work, Frank, is there a need for such help for the engineers?' asked the Managing Director.

'I think it could. We haven't thought of doing it, but support for the fitters could be useful. I mean, as it stands, the maintenance work isn't always done on time, we have to start up with some jobs not completed or sometimes with a vessel still out of action. I'm sure the engineers could use some help. The problem will be, of course, who volunteers and how many of them—if a lot are to do this, we've got a bigger problem than now. And what do we do about the holidays being taken out of the shutdown period? We've got to watch the manning levels, what with sickness and all, but it's probably worth taking a look at it ...'

As reported in the minutes:

Lengthy discussions then followed on the possibility of people taking turns in different years to help during the shutdown, on the problems of managing to work with a smaller shift crew (particularly in the event of sickness) and the possible safety hazards arising from this, and on the feasibility of having a partial shutdown. Mr Campbell said that a good deal more information on maintenance work loads, sickness absence and manning levels was required before a recommendation could be made. Mr Hamilton, an employee representative, raised the point that the committee would have to decide whether the two weeks holiday could be taken at any time during the year, and what period of notice would be required.

The minutes also contain an 'action point':

Mr Anderson will prepare a detailed statement on the implications of a number of alternatives (for the holiday issue) for presentation at the next meeting. Mr Stevenson will discuss the question of 'helpers' with members of the Engineering Department, and the operators' representatives will consult their constituents with a view to reporting their opinions and preferences to the next meeting.

There was a degree of satisfaction at this outcome. It had taken a considerable amount of time but something appeared to be about to be done. At our suggestion, the representatives agreed to 'give further thought to the nature of their duties and responsibilities' and to further agenda items. We urged them particularly to think about issues such as who should be Chairman of the sessions, what should be recorded and how it should be communicated, how frequent the meetings should be, and so on. As we were about to close, Jack Vincent spoke: 'Is it in order to mention a topic I want to take up next time?'

His question was addressed to us, but Ken Stevenson responded:

'Yes, probably a good idea to have some notification, lets us get some homework done.'

'It's the question of moving people around between shifts. There's been a fair bit of it recently and we'd like to talk about it, that's all.'

'Well, I don't think here is the place for that, and, to be frank, I don't think it's anything to do with you,' said Tom firmly, 'You've not been moved ...'

'I know I'd bloody soon object if I were ...'

'Well, you haven't ... *yet*. That's down to me to make those sorts of arrangements, nothing to do with this group.'

'Well', concluded Stevenson, rising from the table, 'Let's have a quick look at it next time. Thank you, gentlemen, a good start, I believe ...'

The outcome of the meeting—some intention to follow up on certain issues—and the meaning attached to the experience by both the managers and the shop floor employees reflected a mood of cautious optimism: a mood decidedly not shared by the supervisor representative nor by the section head, Tom Croker: 'Bloody waste of time.' Accordingly, both he and the supervisors brought strong and steady pressure to bear to have the exercise very much reduced in scope. He arranged a meeting with Mr Stevenson at which he presented a draft constitution for the group which severely restricted its activities, ruling out any attempts to discuss what he took to be managerial or supervisory prerogatives. Within the meetings, he maintained a challenging stance towards every issue he took to be 'illegitimate': 'That's not for discussion here.' Outside the meetings, he sought to influence the shopfloor representatives in the kind of problem they put forward for discussion: 'Don't bother with that, Jack, we can sort that out between us.'

His attitude and that of the supervisors was clear throughout the discussions on the shutdown. The issue was eventually resolved to mutual satisfaction—four people were allowed each year to work as unskilled labour with the Engineering Department (at reduced pay rates) during the maintenance period. Selection was to be by shift and out of the hat (the successful candidate not to be given another opportunity until all who wanted the privilege had exercised it). The resolution of the issue, however, highlighted a number of features of the emergent pattern of interaction within the Working Group. The supervisory group, through their representative, claimed a special status. They approved of the plan to allow some to work with the engineers during the shutdown and argued (on the basis of seniority) that supervisors should have first claim as to whether or not to work. When this failed, they argued for full rates of pay if they worked during the shutdown. Eventually, they had to agree that, whatever the job and whoever was doing it, the same rate of pay was appropriate to all. As one workforce representative put it: 'If I'm cleaning out the vessels and you're cleaning out the vessels, we're both getting the same for it. A labouring job's a labouring job whoever does it.' The discussions around the topic were often heated and marked by the occasional clear declaration of position: 'If that's your attitude, we may as well pack up and go home.' And from the other side: 'I don't care how long you sit here, round this table, we've still got some rights left to us ...'. The confrontation with Tom Croker was short and sharp. In seeking to determine the criteria for the selection for the people for work during the shutdown, he was questioned as the guardian of tradition: 'Don't you worry yourselves about who can work through and who can't', he said in as avuncular a manner as he could manage, 'I'll do the selecting.' He took resistance to this as a personal affront, the more so when he was asked to reveal his selection criteria: 'Look, first of all, that's my business, not yours. Second, I know what I'm doing. With some people, you can tell, give 'em an inch ... it all depends upon the bloke. That's my decision, anyway, nothing for you to worry your heads about ...'. Pressed by both senior management and the shop floor representatives, he was unwilling to offer any clear criteria but reluctantly admitted that in the past, who worked when, where, and with whom had been decided arbitrarily and, just possibly, somewhat unfairly.

In the third meeting, however, our process orientation was vindicated when one of the workforce representatives suggested that we suspend substantive business and discuss the 'difficult situation' the supervisors had been placed in by the workings of the group. It is difficult to reproduce or recapture the essence of the discussion and it would be foolish to pretend that it resolved the difficulties. The important fact is that it was explicitly recognized and openly considered with all parties to the difficulty present. Issues such as 'undermining authority', 'using the meeting to express personal grievances' or 'to get back at the supervisor' were looked at in detail and often with considerable expression of feeling. No one pretended that the issue did not exist nor that it should not. The outcome was that the workforce representatives offered to be circumspect in their roles, referring issues to the supervisors whenever possible and not acting as channels for personal grievance. In return, the supervisors acknowledged that the workforce had an important contribution to make to the running of the plant and that they, the supervisors, occasionally acted capriciously and without full knowledge. Little more than an exchange of earnest interest but it represented, for us at least, a step in the right direction.

Some further comments upon the early meetings

One way of recapturing the essence of the early meetings—less particular, perhaps, than the detailed reproduction of our notes made at the time, but having the advantage of other perspectives—is to reproduce some comments made by the Managing Director, Ken Stevenson, to the Steering Group some months after the experiment had begun. (Figures 3–5). We also produced a report for the Steering Group which captures very clearly the issues as we saw them at that time:

The worker involvement project

1. Our experiences with the Chemical Plant project confirm that change does not occur smoothly, swiftly and efficiently. Negotiation of a basis for joint collaboration has taken a good deal of time, and there have been continual setbacks and obstacles (practical and interpersonal) to overcome. In many meetings on the way, there has been confusion, vagueness, aggression, suspicion, and ambivalence. Often, in order to make some progress, it has become necessary to retrace our steps or to confront issues that many would have been more comfortable to leave alone. However, as explained above, we believe that to achieve genuine organizational change, such a process, given the present state of knowledge, is essential, realistic, and unavoidable.

2. While only a few substantive decisions have yet been reached in the meetings of the working party, as a result of the progress which has been made in the last few meetings, we feel that there is reason for some optimism for the future. The members have jointly mapped out a future procedure for dealing with agenda items which they all identify with and understand; a network of procedural rules has begun to emerge; there is a strong and public commitment to make it work even from people who were initially hostile or indifferent towards continuing; even Tom Croker and Frank Anderson, who in the short term stand to gain little from the experiment, have expressed a willingness to continue; we believe that more trusting relationships are developing which will enable the participants to begin taking more risks with each other and facing up to issues that have to be resolved if change is to be effected; despite early inhibitions, the operators' representatives have since raised a number of important plant issues which they are eager to discuss and which, together with other issues recently raised by the section head and supervisors' representative, have now been incorporated and prioritized in an agenda for future meetings; agreement has also been reached on the need to reconsider over a period of time the structure, procedures, and composition of the group itself.

3. Nevertheless, despite these encouraging signs, it is still early days. The new patterns that are emerging are very brittle, and, unless protected and carefully nurtured, will be easily destroyed. While we believe that the experiment should be allowed to continue, we think that special attention will have to be paid to the following if it is to have a reasonable chance of success: *the structure and composition of the group*—while pressures will increase to deal with concrete, substantive issues, time should still be set aside to review such issues as the chairmanship/vice-chairmanship of the meetings; the frequency, timing, and duration of the meetings; the power and authority of the group; decision-making procedures; group size and representation; *the style of participation*—to continue to focus the group's attention not only on what they are participating in but also on how they are participating, and how they are conceptualizing their experiences; *company-wide support*—the shop floor representatives will obviously be more motivated if they can see others, particularly senior management,

What has been achieved?	Holiday flexibility policy (Chemical Plant)
What has been learned?	(i) Understanding of objectives (ii) Understanding of the processes by which agreement can be reached (iii) A sense of group identity
What underlying issues have been raised?	The issues which might be expected when the *status quo* has been altered? (i) Conflict which is not necessarily harmful in sensitive areas of responsibility and authority (ii) Revelation of possible areas of discord within working tasks (iii) Difficulties associated with heightened expectations (This is magnified in an organisation where a plateau of numbers employed and little labour turnover are characteristics of the organisation)
What questions have to be answered?	(i) If we go on, where and at what pace? (ii) How do we assess whether the issues raised in the Chemical Plant are typical? (iii) How do we spread management involvement? (iv) What training will people need?

Figure 3   Working Party—Chemical Plant.

Do we go ahead? YES/NO	How do we go ahead? What sort of possibilities exist?	On a phased basis (i) On a divisional basis (ii) On a basis of day work areas (iii) On a basis of shift areas
— YES?	What is the size of the problem?	(i) Chemical Plant experiment covers 25 people. Total numbers in Towcester exceed 600 — number of groups would vary from 6–15.
(1) Because some benefit appears possible on the basis of our evidence	What is the likely size of the group?	9–15
(2) Because we have to prepare for forthcoming legislation	What is the average time spent per meeting?	2 hours (in assessing time as against cost it should be noted that the amount of operator time lost in production terms in the Chemical Plant is minimal as shift workers attend meetings in off shift periods).
	What is an estimate of time spent on meetings if extension is planned?	2700–6500
What other time might be needed?	Training time. Directly related to 'worker involvement' — possibly two-day course — (900–2040 hours)	
What other possibilities in terms of time	Impossible to estimate; however, say that the work of the group indicates the need of additional skills or flexibility training for operator, this would then inevitably throw up the need for 'training'	
Do we need outside help	Our experience to date has shown the value of the 'external agent' as the unbiased observer. It has contributed to any progress that has been made to this date.	

Figure 4   Some assessment of future plans.

showing interest in and giving support to the experiment; *the interpersonal and decision-making skills of group members*—it might become necessary over a period of time (perhaps for the group itself) to design tailor-made education and training courses and to acquire interactive skills so that they might be better able to exercise their representative functions (we were greatly encouraged by the results of the recent one-day visit to the University of Bath by the operators' and supervisors' representatives and impressed by the ease at which they assimilated what we were trying to say).

In summary, we believe that there are solid grounds for continuing with the experiment, and a good possibility that, given support and careful attention, the new structure will contribute significantly to the effectiveness of the Chemical Plant's decision-making processes.

4. Turning our attention to the question of extending the project to other parts of the organization, we believe that the Steering Group should now be reconvened to consider this matter. Two possible areas of development might be considered; the one vertical, and the other lateral. With regard to the *vertical*, Croker and Anderson have expressed a desire for greater involvement in higher level decisions affecting the Chemical Plant and the site in general. This might take a variety of forms—for example, it could be either in the form of ascending participation whereby they could attend and participate in relevant, higher management meetings, or in the form of descending participation whereby certain existing higher management decision-making rights would be delegated to them; the extent of participation could also vary from the provision of more information (through formal or informal briefings and other communications) to their greater personal involvement in decision-taking. Apart from the fact that they have expressed a need for a vertical extension of the experiment, there is another reason why this development should be considered; to a large extent, it will only be possible to enlarge the decision-making prerogatives of the Chemical Plant operators as part of the present programme if the current decision-makers such as the supervisors, section head, and plant manager are themselves given new prerogatives at a higher level, and are given the opportunity to delegate some of their authority.

5. An alternative or (more correctly in our view) complementary development might be *laterally* to other plants or departments on site. The Steering Group might consider such developments worthwhile in view of the progress that has so far been made in the Chemical Plant, the lessons that have been learned, and the fact that the particular approach to change has, in our view, been vindicated. Our personal view is that one further experimental area, e.g. Capsule Plant, should be selected by the Steering Group, and that a design procedure on the same lines as the Chemical Plant should be followed. However, if this were to happen and we were again involved, we would wish to introduce tighter 'controls' for measuring and assessing the effects of any changes over the experimental period. We would also prefer to play a more central role in contacting and briefing the personnel and use different methods for collecting data on their attitudes. We would continue to regard our main contribution as facilitating the process of change itself, and helping the parties to define and work through relevant issues as they arose. In view of what we said earlier about the need to tailor-make a system to the variable needs of the situation and people involved, it is anticipated that a participative system of a different kind might emerge if such a contingency approach were used again. In view of this, it would therefore be unwise to hold any preconceptions about a linked participative process between (say) the two experiments and better to regard them for the present as being separate. The question of rationalization and integration should, we believe, be considered at a later stage.

6. If it were decided to extend the project, the following would need examination: firstly, in view of the emergence of new, hitherto unrepresented interests, it would be necessary to examine the functions of the Steering Group and possibly to reconstitute its membership; secondly, with a proliferation of meetings, the Managing Director might care to redefine the nature of his own involvement, particularly with regard to the possibility of delegating certain chairmanship functions; and thirdly, if we were asked to continue our present

Members of working party		Tuesday 17 February 1976 Steering Group	4 March 1976 First Working Party Meeting	22 March 1976
K. Stevenson T. Croker F. Anderson E. Campbell	Company nominated	1. Composition of working group. 2. Basis of election 3. Agreed Topics 4. Communication to managers	*Topics* Design and modification of Plant Annual shutdown May 10 Shutdown	*Topics* Annual Shutdown Movement of operators within Shift Design and modification of plant and machinery
R. Baker	Elected by Shift Supervisors	5. Procedure for first meeting 6. Working party mechanics:	*Personal impressions* (noted at the time) 1. High level of contribution	Distribution of Minutes *Personal impressions* 1. Reinforcement of initial impressions
R. Hamilton H. Perrett J. Vincent T. Pascoe	Elected by shifts — one per shift	(a) Background information (b) Time taken for discussion (c) Formality/informality (i) Role of outsider	from employee representatives 2. Supervision was uncomfortable 3. Employee representatives saw total problem	2. Apparent general agreement within total group
Professor Mangham S. P. Bate	University of Bath	(ii) Recording of procedure (iii) Circulation of minutes (iv) Frequency of meetings (v) Targets (vi) Evaluation 7. Involvement of Bath University 8. Feedback to Steering Group	4. At prior meeting with supervisors and operators, I. Mangham had difficulty in reconciling interests	

1. Supervisory defensiveness apparent outside meetings, e.g.
   (a) I. Mangham's meeting prior to first meeting
   (b) F. Anderson raising question out of meeting
   (c) R. Baker's direct request to K. Stevenson
2. Defensiveness shown inside meetings by disagreement with minutes
3. General high level of intelligence and awareness by Operators
4. Some degree of uncertainty by wishing communications outside group to be very specific
5. Still very much at 'getting comfortable' stage

Figure 5   Worker Involvement Project

involvement in the present experiment and also become involved in other projects, we would have to find ways of increasing our own manpower in order to make an effective contribution.

I. L. Mangham
S. P. Bate
20 September, 1976

Our internal change agent, Eric Campbell, also presented some questions to the meeting in written form:

It is clear that both for internal and external reasons, there can be no cessation of the project, and that some form of similar exercise must be introduced widely at Towcester.

7 April 1976	*23 April 1976*	*4 May 1976*

Topics
Objectives of working party
Specific proposal on 'holiday
  shutdown'
Safety
Procedure to produce agreed
  minutes

Personal impressions

1. Some dissent on minutes —
   Supervisory defensive attitude

2. I. Mangham contribution
   invaluable defining:

   (a) Preparation and com-
      munication of minutes
   (b) Clear signs of conflicting
      areas of power
   (c) Rules in initial stages
      should be flexible
   (d) Responsible representatives
      must feel confident they
      reflect views of their
      people

Topics
Holiday flexibility
Further clarification of objectives of
  group, particularly defining difference between broad policy issues
  and normal day to day problems
  and grievances
Safety
Agreement on further topics: (a)
  training and promotion possibilities,
  (b) movement of operators, (c)
  productivity

Personal impressions

1. Much greater group commitment
2. Greater understanding of
   interaction of group

Topics
Agreed holiday flexibility policy
  in Chemical Plant
Promotion and training possibilities —
  The members to report back at the
  next meeting with views from all
  levels of the Chemical Plant staff
Safety. Plan to discuss composition
  and operation of safety committee

Personal impressions

1. Much more relaxed atmosphere
2. Commitment and cohesiveness of
   group appears to have been
   established

—working party progress since January 1976.

In the discussion to date, many interesting attitudes have emerged but in practical terms, everything has finally focussed on 'the changing role of the Supervisor'.

In projecting our ideas ahead, attention should be focussed on an analysis of this fundamental point on a plant-wide basis.

Questions which have to posed are:
1. How many supervisors have we?
2. Do they act in a similar way as those in the Chemical Plant?
3. Do the attitudes of the supervisors vary dependent on whether they are male or female?
4. Does shift work alter the attitudes of supervisors?
5. What do we expect supervisors to do in the future?'

There could be no clearer support for the assertion that a 'prophet is without honour in his own land' than the fact that the management, the Steering Committee, and ourselves chose to ignore the points made and the questions posed by the internal change agent. At that time, whilst we regarded him as an important ally within the Plant and a person of considerable integrity, we tended to devalue his contribution since, more often than not, it was lengthy and difficult to follow. Furthermore, it was often preceded by a long 'I've-seen-it-all-before-and-if-only-you'd-asked-me' preamble which made it difficult to pick out the wheat from the chaff. Relations between ourselves and him were made even more difficult by his tendency to begin all conversations with an attack on what he took to be our privileged existence as 'woolly-minded' academics. 'Life in the real world', he would assert frequently, 'is very different, you know.'

A couple of further points of elaboration of the notes which we have reproduced above are perhaps in order. First of all, the reference to 'confusion, vagueness, aggression, suspicion, and ambivalence'. Aggression and suspicion we have commented upon above, but the others we have said nothing about. After two or three meetings, the group clearly ran out of steam; items were not put forward for discussion and a great deal of time was devoted to the minutiae of the minutes. Members seemed very confused over their roles and responsibilities and while they were prepared to discuss them, we came to little agreement. Furthermore, the shop floor representatives manifested considerable ambivalence about the sessions, occasionally swinging within the course of an hour or two between assertions that 'this is all a device to prevent a union getting in and a waste of our time', to comments that 'it's very good to be able to get our points across to the management in this way'. In the relations with their constituents, a similar mixture of confusion, vagueness, aggression, suspicion, and ambivalence was also evident. At one and the same time they felt responsible to them but recognized that 'nobody back there gives a bugger what we do up here'; occasionally they referred to them disparagingly as 'wooden tops' or 'flowerpot men' and at others as 'the lads who know what it's about'. Sometimes, less frequently as the meetings progressed, there was considerable energy and a clear commitment to making 'it work' within the group. Increasingly, there was an apathy, a feeling, as one put it, 'that we are only here for the coffee and biscuits'. We characterized it at the time, optimistically, as several characters in search of an issue and took solace from what we knew had happened elsewhere (Engelstad, 1970):

There is not yet any standard pattern as to how far a project can develop within a single company. In all cases, there have been periods of conflict and stagnation lasting as long as up to a few years. In some cases, periods of bargaining, negotiation, information activities, etc., have led to the establishment of conditions to continue ... in other cases resistance ... has been strong or top management commitment and/or ability to handle the problems have been insufficient and all development has stopped.

By these standards, we appeared to be doing all right!

Events took a different turn after the training sessions we held for the participants at the University (referred to in our report above).

We had two one-day workshops, one for the shop floor representatives, another for the supervisor, the section head, and the departmental manager, Frank

Anderson. At both sessions we tackled the issue of commitment, energy, and style of interaction. The shop floor representatives opened up as to why they were not bringing issues forward: fear of recrimination (they were able to give some examples), inability to frame issues in such a form that they thought would be acceptable for discussion, lack of perceived commitment on the part of managers to actually do something, lack of support from their constituents, and so on. The sharing of these concerns did a great deal to clear the air. Some relatively easy ways of solving some of the issues raised were decided upon, but most of the day was spent considering how the actions of some of the representatives tended to trigger some of the behaviour of management and supervision to which they then objected. One operative, for example, accepted that he 'went in both feet first' and responded to many attempts at discussion either by accusing 'the other side' of double-dealing or retreating into a sullen silence from which he could not be stirred.

Similarly in the session with 'the other side', concerns about the operation of the group and about interpersonal style were addressed, particularly that of the section head, which had already received a great deal of attention within the meetings of the Working Group. There was much discussion about human nature which was taken to be malevolent, but both groups appeared to appreciate the points being made and both asked that we intervened more frequently in the processes of discussion to keep them more formal.

Subsequently, as we indicated in our notes, the group took on a new lease of life. Issues such as recrimination and style were raised in the meetings and a great deal of attention was paid to points of conflict. Questions were asked and information given in a manner which was a long way from the old patterns of assertion, followed by counter-assertion, followed by threat. The section head, particularly, modified his style considerably. So much so that one of his old adversaries within the Plant was moved to comment: 'It's wonderful. We've at last discovered that Old Tom is human after all. You can talk to him now about something; before he just didn't want to know ...'.

A Christmas carol

With the approach of the season of goodwill and the first anniversary of the Group, it was decided by all that a combined celebration–review was very much in order. The Managing Director was duly charged with making the booking and choosing the menu, and the evening in question turned out to be a wildly successful event. (Even now, five years on, it is still referred to.) Perhaps most significant was the 'ease' of the relationships between the people in the room, people who twelve months earlier would either hardly have known each other or would have been on the opposite side of the fence to each other. Not that there had not been—and continued to be—differences between them; but now it seemed that a framework existed for the resolution of some of these differences. The common link between them, one which was remarked on by several of those present, was that they were in a 'learning role', pioneers in the company, moving into an area where no man had gone before! No wonder they had all made mistakes, had got lost at times, and gone back to the start when the going got tough.

Perhaps to the cynical reader these comments may read as clichés. However, it is our view that the evening was a reflection and reaffirmation of improvements that had taken place in some key relationships, an event far removed from the traditional, hierarchical culture of the company, and public commitment by those involved to continue to follow the participation road. A quick glance back to the events described in the previous chapter and at the beginning of this one will be a reminder of how much progress we seemed to have made. Less than a year ago, the Towcester management and workforce had been either indifferent or hostile to the participation project, whereas now, at least the members of the original Chemical Plant committee were beginning to take an active part in extending it further.

CHAPTER 4

Struggling on

In this and the next three chapters, we will trace the growth of the participation exercise subsequent to the experiment in the Chemical Plant. Our intention is to continue as before with a detailed description of what actually happened, although there are a number of theoretical themes which, as they provide a background to the narrative, we need to highlight. For example, in this chapter we have selected elements of the story to illustrate the different sources from which pressures for change may come and the ways in which they may be articulated and applied. Interspersing the narrative we have also included not only some of the events within which we found ourselves and some of the decisions to which we were more or less party, but also some speculations about the values and motives of those involved at this stage of the project.

In this chapter we return once more to the notion of 'felt need' that we touched upon earlier. In particular, we will describe the important shift that occurred from that which had been predominantly an external pressure for change applied by the company headquarters and by ourselves to an internal pressure fuelled by an emergent 'felt need' within the factory. As a consequence, our role (another issue which will receive some examination later) underwent a sea change, away from injecting energy into the programme to that of seeking to prevent too much energy being applied to the programme too prematurely by those converted to its value.

Finally it may be noted that the main theoretical theme underlying that which follows in the next few pages is that of 'situational definition'; the notion, that is, that was introduced in our quotations from our earlier work became more and more important as our work continued and was extended. Increasingly, therefore, we began to see and refer to events and the entire change process in terms of idiosyncratic perceptions of circumstances and how these very perceptions shaped the character and development of strategy, action and interaction.

Moving on ...

As was indicated in the last chapter, the members of the Steering Group began to consider extending the Chemical Plant experiment only three months after the first meeting had been held, although it was to take them nearly eighteen months before any action resulted from their deliberations. The initial, early enthusiasm may have been attributable to the fact that the Managing Director, the Personnel Manager, and the Chemical Plant Manager were all closely involved with the experiment and thus were in a position to assess it and to promote extension of the activity on the basis of first-hand experience. Some of the remarks made at the time suggest that this direct experience of participation had dispelled some early anxieties: 'It's very tiring and stressful but people have been a lot more reasonable than I ever thought they would be'; 'I thought that everyone would be having a go at everyone else—and to some extent they have been—but it's been worthwhile'; 'We have a lot to learn from listening to what some of our employees are saying. Surprisingly, a great deal of it is useful ...'.

Others, not having had direct experience and, perhaps, not wanting it, were far from enthusiastic. Discussions dragged on and on and on. To understand the reasons for the delay, we need to describe in some detail the events which occurred over these months and the role of some of the main actors in them.

We begin with Eric, the somewhat prolix Personnel Manager whose preference for pushing ahead immediately was stated in a paper (already referred to in the previous chapter) which was circulated to members of the Steering Group and to one or two people at head office in London. It will be recalled that his note began: 'It is clear that, both for internal and external reasons, there can be no cessation of the project, and that some form of similar exercise must be introduced totally at Towcester.' The internal reasons referred to were that the potential of the Chemical Plant experiment in bringing about 'a growing sense of group identity' had been revealed; the participants had acquired a better understanding of each other and of participation and the process by which agreements could be reached; previously held fears that 'destructive conflicts' would emerge, that people would be 'negative', that management would have their position eroded, had all proved unfounded. The external reasons were that, faced with the recently published Bullock Report on Industrial Democracy and widespread support in political circles for the philosophy of participation, it was considered that the company ought to be well prepared for the anticipated legislation that would undoubtedly follow.

Eric also had a number of more personal reasons for wishing to extend the project and these emerged during conversations we had with him over these months. After many years of personnel work, he appeared to be convinced of the practical benefits that could be derived from participation (at least as he defined it). 'Things', particularly communications, improved when employees were given a say in management; it was the pragmatic reasons, he said, that were most important; ethical considerations focusing upon the employees' democratic 'right' to be heard were largely irrelevant to him:

'All I know is that where people are asked about things, things are a bloody sight better than in departments where they are bloody well told. There's nothing about ethics there. If you want to get down to fundamentals, it's purely results—not ethics but practicality. I've known it all along, thirty years I've been at this job and, quite honestly, my approach to this is practical. If I got hung up in ethics, I'd never get anything done at all. I'd spend my life philosophizing.'

Such ethics, he stressed repeatedly, were the domain of the academics; those in the 'real world' had no time for such nonsense. Although always expressed in a good-humoured manner (and responded to in a similar vein), these comments, we felt, had a serious intent in that they reflected what we took to be Eric's desire to stake out a personal claim for himself in the project—the 'down-to-earth-practical-man'. Perhaps his repeated assertions of this perspective also served to put us in what he took to be our place—outsiders whose ideas he had seen before. Indeed he stated on more than one occasion that what was happening in the Chemical Plant was little different from the plans that he had conceived many years previously:

'Do you realize that what you are doing now, I could produce something from my desk which I wrote six years ago which shows that this is what I wanted to do. Now you are doing it, but I was working on it years ago.'

Regrettably, he added, people in the company always listened more to outsiders than they did to their own people. Nevertheless, if we could help bring his plans to fruition (while giving credit where credit was due), then he was more than happy to work with us. At the same time, though developing a distinct distaste for his repetitive comments about academics, we were happy to be working jointly with him since he could, we believed, provide an important internal impetus for the development of the project without, at the same time, undermining our own influence base.

Furthermore, he was open about seeking to use the project to carve out a niche for himself in the factory and, possibly, within the company as a whole. His present job gave him little satisfaction; over the years, so many of his responsibilities had been taken over by other people that his chance of being fully and usefully employed depended upon 'special projects' being assigned to him from time to time by the Personnel Director. Participation was one such project and one in which he had a personal interest. As he saw it, the time would come when the company would need to appoint an internal man to co-ordinate and develop the programme. He intended that the job should be his.

It was this mix of personal and professional motives (as we read them) which influenced the way in which Eric viewed the project. In so far as it added up to a 'positive' attitude towards participation, the ground was well prepared for an alliance between him and us which we were eager to cement, particularly at the time when movement to a large scale activity was under consideration. We certainly needed him and, to a lesser but nonetheless important extent, he needed us. Such were his interests that he could be counted upon to give a lead to the company.

This lead was offered in the paper already referred to in which, among other things, he noted the difficulties participation could bring for the factory's supervisors. The paper was received with little or no enthusiasm and, like his previous papers on the subject, was ignored. No powerful voices were raised in support of it, none against it; studiously and politely, the Steering Group avoided making a decision, looking, as always, to the Managing Director for guidance.

Some are more equal than others ...

For him, personal involvement in the Chemical Plant experiment had been 'something of an eye-opener'. He had been surprised by the 'responsible attitudes' taken by the shop floor representatives, and by the quality of their contribution. It was virtually impossible (he said at the Steering Group meeting) to convey the unique flavour of the meetings to people who had not directly taken part. However, he added that this was still early days and the experiment had yet to prove its worth. Two things in particular worried him: the first, that few concrete issues had been successfully resolved; and the second, that participation was an extremely time-consuming activity. He had calculated that if the extension went ahead, between 2700 and 6500 hours per year would be spent on meetings alone. This figure (to him) represented a considerable loss of production time.

Possibly the most important cause of his reticence was the personal risk he presumed to be attached to the extension: he, like the Personnel Manager, was unsure about the level of commitment from his superiors in London and the United States. Undoubtedly, they favoured the idea of participation in the abstract, but that might turn out to be very different from the site-wide application that was being proposed for his factory. As far as he knew, Towcester was the first site to actually move in this direction, and, as a pioneer, it would therefore have to move slowly and carefully. Given the fact that the Chemical Plant experiment had not, in his view, yet proved itself, and given the opposition from his fellow managers and directors, he ultimately decided that the time was not yet ripe for the experiment to take place.

This decision to hold fire was taken in April, and between then and the next meeting of the Steering Group in June, the Managing Director and Personnel Manager met to draw up a more detailed discussion document. This (already referred to in the last chapter) was presented to the group in the form of a list of questions: 'What has been achieved?' 'What underlying issues have been raised?' 'What questions have to be answered?' 'Do we go ahead?' 'What other time might be needed (e.g. training)?' 'Do we need outside help?' Again, little progress was made. The more outspoken directors continued to raise objections about participation obstructing managerial prerogatives, taking people away from their jobs, involving people who lacked the expertise to make sound decisions, etc., while the quieter ones sat back and adopted a wait-and-see attitude. For the first time, however, the Managing Director began to challenge some of the views his colleagues were raising. How, he asked, could they, as non-participants, give an informed opinion about participation? Many of their views, he suggested, would be modified in the light of experience. After all, at one stage he had shared their opinions but now his view of employee participation had changed. Although it was doubtful whether the critics were any more reassured by his arguments, they did have the effect of moving them from the offensive to the defensive. Previously he had tended to sit on the fence but, now that he had come down publicly in favour of participation, the prevailing value for the group moved from the 'against' to the 'for'. To be opposed to the notion of participation was tantamount to being a deviant—a role that might incur more costs than gains. For the remainder of this meeting and during subsequent meetings, the critics became more guarded and less willing to speak out against the extension.

Pressures for the extension were therefore building up, although the decision to proceed was delayed until more information on the company's view, and on the results of the Chemical Plant experiment, could be obtained. Throughout the summer, the Personnel Manager continued working on a central role for himself as the 'internal company expert on participation'. Another long document was produced outlining national developments in the participation debate, and relating developments at Towcester to them. The tone of this document was more urgent than previous ones: legislation on participation was imminent; it was no longer a question of whether but how; the company should prepare itself for compliance with the legal requirement while actively developing a form of participation which best suited its requirements; merely reacting to a government 'blueprint' could be disastrous since there would be no control mechanism over the way the scheme developed and no way of anticipating whether the outcome would be successful.

'If lasting progress is to be made, a slow, controlled, evaluated introduction of change is essential. ... Past experience, particularly in the British industrial relations scene, of imposed legislation has been catastrophic, and consent and consensus is fundamental to any success in this field.'

What is interesting is that the philosophy contained in this document and much of its content appeared to have been taken from our own written evidence to the Bullock Commission on participation. Several weeks previously, the Personnel Manager had asked whether we had written anything in this area and we had furnished him with a copy of the evidence. This he had freely used, presenting it as very much his own view on the subject. Although this appeared to be another example of his desire to be personally identified with the project, we also interpreted it as an attempt by him to maintain our support for it. We, as outsiders, were seen as having the power to define the situation for key individuals in the company, and it was therefore important from his point of view that we should not dissociate ourselves from the report. Our position, in effect, allowed us to define the situation for him; rather than losing control over the project, we stood to gain from it.

However, we strongly resisted being put into the position of persuading people to take the next step, despite the fact that we were in favour of this and did have some influence to bring it about. It was not so much that we regarded persuasion as in some way wrong or, in the longer term, counter-productive, but that it was politically unnecessary. The participation experiment in the Chemical Plant was establishing itself, and was in little danger of imminent collapse. Our belief was that in future months it would become stronger rather than weaker. Continuity of itself would serve the participation 'cause'. Add to this one or two successes in resolving local issues and problems, and the case for an extension was strengthened. To some extent, in looking after the original group we could count on the extension looking after itself. Our task, as we saw it at the time, was to help the participants over difficult hurdles, and work with them in evolving an effective, joint decision-making process. It was for the people themselves to define and evaluate 'effectiveness' and to decide, with our help, on any changes in roles, attitudes, styles, or procedures that might aid this.

As we have already said, by the summer of 1976, the 'demonstration effects' of the Chemical Plant experiment had begun to show themselves. Participation, in the case of the Managing Director, had taken on a new, more positive meaning, while in the case of the Personnel Manager, its positive connotations had been reinforced by the Chemical Plant experiment. At the same time, many of the operatives' and supervisors' representatives were suggesting that people in other departments should be allowed to make their own arrangements for participation. Their attitudes were not wholly altruistic since they had discovered that while they functioned as an isolated, and in some ways privileged, group, they were vulnerable to being treated as nothing more than an experiment and, furthermore, they saw themselves as unable to deal adequately with issues that had a site-wide implication. With regard to this latter point, they had at several points in their history met with a refusal by management to discuss certain issues on the grounds that 'other people are affected by them but at this moment in time we do not have the same facilities for discussing and resolving them'. Our view was that if these various pressures were allowed to grow and could in some way be articulated in participation and Steering Group meetings as well as in informal discussions, the parties would ultimately make their *own*, joint decision to broaden out the experiment, and would be willing to invest time and energy in negotiating a form and timetable for the change programme. Conceivably, if we could hold our patience for a while longer, the whole basis of the programme could be changed from what was initially an imposed ruling that 'you will participate' and an imposed change model, to a situation where people wanted to proceed and wanted some say in how to proceed.

The notion of *total* consensus is, however, somewhat naive, as indeed is the notion of involving all of the interested parties in discussions at the same time. There will always be individuals or groups who will either disagree with a proposal or physically be unable to take part in discussions. For example, in this case, some of the managers and directors on the Steering Group fall into the first category. No amount of argument would have convinced them to enter voluntarily into an agreement to extend participation in the factory. Into the second category fall such groups as head office staff and the mass of employees in other departments who were excluded or who chose to absent themselves from the discussions. Our intention was not to seek to move forward on the basis of total consensus, but to initiate and take part in a *political* process within which people would and could make their views heard, and could respond to views expressed by others. Persuasion, together with attempts to impose these views, were part and parcel of the process of making decisions and taking action, but clearly belonged to the tactics and strategies of the immediate parties and not to our own. Nevertheless, as another interested party with our own preferences, we were seeking to be influential—albeit in a different way. This basically took the form of commenting on any proposals put forward, or drawing attention to a point made by someone else which had been advertently or inadvertently overlooked. The fact that our comments were often persuasive—the result of a combination of what we had said, and the position from which we said it—should not be confused with the concept of persuasion which implies a conscious attempt to get one view—your view—accepted. Furthermore, there was no assumption on our part that the outcome of this political process would be a unanimous, comprehensive agreement. Different people had differing degrees of access to it, and differing levels of skill and power to influence it. The Managing Director, as member of the Steering Group and Participation Committee, as relatively skilled committee man with a position that gave him access to all levels of the organization, was obviously more likely to get his views accepted than an operator in a department far removed from the scene. If change was to be achieved through a political process, then (we reasoned) this process would necessarily be piecemeal, fragmented, and imbalanced, and its outcomes temporary and fragile.

The internal debate continues

The internal political debate on whether to extend the project intensified during the three remaining months of 1976. The Personnel Manager had, by way of his reports and various conversations, given the issue salience in Steering Group meetings and at the director level of the organization; the question of the extension had also been raised as an agenda item for the Chemical Plant meetings, and by this time had received broad approval—the operators' representatives were pressing for it for the reasons given above, and the supervisors' representative, section head, and department manager were arguing the case that if the people below them were being given the opportunity to participate in their jobs and restrict their freedom to make decisions, it was only right that they should be able to do likewise at the level above them; we had also been asked to set down our impressions of what had happened to date and make certain recommendations to the Steering Group about extending the project: on the former we had sounded, it will be recalled, a cautious note of optimism.

Rather than make any particular recommendations, we set out a number of alternative ways of possibly extending the project. In particular, there seemed to be two possible areas of development, the first vertical, which would give departmental personnel the opportunity of participating at a divisional or factory-wide level; the second (perhaps complementary) lateral, which would involve the establishment of participation groups in other departments. In both cases, there was a further alternative, either of using a step-by-step, gradual, experimental approach, or of seeking to implement participation arrangements across the whole site.

We were particularly eager to discuss these various alternatives, not because we had any investment in any single one of them, but because of the information this would generate on the level of commitment to participation, and, more important, on what meaning participation had for the interested parties. We were still unsure at this point whether the project was still regarded as experimental—that is, controlled, limited, and one-off—or whether participation was now being construed in wider, organizational terms. The fact that people were now prepared to use the word 'participation' rather than 'worker involvement' or simply 'working party' was revealing, but we could still not be sure whether the word was legitimate in the organization, rather than departmental, sense. Discussion of the alternatives might, we believed, also cast an interesting light on another aspect of people's definition of participation; namely, whether they saw it encroaching not only on other people's but ultimately also on their own freedom to make decisions. Up to this point, the

Chemical Plant experiment had offered few threats to senior management, but a vertical extension of participation might easily be construed in threatening terms, and give rise to a preference for a horizontal extension of the project.

The fact that the decision to proceed was delayed once more partly reflected a reticence to define participation in wider terms. Nevertheless, there appeared to be other factors at play, which themselves had some bearing on the process of definition and re-definition. The work values and assumptions of certain key individuals seemed to form an important group of 'restraining factors'. As we have already implied, an active commitment to making a fundamental change in organizational practice may well hinge on two types of 'conducive values', the first intrinsic, the second (and more important) instrumental. By intrinsic values, we mean that something—in this case participation—is viewed in moral terms as right, fair, good, etc. In so far as these values may override considerations of personal interest, they may be regarded as altruistic. Instrumental values, on the other hand, derive from the view that doing something or other will directly or indirectly serve a person's self-interest. Restricting ourselves at the moment to the individual, we are therefore suggesting that a person's definition of participation, and the extent to which he will actually participate, will be determined by the degree to which he values it for its own sake, and the degree to which it impinges upon his own goals and interests.

We have already drawn attention to the wide range of values held by the interested parties, and to the ways some of these changed over a period of time. On one end of the continuum were the senior managers and directors who did not value participation from either an intrinsic or an instrumental viewpoint. Even they, however, had modified their instrumental values in the face of the Managing Director's support for the notion of participation. In the middle was the Personnel Manager who from the outset had valued participation in instrumental terms—as a way of improving *his* working life—but who had little time for the altruistic considerations of participation. The Managing Director had come to value participation on both fronts, but was still unsure whether an extension of participation would jeopardize his self-interest. The operatives' and supervisors' representatives of the Chemical Plant committee had, as a result of their involvement, come to value participation as both 'right' and personally useful.

Our belief—confirmed by later events—is that change can occur even when certain intrinsic values are not conducive to that change. The converse, however, does not apply. That is, change will only occur if certain instrumental values are conducive to it. To put it simply, there will be few martyrs to the participation cause. If it is not in someone's personal interest to push it, no movement will occur.

From this, we can begin to summarize where the 'blockages' to change existed. Given free choice, the representatives on the Chemical Plant participation group and the Personnel Manager would have pressed ahead. In contrast, the senior managers on the Steering Group would have discontinued the project. The Managing Director, unsure of the standing of participation with his superiors, would have held fire with the extension. If, for the sake of argument, all of the parties held the right of veto, and all of them agreed that unanimity was a prerequisite to any decision taken, it is very doubtful whether the extension would have been made. The fact that it was made casts an interesting light on the political process of (so-called) joint decision-making. To examine this further we need to continue with the narrative and describe an event which almost at a stroke removed the blockages we have described.

The green light

Towards the end of the year, the Managing Director attended a conference of general managers from all the company's sites in Europe (also attended by personnel representatives from company head office in Cincinnati). A full day was turned over for the discussion of the role of employee participation in the organization, and the Managing Director was asked to give an account of what had happened in Towcester. Since, it transpired, he was the only person present who had actually done anything in this area, he had become central to the discussion. He was delighted with their response. Generous comments were made about his 'courageous decision' to embark on the project, and about his being a 'true pioneer' in the development of participation. Apparently, at the end of the day, all those present had been asked to think about moving in a similar direction.

The first thing he did on his return was to convene a meeting of the Steering Group and Chemical Plant committee, at which he passed on the good news to the members. Thanks, he said, were entirely due to their efforts over the previous twelve months; what we now had to do, he said, was forge ahead, breathe new life into the project; the necessary approval had been given, and we should now seize the opportunity to make participation a success; there was good reason for self-congratulation, but we should be careful not to underestimate the difficulties that lay ahead ..., etc. The discussions that followed showed a marked change of emphasis away from the usual concerns of *whether* we should go ahead to *how* we should go ahead with the extension. What further emerged was an assumption that the ultimate goal was to implement participation arrangements across the whole site. Thus, where numerous reports and meetings and extensive lobbying had failed to move the development on, a single event had succeeded. Not that these various pressures had been unimportant, just that the event had provided the missing piece in the jigsaw—the piece which gave overall meaning to the participation picture.

It cannot be said, however, that the decision to proceed was based on totally shared, or consensus values, since the senior managers still continued to express the view privately that participation was risky and of doubtful value to them. Nevertheless, they did accept that the project had entered a new phase, and that they to some extent had lost the battle in the previous phase. Their concern now was not to attempt to 'sink' the programme, but to try and influence its development in such a way as to gain something for themselves. In view of this attitude it might therefore be said that a minimal consensus to proceed had been achieved.

Early in 1977, both we and the Personnel Manager were asked by the Managing Director to put together some concrete proposals for the extension, which could be circulated to the Steering Group, Participation Group, and managers and operatives on the rest of the site. We reiterated our earlier comments on the various alternatives for the extension, but now that we were more sure of our ground, suggested that rather than merely repeat the exercise with another experimental group, we should consider moving forward on a wider front. If this were to be the case, we said, a lot more internal initiative and skill would be required—we did not have the necessary resources to implement and service the new groups. One possibility was to take a group of department managers and help them to develop skills in the design and implementation of their own participative groups. They would collect their own information on people's preferences for participation and attempt to negotiate with them an acceptable form and terms of reference. We, together with members of the Personnel Department, would 'oversee' these activities, acting more as a resource than an initiator. A reconstituted Steering Group would also have an important role to play: directors and senior manager members (drawn from across the site) would have to be prepared to play a more important role in guiding their departmental managers in designing their participation groups—no longer could they afford to view the battle from a hilltop.

At about the same time, the Personnel Manager circulated a short paper entitled 'Developments in Worker Participation' which began with a statement of objectives:

To consider ways and means of greater involvement of staff at all levels, particularly taking into account:

1) The best parts of present systems within the organization;
2) The lessons of the Chemical Plant Project;
3) Regard for external pressures which could impose changes in company attitudes and methods of communication and consultation.

He suggested that three avenues could be explored and could run concurrently. The first he called the 'topic approach' based on the existing Safety Committee model: a group comprising staff from all levels could be set up to consider single issues. The second was the 'project approach', again using a multi-level group to consider specific one-off projects such as shift work and pay arrangements, and the siting of new departments. Such a group would be given precise terms of reference, and would be disbanded once the project had been completed. The third he called the 'consultative group approach' which would cater for specific and wider 'vague issues' which presently had no natural forum for discussion. A two-tier structure of consultation would be set up in each division of the factory. The lower tier would comprise a number of departmental participation groups, which would operate in similar manner to the existing Chemical Plant group. Representatives from each group would be nominated to the higher level divisional participation group, chaired by the relevant divisional director.

The conclusion to the paper warned that a change in structure, such as that being proposed, was less important than a change in attitudes and, particularly, in management style. For this to occur, intensive training was necessary:

Most critical is not the setting up of a group of this nature but the change in style of management necessary for the consultative framework to be successful. Intensive training for managers in the skills necessary to set up, and obtain the best results from diverse views expressed within groups is paramount. The style naturally will not be specific to the 'structured meeting' situation. It should become a part of everyday behaviour. This in itself could contribute to a reduction in the issues which could be raised in the formal situation.

Unlike previous papers, this one was not merely noted and filed away. The climate had now changed and the Managing Director was eager that the Personnel Manager meet with us and agree on the proposals for the extension. At the meeting which followed shortly after, we expressed satisfaction with the general framework that was being proposed but warned that we should not let it impose any rigidity on the development programme. Although this came out almost as a casual remark, we had privately beforehand shared our concerns about the adoption of a 'structural blueprint' for change. Our fears now were that things would move too quickly, and that we would not have time to evolve appropriate processes of participation or bring about a change in attitudes, styles, and interpersonal relations. In particular, we felt there was a danger of the 'bureaucratization' of participation—a multi-level structure might impose artificial barriers between the shop floor personnel and senior management, and the Managing Director might withdraw to the top of the organizational pyramid. Our decision not to share these fears with the Personnel Manager was based on a belief that the last thing we should be doing was dampening his spirits. There was 'energy' inside the system, the project was finding an internal impetus, and it was important that people set their own directions. Rightly or wrongly, we also believed that we had sufficient influence (in our own words) 'to sink the thing later if it becomes necessary'.

We agreed at the meeting to move to this multi-level participation process through a number of stages. The first stage would involve a new department—filling and finishing/blow moulding (or Packaging Department for short)—the intention being to set up a group on the same lines as the Chemical Plant group. The Packaging Department was selected for a number of reasons: firstly, it was, like the Chemical Plant, in the same manufacturing division; if this group could be established, and if at a later stage the remaining department in the division—the Dry Products Department—could also be drawn into the programme, there would then be a basis for establishing the second-tier divisional participation group. Secondly, the Packaging Department was numerically much larger; there were more than 150 people working in this area, many of them women, some working full-time on days, others (mainly women with young children) working on the part-time 'twilight' shift from 6 p.m. to 10 p.m.; the department was also geographically split between the sterile, antibiotics area, and the larger 'floor' area, comprising packaging 'bands', an office, and a label room; the blow moulding area was virtually a separate department, in which plastic bottles and containers were manufactured for packaging purposes; it was, however, supervised by a section head who was directly responsible to the Packaging Department manager; the supervisory structure itself was much more complex than that of the Chemical Plant; there were three, as opposed to one, section heads, fewer supervisors, but a new, larger group of chargehand-supervisors responsible for various work groups; there was also a small section of maintenance engineers and fitters, with their own section head, permanently attached to the department and providing a service to it. In short, the two departments were very different and because of this afforded us the opportunity to move the experiment to a larger scale, and to acquire new experiences. Thirdly, it was felt—and we would have to confirm this—that the staff would welcome the chance of more participation and more information about factory matters; it was suspected that communications and management style in the department left something to be desired, as, indeed, was the case with levels of productivity.

The Tom Sawyer Principle

The main variant of the Chemical Plant phase was the new and greater emphasis put upon training, not only the training of participants, but also of directors and managers in preparation for subsequent developments. With regard to the former, one lesson we had learned from the chemical group experiment was that elected representatives from all levels would have benefitted from prior training in interpersonal, communication, and influence skills; as it was, many of them had experienced various difficulties in the meetings and it had become necessary to provide some training for them after several meetings had been held. The rationale for the latter, the directors and managers in other departments and divisions, was somewhat different. Firstly, there was the question of meeting expectations: apparently a number of managers had begun to ask 'When will we be done?'. They felt excluded from the Chemical Plant experiment and resented the secrecy and privilege which surrounded it. They also disliked the way that some of the issues now being discussed in the chemical group (e.g. holiday working arrangements) were impinging on their areas. Secondly, there was the question of raising expectations: if, through a familiarization and training programme, one could actually increase the desire to participate, this would augur well for the security and extension of the participation programme, and would provide additional, internal pressures for the change. Our reasoning was therefore based on what might be called the 'Tom Sawyer Principle'—if you can convince others that painting a fence (usually regarded as a rather unproductive activity) can be useful and rewarding, it might be possible to persuade them to do the job for you! Finally, on a more practical note, there was a need to prepare the ground for a further extension of the project; perhaps, as was suggested earlier, managers could begin to develop and implement their own participation programmes, without waiting for us to finish with the Packaging or any other department, and perhaps some moves could be made towards establishing parallel participation arrangements for, say, the managers or section heads as a group, thereby ensuring both vertical and horizontal involvement.

The final thing we had to decide was how to process what we had agreed. We insisted that all interested parties be allowed to receive information about and comment upon the proposals, before putting them to members of the Packaging Department for further discussion, and it was resolved that we should begin with the Chemical Plant group, move on to the Steering Group and the Factory Executive group, and finally get the go-ahead from head office in London. Having completed this, we would suggest to the Steering Group that it reconstitute itself in order to include representatives from the Packaging Department, and then draw up plans for the extension and further training.

Another setback?

The Personnel Manager contacted us some days later to confirm that the Managing Director had broadly approved the plan, and that things were now ready to go ahead. A meeting of the Chemical Plant group was due to be held in two weeks time, at which the proposals would be discussed in detail. Everything appeared to be going well until suddenly something happened which put the future of the project in jeopardy. The first we heard of it was at the Chemical Plant meeting. The Managing Director introduced the meeting, saying that he had an important announcement to make which was strictly confidential and which no one on the site was aware of at that time. He had been offered and had accepted the offer of a new appointment back at home in Cincinnati, and would be leaving the factory in the next six weeks. A public announcement would be made later, but as his recall would create the need for a new chairman, and might influence the project in a wider sense, he had felt that the representatives should be the first to know. His only hope, he said, was that his successor would carry on the good work with participation.

The disappointment and, to some extent, anger of the Personnel Manager came through immediately after the meeting. All the work he had 'done' on Ken, he said, had been partly wasted. Who knows how his replacement would respond. What of us if one of the existing directors got the job?... Our worst fears were confirmed a few days later when it was announced that the director of manufacturing, a staunch opponent of participation from the outset, had been offered the job. 'We're now back to Square One'. 'We're now back to fighting for survival.'

Much to his and our surprise, the opposite happened. One of the first things the new Managing Director, Tony Harris, announced was his desire not only to 'pick up where Ken left off', but to intensify and speed up 'our efforts' to introduce participation across the whole site. The Personnel Manager was duly summoned to his office and asked to brief him on the proposals for the next stage of the programme. Having approved them, he said that he would like to take over the chairmanship of the Chemical Plant committee, and also to take a personal lead in (his words) 'inoculating the rest of the site'. To this end, he would put together a 'slide package' and make a presentation to the relevant groups. While being reassured by this commitment and energy, the Personnel Manager was more than a little worried that control over the project would be transferred to a higher level, with the Managing Director and his immediate staff group of divisional directors making the major decisions on participation. His boss was a member of this group, but he was not, and there was therefore a danger that his own stake in the project might be seriously undermined, and that he might be moved to the sidelines. Apart from possibly losing some of his influence and centrality, he was also uncertain whether such a group had the necessary experience and expertise to make the 'right' decisions. Most of its members had not been directly involved in the Chemical Plant experiment, and few of them had taken much interest in its problems and progress. One or two of the members, we argued, 'don't have a bloody clue what it's all about or what we are trying to bring about'.

The Managing Director's electric light show

In the light of this, he impressed upon us the need to keep a close watch over the project during the following months, to continue to liaise with and through him, to strengthen the Steering Group (of which he was a member), and to press for a formal confirmation of his position as 'Participation Manager'.

Our first sight of the 'slide package' came at the Chemical Plant meeting a few weeks later. The new Managing Director made his intentions clear from the outset: although he had not previously been involved with the group, he now wanted to attend and chair the meetings; he was 'for' participation and wanted to push things along as quickly as possible; to this end, he had put together a plan for the future development of the project—'only a proposal, mark you'—which he wanted the members of the committee to comment on. The first slide gave a deceptively simple definition of participation in bold print:

WORKER PARTICIPATION

MEANS

GREATER INVOLVEMENT

Talking to this slide, he said that involvement to him meant that representatives from all levels of the factory came together to discuss two categories of items of agreed issues—work-related issues and people-related issues. The word 'influence' was mentioned, but to a lesser extent than the words 'information' and 'communications'. Clearly, he regarded participation more as an information-sharing and communications exercise than an influence-sharing process (later confirmed in conversations he had with us). The next slide, in fact, set out the two objectives of participation:

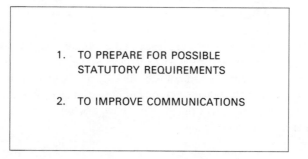

---

1.   TO PREPARE FOR POSSIBLE
     STATUTORY REQUIREMENTS

2.   TO IMPROVE COMMUNICATIONS

The remainder of the slide show dealt with his view of where we had been and where we should be going. The emphasis was very much on structure and rationality: how the project fitted into the formal organizational hierarchy, and how developments—represented again in structural terms—related logically to the organizational pyramid and followed a clearly thought-out plan. If this is what had really happened, then we were impressed! In terms of what was being presented, it was in fact hard to disagree with any of the 'facts'. To us, however, an impression was being given of order, flow, anticipation, logic, intelligibility, and coherence in the change process to date; a false rationale was being put on the experience. No mention was made of the many problems we had encountered on the way, or of the attempt to bring a process rather than structural orientation to the change programme. The presentation, as we have said, implied a plan and an end point which *we* had not been explicitly aware of; it implied a clear direction which we were far from clear about; and, of greater concern to what we did in the future, it implied a 'structural blueprint' which contradicted our views on evolution, flexibility, and 'fine tuning'. While being tangible and comprehensible to the people sitting in the meeting, it appeared to us to be pervasively mechanistic and simple. The danger was that the establishment of a multi-level participation structure might become an end in itself—that if a certain number of committees had been established by such-and-such a date, then the project had been successful, irrespective of the changes which had or had not taken place in management and employee attitudes and the quality of the dialogue between them.

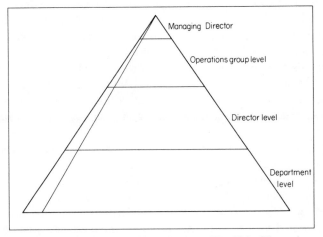

Slide 1   Chemical Plant Pilot Project: 'The Thin Slice ...'

The presentation of the proposed structure went as follows. The first slide depicted the 'thin slice' approach of the Chemical Plant pilot project. The Chemical Plant group meeting had drawn representatives from all levels of the hierarchy from the Managing Director down to the shop floor in order to facilitate communications between them and to provide a learning experience for all. If the project was to be extended to other departments, a repeat of the 'thin slice' approach would not be possible since he, as Managing Director, 'would be doing nothing else but attending meetings throughout the site'. He was proposing, therefore, to 'collapse' the existing chemical group from a thin-slice, multi-level group to a true departmental group, comprising only those people who actually worked in the Chemical Plant.

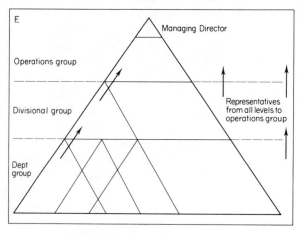

Slide 2   Structure for expansion.

The second slide showed the proposed structure for expansion. In the first instance, attempts would be made to expand the experiment horizontally, preferably to departments in the same division as the Chemical department (Pharmaceutical Production). Once these had been established and were working well, participation would develop vertically in the form of a divisional participation group comprising representatives from each of the three departmental participation groups. Beyond this, other departmental groups would be established in other divisions and would follow a similar pattern of development. Once the final stage had been reached where there would be departmental and divisional groups across the factory site, a third tier would be established in the form of a 'site-wide participation group', comprising representatives from all of the committees. In handling issues, there would be a clear division of labour between the various types of committee. At the lowest level, departmental participation groups would deal only with issues that had departmental relevance and which had either been raised in the department itself or referred down by a higher group. If an issue was found to affect more than one department in the division, it would then be referred upwards to the divisional group for discussion and resolution. Issues with site-wide implications would be dealt with in the committee at the apex of the triangle. From this it was hoped that issues would be settled at the relevant levels, and that opportunity would be given for people to raise anything they liked. At present, the chemical group was hampered because it existed in isolation and was not really equipped to deal with issues which impinged upon other departments and divisions. The new structure would remove this obstacle and broaden the extent of the employee involvement.

The final slide proposed some operating guidelines for the various committees.

Perhaps the most important consideration would be the size of the committees. Any committee larger than fifteen people would become unwieldy, and it was therefore important to strike the right balance between size and representativeness.

Group	Frequency	Representatives	Actions
Site	Quarterly or as required	Reps of all levels and divisions·total 15	Site issues resolved
Division	Bi-monthly or as required	Reps of all levels and departments·total 15	Site issues referred up; division issues resolved
Dept	Monthly or as required	All or reps of all levels depending on group size and type	Division and site issues referred up; departmental issues resolved

Slide 3   Operating guidelines/framework.

The Managing Director ended his presentation by saying that, as the early pioneers, members of the Chemical Plant group would be closely involved in these developments, and would be consulted at every stage. Time, however, was the essence. Things had to be 'speeded up', and to this end, he would 'take the bull by the horns' and direct the operation. ... And now, he would ask them for their response to the proposal.

Several members of the committee were visibly taken aback by this new approach. Ken had been less directive, more cautious. Until now, there had been no clear plan for the future nor, for that matter, a clear summary of what had happened in the past. Ken had also not said a great deal in the meetings, had encouraged a dialogue between the committee members; and now, in the space of half a meeting, they had not been required to say a word. The 'new' man had entered into a monologue with them, and all they had been required to do was sit and listen.

Their response, however, was highly favourable. Without doubt, the slide presentation had given them a useful perspective on what had occurred over the past eighteen months, but more important it was taken as a statement of management's intention to take participation seriously and implement the concept across the entire site. Some doubts had been expressed by the operator representatives at previous meetings about the degree of 'company' commitment to the exercise, and several of them had said that they felt rather lost and did not know where they were going. The section head made a further point, that with the new structure it would be possible for him to have more influence at a higher level and to discuss issues of wider relevance that had hitherto been ruled out of order. All in all, then, the presentation had clarified a number of issues for the representatives, had removed some of their doubts about commitment, and had confirmed their central position in what now appeared to be destined to become a major exercise.

We were then asked to comment upon the proposal. For reasons that we will examine in a moment, we chose not to share our anxieties about 'blueprints' with the group, but instead made some positive noises about the intention to establish a three-tier structure, and said that it all made good sense to us. At the same time, we did point rather mildly to two dangers that might arise: the first, of the 'bureaucratization' of participation, and the second, of rigidly established time limits for implementation of the new structure. A participation scheme could usefully serve the purpose of breaking down some of the traditional barriers imposed by bureaucracy; in the past, Chemical Plant representatives had noted the value of having direct access to the Managing Director and his colleagues, and of not being placed entirely at the mercy of autocratic departmental management; if the existing group and subsequent departmental groups were to be 'collapsed' and senior management allowed to return to their original positions, direct contact with the shop floor might—although not necessarily—be lost. Provision would therefore have to be made for a transition to the new structure, and communications between the various groups closely examined. On the second point, experience had shown that a considerable amount of time and energy was required to achieve only slight progress in changing relationships, attitudes, and 'styles' of operating; while we acknowledged the need to accelerate the programme, adherence to too strict time limits might lead us to skate over these things and to see our achievements merely in structural terms.

After a brief discussion of these two points, the meeting ended in another lengthy monologue by the Managing Director in which he reiterated the position and undertook to continue the discussion at the next meeting. After he had left, we had our usual informal chat with some members of the committee, during which some of their anxieties were expressed for the first time that day. They said that they did not want to get left behind in the new developments and wanted to remain a 'privileged' group in the sense of receiving information about the development and being closely involved with it. In fact, two of the operator representatives offered their services as 'trainers' at the next stage, an offer that we later did take up. There was also some anxiety about the nature and extent of their involvement. During the meeting, they said, they had not been sure whether they were merely being asked to approve the proposal, or whether they could legitimately have made some modifications to it. There were obviously some details about timing, which department would be next on the list, and so on, which they would have liked to have discussed and influenced, but they had felt that their comments were not really being invited. The feeling was that the matter had partly been taken out of their hands and the proposal rather foisted upon them.

Reflections into a tape recorder ...

Returning to Bath after the meeting, we discussed their concerns, and began to speculate more generally on the question of how situations get defined. Ken had refrained from defining the situation for the chemical group—partly because he was unsure about what that definition looked like in terms of prescribing the powers, functions, and overall meaning of participation—and had chosen instead to draw people into the process so that a consensus definition could be 'negotiated' or 'evolved' from their interactions. Progress on this had been very slow and people had been either groping around in the dark or seeking to overcome fundamental differences between them. Nevertheless, an important outcome of this process had been a close association with and ownership of the history and present workings of the participation group. In contrast, and for the first time, Tony, the new Managing Director, had 'come in' with a definition of the situation in the context of the issue of 'where we go next', and appended to it were assumptions about the meaning of participation, the focus of a change programme, the means whereby change is brought about, the role of the Managing Director, and so on. This pre-definition had emerged not from the history of the group (since Tony had not previously been directly involved), but from personal preference and second-hand information collected from some of his close colleagues. Although the operator representatives were at this moment unclear about the source of their anxiety, we felt that it was closely bound up with this 'imposed', non-negotiable definition which had formed the basis of the plan that had just been presented. What we had to ensure was that everyone should be given the opportunity to reflect on the proposal, and that account should be taken of any modifications that might be proposed subsequently. It was also necessary to 'connect' Tony to the history and process of the group since he was still rooted in the traditional company way of thinking about and doing things—a culture which, at a number of points, was contrary to the new subculture of participation we were trying to nurture.

Later, one of us also reflected in a taped conversation with a colleague why we had not expressed our anxieties publicly at the meeting. Three reasons seemed to emerge: first, that critical to the decision to proceed was support from influential figures like Tony; clearly, his terms for proceeding were those stated at the meeting, terms which would also give him some personal stake and some control over the project; better to achieve minimal consensus to proceed than to run the risk of his withdrawing his necessary support; second, that we were confident that we could still exercise considerable control over the project no matter what proposals were put forward; if it came to it, we could possibly switch its direction, and even if it did not come to that, we believed that we could get Tony to modify some of his views; and third, that people inside the organization were now taking initiatives, finding the energy to push the programme on, and that the last thing we wanted to do was extinguish their efforts:

Paul: Remember that we had been priming the thing and pushing it along for the past fifteen months with little support from inside. We sometimes felt that if we pulled out, or missed a couple of meetings, the thing would have collapsed. It's certainly a lot easier for us now. We feel that the thing is ticking along quite nicely—that there's a dynamic within, which is pushing the project forward. Even people in the management structure are beginning to see participation as a possibly worthwhile thing—or an unavoidable thing depending on who you are talking about—and the result of this felt need is that the project is beginning to take off for itself. We can now sever the link with head office in London since they are no longer needed to force people into taking part.

Nevertheless, my immediate reaction to Tony's proposal was 'Oh, Christ! Here's us trying to take a sort of gradualist, evolutionary approach, and now here we are, back at the plug-it-in, standard blueprint approach.' I thought that Tony was going at it far too quickly, and pre-planning in far too much detail before finding out what the people in other departments actually wanted in the way of participation. Perhaps I over-reacted, but for me it did seem to cut across the way of doing things that I thought to be wise. I did get quite hot under the collar about it. However, as we often do, we went along with it—often we say to each other, 'We can let things go on if we please; we can always change them later.'

Sally (*colleague*): I'm not quite sure why you should choose to go along with it.

Paul: Because *we* respected them for taking the initiative themselves, for struggling with the problems themselves, without us having to try to get them to address the issues all of the time.

Sally: So—I'm just checking that I've got it right—you're saying that any step in a particular direction, even if it's not quite the right step, has got to get some recognition, as it were.

Paul: Yes—and support. Our role in the case of that last meeting was to keep them keen, to be supportive, to show that the (to them) outside 'experts' have stood by them, to promote a collaborative climate. But we do still come out later and say that if they do go along a path which we think is wrong, well, we can change it. It's more important that they are now actually doing something, taking initiatives, and trying to move the thing to the next step. It's also highly conceivable that we may be wrong, that we take too black or white view of 'evolution' and 'imposition'—perhaps we too are part of that learning and negotiation process, and that we also have to change.

Before returning to the narrative, it might be worthwhile at this stage to reflect briefly on Tony's apparent change of heart regarding the notion of participation, and to speculate on some of the possible causes. As we have said, in the early days of the Chemical Plant experiment, he had raised numerous objections to it at Steering Group meetings, mainly on the grounds that participation undermined management's right to make its own decisions. Since his elevation to Managing Director, however, he had come out publicly in favour of extending the project site-wide. The question must be asked, how far had his view of participation really changed, and for what reason had he seized the reins so enthusiastically? Some of the answers were in fact provided by Tony himself in conversations we had with him and in a University seminar which he attended at about this time, while others are based on our own inferences.

Firstly, there was Tony's view that, on taking over, there was no going back even if he had wanted to. A major fallacy, he pointed out, was that social 'experiments' could be controlled and revoked if necessary: whatever you do has a lasting effect on the memories of men, and always creates rising expectations which are impossible to control. On taking over as Managing Director, he had inherited an exercise which had been running continuously for the past fifteen months. Those people directly involved had had a 'taste of the good life', and were eager to consolidate and extend their newly found influence. Pressures were also growing among employees who had no participation arrangements in their own departments. A new style of operating had been declared and practised, and it would take a brave man to cut right across this by attempting to restore the *status quo*. If one could not go back, one had to go forward:

'I think you've got to accept that there's risk attached to participation. People's expectations rise fantastically. We were naive to think that by starting as a small, isolated site we could control it. By participating in the way that we have, you declare your style to a great extent, and all the people outside the experiment begin to get a sort of anticipation that we will be moving in their direction. They all want the "goody" you're getting into.'

Apart from these internal pressures, Tony also drew attention to the external pressures of pending legislation on participation. Given these, it was doubtful whether you had any choice in the matter any longer. Better to prepare for legislation than to have to react to a legal directive:

'With the threat of imposed legislation and discussion in all the political parties, I did agree that perhaps it was time that we began moving down the road to participation, and began evolving a scheme at Towcester which suits our participation style—rather than being forced at a particular time to accept a blueprint that would be superimposed on what we have.'

Another reason for forging ahead, he said, was that participation had already yielded some gains to the company in terms of improved communications, and greater effectiveness in coping with situations of rapid technological change. Some months earlier, he said, they had been slightly shaken by the results of an outside investigation into communications within the factory:

'We had a review by the Chemical Industries Training Board, and one of the things they looked at was communications in the factory. We were surprised to hear that in some areas, the indications were that communications were not as good as we thought they were.'

Participation, he added, had proved its worth as a communications device in the Chemical Plant:

'Communications have distinctly improved in the Chemical Plant. People at the bottom do feel more involved in their working day. The quality of answers that managers give to their operators is very much better. They do think much more about the answers they give to people on the shop floor. That in itself has improved relationships in the area very considerably.'

On the issue of the role of participation in coping with change, Tony was confident that, 'Participation has an important part to play in this. If you look at our place within the pharmaceuticals industry, over the last ten years we've been in a situation of almost continuous change—technically in terms of growth and in terms of pressures from the environment. So change isn't new to us. We believe that participation will enable us to cope better.'

Related to this was a further point that there was now less risk attached to the exercise than previously. The management had not 'lost control' of the situation in the sense that they could continue to exercise their executive functions unimpeded; the workforce had acted 'responsibly'; and many of the original fears had been dispelled or exaggerated. In the wider context of the company's paternalistic philosophy, it had been possible to develop participation in a way that reflected and reinforced this philosophy:

'The company is very paternalistic in its outlook and attitudes. It has as one of its maxims that "people count". Participation fits into this quite nicely.'

An important element of this philosophy, which we examine in more detail later, was that 'we as a company know best. We can and do act in the interests of our employees, and it can be said that we are a "caring company".' Within this definition, trade unions had no legitimate role to play—the idea of collective representation by an outside body was regarded as unnecessary and undesirable:

'I wouldn't say that we're anti-union, but we would prefer to work without unions. One of our policies is that we try to work with people on an individual basis.'

Participation organized from within was clearly one way of coping with the demand for more involvement by employees without letting the union in.

From these comments, it can be seen that Tony had elected to define the participation project in a way which was conducive to his and the company's values and goals—something which would serve as a communication mechanism and a substitue for outside union interference. Thus the relevance of the earlier quoted phrase: 'evolving a scheme which suits our particular style'. In this sense, participation was not seen as leading to any fundamental change in factory or company philosophy or practice, but fitting in with and reinforcing it. Most important, as an influence-sharing mechanism, participation did not have a very rosy future: any fundamental challenge to the existing authority and power relations within the organization would not be tolerated.

Given the fact that internal and external pressures prevented him from 'going back', Tony had apparently elected for a different option: he would take control of the programme and ensure that his view of participation became embodied in practice. In the words of Weinstein and Deutschberger (1963), his central strategy would be 'structuring the situation for other people's perceptions'.

Our view at the time was that this definition did not accord with the meanings being put on participation by employee representatives and many middle and senior line management—nor our own, for that matter, and consequently, that if it were imposed unilaterally upon people, it might create serious problems at some point in time. Our role during the following months would be to try to achieve some kind of consensus definition for the next stages of the project which provided, at least minimally, for the expression and implementation of the various parties' goals—

including Tony's. It could be expected that conflict and disagreement would be inherent in this new stage of 'meaning negotiation'. In retrospect, however, it must be said that we seriously underestimated the difficulties involved in bringing this about, particularly in the case of getting powerful people, such as Tony, to 'move' significantly towards some kind of compromise view.

During the months following Tony's première at the Chemical Plant meeting, the slide show was repeated at meetings of Tony's directors' group, the Participation Steering Group, and later at meetings with the management of the Packaging Department and section heads across the whole site. A summary of the company's intentions was given in the factory news-sheet, preceded two days previously by a 'briefing' to all employees stating the company's proposal to extend the exercise into the Packaging area (see Appendix III). Company head office was also informed of our intentions to extend the programme. The final action was to reconstitute the Steering Group, so that the head of the Packaging Department would be able to attend.

A rubber framework

Although during this time we did not challenge fundamentally Tony's views on participation, we were able to impress upon him the need to record the plan as a framework rather than 'blueprint' for action. New slides appeared, along with a modified script for the presentation. For example, one new slide stated:

```
Company Approach –

GRADUAL

EVOLVED

RATHER THAN BLUEPRINT
```

Increasing emphasis was given to words like 'flexibility'; and 'this is only a proposal—whatever comments you have, please make them. We need everybody's views.' Perhaps the most telling new phrase to emerge was, 'These triangles should be seen as a rubber framework'. The consummation of this significant move by Tony away from the somewhat mechanistic view of the programme to the organic one that we were seeking acceptance of came at the University seminar to which we have already referred:

'The presentation only provides guidelines and frameworks on which you build something which suits you. And I think that the guidelines we have set may not have been relevant three years ago and may not be relevant three years hence, because you're going to be into different influences from outside, different situations of change, under different pressures. You've got to be loose on this. You can draw up fancy triangles, but when it comes down to it, you're going to have to see what works.'

The practical confirmation of this came at the next Chemical Plant meeting. Tony's original proposal had been to 'collapse' the group to a purely departmental group composed of only departmental personnel. The head of the department would take over the chair from him, and he would continue to take an active interest in the group's affairs from a distance. At the meeting, the supervisor and operator representatives argued strongly against this on the grounds that they would be thrown to the mercy of local managers who might easily revive their previously autocratic styles of managing. They also insisted that they were not going to be cast adrift from the next stage of the development. One of us was present and asked to comment. The comment was reported in the minutes of the meeting:

Paul Bate felt that it was too early to collapse the existing Chemical Plant group. He saw no reason why the Chemical Plant should not have a departmental group, but thought we should still have the existing working party as a sounding point. To extend participation around the plant, we must use the expertise we have established in the existing group. He also felt that at the beginning we must keep the whole structure as flexible as possible until the new groups are working satisfactorily.

This view, to some extent a compromise between the Managing Director and the operator representatives, was accepted. A departmental group would meet every two months and discuss purely departmental issues. Every other month, a full meeting of the existing 'thin slice' group would take place and would be chaired by Tony. This group would oversee the participation project and would also deal with issues of wider relevance in the factory.

Such a process, in fact, was established immediately afterwards, and it is to this that we refer in later chapters. One interesting postscript was that one of the first things the new departmental group decided (contrary to Tony's intentions) was that the departmental manager should not chair the meeting. The unanimous decision of the committee was that the chair should be taken by the (in their view) less partial Personnel representative.

CHAPTER 5

Two lovely black eyes

Having reached agreement with all of the people involved in the original Chemical Plant experiment—Steering Group members, managers, Participation Committee—that the next stage of the programme should be the introduction of participation into the Packaging Department, we met with the Personnel Manager to discuss the details of the extension. We all recognized that the situation was now very different: there was now a desire to establish joint committees in all departments and to use these as the basis for second tier divisional committees and the third tier site-wide committee, but, above all, there were some valuable experiences with the Chemical Plant project that we could reflect on and learn from before launching ourselves into this next stage. In this chapter, we follow through the story of the Packaging Department project from our meeting with the Personnel Manager to the inception and working of the new committee. The significance of the chapter heading will emerge as the narrative unfolds.

Do's and dont's

Prevalent in our minds at the time were some of the mistakes that had been made or problems that had arisen during the initial stage of the change programme (and here we are referring to mistaken assumptions as well as actions). Nevertheless, there were also proven strengths in some of the things that we had done and we were eager to incorporate these into the change programme for the Packaging Department. To begin with a brief summary of the problems, these may be re-stated in the form of 'pitfalls to be avoided':

(1) Don't rely on management communications with the shop floor: while the content of company briefings had been, in our view, informative and factually correct, some managers had not been able to restrain themselves from making misleading 'asides'—for example, 'you won't of course be able to talk about ...', 'we tell you who your representatives should be', 'we decide the structure of the meeting', etc. At the same time, their interpretation of the response to these briefings had proved suspect—for example, 'they didn't seem to be very interested', or, 'there don't appear to be any really "burning" issues', were views which later turned out to be very wide of the mark. The chemical project had highlighted the point that 'the answers you get depend to a great extent on who asks the questions': an accurate appraisal of shop floor issues and problems would not be possible if the perceived

cause of the problems was in fact the people who were asking the questions. Unfortunately, the concept of 'briefing groups' was far too deeply rooted in company philosophy to prevent its use in the Packaging Department, but, as we shall see, we did take certain steps to try to avoid some of the earlier problems that arose in the Chemical Plant.

(2) Pay particular attention to the views and actions of middle management: the section heads and supervisors in the factory were a key group from the point of view of setting the climate and style of industrial relations. It was this group, we had discovered, who felt most threatened by the introduction of arrangements for employee participation, and who could seriously harm them if they chose to do so. We were now in a better position to appreciate their dilemma: they had only very limited participation upwards and were continually being 'squeezed' to implement policies or decisions made by the senior management. Through participation, shop floor employees would (they presumed, probably correctly) be able to squeeze them from below and take away the present freedom they had to make some departmental decisions unilaterally. As one section head had remarked to us, 'Previously we were in the guillotine, but now we shall be in the nutcrackers.' Again as we shall see, we devoted more time and energy at the second stage to discussing their problems with them, to seeking to allay their fears, or, failing this, using various means to give them our perspective on what might happen. It was also an awareness of their unenviable position that later led us to explore the possibility of alternative arrangements for their participation as a group in higher level decision-making processes.

(3) Be clearer and more realistic about the purposes and methods of prior information-gathering: little needs to be added to what we have already said about the painful lessons of the Chemical Plant data-collection stage, except that it was oriented too much towards the academic researcher and far too little towards the practitioner. The data had little meaning for the parties when it was fed back and played no part in what happened subsequently. This time we abandoned all vestiges of the 'scientific' approach—a structured interview format, rating scales, a comprehensive list of decision-making items, and so on—and replaced it with a more open-ended, 'sensing', 'antennae-waving', or exploratory approach. 'Research' was really too strong a word to describe what we now wanted to do. 'Testing the water' might be more appropriate in so far as we wanted to get a 'feel' of what was happening in the Packaging Department—what issues were of central concern to the employees, what particular problems they had, how they reacted to the general notion of participation, how they viewed the company, their jobs, the management, and so on. At another level, we were exploring and to some extent trying to influence, their level of commitment to the change programme. We were not expecting to be overwhelmed by a strong and well-articulated desire for 'participation', since we had already learned that people can hardly yearn for something which they have never experienced directly, and which has no real meaning for them. Unlike the first time, it was not our intention to feed back a comprehensive, in-depth analysis of shop floor attitudes to participation, but to provide some informed opinions about (a) whether there were any issues and problems that were not being dealt with satisfactorily through the usual channels, (b)

whether people were in favour of 'giving participation a go' in the sense of choosing representatives for the new committee, and using them to raise items for discussion, and (c) the structure of the proposed joint committee (size, representation, constituencies, etc.).

(4) Don't throw people in at the deep end: many of the people on the Chemical Plant committee had been ill-prepared for what happened in the early meetings— they had not anticipated many of the problems that were to emerge, and had not worked out ways for handling them; in the absence of any guidance on how to play their new representational role, several had waded out of their depth, while others had 'played safe' by persisting with their usual ways of behaving. In the light of this, we were committed to preparing the representatives as best we could beforehand, not 'training' them as such, but exploring with them their fears and uncertainties about participation and suggesting various ways of overcoming them.

These were some of the pitfalls we wished to avoid, but there were also certain 'good points' of the Chemical Plant experiment that we wanted to retain:

(1) Make contact with shop floor personnel at the earliest opportunity and clarify your role with them: an unforeseen consequence of the drawn-out interviews with the Chemical Plant operators had been the forging of a link and degree of rapport with them which later proved useful. Perhaps most important, by establishing a direct link with them, we were able to form a relationship that was independent (and seen to be independent) of the existing manager–subordinate relationship. Having made it clear to them that we were not 'agents' of management, and that we would not be reporting back any comments that could be attributed to individuals, we had found that they were quite prepared to 'open up' and share their perceptions with us. Why they *were* prepared to take us at our word was a question to which we did not know the answer, although we sensed that what we were doing and the way in which we were doing it was seen to be so different from the customary 'management' way of doing things that they could not possibly write us off as management 'agents'. The fact that we had spent time with them (particularly on the night shift), actually appeared to listen to them, not 'taken sides', not tried to impose anything on them, was clearly a violation of the stereotype that they had rightly or wrongly built up of the management (i.e. distant, rigid, uncaring, obdurate). Or, on the other hand, it might have been a case of them using us to carry a message back to the management that they had found impossible to give direct.

If the management reason for using us was to collect information which they could not easily gain access to, and if the operatives' reason for talking to us was to convey their feelings back, we also had our own reasons for making direct contact and for acting as go-betweens. Firstly, in being the sole link, we could control the nature and flow of information between the parties, using it selectively to bring about the responses that we wanted and believed to be the most desirable. Any of the initial ideals that we had held about neutrality and objectivity had been abandoned in the face of what we took to be the political realities of the situation and the inclinations of influential people (i.e. ourselves) to use their influence to achieve ends which they believe to be correct. Information of the kind that we were collecting, we had decided, could be powerful if used in the right place at the right time. Secondly, direct contact with the shop floor was essential to *our* understanding of what was going on and what issues would have to be considered in the future design of the change programme. By no stretch of the imagination would we have been able to piece together an accurate picture of the department from the comments of the management alone.

(2) 'People support what they help to create' (Sherwood, 1971). One of the more depressing sides to our conversations with the Chemical Plant operators had been our repeated exposure to what we termed the 'moaning and groaning script'; people would almost automatically pick on the negative aspects of their work—'no one ever listens to us', 'you wouldn't believe some of the crazy things that happen round here'—comments which seemed to be made deliberately in order to present the company in the worst possible light. Everything that was wrong could be attributed to someone else, usually the management; the operators were merely the passive recipients on whom troubles were piled, the offended and innocent parties who were powerless to prevent these things happening. What had concerned us about this, from the viewpoint of introducing participative processes into the department, was the freedom they currently had for abdicating all personal responsibility for what happened in the department. By not involving them in the decision-making process, management had laid itself wide open to accusations of error and incompetence. To avoid this happening to participation when and if things went wrong, we sought from the outset to draw the operators into the change programme and to engender a sense of ownership of and responsibility for its future course and direction. Their actually having influence was, of course, central to this, for if they could see no concrete examples of their impact on it, then understandably they would not have identified with it.

Working it through

While we were eager, for the reasons we have given, to continue with this philosophy of 'participation for participation', we did appreciate the practical difficulties of doing this in the Packaging Department where there were 126 employees. In order to cope with the large numbers, we decided that two separate lines of attack should be adopted. The first concerned what we would do: initially we would meet everyone and make it clear that we would genuinely endeavour to incorporate their preferences in the new structure; we would then give them time to think about the proposal and meet them some weeks later to discuss their views in detail; once the meetings were under way, we would also attend some of the pre-meeting sessions with their representatives and try to deal with any queries raised; in addition to this, we would also try to review the project with them at regular intervals to determine what adjustments needed to be made. There were obvious limitations to this which made a second line of attack necessary: our intention was that the elected representatives should, in addition to their normal representational duties, perform a regular review role—reporting to us the views and reactions of their constituents and alerting us to any problems that were arising. For this to succeed, we would have to set aside regular times for private conversations with them. The sum total effect of all this, we hoped, would be the operatives' disinclination automatically to attack a process which they had sanctioned. Unfortunately, as we shall see, we had only limited success in getting the operators to identify with and feel a sense of ownership of the change programme, and the development was marked by their increasing alienation from it.

Having thought through these various issues, we were able to sit down with the Personnel Manager and draw up a rough plan for the extension. The plan was as follows:

(1) Meeting with departmental management team—head of department, section heads, and supervisors.
(2) Briefing by senior management to all employees.
(3) Meeting with chargehands as a group.
(4) Meeting with all operators in 'natural' groups (day and evening shifts).
(5) Meeting with department fitters and engineers.
(6) Report back to management team.
(7) Report back to Steering Group.
(8) Report back to operators and chargehands.
(9) Nomination and election of representatives.
(10) 'Training' session with management representatives.
(11) 'Training' session with shop floor representatives.
(12) First meeting of the new Packaging Participation Committee.

The department

As a preliminary to what follows, the reader might find useful a brief description of the department and some of its main characters. As with the Chemical Plant, the management chain in the department is long. Like his counterpart in the Chemical Plant, the head of Packaging (Michael) reports to the Manager Production Services (Charles), who in turn reports to Simon, the Director of Pharmaceutical Production. The organization chart (see Appendix IV) shows reporting lines below Michael.

In contrast with the one section head in the Chemical Plant, there are three in the Packaging Department, one responsible for the manufacture of plastic bottles (Bert, a man if his fifties, who was, in fact, replaced by a younger man during the course of the exercise), one in charge of the department's engineering section (Ernie, a younger, relatively new man to the department), and one responsible for a wide range of production activities—labelling of packaged tablets and capsules, cleaning, porterage, clerical work, and packaging itself (Fred). The packaging activity divides into two main parts and into two geographically separate areas: more than eighty female employees work on mechanized 'bands', either filling cartons with tablets or capsules, or 'finishing' the packaged product. The main area where this is done is known simply as the 'floor', a spacious area divided between ten production bands, each with approximately eight operators. The other area is known as the 'sterile' or 'antibiotics' area, screened from the rest of the factory, where 'Dunromin' and penicillin products are packed for despatch. Fred, the section head for both areas, is the central figure of the department, a large man who rules his empire through two section supervisors (Ron and Arthur), and fourteen female chargehands.

Certain aspects of the organization are worth highlighting for the story that follows: firstly, a predominantly female workforce is supervised exclusively by males, and the age spread of operators and managers is wide; secondly, Michael and Ernie are fairly new to the department. Fred is the 'old stager', who for many years ran the department and reported directly to the Manager Production Services. Not surprisingly, during this time he had left a strong personal print on the department, and had been able to control almost single-handed most of its operations. The arrival of Michael and Ernie, both much younger men, had created difficulties for all concerned. In Ernie's words:

'Michael and I were brought in last year—before that it was Fred reporting direct to Charles. When Michael was put in, Fred found this very difficult. Fred used to have the office ladies generating figures—he still does, for that matter—and he was the only one who could understand them. He had total control. We've been trying to get things more centralized so that we can understand and have access to what is going on.'

The extent to which Fred *still* had control despite the changes that had occurred in the formal structure, and the extent to which Michael was prepared to 'manage' Fred and the rest of the department was something which had a considerable bearing on the way in which the participation programme developed.

A third aspect of the structure worth noting is the strategic position occupied by Ron and Arthur, the section supervisors who had most direct contact with the shop floor. Supported by Fred, they could effectively filter out communications between the girls and the senior managers, and could insist that there be no 'short-circuiting' between top and bottom. Thus, like Fred, they had considerable freedom to decide how the various sections should be run and could put a very personal print on the proceedings.

Finally, the separation between the day girls, twilight girls, and the engineering section should be noted. There was little or no contact between the eight-hour day girls and the 6–10 p.m. 'twilight' girls, and frequently there were complaints that the one shift had left a mess for the other shift to clear up. There were also some tensions between the male fitters and female operators, with the former often being accused of sitting in the workshop adjoining the main floor reading the newspaper and drinking tea, instead of repairing or maintaining machines that were frequently breaking down.

Preliminary meetings with the management team

Our first meeting with the management team started rather badly—although it was not without its humorous side. Tony, the Managing Director, had thought it important to put the official seal of approval on the project by spending a brief time with the team and ourselves in order to, as he said, 'set the scene and gee them up a bit'. What followed was recounted to a colleague (into the tape recorder) shortly afterwards:

'Well, here we all were in the Managing Director's parlour—a gigantic room about eight times bigger than this one, typically American, you know, and really a bit overbearing—not the sort of place that these people visited frequently. And here were two strangers from a distant university and the Personnel Manager. Tony's introductory spiel outlining what had happened and what we now wanted to do was most impressive—but he didn't seeem quite to know how to finish. "I shall be leaving you in a minute", he kept saying, but could not bring himself to actually go. "Now, I want you to be completely open and frank with them (do you hear me?)" ... "Well, I'll be going now and the Personnel Manager will be going with me" ... and so on. If setting them at ease had been his intention, this was the last thing he had done. I know that if my Managing Director was *telling* me to be open with two strangers, this would be the last thing I would do. By the time he did leave, everyone was keyed up for something big to happen!

'Our part of the meeting began disastrously. We had decided beforehand to take in a tape-recorder to get a fuller record of what happened in the Packaging Department, and feeling that, given the choice, the people would decide not to have it in, we did present it to them rather as a *fait accompli*. Well, Iain plugged it in, switched it on, and nothing happened. So there he is trying to figure out why it won't go and saying, "While I'm trying to get this going, Paul will fill you in on the background to the participation project." So I begin ... and in the meantime, everyone's eyes are firmly fixed on Iain and the tape recorder. My attempts to bring the thing back into line finally failed when Iain disappeared under the desk looking for another plug. By this time, everyone's eyes had switched to the backside sticking up from the desk. The final *coup de grace* was delivered by Fred, the section head, who, like his colleagues, had not uttered a word since coming into the room, and who had become redder and redder in the face, when he finally muttered, "Why do we need this when it's been a bit of a flop in the Chemical Plant?" ...'

Needless to say, we made little progress in this meeting except to identify (and possibly add to) the managers' anxieties about the proposed participation scheme. Their main objections were that (a) there was already a great amount of participation in the department, and there was little need for a formal committee system; (b) existing communication mechanisms were more than adequate, and there was a danger that a participation committee would merely duplicate business currently being dealt with in supervisors' and Health and Safety meetings; (c) the shop floor people were neither capable of nor interested in greater participation: 'You have to appreciate that many of our female employees are of a much lower grade and calibre than Chemical Plant employees, and there's a good deal of apathy, particularly among the older ones. We've tried holding meetings before but people were just not interested'; and (d) there weren't any really burning issues that could be raised, and whenever there were, 'we're always accessible enough to deal with them'.

Although the temptation was there, we refused to let ourselves be drawn in to the 'sell and tell' about participation or into commenting on the points they had raised. We did suggest somewhat mildly, however, that other people might not see things the same way, and that there might be some personal advantages to them which they may have overlooked. Nevertheless, if, at the end of the day, they decided not to participate, then this was their choice and no-one would challenge it. The meeting broke up after an undertaking by us to meet them at a later date and give a summary of our discussions with the rest of the workforce.

A free choice?

Returning home after the meeting, we reviewed what had happened and speculated on the stance we should adopt towards the supervisors in future. The issue seemed to centre around the question of 'free and informed choice', Argyris' (1970) persuasively simple maxim on organizational change. What was 'free' in the case of these people and how desirable and realistic was it? Clearly they were being given a free choice about whether or not they personally wished to participate, but how much actual freedom did they have to choose freely? There was an implied limitation in that they could not make up the minds of other groups, but, more important, given the enthusiasm of their superiors for the scheme and given the possible high costs of their non-involvement in it, their freedom to make free choice appeared to be merely hypothetical. They were, after all, regarded as 'management' and expected, regardless of personal preference, to carry out the wishes of the company. If they were not in a position to make a free choice, we also believed they were not in a position to make an informed choice. They had not directly experienced participation and had not apparently talked at any length with people in a similar position as themselves who had. Clearly there were limitations to the amount of information we could provide on how a supervisor or manager 'felt' about the participation process.

There appeared to be a parallel here, we remarked, with (of all things) the parents who want their child to learn the piano: given the freedom to choose, the youngster would in the majority of cases decide not to go to piano lessons, preferring to carry on with the things he already enjoyed doing. Even if he were persuaded to go for lessons, the long hours of practice and feeling that he was not getting anywhere might lead him to give up. The decision for the parents is whether to compel him to carry on against his wishes or respect his preference to withdraw. Clearly not having experienced the pleasures of playing an instrument well, he can hardly feel any strong, positive attraction towards going for lessons or persisting with them when the going gets tough. In other words, initially he is not in a position of informed choice and premature withdrawal might in later life be considered with great regret. On the other hand, the risk attached to his parents insisting that he carry on is that he goes through a series of difficult and dissatisfying experiences, only to find that he hates playing the piano, or would have preferred to learn the trombone!

Like the parent in this illustration, we, for a number of reasons, wanted the supervisors to participate in the scheme, and believed rightly or wrongly that, as of that moment, they were not in a position of informed choice. Perhaps, then, our strategy should be to let information precede free choice—encourage them to 'give it a go', while respecting their wishes to pull out at any time. The problem, though, was that we were not in a position to provide the relevant information. Recognizing this, we decided to invite the management team to meet a supervisor and the section head from the Chemical Plant who had first-hand experience of participation and who could give a 'warts and all' view of this experience.

In the event, they were happy to do this and a meeting took place shortly afterwards. The record of this meeting tells its own story, but it might be worth noting, in contrast to our initial meeting, how much more meaningful this meeting was in terms of drawing out the real anxieties the supervisors felt, and of imparting to them the essential flavour of what was to come.

After some preliminary discussion about the role of the representative, Ron, the section supervisor, began to express some concerns about his position in the participation meetings:

Ron (*to Ray, his counterpart in the Chemical Plant*): How much defence work do I have to do in these meetings?

Ray: What do you mean?

Ron: Well, if my people say, 'Ron, you keep moving me around between bands', I have to defend myself. I'm asking you how you defend yourselves in the meetings.

Ray: It's true that in the first few meetings we had to defend. We lost a lot of ground, or at least seemed to. We were used to making decisions without being questioned, and understandably we were pretty upset at first. But gradually we began to see some value in explaining our decisions, and got used to having to do this. I suppose *we* began to get educated as a result of sharing attitudes.

Tom (*section head, Chemical Plant*): We have not achieved much in concrete terms, but now we can all at least talk to each other—which is bloody important when you get down to it. You will get very involved—emotionally—and there will be problems, but things will start to come. You as supervisors will be able to raise your own issues and get something out of it.

Paul: Would you say, Tom, that things don't get more difficult, but perhaps a little easier?

Tom: I wouldn't actually say that, but what you are doing is actually treating people as human beings.

Fred (*without much conviction*): I'm sure my life is going to be easier. I've spent ages and ages talking to people explaining what's going on, and it's been worth it.

Tom: Like you, Ron, we used to move people from shift to shift—it was a unilateral decision. This issue came up very early, there was a lot of discussion and it was agreed that in future if a person was moved from shift to shift, we would have to give reasons. You must remember that a person can ultimately say no, and you can't really do anything about it.

Ron: Well, don't you think you've then lost something, and can't do your job properly? What the hell do we do with people who, as a result of the new system, refuse to move?

Paul: People aren't going to refuse as a result of this. All you're being asked to do is give reasons. There may be advantages for you in this—people may have a better understanding of your problems, and may be less inclined to blame you.

Ray: Look, Ron, there may be things you've been doing for twenty years or more which you automatically think are right. Then someone says your views are stupid, and that shatters you. But then you look and very often you find that he's right.

Tom: You are going to get sniping until people get rid of their 'chips', but after that you'll find that you can actually talk to each other.

Fred: Would you say that relations with the operators are better now?

Tom: Definitely, yes. And I'm doing my job better now. I think more about the decisions I am making and their implications. And don't forget that you can use these meetings to bring up things with your managers, and like you, they have to explain themselves.

Ron (*unable to contain himself any longer*): Look, I'm paid to do a job of work, why should *I* explain and be answerable to everybody else? I've got a job description which says what I do. Why should the girls question me?

Paul: If Fred makes a decision that you think is wrong, do you not think that you have the right to question him? The girls have the same right, surely?

Ray (*Laughing*): I was saying exactly the same thing that you are now saying, Ron. I used to get very annoyed and think why are they allowed to question me like that? But it works both ways, you know—not only do I involve the operatives more, now I get more involved with Tom and the people above him.

Ron: Now you're talking. There's a lot of people higher up who have got a bloody lot to give us.

Tom: Well, there you go—there's probably a lot of people on the shop floor saying 'I want a bloody lot from Ron Brass' ...

(Discussion then moved on to how issues got raised at meetings and the sort of things that had been dealt with in the Chemical Plant. After this, the meeting ended.)

The above extract underlines quite clearly the fear that the supervisors—and particularly Ron—had of losing their freedom to make their own decisions, and the feeling that their subordinates had absolutely no right to meddle in *their* jobs. It can be seen that the whole notion of participation was alien to their conception of the role and rights of a manager. While they were still highly sceptical after the meeting (and understandably so), we did feel that they had begun to be more aware of and to reflect upon views and assumptions that they had always taken for granted as being inherently right and indisputable.

The presence of Tom and Ray had turned out to be particularly powerful. After all, here were two of their colleagues in the same boat as themselves actually defending the participation programme, and challenging their grounds for resisting it. Here was a new pressure to add to existing pressure from the 'company' side to go the participation way, and here were people who were not only saying that they would have to abandon some of their traditional ways of doing things, but could in fact derive some personal benefit in terms of greater involvement in decision-making at the higher level. In short, here was a clear invitation for the supervisors to take a long and hard look at their 'instinctive', habitual notions of management and participation and, as a result of this, to possibly re-think (i.e. re-define) their personal situations.

What's in it for me?

The third and final meeting with the management team took place a couple of weeks later, its purpose being to discuss the views and issues which had emerged from our meetings with the shop floor personnel (then complete), and in the light of the discussion, to agree on an acceptable form for the new participation meeting. We were immediately struck by an apparent change of heart by some of its members, and by Fred, the section head, in particular. Whereas previously they had seriously questioned the desirability of participation, they now seemed to be assuming that it would happen and that consideration of the 'how' rather than the 'whether' was more important at this meeting. It seemed as though, having reflected on the arguments that had been put forward and on the mounting pressures to introduce participation, they had made a crucial decision to swim with rather than against the tide. Perhaps the meeting with their counterparts in the Chemical Plant had settled the matter, or perhaps their change of heart had more to do with the recent company brief to all employees, giving a formal undertaking to introduce participation in the Packaging area. There had also apparently been some 'leaks' from our meetings with the shop floor personnel which may have contributed to this attitude. Perhaps it had been the combined effect of these factors rather than any single one which had led to a change of heart.

Whatever the cause, each member of the team had chosen to rationalize the decision in a different way (although what they all had in common was a desire to show that they were neither being coerced nor inconsistent). Michael, the head of the department, gave the impression that he had always been for participation, but had thought it necessary to adopt a devil's advocate position in order to promote an all-round debate. Furthermore, being 'responsible' for his supervisors, he had felt it necessary to represent their fears and anxieties to ourselves and the senior management. Fred's new stance was particularly interesting, since it allowed him to remain personally sceptical and to adopt a wait-and-see attitude without incurring the displeasure of his superiors. Regardless of his personal feelings, he said, he had a dual loyalty to the company and to 'his girls'; if the management wanted participation, it was his job to bring this about; if his girls had issues that they wanted to raise, then it was his job to help them to raise these issues. 'We've got to get it right', he kept saying in the meeting, 'We've got to make sure that the constituencies are not too big and we've got to make sure that the girls get adequate representation. I'm particularly worried about the involvement of my chargehands and supervisors like Ron and Arthur. I don't want them left out; the supervisors as a group need to be represented, even if that means they have a chance to disagree with decisions I make.' This move from critic to champion of the participation cause was greeted with surprise and bewilderment by the people present at the meeting, ourselves included.

Ron's and Ernie's attitude was 'If this is going to happen—and let's face it, it's going to—we're going to make sure that we get something out of it for ourselves'. In the case of Ron, this meant more personal influence on decisions made by Fred, Michael, and the senior management, and in the case of Ernie, of getting more co-operation from his fitters, and a better relationship with the production people.

Whereas previously we had been worried that the management team would choose not to nominate anyone to the new committee, the problem we now had was that everyone wanted to sit on it. Some minor squabbles over this broke out at the meeting, with Fred arguing that having the largest empire entitled him to a seat, and with Ron saying that, as many of the issues raised by the operators seemed to concern him personally, he should be allowed to handle them in person. While everyone agreed that there could only be one representative from the supervisor and one from the section head level, no one was prepared to stand down. Our reaction was to suggest that they discuss the matter further after the meeting and inform us of their choices. Subsequent to this, we would meet the representatives and talk further with them about the sorts of things that might happen in the participation meetings.

One week later, we arrived at the appointed time, only to be told by Michael that the section heads and supervisors had agreed to 'take turns' at representing each other, having failed to make a single choice. We said that continuity was essential to the success of participation and that they should therefore try harder to reach some kind of agreement between themselves. Despite his requests to see them all again, we said that the purpose of our meeting was to discuss representation with the representatives, not to see them all again and make a choice for them. He was visibly upset by this but agreed to take our message back. At the same time, he raised some concerns about his position in the participation set-up. He had been alarmed, he said, by some of the comments from the shop floor that we had fed back at the meeting (more of these later), and had since then made his own investigations and confirmed their accuracy. Many complaints had been directed at his management team, particularly Fred and Ron, but the problem he now had was how *he* could manage his management team; if he publicly agreed with the criticisms, he would be betraying them, but if he did nothing about them, he would be criticized by his superiors. Previously the problems of the department had been kept internal, but the participation project was turning over stones and exposing the problems to a wider audience. He would be responsible, so what could he do, he asked, to sort out the problems?

Our view, we said, was that the source of his problem was that he was responsible for a team which, by his own admission, he could not control. Fred was still effectively running the department, but it was he, not Fred, who would be blamed for things when they went wrong. The question was, did he want to run the department, and if he did, from what source could he draw on the necessary authority, and how could he use the new participation set-up to assert it? He readily confirmed this view and said that Charles, his superior, was the main source of authority in the department: he was the 'manager', with the potential authority, who had left him with no authority, to do the managing. Following on from this and further discussion with us, he decided to try to put authority before loyalty to his operational team, and to try to take some of the influence away from Charles in order to do this. His key task, he said, would be to assume the chairmanship of the new participation committee, and seek to influence events from there. In this role, he would have direct access to members of the shop floor and could use them to exert pressure on Fred and Ron.

In the event, Michael was not successful in being appointed to the chair. It was decided that initially the Divisional Director should occupy this position until the group could be collapsed to a purely departmental committee, at which time Charles would take the chair. Nevertheless, as we shall see, our meeting with Michael was not without its impact; firstly, it clarified in his mind the source and nature of his problem, and the magnitude of the task to resolve it; as he remarked after our meeting, 'Thank you, gentlemen. After that I don't know whether I'm reassured or more worried. I suppose it's because I now see the job that lies ahead of me.' And secondly, it settled the question of his involvement in the participation committee, since he saw it as a way of bringing about the situation he desired.

The postcript to our meetings with the management team was that its members were finally able to agree on the respresentation for the Participation Committee. Fred, as we had anticipated and hoped, was chosen as the section head representative and Ron as the supervisors' representative. Michael would also sit in his own right as head of department, while Charles for the moment would be excluded.

Briefings to the shop floor and the initial response

Shortly after our first meeting with the department's management team, the official briefing (to which we have previously referred) of all employees on site took place. As usual, the briefing process was carried out with almost military precision: directors and managers on site were instructed to commence at exactly 09.00 hours and to have completed the brief by the end of the second day. The briefing guideline, written by the Personnel Department in consultation with ourselves, was

not to be read out to staff, but used as a quick guide a) prior to the briefing meeting, and b) during the meeting as a discreet check. As far as possible, brief the matter in your own words, with normal style and phraseology, so that your discussion is natural, EXCEPT that certain words and phrases in the written text are underlined; these should be retained in your own version intact, since they are more critical in retaining the correct emphasis or interpretation in the matter.

(See Appendix III for a full text of the briefing to employees.) The rationale for this rigid procedure was that a consistent and accurate message should be put out to all employees, free of personal interpretation, and not giving special treatment to any particular groups. Its purpose, apart from giving information, was to receive information back that would help the management to plan the implementation of the change.

So much for the theory. The practice, as we had previously discovered to our cost, was somewhat different. Unable to prevent this hallowed ritual from taking place, we had opted for the second best: rather than wait any length of time, we would follow up the brief immediately and establish direct contact with the shop floor of the Packaging Department. By doing this, we hoped to avoid some of the early confusions that had arisen from the briefing procedure. In the event, such a course of action proved fruitful.

After the briefings, a number of managers told us that everything had 'gone off without a hitch'—everyone had been seen, and the agreed message—nothing more, nothing less—had been given. The response had been favourable—that is, it had not been unfavourable—that is, no one had actually said anything—the conclusion being that there were no objections to the proposal and no burning issues awaiting the fire brigade. The impression, in short, was of a complaisant and passive workforce, ready and willing to co-operate in the new arrangements for participation.

Within a very short period of beginning our discussions with the operators (in groups of eight to ten people corresponding with various sections in the department), we found that things were not the same as we had been led to believe. In fact, one of the first groups seen (blow moulding operatives) had not been briefed at all: 'You talk about communications. Well, that shows the situation we're in, doesn't it?' More seriously, in some cases the brief had either been embellished, deliberately or as a result of management misinformation, or had been wrongly interpreted by certain employees. Whatever the cause, some critical points of the message about participation were, in our view, factually incorrect. For example, virtually everyone had been led to believe that they had little choice in the matter of whether participation actually came into their department—they had been chosen, and that was that; the scheme would be decided on by the management, and they would be expected to go along with it. Although we and the management obviously favoured acceptance of the idea, we had always insisted that (as with the supervisors) people be given the right ultimately to choose or refuse to participate. Unfortunately, this right had not been clearly spelled out in the briefing, and many people had already formed the impression that this was just another management exercise, of which they were being informed rather than consulted.

On one or two other points, we concluded that attempts had deliberately been made to 'define the situation' for employees in a way that best suited the management and its control of the project. Some employees, for instance, claimed that they had been told formally at the briefing and informally by members of the management team that people would be nominated rather than elected to the committee, or, at the very least, management would have a good deal of say in who was chosen. In one or two cases, the operators had raised this point with us privately after the meeting in order to avoid being seen as 'troublemakers and stirrers' (their words). Some attempts had also been made to pre-define the powers of the new committee. For example, one of the engineers was under the impression that 'we can only talk about things they want to talk about—and we shall be in minority anyway', while another claimed, 'We've been told that this experimental committee is not going to be as high-powered as the one in the Chemical Plant.'

Our reaction was to spell out the facts of the project as *we* saw them, in the hope that this would clear up any misunderstanding that had arisen. At the same time, we went back to the Steering Group and drew their attention to the problems. With an eye on the next stage of the process—the election of representatives—we asked them to instruct the management team not to interfere in the choice of people for the committee.

If, as a downward communications device, the briefing system had proved faulty, as an upward communications device it was, in our view, useless. As we shall show in the next section, the employees in the main were not passive, accepting, and contented people that we had been led to believe. Although they may have acted in this way when the management had been present, their response, we believed, did not reflect their real feelings, but was in fact conditioned by the presence of the management.

Meetings with the operators and their views on participation

Since it would be impossible to report in full the results of our discussions with the hundred or so employees, we have selected extracts of conversations with a sample of the groups in order to illustrate the issues which mainly concerned them and their feelings about various aspects of participation.

As predicted, the term 'participation' had little meaning for most of the employees outside the worker director proposals they had read about in the press. Therefore, our initial task, in most cases, was to try to say what it meant to us, and by relating this back to their world of experience, help them to put their own meaning to the concept. To set the scene for what follows, we usually began with an explanation of who we were and what we were doing in the company, followed by a brief account of what had happened in the Chemical Plant and what was now being proposed for the Packaging area. The introduction usually finished with a general definition of participation which stressed that it was about information-sharing and influence-sharing with the shop floor ... more involvement ... better communications ... a better dialogue and relationship between workers and management. We then asked the general question—'Well, how do you feel about it?'—which was followed by a pregnant pause, during which people stared downwards twiddling their thumbs, and we became increasingly anxious. Finally, someone took the plunge, muttered something and triggered-off an almost overwhelming response from the rest. After that, we had little to do other than sit and listen, and from time to time bring the discussion back to the participation proposal.

The first extract from a meeting with the ten chargehands in the department gives a fairly typical illustration of what might be called the 'moaning and groaning' or 'futility' script which we encountered with virtually all the groups: 'What's the point of participating? Nothing ever happens. Nobody takes any notice of us. Things just get squashed. It has never worked in the past, why should it now? The management conspire against us. They give us hell for the sake of it. We're not treated like people. Nobody's interested in what we want out of our jobs', etc.

Chargehand: Do you really think anything constructive will come out of it—will some action result or will 'they' conveniently forget as usual?
Iain: I don't really know at this stage. I believe something can come out of it.
Chargehand: Too often things are brought up and then squashed.

Iain: Is there a strong feeling among people to participate more?

Chargehand: There *is* a feeling that your views are not taken up. If the section head doesn't agree with or sympathize with the issues and problems you raise, it never goes any further.

Chargehand: We want our views to be taken notice of. It's not so much that we want more influence, but more a matter of just being taken notice of.

Iain: What sort of issue are you talking about?

Chargehand: Well, grading for example. There is a grievance procedure, but the section head can still effectively prevent a grading grievance going any further than him.

Chargehand: There used to be meetings with section heads (without the managers), but things just got squashed at these meetings. In the end, chargehands just sat there and didn't bother putting anything forward. The meetings deteriorated. Now we don't meet with section heads or managers.

Iain: Would you like to see the meetings with section heads revived?

Chargehand: No, not really. It would be a waste of breath. They squash everything.

Chargehand: No wonder there's a lack of interest.

Chargehand: We're just left to get on with things.

Chargehand: One of the basic problems is communication.

Chargehand: Yes, we would like to have more information.

Chargehand: Things used to be a lot better before the present managers came. You were treated like a person then. We feel like part of the furniture now.

Chargehand: More co-operation is what we want—when you tell someone about something, you want them to do something about it. We want management to understand better some of the general hassles that occur on the shop floor.

Iain: You feel 'they' don't know enough and therefore don't care?

Chargehand: Yes. We need better communication in general.

Iain: How much influence do you have on work scheduling, distribution of labour, and so on?

Chargehand: None at all. People get moved about a lot and we have nothing to do with it. Ron and Arthur do that—that's why they're so popular! (*Everyone laughs.*) This is a great source of frustration. The girls themselves don't like to be moved around. Arthur and Ron don't seem to plan or organize things properly. Ron is the more aggravating of the two. He really does just do things to aggravate. His manner is generally unpleasant and impersonal. If we're left to do the scheduling, everyone is happy. The atmosphere is nicer.

Chargehand: The trouble is that we're left to the mercy of Ron. He and Fred have been together for a long time. You can't take things to Fred about Ron, they're far too close.

Chargehand: Like a couple of kids, in fact.

Chargehand: We just give up.

Chargehand: We just don't bother to say anything any longer.

Chargehand: There is a bad atmosphere.

Chargehand: We used to keep going on about things that needed doing—like the lighting—but nothing got done. In the end, we don't care. ...

In the meetings with the operators themselves, the issue of moving girls between production bands came up repeatedly. Ron, in particular, was accused of a number of things—of being short-sighted, disorganized, and even slightly sadistic, and of having 'favourites' who received special consideration.

Operator: The issue of moving girls around is always taken above our heads.
Operator: Yes, this is a real source of annoyance.
Operator: We used to be put on permanent bands, but that is no longer stuck to. Girls don't like moving about, and there often doesn't seem to be any sense in it.
Operator: We're never told why we have to move so often.
Operator: When Shirley (*the chargehand*) is in charge of this, things run beautifully. So we know it can be done. And she shows an interest. Why can't other people do this?
Operator: And then the supervisors complain that work is not going out and is not up to standard. What do they expect after all this messing us around?

And in another meeting:

Operator: We would all definitely prefer to stay on one band.
Operator: Yes, you feel you need a home. When they move you around, you feel like a duck out of water—like a new girl just starting on the job.
Operator: The trouble is, that if they see you're happy, they move you—'Let's wipe that smile off *her* face.'
Operator: And if your face fits, you stay there.
Operator: If you show you don't like that band, you can count on being there for ever!
Operator (*to us*): Is this the kind of thing you're saying we could have more influence on with the new set-up?
Paul: Yes, this is the kind of issue you can raise. And you can ask the management to explain why they move people around so often—there may, in fact, be a good reason for it, and there again, there may not. We want the views you're now expressing to us to go higher up the organization. To get some action taken. We want to try to take out the filters, and improve communication up and down—to provide an opportunity for you to influence decisions that concern you. But we don't want it to be seen as a platform for moaning and groaning. We want issues to get raised and a general attempt by everyone to resolve them. It's easy to blame the management, but they may not be fully aware of your problems and the way you feel about them. The first stage is to make people aware of these problems.

It was during a similar conversation with another group that the issue of 'black eyes' was directly alluded to:

Operator: It's all well and good you telling us to speak up for ourselves at a meeting, but it really wouldn't be worth our while. Our life wouldn't be worth living.
Iain: What do you mean?

Operator: If you worked here, you would know what I mean. (*Everyone nods.*)

Operator: Take the people in penicillin, for example. They have a reputation for sticking up for themselves, and look what happens. If they see that you have got views—are a bit bolshie—they pick on you. You get all the bad jobs.

Operator: And black eyes into the bargain!

Operator: People need protection.

Operator: I've heard that this is why people in the Chemical Plant never use the Participation Committee. It's just not worth their while—why put yourself on the line for something which you know they'll only go along with if it suits them? It pays to keep your mouth shut.

The engineers had their own story to tell:

Engineer: At the moment, we get blamed for everything that goes wrong on the machines. But the fact is that we're not consulted about new plant. We understand the machines and how they work far better than the management, but the project engineers never consult us.

Engineer: That's typical of the way we're regarded in this place. It's all production. We're seen as the necessary evil. Our views are not considered at all.

Engineer: There's a strong 'them and us'. We do get blamed for everything.

Engineer: Yes, we do get a lot of stick if we hold people up. Production errors are not jumped on nearly as much. We definitely feel the scapegoats.

Engineer: And do you know, a lot of our call-outs are for trivial, boring things. The girls could do a lot more to help themselves. They ought to be more involved with their machines.

A general complaint was that 'people never tell you anything'—that one either had to ask or rely on rumour:

Operator: There are some part-timers working with liquids. The section is closing down and being moved to Germany.

A number of other issues came up at the meetings which should be briefly described here. The first was the problem of machine breakdowns and, related to it, poor relations that existed between the male engineers and the female operators:

Operator: We do have a lot of breakdowns. I think this is because they try to rush things through too fast, and don't service the machines enough.

Operator: Some of the machines are a load of rubbish anyway. Nobody asks us what we want, but we're the people who have to work them. We had one example recently where we were told that a new machine would be installed by an exit door. We complained that it would be too near the door, and that it wouldn't work properly anyway. But they didn't listen. We've now got the machine, and predictably it doesn't work. Every now and again we have to climb on the top and bang the stainless steel slats with a lump of wood to free them. You ought to see the mess. Also the girl who has to work the machine is knocked over every time somebody walks through the door. It's bloody ridiculous!

Operator: And when a machine breaks down, you have to wait ages for an engineer to come and repair it. They only come when they're ready.

Operator: They also have their own favourites. If you moan, they don't come.

Paul: Do you know why?

Operator: No. You hear all the tales but you don't get the real story.

Operator: We don't get told anything.

Operator: All the information we get has to be asked for, or we get it eventually by word of mouth. Communication is very bad.

Operator: We don't like second-hand information. Michael or Fred should be telling us, but we hardly see them.

Not only Michael and Fred, but also the chargehands came in for a good deal of criticism for not feeding information back:

Operator: We don't have any meetings with anybody at the moment. The chargehands do. They are supposed to come back and inform the shop floor. Some are better than others at doing this.

Operator: We only get to hear things they want us to hear. Some chargehands, when asked, say everything is confidential—not for our ears. Other people give the information grudgingly—in not a very pleasant fashion.

Operator: Certain people do get told what is happening by the chargehands, but others get told nothing.

Iain: Why are some of them reticent about telling you things?

Operator: You tell us. I don't really know. They seem to think it's private, for their ears alone. It makes them feel important, I suppose.

Operator: And so you end up hearing more about your department from another department.

Almost always, the conversation drifted back from the problems to the issue of participation itself, with the employees themselves exploring the association between them. They would ask, 'Is this what participation is all about—you know, finding out more about what's going on, and getting your problems raised?', and we, in reply, would confirm that participation indeed meant problem-solving and information-sharing, leading to a better industrial relations climate in the department. As the concept acquired more meaning, people began to speculate on the detailed issues and problems of participation in practice. The following extract from a conversation with the engineers is fairly typical:

Engineer: I'm not really sure how it works, and why it should be any different from what we've got now. For example, I've noticed that in the Chemical Plant committee, there's a 6:4 ratio in favour of the management. Does this mean that the operatives get put down every time? You see, that's what happens here now—we *are* free to bring anything up, but getting it sorted out in our favour, well, that's a different story altogether. You see what I'm getting at? Where is the extra power to come from?

Paul: I would accept that, in power terms, you are at a disadvantage, and it's doubtful whether, certainly in the short term, you will be able to argue on equal terms with the management. You certainly won't get your way all of the time. What participation hopefully does is discourage management from unilaterally making decisions—it gives you the right to raise anything you want to raise, and it obliges them to discuss things with you; they are obliged to give reasons for their decisions or preferences, and you have the right to question—and carry on questioning—these. The discussions are also public in terms of minutes: all of these things should discourage management from doing things without prior consultation with the shop floor, and stop them hiding behind their so-called prerogatives.

Engineer: Well, we would want our own representative on the committee, someone who could represent the engineers as a group. We would also like to see a 50:50 arrangement, so if there is a stalemate, we can take the issue higher without having 'it's not company policy' thrown at us.

Engineer: We've got to be able to get to the directors' group—not landed with just the departmental management. We've got to be able to get things outside the department. We need the Divisional Director or even the Managing Director on the committee.

Engineer: And we shall have to be careful that things don't get pushed through with the supposed stamp of approval of the 'workforce'.

Engineer: We shall begin by raising local things—such as the putting in of new plant, and relations between fitters and the production girls.

Engineer (*to us*): And what about you? Do you have any influence in the company?

Paul: We would like to think so. We shall be there as umpires, seeing that there's fair play. We will not always be taking the same side. Our concern is not only that you have more information shared with you, but that you have more influence at the end of the day—the position we adopt will be ruled by that consideration.

One month after the preliminary meeting with the shop floor groups, we came back once again to discuss the details of the composition of the committee. We had asked them to go away and think about this, bearing in mind the need to form a committee that was truly representative but not too large, and in most cases they did come back with some views on this. Finally, we were able to agree the following list with everyone concerned. This list, we need to stress, was not imposed on anyone, but slowly evolved from the discussions we have outlined.

Composition of Packaging Department Participation Committee

Director Pharmaceutical Production (Chairman) – Simon
Personnel Manager – Eric
Head of Department – Michael
Section Head (1) – Fred

Supervisor (1) – Ron

Consultants (2)

Chargehand (days) – Shirley
Chargehand (twilight) – Ethel
Blow moulding rep. (days) – Mary
Blow moulding rep. (shift) – Charlie
Label room/Porterage rep. – Maggie
Main 'floor' reps (2) – Joan and Margaret
Penicillin/Dunromin rep. – Sheila
'Twilight' rep. – May
Engineering rep. – Alan   Total = 17

For ease of identification, we have also appended the names of the representatives who were elected as a result of a secret ballot of all departmental staff. Nominations had been invited for each section and where there had been more than one nomination, the ballot had been held. Members of the management team had been told to keep well away while all of this happened, and not to interfere with the electoral process in any way. Shortly after the elections, a 'training' session with all of the shop floor representatives was held (i.e. the bottom group in the above list). It was agreed that we should chair the meeting and that only the Personnel Manager should attend from the company side.

The representatives' training session

The purposes of this session were to provide more details about the background and progress of the participation programme, to explore with the representatives their fears, anxieties, and uncertainties about participation, to work on some of the basic skills of representation, and to draw up an agenda for the early meetings. The success of the session hinged on our being able to deal with issues in a way and in a 'language' that could be readily understood by the people present, and what better way of doing this (we reasoned) than by inviting some of the worker representatives from the Chemical Plant to give their view of participation. This was not difficult to plan since three of the Chemical Plant representatives had already volunteered to give their services. It was therefore agreed that we would spend the first two hours or so on our own with the new people, drawing up a list of issues to be dealt with during the course of the session, and have the Chemical Plant representatives join us after that to give some general impressions and to comment on the points that had been raised. The problem, of course, was that we could not predict what the representatives might say—that they might easily scare some of the new people into withdrawing from the project. The obvious solution (and temptation) was to brief them beforehand, but it was decided at the time that there was a greater risk in taking the 'naturalness' and spontaneity out of the proceedings. Therefore, in the event, we decided to let things take their natural course—a decision which afterwards we were glad that we made.

After a brief description of the background to the project by the Personnel Manager, we got down to identifying the new representatives' fears and anxieties about participation. These flowed out, and after a short period of time, we had produced the following list:

Issues

1. Fear of 'black eyes'—recriminations and comebacks by certain managers.
2. How issues get raised—do they have to go though the normal channels first?
3. What does the company want to get out of it—keep the unions out?
4. Do we have to have firm proof of things before raising them at the meeting?
5. Will the company do anything about the issues raised—what powers do we have?
6. Why hasn't this happened before when we asked for it—how genuinely committed is the company?
7. Fear of polarizing into a 'them and us' situation.
8. What 'style' do we adopt—moaning? confrontation? asking?
9. What do we do when things get rough and people get tough?

What we then tried to do was work through each item on the list, clarifying it, examining its foundations (e.g. real or illusory? inevitable or avoidable?), and 'rehearsing' ways of dealing with it with the people present. The rehearsal was intended as a simulation of the meeting itself, people were encouraged to take a concrete issue and say how they would go about dealing with it; we would then comment and explore alternative ways of handling it.

To illustrate this process, we can focus on the issue which prompted most comment—the fear of black eyes:

Iain: Perhaps, Maggie, you can explain what you mean by 'fear of black eyes'.
Maggie (*Nodding furiously*): Oooo ... ooh. (*Followed by everyone nodding knowingly and murmuring in a chorus—'Oooo ... ooh'.*) I don't know whether I should say, but, you know, black eyes—recriminations after the meeting, people coming back on you and making you pay for it.
Iain: Can you be a bit more specific about who gives the black eyes?
May: Bloody Fred, of course.
Ethel: And Ron.
Maggie: You see, if Fred is sitting there, we will be frightened of putting a point forward. He will be thinking 'they're going at me'. He's going to wish he'd never come.
Sheila: And us!
Maggie: You see what I'm getting at? How do we put points that are personally critical of Fred?

May: Especially when he has already told us that the meeting is not a place for moaning.

Maggie (*to us*): You see, we've got a boss who cuts you off dead; nobody can talk to him.

Iain: Let's look at that point. What is being proposed is a new way of doing things. There are going to be difficulties; the old structure won't change overnight. Don't get too high expectations, Fred ain't going to change just like that. There are two ways to change, the one by evolution and the other by revolution—and I happen to believe in the former. But I also believe that most people by nature are good; few inflict pain and suffering for the hell of it; I have a fairly optimistic view about human beings. That being said, we do have to look very carefully at the way we handle people like Fred.

You can't guarantee that there won't be recriminations, but there are safeguards to reduce the likelihood of this happening. The first thing to bear in mind is that the thing is public—by raising things at meetings, you may in fact be more protected. At present, things are private and it's this that gives managers the freedom to take revenge. So the first message is have courage, use the public thing as your safety guard.

There are also things you can do in the meetings to prevent recriminations— and this is linked to the second issue of how issues get raised. I would initially advise caution; we need to handle the first few meetings carefully. Nevertheless, if things do get tough, you have a second line of defence in us. We want and need to know of any difficulties you are having—if you don't tell us, we can't do anything about it. There are people above who will be keeping a careful eye on the development—if they know, they can do a lot to keep the pressure off you. The first thing you've got to do in the meetings themselves is try to put yourself in the supervisors' shoes. Ask yourself why they behave as they do—for example, they may be defensive and anxious (just like you) because they feel they are the losers; that they are losing their power to you. We need to put ourselves in their position and see that they may feel threatened. If this feeling is causing them to act aggressively, the obvious solution is not to back them into a corner.

Eric (*Personnel*): And they will behave aggressively if you let out a full tirade of moans and abuse—try not to be 'negative' or too critical.

Maggie: We know Fred knows what we think of him.

Eric: You *think* he knows—but he may not. Anyway, if he does know, why do you need to spell it out to him?

Paul: A level of trust needs to be built up very slowly, and carefully; it can be spoilt very easily. Remember, it will be your meeting—one you have helped build up— if it gets spoilt, it will be everyone's loss. Just staying on the 'how things gets raised' issue—and this is connected with the black eyes issue and number eight, the 'style' we adopt—can I ask how you might go about dealing with the problems of moving girls between bands?

Joan: Well, I suppose we would put our point of view—present our case to the management and say ... (*Here she goes through the argument.*)

Iain: I think the skill lies in firstly being clear to everyone what the issue is—don't assume that everyone knows what you're talking about; secondly, in thinking beforehand, 'If I was in their position, how would I react to this?', thirdly, avoid the 'crunch', although the temptation may be to unburden your feelings on someone—try to avoid being too personal—most people know you're talking about them even though you don't explicitly point it out; finally, try to avoid the natural tendency to make statements—these usually put people on the defensive; questions are often better—the innocent question can be very powerful, since it puts the onus on people to give an answer...

Maggie: I take your point, but it's still not going to be easy. Poeple are afraid to speak up in front of their bosses.

Paul: Can I just ask you, Maggie, whether in fact anyone has actually been given a black eye?

Maggie: I can't think of any concrete examples—I suppose it's the fear of getting one that prevents it happening.

Paul: Yes, this is what I'm trying to get at. You may be right—come the crunch and someone may get a black eye, but there again, we may be wrong. What we shall have to do is slowly and carefully move to an answer.

The other issues on the list were handled in the same way, the intention being to get the people present to examine aspects of their 'stereotype' of the management, and to think about alternative ways of handling the relationship with their bosses. Implicit in this was a desire to make people more aware of the skills involved in handling this relationship—listening, empathy, political, articulation, etc.

The chemical representatives joined us for coffee and after a brief introduction from ourselves, began to relate their experiences. As the conversation developed, we were able to withdraw to the sidelines and watch what, for us—and we suspected also for those taking part—was a quite remarkable event. Two years previously, the same three people had been in the seats that were now occupied by the newly elected representatives; they had expressed similar fears and anxieties about participation, and had perhaps been more suspicious and doubtful; but now, here they were taking initiatives, rather enjoying their new status as 'trainers', and fortunately talking in a positive and meaningful way about the participation programme. In no way could we have nurtured a similar quality dialogue. An extract from this part of the session is reproduced below, which regretfully does not capture the total essence of the event:

Shirley: Tell me, Jack, have you found it worthwhile?

Jack (*rep.*): Yes, definitely. You can now get things done, so long as you're not too aggressive, and don't get too personal. People soon get to know who you are talking about, even if you don't actually say who it is. It's all a bit like being in court—you say your bit; you're allowed to say your piece, and nobody will cut you off mid-stream. You've got to speak up—and be careful of these guys (*pointing to us*), because if you start to say something and then stop, they will make you bring it out!

Huw (*rep.*): You can also say things without comeback.

Jack: Mind you, the first two or three meetings were terrible. We got very heated. But slowly it got better. Now we can raise the same issues and people will accept criticism.

Joan: Can you say something about the problems of reporting back to our members, especially the problem of their lack of interest.

Jack: Yes, this is a very difficult one. You've got to represent, you can't just put your own case—which is tempting sometimes, when your people don't show any interest. At the other end, you've got to go back and say what happened without twisting it. The representatives really need to get the story straight before they go back.

Joan: But how do you get over their apathy?

Jack: Some you can't get through to, and never will. But generally you try to chat to them, regardless of their level of interest. And keep doing it. Things do get easier when you can talk about things that they're interested in.

Alan: What about the management—do they bring up gripes?

Huw: Not very often. They usually wait for ours.

Alan: So it's one-way?

Huw: Initially, it is rather like that, but later you begin to work things out together. A lot of things are joint, with no real vested interest on either side. Either side may originally raise them, but after that, we regard them as joint problems to be solved by the Participation Committee.

Alan: I detect from what you're saying that many of these things could happen rather than are happening at the moment. The question is, do the management use the committee to raise their gripes?

Trevor (*rep.*): Let me say, it's starting to happen. They are bringing more and more things to us—major plans on departmental alterations, for instance. They bring along the plans voluntarily and ask us for our comments. It's true that we haven't had all that much two-way traffic, but it's slowly coming.

Iain: This meeting is an example. The management wanted to extend the project, checked it out with the Chemical Plant people, and then asked them, 'How do we do it?' They said, 'Well, let's talk to Packaging'—and this is what is happening.

Trevor: Early on, the supervisors tend to feel their position is being undermined. But when they realize this ain't necessarily the case, realize that you want to get things done rather than get at them, they also get involved.

Sheila: The trouble with our lot is they're stubborn, make mistakes, and refuse to admit they're wrong. In our department, things are just not thought out. We tell them something or other isn't going to work, but they carry on regardless. They keep saying it must work, look how much it's costing.

Trevor: Well, now we want to know about projects before they happen. We want the blueprints before anything has been done about them.

Sheila: But they won't reverse their decision even if they see it's wrong.

Trevor: At the moment, that's probably the case. But you don't presently have the correct forum. Mostly, if you've got a problem, it's you against them. You will now have allies and a place to make your moans public. You will have a wider audience and they will know this and be more careful.

Maggie: Let me ask how much 'say' we will actually have. What I'm getting at is, if you decide something as a committee, will the management still go ahead and do it their way?

Trevor: It's true that you may decide something as a committee—management and workers—but find that people higher up decide to do something else. But if it doesn't work, they, not us, are responsible. When this happens, they're usually quite happy to use us more, pay more attention to us. It's a case of them having learnt a lesson. The temptation—if you'll pardon my French—is to say 'bugger you', but it should be a case of us being prepared to take on collective responsibility and get it right for the next time.

Jack: With the meetings, at least you'll know that things have gone as far as they can go—to the Managing Director if necessary. Now, the line manager can't just say no and that's that.

Maggie: But what it boils down to is a question of personalities. You can't change these.

Iain: You may be right, but you can change relationships.

Huw: You wouldn't say that if you could see Tom now. He's a new man—milder, more concerned about how we feel. He consults with us whereas at one time he just used to tell us. This change would not have occurred had it not been for participation.

Jack: But it also means that you have got to change. You all know me—and these gentleman (*to us*) will confirm it. When they first came to see me, I was effing and blinding, saying it would never work, didn't want to know. And in the early meetings, I was like a bull in a china shop, always getting myself into trouble. We used to have an arrangement where if I was getting into deep water and not knowing it, one of them would kick me under the table! I would like to think I'm different now—quieter but probably more influential.

Huw: My message simply is that I want people to support this. I have been very glad to be part of it.

Trevor: I would support what is being proposed, too. Your commitment is really crucial.

Paul: Before you go, is there any particular advice you can offer?

Jack: Mine is, get your facts straight before you start, or you'll be made to feel a right Charlie.

Trevor: And make sure you know your procedure inside out.

At this point, we broke for lunch, although the discussion between the Chemical Plant and Packaging representatives continued throughout the break. Having re-assembled, we took stock of where we were. Several people volunteered the view that the morning's session had been excellent in giving a better understanding of what participation was all about, but there were still one or two who persisted in using the event as a moaning and groaning session—a way of letting off steam about their bosses. The difference was that some of the others rounded on them and suggested that they 'give it a break'.

Rep.: Well, we shall be able to get them on their toes now. I can't wait!

Rep. (*not really listening*): My complaint is that some of our bosses don't even say good morning to us. In the morning they just walk straight by. That really gets up our noses. Aren't they ever going to talk to us in here? They really are out of this world!

Rep.: Look, isn't it about time we cut this out and got down to the matter in hand. My preference is to try and get some issues out for the meetings. We're not going to make any more progress on the other thing at this meeting. (*All agree, except the one representative who continues muttering 'and they call themselves gentlemen', 'really, it gets you, it does', etc.*)

And so, the rest of the afternoon was spent listing issues for future meetings. These were then arranged in a rough order of priority, and agreement reached on which issues should be dealt with first. Most people obviously wanted to raise initially the 'burning' issues, but we suggested that it might be better to wait until the meeting had settled down and people had had the opportunity to establish themselves. This suggestion was accepted and the following agendas agreed:

Agenda for first meeting
1. Process for communicating back to constituents
2. The grievance procedure—what it is, and how to use it
3. The role of the Personnel Department—right of access to it
4. Canteen arrangements and food dispensing machines
5. Banking facilities on site
6. Entrance gates
7. Xmas wages
8. Lighting in the Label Room.

Agenda for second meeting
1. Issues around unpaid leave and sick pay arrangements
2. Lack of communication between sections, particularly Production and Engineering: resulting feeling of isolation
3. Job grading and problem of moving people between jobs
4. Storage facilities in the Label Room
5. Manning arrangement for twilight shift
6. Changing room facilities
7. Shower facilities
8. Heating

Agenda for third meeting and others
1. Issues of responsibility for inspection
2. Does the company want quantity or quality?
3. Shift manning
   plus any other issues carried over or raised in the meantime.

During the week remaining before the first meeting, we held further discussion and counselling sessions with people around the site—the Managing Director and other members of the Steering Group, the Departmental Management, and the Divisional Director who would be chairing the meeting. In the case of the latter, we spent a good deal of time explaining how we saw his role as chairman, emphasizing the importance of 'biting his tongue', keeping the meeting to the point, drawing people into the discussion, promoting openness, keeping temperatures down, not automatically siding with the management, sharing information, insisting that reasons be given for a point of view, and so on. He was clearly anxious about the high level of feeling that was running about the quality of his management team, and about his ability to keep the meeting in order, and asked us to help him if he ran into difficulties. We agreed and took the opportunity to explain the way we saw our role in the meetings, notably to help people to get their issues out on to the table and to get a meaningful dialogue around these issues; generally, we would be aiming to keep the initial meetings low key, although later on there might be a need to be more direct and confronting—towards him as much as anybody. The meeting ended with us agreeing to see him briefly on the day and to quickly run through the agenda items with him.

Thus the scene was set: everyone had been seen and everyone, tentatively, was prepared to 'give it a go'. The atmosphere in the department on the Friday before the Monday meeting was rather like that of a dentist's waiting room—people nervous and not really saying very much to anyone, not really knowing how painful the forthcoming experience would turn out to be.

CHAPTER 6

Sweet and sour

To everyone's relief, the first meeting turned out to be a fairly low key affair, partly because of the non-emotive issues that were considered, and partly because of the participants' eagerness to avoid saying anything that might cause friction. However, as one would expect, different people reacted in different ways: Ron, apparently having decided to play a waiting game, said nothing, as did several of the operators' representatives; Fred, to everyone's surprise, was helpful and supportive, even on a couple of occasions admitting some personal mistakes and taking sides with the operators; Simon, the chairman, was also eager to demonstrate his commitment to making the participation meeting work—or, at least, not to be seen to be indifferent towards it; and Eric, the Personnel Manager, tried very hard to draw people into the meeting and to get issues raised for future meetings. In short, the early signs were encouraging. People, it seemed, had thought hard about their customary ways of dealing with each other, and were trying to demonstrate that they were capable of going about things in a different way—the operatives, by refraining from the 'moaning and groaning'—'what are you going to do about ...?'—and the management by trying to dispel the view of themselves as uncaring, selfish, and heavy handed.

A pattern for the early meetings soon began to establish itself, and it is to a description of this that we now turn. The first aspect of this—an attempt by the parties to establish a more 'humanistic' stance towards each other—has already been mentioned in the context of the first meeting. This, in fact, continued for the following three meetings or so—at least on the surface. Even Ron began slowly to emerge from his shell when he realized that no one was actually attacking him or his position. Fred continued to develop his 'champion of the girls' role (thereby avoiding any fundamental clashes with the representatives present), while Michael, to some extent, also publicly separated himself from the management side, and began to function very much as an independent. One or two of the girls found this humanism more difficult to swallow: they had always been used to presenting issues in the form of a complaint, or a request for the management to resolve them, and had expected— and had usually received—a negative or grudging response. Now that the management members were acting in a very different way, the girls found this approach somewhat inappropriate: confrontation could only exist if there was something or someone to confront, or something or someone to confront you; this clearly was not happening in the meetings, and the danger was that to persist with a confronting style was tantamount to running at a closed door, someone opening it at the last moment, and you falling flat on your face. The fact of the matter was that there was now a pressure on them to adopt a different role, one which implied a joint approach to problem-solving and a joint responsibility for any decisions taken. What made it difficult for them to take on this new role—apart from any previous experience of it—was a lack of conviction that the management style had genuinely changed. Some of the girls felt that the managers were only 'putting it on' for the meeting and for us, and that to be drawn from an oppositionary to a collaborative role was to be exposed to and hoodwinked by the management. What we are saying (and this is a point that we come back to and discuss in some detail in a later chapter) is that in the early stages there was literally no script for collaboration between the parties, but yet a strong 'situational' pressure (implied by our presence and the whole notion of participation) for people to collaborate. In dramaturgical terms (Mangham, 1978), the evolutionary process we were trying to engender during the early meetings was one in which people moved from the traditional 'conflict' script to the collaborative script—a process akin to drafting and re-drafting the lines of a play, people rehearsing new roles, with ourselves acting as both director and prompter to the players. To put this on the right footing, we had attempted to set the scene before the meetings began, at this point occupying a variety of roles ranging from ghost writer and choreographer to scenery manager and impresario. The show was now on the road and the central task was to bring out the 'best' in the players—a best which would ultimately be judged by the audience and critics waiting in the wings.

Although progress was painfully slow during the first five months of the project, most of the members of the meeting did acknowledge that relationships between them had improved. The only reservation was, as we have already said, that a good deal was being suppressed, and that behind a thin veneer of bonhomie, people were their same old nasty selves! The following comments made privately to us illustrate various people's feelings at the time:

Ron: Actually I'm very happy with the way the scheme is going. I was not too sure at first, a bit concerned about it, but now it's here, I'm glad we've got it. I do think things are better than before—with the girls, I mean. I think it may help to make my position easier, you know, clarify what I'm supposed to be doing, reduce some of the ambiguities, help me see where I stand. Mind you, I do think Fred is very worried. The other day we were talking about some unrelated thing and he started sounding off about participation. Actually, I do think things between me, the girls and Fred will be better now. You see, Fred used to stop any suggestions of complaints that I made—used to apply the guillotine—just stopped things dead. He's now beginning to ask people about things, rather than merely imposing them.

Q.: What about the way the shop floor representatives have responded?

Ron: Well, I've been surprised really. They have behaved better than I thought. Most of the points they have raised have been sensible. But I don't think they're presenting their case as well as they could. But it's early days yet, it takes time. I thought the air would clear after two or three meetings, but now I think it will be about twenty.

Operator: It's encouraging to see Michael and Simon taking a constructive approach, but we really need to get Fred and Ron more involved. They are too cautious, too aware of each other's presence. I would like to see them coming with issues of their own, instead of just responding to ours. But really I'm quite happy with the way things have gone.

Operator: I really am surprised by the way Ron and Fred have reacted. They are far more friendly, and far less defensive and aggressive than I expected. They do seem, well, you know, just more friendly. We don't feel so keen to attack them now. We are not the sort of people to want to hurt people's feelings anyway. This does sometimes put us in a bit of an awkward position—we want to raise something but know it will upset somebody; so we don't raise it. It's all a bit awkward sometimes when you know how people will react. Ron, for example, is more friendly but just as silly—he can't run the floor really—but how do you tell him that? We don't know how to raise an issue without attacking them personally.

Operator: Yes, things have got better between us and the management. Now in the meetings they let you say your piece, and you know that someone is listening. They don't block things off as they did before.

Michael: The reps have responded better than I thought they would. Their case has been presented quite well. But it's all been a bit slow, possibly because of Fred. He's worried, you know, definitely not a convert yet. What worries me a little is that the shop floor reps are using the meeting to get access to the top management through Simon, so they end up participating with top management but not with me. I'd like to see the whole thing collapsed down and I take the chair. There's several people sitting round that table—Fred is one of them—carrying on with the collaborative working party atmosphere but really holding back to bursting point. Production pressures on us are very great at the moment and I'm afraid that this might finally burst the bubble.

Operator: Fred is a lot more friendly. He actually says hello now, and he doesn't shut the door in your face. We see a lot more of Michael, too. Eric does go on a bit, but he's OK. And Simon—I was expecting him to be less helpful than he has been. After all, he is the senior management.

Fred (*If, as the others suggested, he was very uncomfortable about the scheme, this did not come out in his comments to us.*): I'm all for participation, people have the right to a say and some influence. I feel OK about the meetings so far, but would like to participate in things that concern me and the people I represent. We need to get this extended site-wide. There's too many petty grievances at the moment, nothing in it for me yet. But, I am trying to help out wherever I can—if Ron is being a bit unjust, I can have a private word with him. If people want to come to me, I'll give them information any day of the week. Joan is already doing this outside the meetings.

Operator: Yes, quite happy really. Ron is still doing things that put the girls' backs up—he is still very rude to the girls. But he is being more careful now. The other day he said sarcastically, 'I've got to be careful with you now, haven't I?' But Fred is very different. Now he will listen to you, whereas before if any points or suggestions were made, he would just say 'Rubbish' and put you down. I just wonder sometimes how far people like him have changed deep down.

Therefore, to summarize, there were signs in the early meetings of an attempt by the parties to establish a collaborative relationship with each other—to be more accommodating, more concerned for personal feelings, better listeners, and generally more supportive of each other. This at times, in fact, meant that they deliberately refrained from being open about their feelings or disagreements—'biting their tongues', as we put it to them—until the meeting had developed sufficiently to handle the more 'thorny' issues. Clearly, one unfortunate effect of this holding back was that the parties were uncertain about the depth and strength of the new bond and the amount of weight they dared put on it. On balance, however, given the strong feelings that existed, we decided that this was preferable to seeing the meeting collapse under the weight of openness and absolute honesty. The 'absolute truth' at this stage would have been unhelpful; some things were best left unsaid.

Another aspect of the pattern of the first few meetings was the normative one of evolving a system of procedural rules for participation—in short, the constitution-building activity or process. This activity tended to run parallel with the substantive activity of actually raising and attempting to resolve concrete issues in the meetings. At first, people found it strange that no pre-set, operating guidelines existed for participation, and that they were being asked to help draw them up, but soon it became part of the natural course of things to spend time on procedural issues. By the end of three months, a broad framework had been agreed which included the following: meetings would be held every three or four weeks, minutes would be taken and circulated to everyone in the Packaging area within two to four days of the meeting, as well as displayed on notice boards, and agenda items would be formally submitted before the meeting. In response to a backlog of issues that built up during this time, it was also agreed to have a twenty minutes (maximum) question time for issues that could be resolved fairly quickly without going through the agenda procedure. The procedure for reporting back was also important in the light of the large number of people in the department: the representatives successfully negotiated two fifteen-minute 'slots' during work time, the first for feeding back immediately a verbal summary of what had happened at the meeting, and the second, a pre-meeting as it was called, which was held shortly before the main meeting in order to formulate issues for the agenda. In the first instance, the management had expressed a preference for these meetings to take place during natural breaks—coffee or lunch breaks or machine down-times—but Fred had insisted on regular slots during normal working hours, when, if necessary, the machines should be closed down. As a result of this, the pre- and post-meetings became established as a regular practice in the department, and a novelty for the factory.

In the first instance, procedural/constitutional matters were taking up nearly half of the total meeting time, but as they became established as normal practice, far more time was taken up dealing with actual issues raised by the representatives.

Another aspect of the early pattern, alluded to in the extracts of conversations with the representatives, was that the meetings tended to be one-way: the shop floor people would raise items and the management would react to them in one way or another. Very few items were tabled by the management, a result in Fred and Ron's case of their wait-and-see stance, and in Michael and Simon's case of a desire not to swamp the meetings with their own issues. However, with the realization that the meeting was here to stay and could perhaps have its uses, more management issues began to creep on to the agenda. For example, at about this time, Simon and Michael were coming under pressure from their superiors to reduce production variances in the department, and were becoming increasingly concerned that Packaging was being treated as the 'brush end' for the factory's problems. Their reaction was to raise the issue at a participation meeting and use the representatives to take the message back to their constituents that greater efficiencies were required, not before the representatives had pointed out that the term 'variances' meant nothing to the people on the floor. After further discussion, it was agreed that someone from the quality control department should hold meetings with groups of people on the shop floor, explain the term, and point out the seriousness of the problem. Meanwhile, members of the Participation Committee would seek to discover some of the causes of the high level of production variances. This, in fact, did happen and an impressive list of possible causes was drawn up for further investigation.

In the main, the early meetings were more of an information-sharing rather than an influence-sharing kind. Any influence-sharing that did take place was confined to fairly minor 'hygiene' issues—tokens of goodwill, as we labelled them. At the time, we (and the representatives) were not too worried about this, since we believed there to be a genuine need for basic information that hitherto had not been made available to the shop floor, and a very good possibility that, given time, the meetings would naturally evolve into influence-sharing mechanisms, giving employees a good deal of say about major issues.

The importance of participation as an information-sharing mechanism should not be underestimated or looked at too unfavourably against its big brother, influence-sharing. As the following example will show, the sharing of information about such things as the formal grievance procedure can be pretty revealing:

Joan: I have raised this one because people don't know what it is or how to use it.
Eric (*handing out a written summary of the procedure*): This procedure has been going since 1972. It's all pretty straightforward and typical of other companies. (*Goes through it.*) We want people to use it if necessary—be free to raise things freely without any fear of recrimination.
Joan: Well, this is a help. I didn't know this existed and I'm sure my girls still don't. I'll now be able to show it to them and explain it.

Sheila: On paper it might look straightforward, but it doesn't work like that in practice. We have a grievance, we go to Fred, and he says 'no'—our recent complaint about the new machines is an example—it went to Fred, came back, and went back again—the machines are still not OK. So what do we do?

Fred: We are aware of that particular problem and we do want to get it right. But I do take your point, Sheila.

Sheila: But we want to know if something is being done.

Michael: It's actively being looked at, let me say that.

Sheila: But it's not enough for you to say that.

Michael: We agree, in the case you quote, that things got away. We moved too quickly and we didn't get the money right.

Eric: Don't concern yourself, Sheila. A group has been set up and is now actually looking at this.

Sheila (*getting excited*): Well, *we* didn't know that! Why not tell us that somebody is looking into it? At least now I've got something to tell my people.

Paul: Perhaps it might be worthwhile to clarify what is happening now with regard to people using the grievance procedure.

Sheila: The fact is they're not. People wouldn't dream of going to Fred. They see him as the ogre type! (*Everyone laughs nervously.*)

Fred (*apparently taking it quite well*): Well, if they don't come to me, how am I supposed to know their problems?

Maggie: Can people come direct to Fred over the chargehands' heads?

Simon: I suggest they try the normal system of one-to-one with their chargehands but they can take it higher if it doesn't work.

Eric: From what you say, some people obviously don't want to take things even to the first stage. I don't suggest we open this one up now. Perhaps we should work it through at a later meeting.

Simon: I think we should accept Eric's advice there.

Shirley (*ignoring this*): Is it possible to go straight to Personnel without going through a third person in the department—say, Fred?

Fred: If it's nothing to do with work, then yes; if it's related to work, then I think you should come to me first.

Michael: I feel that everything should go through the supervision. After all, it will ultimately have to go back to them if anything is to be done.

May: But some people may not want to go to Fred. They may be frightened.

Ron: It's straightforward to me—you have only to come to me and say you want to see Personnel. Simple, isn't it?

Maggie: No. Some people wouldn't come to you and ask that, and most don't know their personnel representative anyway.

Michael (*incredulous*): Are you telling me that you don't know who your personnel man is?

May: Not until last week when he brought some contracts round. It's the first time we had seen him.

Paul: Are we saying that, while it's desirable to raise an issue through the supervisor, everyone does have the right to contact Personnel direct and have a confidential meeting with them?

Alan: Yes, that's what I want to know—is that kind of meeting feasible now?

Eric: Yes, definitely.

Alan: Well, that's clear for the first time. That reassures me and will certainly reassure my people.

Paul: So, to summarize, you do have the right of direct access to Personnel, the right to a confidential interview, but out of courtesy, see the supervision whenever you can. As Fred says, he can't sort out your problems unless he knows about them.

The effect of this interchange was to make the management realize that the grievance procedure was not as simple and straightforward as they believed it to be. It had not really occurred to them that a policy document, no matter how clearly written, would have little impact if either people did not know of its existence, or found it to be unworkable in practice. They had also discovered, almost incidentally, that people hardly knew their local personnel representative, and were unaware of their right to contact him directly. For the worker representatives, the interchange also provided information about the procedure and their rights of access which hitherto was not known. Going back to the discussion preceding this extract, one might conclude that, at such times as these, information-sharing can be pretty influential.

A further characteristic of the early days of participation in the Packaging area was that a mass of 'hygiene' issues—issues concerning the work environment—were brought forward by the representatives, while the major issues which had been mentioned in our initial meetings with them were kept in the background. This was partly due to us recommending that they concentrate on low-risk issues first, but also, we believe, due to their preference for 'rehearsing' their roles on such things. Initially, the management were also quite happy to concentrate on these and to chalk up some early successes for the participation group. As a result, within the first three months of the programme, the following kind of issue had been resolved to everyone's satisfaction: extra tables in the canteen (as one representative remarked, 'These were wheeled in literally minutes before the participation meeting'); lighting in the Label Room; showers repaired; lifting machinery purchased for blow moulding; hot water in blow moulding; and consultation with the shop floor about a project to improve the machines, improve the cleanliness, and reduce the dust in the penicillin/Dunromin area. The bonus for the girls was that they had something substantive to take back to their constituents, many of whom were still sceptical about the success of the scheme. As one remarked, 'Yes, we can see little things happening. For example, Michael came down the other day and showed us the plans for some new machinery. The girls were interested and pleased that someone had actually taken the trouble to come and explain, and to ask them what they thought about the plans.'

The problem that we had not anticipated was that, rather than remove the backlog of hygiene issues, leaving time for more substantial ones, the meeting tended to spawn more and more of them at an alarming rate, in fact. The girls began to complain about not being given the time to raise all of their constituents' issues, and of having to go back to them empty-handed. The supervisors became increasingly concerned that many of the items being raised drew people's attention to things they should have been dealing with during the normal course of the day, and that the Participation Committee was being used to short-circuit the normal channels. Our reaction was to ask why, if the normal channels were working successfully, should there be such a backlog and why did people prefer to come direct to the Participation Committee with such issues—the implication being that perhaps the quality of supervision left much to be desired. The senior management's preference was for us to endorse their view that the normal channels should be used first, but we pointed out that one had to face up to the reality that people in the past had not been prepared to use the normal channels, and there was no reason to suppose that they would in the future; either we returned to a situation where grievances were bottled-up, or we accepted that, for the moment, the Participation Committee provided one outlet. Discussion about this continued at a meeting of the Steering Group, at which we drew attention to the major problem (as we saw it) of poor quality supervision in some but not all cases. At present, we said, many supervisors could not be relied on to resolve the issues that were being raised: what was needed was some kind of training programme for developing a range of technical and interpersonal skills, or, in extreme cases, consideration of the possibility of moving some supervisors to another department and a less difficult job; if the quality of supervision could be improved, there was a good chance that many of the issues currently coming to the participation meeting could be resolved through the normal channels; improving the quality of local personnel representation would, we thought, also improve the situation. Many people at the meeting were visibly alarmed by what we had said, but no one actually disagreed with it. In the event, however, it was decided not to make any radical change in the supervisory structure at that time since people might associate these with participation, and begin to see the latter as something of a threat. For the moment, it seemed, the participation group would have to try to cope with issues that would normally be filtered out by the supervision.

It was at about this time, six months or so after the scheme had begun, that things seemed to enter a new phase. Whereas, despite early problems, the meetings had registered some successes in improving relationships and resolving hygiene problems, the next stage was marked by much more fundamental problems which shook the whole foundations of the scheme. In reality, there was no clear cut-off point between the two phases, but more a gradual change in the balance between success and failure.

The gathering storm

Perhaps the turning point for the group occurred when attention began to be switched from fairly uncontroversial, 'local' issues to more controversial issues with wider implications for the factory. The expectation had always been that this would naturally happen, but there were very different points of view about when it should happen. The shop floor representatives, as we have said, were quite happy to move forward slowly and evenly, giving themselves the chance to find their feet in the meetings. The senior management, too, were happy to wait until such time that the group could take on more 'meaty' issues, or until the higher divisional or site-wide committees had been established.

The pressures to move more quickly to the more difficult issues came from three sources: the first was the supervisory element of the group, who wanted less talk about decisions taken locally by them, and more talk about decisions currently being taken by higher management; the second was an inevitable consequence of the participation experience itself and had been referred to in the literature as the 'salted peanut paradox' or 'the taste of the good life'. As the meaning of participation becomes more clear to the participants, and as the success rate in resolving issues improves, expectations of even greater, better things begin to emerge; what previously is regarded as a major achievement becomes, in an historical perspective, relatively trivial and unimportant; rather than being satisfied with what they have achieved, people merely expect more and more. The shop floor representatives, in this case, were the people who expected and began to press for more. And as they began to force the pace, some of the senior management became alarmed that they were losing control over the meeting and their own prerogatives. Their situation was not helped by the supervisors' representatives who joined forces with the shop floor representatives to push for more, and which led on more than one occasion to Simon, the Divisional Director and chairman, remarking: 'It's the attitude of Michael and Fred that worries me in the meetings. They seem to forget that they are members of the management team, they are not acting like proper managers.' The third pressure came from the shop floor itself in the form of complaints that nothing of importance was happening. This, we believe, lay behind the representatives taking an increasingly tougher line in insisting that they be given time to raise the more important issues, and yet still be allowed to add to the pile of unresolved 'hygiene' issues.

At the time we did in fact talk to some of the shop floor workers about their attitude towards the participation scheme and were able to confirm the pressures being put on the representatives to achieve more for them. As the following illustrations show, the main complaint was that nothing had happened and nobody (i.e. the management) had actually changed; evidence, people believed, of a lack of management commitment to the scheme:

Q.: What's your general feeling about how the scheme is going?
Operator: Well, it's not, is it? Nothing much seems to have happened.
Q.: What about things like the lighting and the heating?
Operator: Yes, but that's not very much.
Q.: Have you noticed any change in supervisory style?
Operator: No, they're just the same. They still treat us in a rude fashion. The other day, Ron whistled to one of the girls to come. He didn't even call her by name. We still never see Michael. He doesn't speak to us, doesn't even say good morning. The girls are beginning to think they brought you in to keep the unions out, that they are not really interested in involving the girls. When I read the minutes, I

always think the management have their answers all ready—they seem to be able to give a snap answer, and that's that.

Q.: Have you noticed any change in Fred and Ron?
Operator: No, none at all. They're just ignorant.
Q.: Some of the representatives feel they have changed—that they act more pleasantly at the meetings.
Operator: Yes, they may act differently at meetings while you're there, but what's the good of that to us? I doubt whether they will ever change with us.

Operator: Nothing has happened really. Management won't change things if they don't want to.
Q.: Well, some things have been done, haven't they? Like the heating and lighting.
Operator: Yes, something was done, but it's as bad as ever now.
Q.: What about the decision to provide banking facilities on site?
Operator: Yes, but we asked about that ages ago. It was promised early last year.
Q.: Have you noticed any change in the supervision?
Operator: Well yes, Ron is a bit better, at least not quite as bad as he used to be. He tends to keep out of the way more than he used to. But Fred is just the same; neither he nor Michael bothers to say good morning. The only time Michael wants to tell you anything is when he wants to point out how much a thing costs.

Operator: The company are only doing this to prevent the unions getting in. Tony Harris is always nice and polite when he comes down, but you never know whether he's being two-faced or not. I also think Simon gets all his own way at the meetings and only discusses things if he wants to. No, I'm not at all sure whether they're committed to the scheme.

Operator: No, I don't think much of it, to be honest with you. Nothing's happened. People just use it as a way of skiving off work and having a lark about. We're still waiting for the water fountains and the heating is terrible.

There were also a number of complaints that the pre-meetings had given rise to frictions between the girls:

Operator: The meetings we have with Joan have got bitchy too.
Q.: What, among the girls, you mean, or with Joan?
Operator: Yes, amongst the girls. One group says we should have this and another says no.
Q.: Presumably the differences have always been there, though?
Operator: Well, yes—but this participation thing has brought it all out. Before it was just a few individuals, now it's groups.

What is interesting from the point of view of these comments is that the 'hygiene' issues that had been dealt with at the meetings somehow did not count. It was as though the original, Herzbergian meaning of 'hygiene' applied—that resolution of hygiene issues reduced dissatisfaction and negative feelings, but did little to increase satisfaction and more positive feelings towards participation. In fact, many people had forgotten that some issues had been resolved at the meetings, while others complained that improvements had mostly been temporary. Clearly, what was happening did not accord with people's expectations of what would, and should be happening as a result of participation, although we also suspected that people were so immersed in the moaning-and-groaning script that they literally did not know how to (or want to) respond to the few successes that had been achieved.

As pressure from the shop floor began to build up, the representatives responded by reviving some of the issues from the original agenda list which they hoped would be of sufficient concern to their constituents to capture their interest and to gain a plus mark for the participation scheme. Canteen facilities was one and the issue of 'unpaid leave' another. The story of the troubled passage of one of these items will be dealt with in Chapter 8—together with another item which came up later, that of an early finish to the working day. As a prologue to this story and as an epilogue to this chapter, we can say that these issues were handled very badly and resulted in a crisis for the group which threatened to push it into obscurity. Initially, a reticence on the part of management to open up the issues for discussion at the meeting led to a good deal of frustration which was later compounded when decisions were made which directly contradicted the wishes of the majority of the people in the group. A point had been reached when the management were being asked actively to demonstrate their commitment to the notion of participation by respecting the wishes of the group. In the final analysis, they refused, thereby underlining for everyone the wide gap which exists between the preaching and the practice of participation.

CHAPTER 7

But can it boil milk?

At about the same time that the storm clouds were gathering over the Packaging Department's participation group, we and the members of the Steering Committee began to give some thought to extending the programme laterally and vertically in the organization. In view of the difficulties the group was experiencing, it may appear rather odd that everyone was eager to press ahead, even to accelerate the pace of change, rather than to call a halt until these difficulties had been overcome. Part of the explanation for this can be found in judgement made at the time that a rapid expansion of the programme would actually contribute to a solution of the group's problems. It is the reasoning behind it that we examine briefly below. The other part can be dealt with fairly quickly here. First, it must be remembered that, by this time, the Chemical group was running smoothly, and was receiving the support of all levels of the department. Undoubtedly, it had the effect of maintaining people's faith in the notion of participation, and made it easier for them to look upon the Packaging Department as being untypical and having problems which did not occur elsewhere to such a degree (e.g. it was particularly large, had a high proportion of female operators, and had a relatively poor record of industrial relations between the supervision and the shop floor). Second, the question of the extension was arguably a case of Hobson's choice; there was expectation site-wide of participation being implemented in every department, and other groups not presently in the scheme had asked repeatedly why they had not been 'done'; the Chemical Plant committee itself was also making known its feelings about expanding the programme as quickly as possible. Faced with these pressures, the senior management would have found it difficult to call a halt to the programme, and virtually impossible to scrap the groups already established. The final point was mentioned in an earlier chapter: for personal and professional reasons, the Managing Director and Personnel Manager were determined to implement their 'master plan' ('Tony's Triangles', as it had come to be known, after repeated showing of his slides), and had already acquired kudos for what they had done from the company at large and outside bodies such as the Industrial Participation Society and the Chemical Industry's Training Board. Given this level of approbation, and a genuine belief in the value of participation, it is not really surprising that the slow progress of the Packaging group had done little to quell their enthusiasm.

In what way would acceleration and extension of the programme actually help the Packaging group over its difficulties? Possibly the best way of dealing with this question would be to work back from a rough one-year plan which was largely the outcome of discussions between the Personnel Manager and ourselves from May to July 1978. (It is important to note that, by this time, partly because of the Managing Director's strong personal involvement in the project, and partly because a framework for the whole programme had previously been worked out and agreed, the Steering Group was no longer 'steering' as it had done before; meetings were called infrequently, and then mainly in order for us to up-date the members on what had been happening and to get a rubber stamp for decisions that had been taken in one-to-one meetings. Nevertheless, it still served a useful purpose as a communications device, particularly for new members who were co-opted when the next stage involved their areas, and also as a forum in which support could be marshalled and any opposition institutionalized.)

The agreed plan was as follows:

(1) Establish a new participation group in the Dry Products department (target date October 1978).

Two of the three departments in the Pharmaceutical Production division had already been introduced into the participation scheme (Chemical Plant and Packaging). If the third department, Dry Products, could also be brought in, the ground would be prepared for a second-tier divisional group. At present, the Dry Products department was therefore the odd man out, and this in itself had created some problems. Some of the employees in the Dry Products area had complained that the two existing participation committees had been discussing issues which concerned them, and were asking why they should not have the same kind of forum. Meanwhile, members of the two groups were finding that the absence of Dry Products was leading to a restriction on some of the things they could discuss, in that certain issues with divisional-wide implications were being ruled out of order by the management. Confinement to in-house or departmental issues was causing some frustration and stultifying the process of evolution towards matters of wider concern. From an organizational point of view, it also seemed logical to set up a Participation Group for the Dry Products people: their department occupied a central position in the production chain of pharmaceutical production—the Chemical Plant produced dry powder chemical for capsules and tablets, and passed this on to the Dry Products department where the powder was mixed with starches and other ingredients, dried, pressed into tablets or filled into capsules, and then sorted and tested; finally, the Packaging department would receive, label, and pack the final product. If the committee structure could be brought into line with the production organization, it would become possible for the whole range of production issues to be dealt with in the same way.

(2) Establish the first divisional participation group in Pharmaceutical Production (target date December 1979).

As we have said (and this we will try to illustrate further in the next chapter), frustrations had arisen in both groups as a result of their inability to deal satisfactorily with items that had divisional-wide or site-wide implications. The management had insisted that they could not be expected to make decisions for people who were not involved in the scheme. This, they said, was one of the problems of the 'incremental', evolutionary approach to change that had been adopted: there would initially be groups with privileged access to the management who would have to be patient in their demands until such time as the privilege could be extended to others and there was the additional problem that groups would be in differing stages of development and might, when the time came to build divisional and site committees, experience difficulties in working together. Many of them would have been happy with a slow movement towards the higher level committees, but faced with the danger of shop floor and supervisory disillusionment with the scheme, they decided that it would be better to bring the target dates forward. This is what we meant when we implied earlier that the decision to extend and accelerate the pace of the programme was taken because of, rather than in spite of, the difficulties the Packaging group in particular were experiencing.

(3) Establish new participation groups in departments within other divisions of the factory (e.g. Engineering group, 1979; Capsule Department, 1980)

It had taken a good deal longer than anyone had anticipated to reach the point that we had now reached. Several of the directors had expressed personal disappointment about the speed of progress, and they were also afraid, they said, that factory employees would get tired of waiting for the final, grand structure. We, also, had begun to realize that if we continued to proceed from department to department, in series, the programme would drag on for years. Our main concern, however, was about the future development of existing participation groups: if the situation continued where site-wide issues could not be handled within the groups, and no mechanism outside the groups existed for dealing with them, there was the danger that everyone would become disillusioned. Obviously, there could be no site-wide committee until departmental and divisional groups had been established through the factory, and even at this point there were likely to be extreme difficulties in linking groups which were in different stages of evolution. The solution seemed to be to introduce and develop new participation groups in parallel, and not wait until one group was working well before moving on to another. The problem, however, was resources to move forward on a wider front. An inordinate amount of time had been needed to set up and run the two existing groups, and there was a very real danger, in opening up new areas, of our not being able to manage. In fact, it was around this time that we began to have visions of those athletic, misguided people who spin plates on canes for a living—the intention being to spin as many plates as possible and to keep them spinning by rushing back to those which are about to fall off for lack of momentum, and giving them an extra spin. Our worry was that we might set too many plates in motion and be unable to prevent some falling off and breaking.

In the event, it was decided to call on the services of two additional university staff, who would act as 'scouts' in new departments and collect the necessary data for planning the change. Having become familiar with the situation, they would then begin to engage in wider consulting activities with new and existing groups. A division of labour between ourselves and the Personnel Manager was also agreed: he would focus his attention on maintaining the Chemical Plant group, and we would divide the remainder of the work between ourselves.

(4) Participation arrangements for section heads

As we have noted on a number of occasions, many of the middle managers criticized the departmental approach to setting up participation on the grounds that everyone became involved in their jobs, while they had no opportunity to participate upwards in their superiors' jobs. Participation, they said, also made them more visible to the senior management and often subjected them to increasing pressures from above. At this time, we were inclined to agree with them, and felt that the departmental groups might run more smoothly if they were given the opportunity for upward participation. The section heads were an extremely important group in the factory in so far as they, perhaps more than any other single group, could set the climate of industrial relations with the shop floor employees. If they could be encouraged to adopt a more participative management style in the meetings themselves and in their day-to-day dealings with the shop floor, we believed this would have a major impact on the social organization of the factory. Because they were so critical to the success of the programme, we believed that it might be advisable to make alternative arrangements for them to participate as a group, and not wait until the site-wide group had been established.

There was also another area in which their participation might have considerable impact, namely, that of senior management. Up to this time, the senior managers had been able to distance themselves from the scheme, to leave the groups to discuss departmental issues without encroaching upon their own decision-making prerogatives. In fact, it would be fair to say that participation up to then had had little or no impact on the manner in which they made decisions. Their view on this seemed to be that it was right and desirable that participation meant that people participated in everybody's job but their own. When, on one or two occasions, the groups had strayed into their 'patch', they had been met with an extremely defensive reaction. For example, when the Chemical Plant group raised the question of shop floor entitlement to private medicine under BUPA, the directors at a Steering Group meeting reacted in a telling manner:

Director: How do we react to their desire to discuss BUPA?
Director (*grinning*): Easy. We tell them they can't.
Iain: How do you think they will react to that?
Director: That's their concern, not mine. The group was not set up to discuss things like this. We should tell them as much.
Director: Yes, I think we are going to have to give them some guidance about the proper things for discussion. (*To us*) Could you do this?
Iain: No.
Director: Why not?

Iain: Because this isn't what participation is about, and would in fact be doing the thing we're trying to get away from.

Director: Which is …?

Iain: Telling people what's good for them.

Director (*ruffled*): Oh, come on! What they're raising is silly and stupid. They've got no right.

Iain: Stupidity is not exclusively a management prerogative, you know. (*Meeting collapses under a wave of laughter.*)

Iain (*continuing*): No, I'm being serious. Participation is not just about discussing things we want to discuss. At the very least, we should go back to the group and say why we're not prepared to talk about BUPA—give reasons. One reason, I suspect, is that not even you can make that kind of decision—that it has to go back to the States. I doubt whether the people down there will be aware of that. If they were aware, then it's likely that they will decide to withdraw the issue. Frankly, I think the time has come when we as a group have to accept that participation may mean that we have to think deeply about what we do and how we do it.

Director: Be that as it may, these people have to be told that they can't discuss everything under the sun.

Iain: I wasn't aware that they wanted to.

Director (*not listening*): Frankly, if some of them are under the impression that they can, I think they're working in the wrong place. If they don't like it, they should go elsewhere …

The reader must excuse this brief diversion from what we were saying about the section heads, but we do believe it illustrates the reasoning behind our plan to use this group as one way of exposing the senior management to the participation notion. Members of the shop floor had continually questioned the senior management's commitment to the scheme, and we felt that it was about time that this was demonstrated.

(5) More work with the senior managers—'freeing it off at the top'.

In view of the above, it is not surprising that we began to give serious consideration to what needed to be done at the senior management level of the factory to ensure the growth of the participation programme. Our feelings were that we had spent too much time at the grass roots level, and not enough at the higher level. If the project was to continue to grow, we believed that a good deal of preparatory work with the senior management was necessary.

Some months before, in fact, we had held a one-day session with the thirty-two senior managers on-site to familiarize them with the participation concept, to deal with any questions or anxieties that they had, and to begin to identify (in this case, through a couple of group exercises) the skills required for the management of participation. Some follow-up to the session had been intended, and we even had some vague notions of selecting a small super-group of young, dynamic managers to go out and act as participation missionaries in the as yet uncharted regions of the factory. Such was the intention, but not the practice: we were already spending more time on the project than we had intended, and the reactions of some of the managers at the session had done little to endear them to us. Some of the chosen people had even had the temerity to ask what we were doing there when they were already participating and could quite well manage their own affairs.

Pressed, however, by the Personnel Manager, who at the time had more energy than ourselves, and by a growing realization that chipping away *ad infinitum* at the base of the pyramid was unlikely to have any visible effect on its overall shape, we let ourselves be talked into holding further sessions with junior and senior management during the following twelve months, and also into taking a closer look at the workings of the Operations group of directors.

Before getting into a description of some of these activities, it might be worthwhile to reflect briefly on our original metaphor of the journey to the Golden City of Participation. We had reached a crossroads (more a Spaghetti Junction?) on our journey; we were tired and the Golden City seemed as far away as when we had first started; the 'low' road stretched out long and winding before us; the 'high' road swept upwards into the mountains, possibly offering a short cut, but also more tiring and perilous. Which to take? Why not take both? How? Well, there's two of us, isn't there? True. ... And so the two travellers who had accompanied each other on a trip which had lasted more than two years bade their fond farewells and strode off into another chapter of adventures, each going their separate ways.

Dry Products Department

The terrain of the low road was thankfully familiar and good progress was made. With one exception, it was decided to use an identical sequence of activities for establishing the new participation group to that used in the Packaging Department, i.e. brief supervisors—brief all other employees—private meetings between ourselves and groups of employees to ascertain views, collect issues, and to make ourselves known to them—proposals back to Steering Group—elections—initial training of representatives (with representatives from the Chemical Plant and Packaging areas)—first meeting. The exception was that we would attend the initial briefings and hopefully be able to avoid misleading impressions being given by the management. In the event, we were able to reach this end point more quickly than we had anticipated, partly because, as we have already noted, the terrain was familiar, but also because the number of employees was smaller (sixty-seven), was mostly male (and tended to gossip less), and because we were able to explore their issues and discuss the structure of the group at the same time.

It is not our intention to bore the reader by repeating ourselves, so what we have done (against this background of similar events) is pick out features of the landscape not previously alluded to. In certain cases, however (and here we do not apologise for contradicting ourselves), we have deliberately re-traced some old steps in order to emphasize recurrent patterns which seemed to be emerging.

Lest the reader should be confused about the relative time during which all of this was happening (which in actual time was between October and November of 1978),

116

the Packaging group was just entering its turbulent period, when a number of people began to question its value—the period of 'The gathering storm' as we referred to it in the last chapter. This chapter, in fact, will lead us to a similar end point, and will provide a lead-in to the next chapter in which the problems and crises will be considered in some detail.

Initial briefings with supervisors: an illustration of how the participation issue was being presented by the management, and how people reacted

The briefing given by the Divisional Director contained a hotch-potch of now familiar 'buzz' words and phrases which had been picked up *en route*. What is important is that, properly digested or not, they were very different from the words and phrases used in the case of the Chemical Plant, prior to the actual experience of participation:

'A lot of people talk about participation without really knowing what it means—and I include myself in this. But what I think it does mean is trying to get people more involved in things that are going on. These slides' (Tony's notorious 'Triangles') 'might help ... it's flexible ... it's a learning exercise for everyone ... it's not easy ... it's not a substitute for normal supervisory channels. ... We've had some frustrations, but some have arisen because it hasn't properly developed site-wide. ... Now's your chance. You've been arguing that you're underprivileged, that you haven't been able to contribute. But now you'll be privileged. And' (nodding knowingly), 'mark my words, people will get on at you for being privileged.' (Throughout he has been twitching nervously, but the twitches now increase in their intensity when several of the supervisors remark that nothing has happened, and then ask him to give examples.) 'It's difficult to pick on concrete examples but' (evading the question) 'the idea is to reach some kind of agreement. Don't let me kid you, you don't always get that agreement. You know as well as I do that the world just ain't like that. ... No, it won't solve everything, but we hope it will create a more civilized atmosphere in which people can work.' (Going back to the question) 'There have been successes. I'll tell you what I'll do. I'll bring along a list of the issues which have been resolved in the meetings. The success of these meetings really depends on you being open and frank about things—there should be no fear of black eyes.
'Let's be clear, we're not forcing this upon you. If after Paul and Bob' (our Research Assistant) 'have spoken to the operators they or you don't want to participate, then that will be it.' (At this point, a supervisor questions this: 'You are dictating to some extent. If we say no, we don't want it, then we're left on the outside.') 'It's not as black-and-white as that, but it's true we would be disappointed if it was rejected here. What we're not doing is imposing any blueprint. It's a question of trying it, seeing how it goes, and fitting it to our needs. ...'

Although the presentation was somewhat muddled, it can still be seen how a good deal of our 'intellectual luggage' had been picked up by the people like the Divisional Director (and he was no exception). For example, in the above extract, one can identify indirect references to notions of 'free choice', initial expectations, 'interpersonal goals', and contingency. At the risk of appearing unkind (and arrogant), one could even suggest that this director and some of his colleagues had been reduced to being the baggage porters for our expedition—we got the pleasure and the protection, and they got the hard work.

Without repudiating entirely some of these suggestions, we do need to point out that we, at least, were still pulling more than our weight in the follow-up sessions to the briefings, and still having to bear the burden of employees off-loading things that they had concealed while the management had been present. For example, the follow-up meeting with the supervisors several days later soon fell into the normal pattern of people looking for every reason under the sun for not participating, but at the same time making certain that they did not lose the opportunity.

The first reason was that adequate machinery already existed for handling issues and grievances:

'We already have the machinery for handling all the gripes. Participation is just a grandiose idea—the dream of the Liberal Party and now the Socialists. I think it's all a load of rubbish. There's enough machinery as of now without burdening it down with such daft ideas.'

Then there was the point of view that decision-making was for the managers, not for the ordinary working person:

'All we would be doing is taking things off the management which they should be doing. It's their responsibility, not ours, and they get paid for it. Why should we bother?'

This was followed by the customary reference to participation as a way of keeping the unions out:

'Come on now, come clean. All the company is doing is looking to the future, making sure the unions can't creep in through the back door. The way things are going, we might all be better off in the union instead of getting caught up in another of their ploys to get us involved in things which are not in our best interest.'

Tied in with this was the feeling that the management was not really committed to genuine participation, whatever genuine might mean:

'The management don't really want it to work, you know. They're only using it as an early-warning system—a way of forestalling the unions.'
'Yes, I agree. I mean, why did they come to you? Why didn't they just come to us and say "we want to set up participation"? The fact is they don't want to get their hands dirty.'
'It's obvious to me why they didn't take the initiative, and it's not just the unions thing. Someone is pushing them from behind to do something they don't really want to do. I reckon you guys are government sponsored, and all they're doing is paying lip-service to the government.'
'You could be right. There's a lot of talk about nationalizing the pharmaceutical industry, and the company don't want to put anyone's backs up. Give them a chance and they'd be off this in a flash.'

They were also of the opinion that the new group would be virtually powerless to influence anything or anybody—witness the lack of progress of the other groups:

'The only thing we've heard from the other groups is that it's all a waste of time. Workers' ideas will be vetoed if they don't agree with them.'
'Yes, there's always that bloke at the top of the pyramid, a director who can veto 800 people.'

'It would be an uphill battle. You always end up running into people playing politics. You watch, they'll make sure the committee is top heavy. You wouldn't get me on to it for love nor money. All they'll do is put their foot down and say no.'

'Frankly, if a job comes up somewhere else, I'm off. I'm pissed off with this place. And participation ain't going to change it.'

'You can tell how people feel about it. You see, we have had a lot of feedback from the other groups, and it's not good—well, our impression is not good. My impression is that it's the same old questions and the same old answers every time.'

'It might work somewhere else, but not here. It's not like the Post Office. There's more buck-passing here, and you never get straightforward answers. You ask where the block is: that's what we would like to know.'

And finally there was the now familiar issue of 'black eyes':

'I suppose you know that this company has a little black book. If you're a bad boy, in goes your name. How can you be expected to speak your mind when you've got that hanging over you?'

'Yes, people are scared. I mean, we're taking a risk talking to you like this. We've only got your word that the things being said won't go back to the management.'

Having put forward a strong case for not participating, the group moved on to the equally familiar stage of discussing how they would actually participate when the group had been set up—from rejecting the assumed terms of participation of the management to setting out their own terms and preferences. Thus, from the viewpoint of 'felt need', it was possible to construe this apparently contradictory behaviour as a felt need for a particular kind of participation (influential, open, wide-ranging) and a 'no felt need' for another kind of participation (manipulative, devious, and limited) which they believed the management were seeking to impose on them. In other words, their initial hostility was not, in our view, an out-and-out rejection of the scheme—more an attempt to tailor it to their own requirements.

Meetings with the management team

The managers of the new department (see Appendix IV)—Kingsley, the departmental head, and Frank and Roger, the two section heads—were less defensive about the idea of participating than had been their counterparts in the Packaging Department. They seemed to expect that 'it' would happen regardless of what they said, and did not seem too bothered about this. Perhaps the main reason for the difference was (as we discovered later) that relations with the shop floor were fairly good, and there was less fear of being exposed at the meetings. The three personalities involved were also very different: Kingsley was a mild, quiet man in his fifties who had a reputation for being farily easy-going with the shop floor personnel, and generally a very helpful person; Roger was similar in age and stature to the famous Fred, but had never actually been in charge; and Frank was a fairly young, intelligent man, who, being destined for higher things, would not, even if he had wanted to, have challenged the party line. Thus, our meeting with them was a low key affair devoted almost wholly to structural details.

Meetings with the operators and their views on participation

Because the chargehand-supervisors' reactions to the proposal had been nearly identical to those we had encountered in the Chemical Plant and the Packaging Department, we had expected the meetings with the Dry Products employees to follow suit. Such was not to be the case: the operators on the whole were fairly indifferent and off-hand about the whole thing—yes, that would be nice; yes, it sounds a good idea, but well, you know, nothing much will come of it ... etc. 'What's the supervision like round here?' we asked, trying to stir them into some kind of action. 'Oh, not bad', they replied with a yawn. And taking another tack, 'Do you find things you raise get blocked?' 'Yes', came the reply—followed by another yawn. 'Well, would you like to enlarge on that?' 'Yes, things do get blocked.' 'Oh, thank you. Are there any issues you could raise at the new meetings?' (Yawning) 'Yes, hundreds, but there's not much point, is there?' 'Why not?' 'Well, things get blocked, don't they?'

It was about this time that we began to long for the much-cursed moaning-and-groaning script—the good old days when the sparks used to fly and we could indulge our fairy godmother fantasies. The truth was that this new 'take it or leave it' script was proving more difficult to cope with and far more damning of the participation proposal than its predecessor. Asking ourselves after the meetings why these people had reacted differently, we settled for two possible reasons: first, there were issues, but no burning issues to fuel the participation fires—people were relatively contented with the work and the supervision; and second, they seemed to have generally lower expectations about their work and a low attachment to it—if there were problems, these were to be expected, and 'what the hell anyway, we only come here for the money'.

Fortunately, there were several people who did not go along with the majority view and who, ultimately, allowed their names to go forward for election to the committee. Predictably, one of their recurrent problems as representatives was coping with the apathy and indifference we have described.

The only exception to the rule, apart from the chargehand-supervisor group, was the night shift group which reacted with healthy aggression towards the proposal. In its members' view, everything that could be wrong, was wrong: there were dust and fume problems, lighting problems, safety problems, problems in errors in wages, problems with the music that was piped through the ear protectors that they wore, problems with the fork lift truck, cooking facilities, vending machines, overtime, and unpaid leave. Possibly what made them different from the rest was that they had a particular grievance about being the 'forgotten men' of the department, and a particular leader ('Maurice and Mouth', as someone dubbed him) who had taken it upon himself to champion their cause for recognition. Not knowing at the time about their particular grievance, we had played straight into their hands by sending someone else to interview them. However, after repeated requests, we did agree to go on the night shift and hear their grievances.

Composition of the Dry Products Participation Committee

After much toing and froing, and arm-twisting, we were able to agree a structure of representation for the new committee, and to arrange for the election of its members. It will be noted that the committee was smaller than the one in Packaging, a consequence of the smaller size of the department, and of a deliberate intention on our part to make it more manageable:

Director Pharmaceutical Production (Chairman) – Simon Teffler
Personnel Manager – Eric
Head of Department – Kingsley
Section Head – Roger
Supervisor – Dave

Consultants (2)

Operator reps – Becky, Herbert, Dan, Peter, Steve, Kieron

The representatives' training session

As before, we spent a day with the operators' representatives shortly before their first meeting in order to explore any anxieties or worries they had about participating and to discuss with them some of the possibilities of the new scheme. The services of the Chemical Plant representatives were called on again, and two members of the Packaging Committee were added to their number.

Before their arrival, we raised the question of black eyes with the new people, asking them whether they foresaw any problems in speaking openly to the senior management, and the supervisory members. Most replied that they did not expect to have any major difficulty on that score, since they had in the past been members of other committees and had learned how to cope with 'the other side':

Dan: No, there's no problem there. I have sat on other committees, and am quite used to dealing with the management. There are difficulties at first, but they disappear. It's really a question of getting to know the person. Most people are OK once you've got to know them.

Paul: How about the supervision? Any chance of them making it difficult for you when you go back after the meeting?

Becky: No, they're not a problem. My supervisors are good. They're on the side of the workers. They would back me up if I ran into any difficulties.

Herbert: It all boils down to the way you deal with people. You have to treat everybody as an individual and a human being. The way you deal with a person depends on what he's like.

Dan: What is important, I think, is that you shouldn't be afraid to speak your mind.

Paul: That's easier to say than do sometimes.

Dan: Yes, it's easy to say—but it all depends on the way you approach it.

Steve: I would go along partly with what Dan is saying. We would probably all be quite straightforward with people we work with—but higher up, they aren't always direct, so why should we be?

Paul: I don't think you always should be. I agree that's what we're ultimately aiming for, but it may not be like that initially. You may need to be devious at first, not as open and frank as you would like to be. Because some people may be defensive, you may have to play it cool for a while.

Our reason for including this extract is that it does, we believe, underline both the difference between the Dry Products and Packaging Department representatives, and our movement from the traditional 'openness–trust' view of organizations to one which emphasizes their devious-political nature; while openness and trust were still admirable ideals, we found that the last thing people were in the participation arena was open and trusting. What we were therefore aiming for initially was a situation where people 'felt their way', got a clearer picture of what they wanted out of participation, and how others might react to various approaches to getting it. In power terms, the representatives were at a major disadvantage and the only way, we believed, that they could ultimately exercise some influence was through the acquisition of political skills. With these, people could take full advantage of the little power that they had.

The discussion about political/influence skills continued after the people from other groups had joined us:

Jack: If you're going to have maximum impact, you've got to bring up issues that have a solid foundation. Get your facts straight. You have also got to pursue things—keep at it. Never let them drop anything. Another thing is, save the small things for normal procedures and go for the big issues.

Trevor: Yes, I agree with Jack. Make sure the small issues are sorted out locally, and leave yourself time for the major ones. If you get the two mixed up, you'll get nowhere. The deeper you can get into an issue, the more difficult it is for them to drop it.

Joan: We had—and still have—this problem; lots of small problems, lots of small things on the agenda, with everybody fighting to get their things raised. We try to cover too much, and keep jumping around all over the place. We end up getting nowhere with nothing, and everyone leaves the meeting with nothing concrete to show their people.

Jack: That, I think, is the big difference between Joan's group and ours. The Chemical group pursue things, and don't drop them. My impression is that the Packaging group let things go, or raise far too much in the first place. And they accept the answers too readily. Another thing—you need to stick together, give each other support, don't go in just riding your own problems; get together before and agree on the important items you're going to push. It's fatal when you go in and fight each other for some air time.

Charlie: I would agree with Jack that we accepted things too easily, it's just a thing you naturally do—you know, a feeling that they reserve the final right to say yes or no. You have got to challenge. You have got to get into the way of keeping things going, and you've got to get things out. I work on the view that if you keep raising the same thing time after time, they will finally give way. But all this is embarrassing at times: in meetings before, the management have tried to close something down, get it taken off the agenda—and you raise it again. It can make the atmosphere feel pretty icy. It does take a lot of nerve and a thick skin.

Trevor: The worst thing you can do is say 'Sod participation' and jack it all in. Things can get very heated, and at times you're going to get frustrated because you don't seem to be getting anywhere. But don't give in. Now I feel we have won. At last our problems are getting discussed properly, and we're getting something out of it. Now the word 'no' in participation is taboo.

Charlie: The line I take is persistence lowers resistance.

Steve: I see that. But I'm still not clear how you can get into factory issues or issues which may even involve Alpen Industries.

Trevor: There will be some issues at your level that you can't sort out. You may have to shelve them until the thing spreads site-wide.

Charlie: I'm not sure about that. Should you have to wait until the thing is site-wide before raising site-wide issues? Surely, if anything affects your department, it should be raised. If it does have wider relevance, it should be up to the management to raise it further in the right quarters. What you've got to be careful of is not letting the management fob you off with 'sorry, you can't discuss this, it's a site-wide issue'—as soon as they put the site-wide label on it, it's dead. Try to put any other label on it but site-wide. Don't let them tell you that a departmental group can't discuss wider things. See it as a departmental group discussing departmentally relevant things which happen to have wider repercussions in the factory.

Turning away from the political skills involved in defining, presenting, and processing an issue, the representatives moved on to the related question of allies:

Becky: What about disagreements between yourselves in the group. How do you cope with this?

Jack: This can be fatal. If they see you're divided, they will be happy to sit back and let you get on with it. Try and get it all together, get some agreement between yourselves before you go in.

Charlie: That's easier said than done. Even if people agree with a point you make, they rarely back you up. It's particularly true in my case where there's some friction between my lads and the girls. We're trying to get round this one at the moment by informally meeting together before the meeting itself.

Jack: And on the other front, you should be trying to get the local management on your side, so that you can all put a case to the senior management. They will see that you're together on something or other and will think twice about turning you all down. It won't be easy at first and when you've got a person like we had—a self-styled autocrat ... you've got problems!

Paul: Remember when you talk to your managers, they say the same thing as you—

'We push things but they don't get anywhere'. One strategy is to support their interests—not always your own—because if you support them, they may support you.

Jack: Definitely. Tom now does this, you know, comes to us before a meeting and canvasses our support.

Charlie: We've got a long way to go on this. Fred has changed slowly; there was a time when he wouldn't even pass the time of day with you, but still we need to get together on more things. I have more of a problem with Joan: her girls often have a different view from my lads. She has to represent that view, and I have to represent mine. If these views clash, then me and Joan will clash.

Trevor: If you clash, well, that's participation. The thing is what you do with that clash. To begin with it might be better to deal with things where there is a measure of agreement, and you can present a unified front. Later the meeting will be in better shape to allow disagreements to occur without leading to any permanent rifts.

Finally, another aspect of the political process was managing the people you represent:

Iain: When someone gives you an issue, check it out. You might get only one side of the story, or a person may not feel as strongly about something as you were originally led to believe. Test the water, sound out other people, try to come to some conclusion about the nature and seriousness of the problem.

Before you can get their support, you need to get their interest. Pick on things where you know you can make a big hit, and don't fall into the trap of only representing your interests.

Charlie: It will be an uphill battle getting the interest of people on the shop floor. It takes a long time to change them. What you've got to do is tell them what went on even though they may not want to hear. Keep canvassing them for issues. Don't let them trap you into raising your own things and then criticizing you for not representing them. When they say things are not happening, tell them why. Not being directly involved, they just can't appreciate why things take so long to sort out. Try and help them understand that participation takes a lot longer to get working than people expect.

Again, the existing representatives had made an invaluable contribution to the session, bringing out and dealing with issues in a way that no outsider could have equalled. They had, in effect, successfully reduced complex notions about the politics of participation, the definition and articulation of issues, and the role of the representative to a level which everyone could understand and apply to their own situation. All that remained after this was to draw up a list of items for the first few meetings, and re-cap on some of the points that had been raised.

As a final note to this session, we should perhaps point out one unanticipated consequence of this session. Although it had been designed with the Dry Products people in mind, the two Packaging representatives told us afterwards that they had also learnt a lot about the participation process, particularly about the need to think more carefully about the ways and means of raising items and of having maximum impact on the meeting.

The early meetings

The first three meetings of the new Participation Committee got off to an excellent start: a number of 'hygiene' issues were raised and rapidly dealt with; work began on building a procedural constitution for the group—agreed rules on agendas, minutes of meetings, feedback to constituents, and so on. In this respect, the pattern was very similar to that of the early Packaging meetings, with the important difference that the level of communication between the members was a lot better. By this we mean that virtually everyone became actively involved at an early stage, and the level of contribution between the members was about even; there also seemed to be less hanging back—less fear of black eyes; issues were raised in a fairly low-key manner and discussed in a fairly level-headed way; rather than say or imply 'here is the issue, what are you going to do about it?', the shop floor representatives tended to raise issues in the form of 'here is an issue, what are we going to do about it?'—more collaboration and less them-and-us than in the Packaging group. The new members also showed less deference to the managers present, quietly refusing to bow to their better judgement, digging in, and insisting that their point of view be listened to. All this in a manner which helped the managers to come off the defensive, to unstiffen, and, as they themselves said, to enjoy the meeting instead of seeing it as something of an ordeal.

Everyone, it must be admitted, had an air of self-congratulation and optimism, us included. The representatives themselves told us privately that they had been pleasantly surprised by the management's attitude:

'They have been more friendly than I expected. I thought it might be a bit like shop stewards meeting the managers—you know, more formal and more arguing. It has not turned out to be like that at all, really.'

'Yes, I'm very happy with it. I thought I might have problems in my role of representative but everyone has been very helpful—more helpful and kind than I imagined.'

'I'm starting to enjoy it. I think it's starting to go well. I wasn't too sure at first—you know, I'm not very good at talking like that, I'm not a committee kind of person. But now I'm quite happy; I feel I can sit down, settle in, and begin to present the views of my members.'

'The atmosphere is good—more friendly than I thought. Some issues have not been tackled yet—the bigger ones that is—but it will come. I'm not too bothered about that as yet, because I see it as a case of me feeling my way, finding out what makes the others tick.'

Unfortunately, because things were going so well, we tended to push from our minds the fact that the Packaging group had gone through a similar, if not quite so pleasurable, 'honeymoon period', when everything in the garden was lovely, but after that had entered a long winter of discontent. What we failed to consider was the possibility that the new group might follow a similar path. As we shall describe below, this did in fact happen.

But can it boil milk?

The issue that caused all the bother was first raised by the operators under the agenda heading: 'Canteen facilities at night'. Since it appeared to be another, minor 'hygiene' matter affecting only a small number of people and having no site-wide implications, everyone believed that it could be resolved fairly quickly. Members of the night shift (and here we should have been more on our guard after our earlier exchanges with them) had complained that the vending and hot meal facilities available to them were unsatisfactory: the vending machines were frequently empty when they arrived, and they were not able to purchase snacks for eating during the shift. Over the years, however, they had made their own cooking arrangements—a room little bigger than a broom cupboard had been taken over and an electric cooker installed for warming up milk for coffee, soup, baked beans, and pre-cooked snacks brought in from home. Their complaint was that the facilities were unsatisfactory. What they wanted was similar to the facilities currently being enjoyed by neighbouring Capsule Plant workers—a proper kitchen and eating area, a fridge and storage space for food, and somewhere private to sit down.

What follows is an edited version of the conversations that took place during four of the meetings:

Simon (*Director and Chairman*): It's getting late. Can we leave the next item till next time.

Dan: No, not really. The canteen arrangements for the night shift is a very important issue. They are very angry.

Simon: What are they angry about?

Dan: The vending machine is always empty. I've personally been checking it for the past two weeks, and it's always the same.

Kingsley: Yes, I agree. I checked on this last night.

Eric (*Personnel, responsible for canteen facilities*): You know, that's not right. It's not always empty. I've checked it for myself.

Dan: At what time?

Eric: At all times.

Dan: You see, if you check the machines at 4.00 p.m. they usually are well-stocked. But what the day men do is empty them before they go home. It's cheap food to take home. That leaves us with nothing.

Eric: Look, Dan, you know as well as I do that we don't live in a perfect world. Don't you try to tell me any other.

Dan: I don't intend to.

Roger (*Section Head*): Why can't we open the canteen at night? There's enough people in the factory on shift to justify it.

Simon: I think we need to consider other alternatives first.

Dan: What the men really want is good cooking facilities. They have supplied a lot of equipment, but it's not very satisfactory at the moment. They brought it in because they didn't want to have to eat cold sandwiches every night. You need a hot meal on shift. What annoys them is that the Capsule Plant have an ideal facility paid for by the company.

Kingsley: What about the old Elina Marty room? It's never used. Couldn't we get that converted? It's large and it's private.

Simon (*jumping in very quickly*): What about an infrared cooker in place of the one you have now—you know, a microwave oven? It would be quick, clean, and efficient. Actually, we have already given a lot of thought to getting one. Eric, I believe, has been looking into it.

Dan (*ignoring the suggestion*): Most companies have a sub-canteen facility. The men feel very strongly that they should have one.

Steve: And they would be prepared to pay their way.

Simon: What about an infrared in place of the cooker you have now?

Steve: People don't want a microwave oven. They want their own place to do their eggs and beans.

Simon: But couldn't we do a trial run with a microwave?

Dan (*smiling*): Yes, but once we've got it, we've got it for good. Look, if we don't want it, we shouldn't have to have it.

Simon: But you've got to give it a fair hearing. I think you need to go back and consult your people about this.

Steve: That's fair enough. We can also ask them about the idea of converting the old Marty shop, or possibly of extending outwards from the Dry Products lounge.

(Meeting ends)

After the meeting, we were fascinated to discover why Simon, the chairman and director, had been so in favour of a microwave oven. His comment to us was that there was a good deal of time-wasting on the night shift with people cooking their own food: a microwave would be quicker and would not need a worker to act as cook as such. If they had their own room, he said, even more time would be wasted. It is worth noting that none of these points were raised at the meeting itself.

At the next meeting, tempers began to fray:

Herbert: I've been back to my people and they don't want a microwave.

Steve: Mine neither. They want better self-catering facilities.

Simon: But the main advantage of the microwave is space-saving.

Dan: Look, I don't know what we need to argue about. Capsules have had the facilities we want for years. We've been behind for ages. Why do they come in for special treatment? Our night shift is completely forgotten about, nobody listens to them. They are saying we don't want the ruddy thing. Why try to put it in when they don't want it?

Simon: But why don't they want it?

Steve (*raising his voice*): Simply because the cooker they have is perfectly OK. How do I make it clear that it's a room they want, not a new cooker?

Kingsley: I do think we should give the microwave a fair hearing. Perhaps we ought to check with people.

Dan (*also raising his voice*): Look, I've just done that. I have spoken to my people.

I've come back to you to state that they don't want it. And that's final.

Eric: Hang on, Dan. Apart from wanting their own room, are there any other reasons why they don't want it?

Dan: Yes, they think it's dangerous. Some of them have read in the papers that the rays cause cancer.

Eric: Well, that's just not the case. We have looked into it.

Dan: Another thing is that it won't do the job. It only warms up pre-cooked food. It can't actually cook things.

Eric: Says who? Yes it can. We really must get our facts straight, you know.

Herbert: Just tell me one thing. Why can't we use the Marty room?

Simon: Because it's used as a conference room.

Herbert: But conference rooms are not used at night. How can they be when few managers have ever been seen after 4 o'clock?

Simon: Now come on, be fair.

Herbert (*moodily*): That's the way we see it.

Simon: OK. It seems to me that there's some confusion about what a microwave can and can't do. I think we should set up a sub-group to look at this—say Eric, Steve, and Dan. Let them look at the various alternatives and report back.

Dan: That sounds reasonable. But you must appreciate that people are getting impatient and asking why this is taking so long to resolve.

Kingsley: I would consider that to be a healthy sign. The men are sceptical about participation, not really that interested. If we can get some action on this, we will have a trump card. If the men can see us taking action, they may begin to believe participation is actually doing something.

Steve: Yes, that's true. But they're not very happy with our progress so far.

Simon: Look, Steve, don't let me give the impression that we're putting this thing off and saying you must have a microwave oven. I'm completely open-minded about it at the moment. Let's have patience for a little longer and see what the sub-group can find out.

(Discussion ends)

During the course of this meeting, it became evident that the group was no longer talking about the specific issue of canteen facilities for the night shift—that the issue had begun to take on wider proportions, to symbolize and act as an outlet for deeper issues. There was, for example, the issue of privilege first raised by Dan. He had implied that the problem of cooking facilities was symptomatic of a deeper grievance that the Dry Products department was the poor relation of the factory, people in the Capsule Plant worked in relative luxury, and were given things without even having to ask for them. The night shift workers had a particular grudge that they were blatantly ignored—they never saw the management, no one was concerned about them and their problems, etc. To them, it seemed, the cooking facilities issue was one of many examples of this wider grievance. (This was confirmed when we met them several weeks later.) Herbert's poignant remarks about the conference rooms not being used at night are particularly revealing in this respect—as he explained to us later, very few managers came in on the night shift to see what was happening, and this was taken by many of the men to be a sign that the management were not really interested in them. Finally, the operators had begun to see the issue as a test case for participation—a way of finding out how committed the management actually were to implementing a majority recommendation of the group and the preference of the night shift people, and a way of discovering how much influence they really had when it came to the crunch.

To continue with the story, the next meeting started well, with a comprehensive report from the sub-group which examined three alternative solutions to the problem. From the very first comments of the Personnel Manager, it became clear that the managers had capitulated on trying to impose their own preferences. First victory to the representatives. Unfortunately, much of the goodwill built up was to be undermined by an incident which occurred towards the end of the meeting:

Eric: Well, I think Steve and Dan will agree with me that we've made some good progress on this one. Let me report on the thoughts of the sub-committee. The first point we accept is that the facilities in Dry Products should be as good as those in other areas. The second point is that we have to do what people need and want.

The first alternative is to adapt and improve existing facilities. This might be accomplished by purchasing some different equipment like a microwave oven and a cupboard. But space is very limited, we all agree. The estimated cost for implementing this proposal would be £200–£300.

The second alternative involves converting part of the Marty room, and providing self-catering facilities—cooking equipment, a sink, and an extraction system. All of this could be installed for about £700–£900.

The third alternative would be to modify a section of the existing DP lounge, constructing a room in the space to the right of the entrance. This proposal has been estimated at £1500–£1800.

My two colleagues here have gauged the opinions of their members, and the general view is that alternative two would be best.

(Discussion follows, and everyone agrees to go for the second alternative—the one preferred in the previous meeting by the operators' representatives.)

Simon: OK. We've got to move quickly on this one. What we need to do is raise this formally as a capital request, get Engineering to take it as a project and do a proper costing. I know you feel this has been dragging on, but the earliest I can get a request in is a month's time.

Dan: Well, that's OK. So long as I can tell the men that something definite is being done.

(Further discussion ensues, about the details of the proposal, where crockery would come from, and so on.)

Dan: While we're on the subject, the vending machines are still not being filled up for the night shift.

Eric: I can assure you that they are.

Dan: I'm afraid I have to disagree with you there.

Roger: The answer is to get them filled up more often.

Eric (*impatiently*): That's all very well, Roger, if you want to go and fill them ...

Simon (*shakes his head*): Come on, hold on a minute.

Dan: The fact is that the machines are not always full, even in the afternoons. The woman doesn't always fill it up then.

Eric: Yes she does, I've seen her.

Dan: No, I'm sorry ...

Eric (*angrily, turning on Dan*): Look, I'm telling you, I've seen her.

Simon: Hey, hold on.

Dan: I don't want to argue about it. If you come down to our place you will see.

Eric: Right, I will, I'll check it myself.

Roger: I can't understand it. The fact is the machine is often empty.

Eric (*snapping*): What do you mean, you don't understand?

Paul (*joking*): Belt up, the lot of you. Things are getting a bit high. Clearly the conflict between you is over the facts—as yet, as far as I can gather, there's no actual conflict of interest between you. I'm sure everybody wants to get the machine sorted out. If the conflict is over the facts, the best thing, it seems to me, is find out the facts—together if possible.

Eric (*rounding on Paul*): Yes, that's all right for the world of the academic, but it's not like that in the practical world.

Paul: I was of the impression that what I was suggesting was immensely practical.

Eric: OK. I accept that. But you can't please everybody all of the time; you know that as well as I do.

Paul: I don't think anyone would disagree with that, but I'm not sure where that gets us in the practical world.

After this exchange, the meeting was soured and came to a rather abrupt end. Eric was disappointed, perhaps thinking it unfair that after spending a long time participating with the sub-group he (or more precisely, his area of responsibility) should be treated so roughly. 'People are just never satisfied', he exclaimed after the meeting, 'they really should get their facts straight.'

By the time the next meeting had come round, the issue of canteen facilities at night had entered a new phase. Simon announced that a resolution was imminent: the Engineering department had taken it up as a project and were 'running with it'; the various alternatives put forward by the group were being considered, and the sub-group would be kept fully informed; 'everything should now go forward quite straightforwardly', he concluded, 'capital approval should be obtained next month'. The representatives expressed satisfaction that 'at last something is being done', and that 'we can now tell our people something positive is happening'.

What they (and we) failed to realize at the time was that the issue had effectively been taken out of the hands of the Participation group, being referred sideways to another department (Engineering) and upwards to a directors' group (the 'Technical Committee', responsible for all decisions on major capital expenditure). They were obviously aware that the issue had gone 'outside'—and acknowledged that this must happen—but were under the impression that their preferred alternative would be approved and rubber stamped by the Technical Committee. What they did not foresee were these committees starting the process of considering alternatives all over again, and virtually disregarding the recommendation put forward by the Participation Committee. This, in fact, is what happened, leading ultimately to a decision being made which was diametrically opposed to the wishes of the Participation representatives.

The crunch came at a meeting of the Participation group a month later:

Eric: Mark (*senior manager responsible for canteen arrangements across the site*) has come up with four alternatives *vis-à-vis* building alterations. The first involves modification of the old Marty room; the second, modification of the under-stairs area; the third utilizes the existing area with certain modifications; the fourth involves 'breaking' into the plant room itself. Dan and I have discussed these with him. I now suggest that we let Mark go ahead with the capital request, making his recommendations.

Steve: Mr Campbell, I was under the impression that we had agreed that the Elina Marty room was the best alternative.

Eric: That's your preference—your individual preference. I'm not sure the Technical Committee would necessarily accept that preference.

Steve: But Mark doing this extra work, why ...

Eric: But it's the way the Technical Committee work. You've got to come to understand how the Technical Committee operates.

Steve: That's the problem—I'm beginning to. Then we have wasted two months. We've spent two months making a choice, and now that choice is irrelevant. It strikes me we should have had the Technical Committee people in from the start—or the engineers, or whatever. Now we've got ...

Eric: As I've said, you have expressed your preference. There are a number of other factors like costs, time, and so on that we now have to take into account at the next level. What we are now doing is refining. The Technical Committee will take account of everything and then make a decision.

Steve: If you ask me, we already did that—you asked us to check out opinions—we did that; you asked us to make a choice—we did that. What happens if they make a choice that isn't acceptable to the men? There's a real problem now because the men thought that the choice had already been made.

Simon: I know it might appear that we're backtracking, and I realize that this is an item that people are interested in—and that you will have difficulty explaining it to the men. I don't want to make an arbitrary decision. I'm open-minded. That's why I want you and Dan to sit down with Mark and Eric Campbell, and look at the pros and cons. With hindsight, I would agree that we should have involved Mark earlier, but I'm still optimistic anyway that our recommendation will be accepted.

Steve: I can appreciate that we can't have things entirely our own way—that we may need a compromise between what the group want and what the management want. What I don't want is for the item to go to the Technical Committee and then they say this is what you'll jolly well have.

Simon: No, I won't let that happen. I'm on the committee, and will be asked to justify the recommendation. That's why I need all your comments.

Dave: I really don't know where all this is taking us.

Dan: That's what bothers me. It's gone on so long. People are saying it's being pushed under the carpet.

Eric: What you have to appreciate is that in your daily lives you get involved in immediate decisions. Simon and I are involved in things where the decisions may take two years to pass.

Steve: And what you have to appreciate is that we're just about to get a lot of stick.

Thus, it was beginning to be realized that the participation group was not a decision-making body. Clearly, it could discuss and make recommendations, but anything over and above that was, in the present order of things, out of the question—the rules of the game being that decisions were the prerogative of a top-level, specialist, directors' group. In a situation like this, it is attitudes rather than rules that are important: if Eric and, particularly, Simon had been prepared to back the committee's proposal, and if the members of the Technical Committee had been responsive to a 'participative' style of operation, it is likely that the group would have been more influential. Unfortunately, as we had discovered on previous occasions, the concept of participation was entirely alien to the majority of directors sitting on the Technical Committee, and it was unlikely that much attention would be paid to the participation group's recommendation. Furthermore, even though Eric was firmly committed to a participative approach, he was not a member of these higher-level decision-making bodies, and was therefore as powerless as his fellow group members. There was also another issue relevant to both him and Simon, which we describe in more detail in the next section: in brief, this was that it took a brave man to disagree with the majority view of powerful people in the factory and company at large; the deviant, non-conformist always ran the risk of being passed by in the promotion stakes, whereas the conformist, 'company man' always stood a better chance of getting on. A manager put it in a nutshell: 'If you want to get on in this place, don't, repeat, don't think—and never, but never, disagree.' It was unlikely that either Simon or Eric would put much force behind the group's recommendation in the event of a different decision being taken—neither, understandably, wanted to cause much of a noise, particularly over an issue which did not affect either directly. It is also worth remembering, finally, that the present decision-making structure allowed Simon to pass the decision to someone else and maintain face with the shop floor representatives: if an unsavoury decision had to be taken, it did not need to be taken by him, merely referred upwards to the safety of an anonymous top-level group. In short, given the present state of affairs, he never needed to have to say no in the Participation Committee.

The death knell had been sounded, and all that remained to be done at the next meeting was to give the issue a decent, if not uneventful, burial. The meeting began with an announcement that people had feared and expected:

Eric: We may have fallen down on this one. Dan and I—would you agree, Dan? (*Dan doesn't respond*)—had a constructive meeting over the proposals from the project engineers. ... Steve, unfortunately, was away and we didn't actually manage to get together. Well ... Mark took account of your views when he submitted his capital proposal to the Technical Committee. ... The, er, proposal that has been agreed is to modify the existing area ... and, and, er ... instal a microwave oven. I did pass this message to Steve, but he didn't give me any feedback. But Dan has. As he said at the last meeting, what was most important was to get something done. Well, something now has been done, isn't that right, Dan? (*Silence*)

(*Continuing*) It's interesting, actually, we did seek the expert assistance of our canteen people, and they definitely advised the microwave oven. They say it's OK. Actually, I recently had the opportunity to look at one, and there's really a lot of versatility, a lot of smoothness. ... (*Long silence*)

Dan: Be that as it may. My men don't want a microwave oven. They are dead against it. I mean, it won't do toast. And can it boil milk?

Eric (*elusively*): It can do most things.

Dan (*impatiently*): But can it boil milk?

Eric (*elusively*): Well, it does a lot of things. I had a lovely roast beef and three veg when I was over looking at them.

Dan: But the night shift blokes don't eat roast beef and three veg! It's things like soup, toasted cheese sandwiches, boiled milk. The next thing that will be suggested is that we change our eating habits to fit in with the new oven.

Simon: Hold on a minute. Are we clear, Eric, what it will and won't do?

Eric: Well, not exactly, not exactly everything. But we have, in fact, hired rather than bought one, so that everyone can give it a trial period.

Dan: And that has already been done?

Eric: Yes.

Up to this point, only three of the committee had been involved in the 'discussion', but now everyone came in:

Peter: People are absolutely disgusted by the way this thing has been handled. They feel it was all decided a long time ago. We said time after time we did not want it, and now you've bulldozed it through.

Steve: Yes, my group are one hundred per cent against. They are disappointed with the way things have been done.

Paul: Perhaps we should go round the table and get everyone's views.

Dan: People want a conventional cooker. Ours is nearly new and works quite satisfactorily. We're now going to lose that, and our canteen room.

Steve: There's been no participation at all, really, in the actual decision that has been made. We've been strung along. (*The rest agree.*)

Simon: I would have thought the microwave would have helped. It's quicker. We can get more throughput.

Steve: That may help you but it doesn't help us.

Eric: People might think Simon and I have a bee in our bonnet about this. What we did was ask our expert canteen staff and a catering company. We said, what would you advise, and they said, the microwave.

Steve: Well, it's hardly surprising that a company should recommend its product. And anyway, on our side, we've got the opinion of experienced, expert shift staff-workers, if you like; people who know what they're talking about. They, after all, are the consumers.

Eric: What we've got to get down to now is arranging a display.

Steve: Well, that's not my problem now, it's yours. The way things have gone has destroyed a lot of confidence in the participation meeting. We could have probably got the same facility without ever having come to this group—through the normal channels.

Simon: I agree, it could have gone that way. But the advantage of this is that it gets things out on the table. We've all got our opinions out, and that's a good thing.

Dan: Well, that's where we disagree.

Steve: It's destroyed all confidence. People will now say, 'Oh, I told you in December it wouldn't be any good.'

Dan: That's what they will say.

This continued for another twenty minutes or so. At this point, we tried to get the group to go back over the issue, and try to find out where things had gone wrong. On reflection, people agreed that the major mistake had been to let the issue slip out of the meeting, first into a sub-group, and then into the normal decision-making channels; if this was to be avoided in the future, people would have to 'come to' the participation meeting, rather than it to them. As one member remarked, 'We just farmed the issue out, just avoided it. Perhaps it should have been kept in here.' On the more general question of how, at the end of the day, they could acquire more influence, the group drew a blank—either 'things' would have to change dramatically in the factory, or the group would have to content itself with being a talking-shop rather than a decision-making body. The problem now was managing the very different expectations that people had formed about the nature of participation: the representatives had agreed to participate on the assumption that the committee would be influential, and for similar reasons the shop floor had also agreed to 'give it a go'. These expectations had now been violated, creating a personal credibility problem for the representatives, and reinforcing everybody's prior belief that it would all be a 'waste of time'. In short, the group had not only made no progress, it had gone three paces back behind the starting line.

What this event underlined for everyone was the considerable distance we still had to travel before reaching the Golden City of Participation—indeed, our feelings at the time were no doubt not dissimilar from those of the other participants: fatigue and a dropping off of enthusiasm. Just when the rainbow's end seemed in sight, something happened that put it further away than ever. Again, perhaps not unlike the others, we considered crawling into a ditch and giving up.

CHAPTER 8

A change of climate

What became known as the 'Great Microwave Affair' was by no means an isolated incident; throughout the organization, earnest, well-intentioned managers were ardently, and only too effectively, seeking to 'help' the participation programme and, in so doing, unwittingly promoting similar crises to that outlined in the previous chapter. As we have indicated, many of the members of the Dry Products group forcibly expressed their dissatisfaction with the decision-making processes they considered themselves subject to, and in other groups, similar expressions of discontent and disillusion were to be heard.

The Packaging group, which had begun in an atmosphere of sweetness and light, was now marked by an air of bitchiness and demoralization. Two issues, both seriously mishandled, had brought the group low. Some of the members had threatened to resign and several of their constituents on the shop floor chose to withdraw their support for the programme.

Furthermore, section heads and senior supervisors across the site had met and had voiced—albeit only to us—their protests about the way that the participation programme had been handled. A series of two-day meetings with groups of them had confirmed how exposed they felt as individuals; the programme, they had argued, had begun from completely the wrong 'end'—bottom-up rather than top-down. We, they pointed out, had been misguided in encouraging people below supervisor level to participate in the supervisor/section head's jobs without providing opportunity for the latter group to participate, in turn, in the jobs of their superiors. Having expressed in relatively strong terms their contempt for the programme and their hostility towards us, they had gone on to suggest that they should be given an opportunity to meet with the Managing Director on a regular basis in order, as one of them put it, 'to get some bloody participation for ourselves'. This request, which we conveyed somewhat less graphically to the Steering Committee, was ignored which, not surprisingly, had the effect of stimulating those who had made it into expressing more disenchantment with us, with the management, with their subordinates, and with the programme.

Members of the Steering Group had become alarmed by these developments, not least because their role and position in the programme as directors had come under attack. Some individuals in particular had come in for personal criticism, either for the way they had handled the meetings, or for some of the answers they had fed back to the groups. Their response, as we shall see, was to blame all and sundry for their unreasonableness, and to pick out certain individuals—the 'troublemakers'—to bear the brunt of their attack. Accusations, most of them behind the scenes, were also flying in our direction. We were blamed for not helping them avert the problems they had now run into; one or two people began to express some doubts as to our competence and some suggestions were made that the process should be controlled internally.

The participation programme had clearly moved into a new phase. Although during the previous stages progress had been jerky and uneven, there had nevertheless been some positive movement forwards: groups had been set up and were meeting regularly; they had tackled a wide range of issues and, more importantly perhaps, had begun to learn how to deal with each other; there had been a growing internal commitment to move the programme to a site-wide conclusion. In contrast, we had now moved into a period of doubt and dissension; it seemed that many people no longer wished to travel with us.

In order to understand more clearly the nature of and cause of the problems, we need to return, for a moment, to the development in one other group—Packaging.

Packaging re-visited: the unpaid leave and early finishing issues

The story of the decline in the fortunes of the participation programme really begins in January 1978 in the Packaging group, six to eight months before the microwave oven issue came to a head in the Dry Products group. Since the story virtually speaks for itself, we have decided to describe it in diary form, picking out important events or dialogue as illustrations of the issues in contention. We also include from time to time some of the comments made by the representatives to one of our research students, Bob Westwood, who was monitoring the process.

January 1978

The issue of the company's unpaid leave was raised at the very first meeting of the Packaging Participation Meeting. Fred, the section head, asked for clarification of the issue. His understanding was that all employees were given ten special 'Alpen days' holiday per year in addition to basic holiday entitlements which could be used up throughout the year in the form of days off for uncertified absence. He was unsure as to whether this was a blanket entitlement or whether unpaid leave was only granted at the supervisor's discretion. If the latter were the case, which he believed it to be, were there circumstances in which paid leave could be granted (and if so, what were they?), or in which unpaid leave could be granted without employees losing some of their Alpen days? Finally, he asked what happened if someone had used up their ten Alpen days and still needed unpaid leave. The shop floor representatives who were present confirmed that unpaid leave was a very emotive issue and that people were very unclear as to their entitlement. It was agreed to discuss the item in full at the next meeting.

February 1978—meeting of the Steering Group

It was noted that the present policy in fact stated that there was no unpaid leave within the company, but this was clearly at odds with the reality since from time to time, employees were granted unpaid leave with or without loss of their Alpen holidays. It was agreed that the policy needed to be modified with the term 'authorized absence' replacing the words 'unpaid leave'. The policy would read that authorized absence 'with or without pay may be granted in very unusual circumstances by supervision after discussion and agreement with Personnel'. This message would be fed back to the next participation meeting with a statement to the effect that the whole question of 'authorized absence' was currently under discussion for the new Employee Handbook and would be clarified.

Clearly, at this time the management were unwilling to clarify the issue any further. Rather, they wanted more time to decide (unilaterally) on a new or modified policy which would then be communicated to employees. The approach to the Packaging group was to give some information and hope this would suffice.

Meeting of the Packaging group—February 1978

In the event, things did not go as smoothly as had been anticipated. The chairman-director tried to close the discussion down on the basis that 'this is a site-wide issue that can't be dealt with satisfactorily in a Departmental meeting. We want consistency across the whole of the site. All I can say at the moment is that it is not our policy to encourage unpaid leave, although we recognize that there may be occasions when it becomes necessary.'

The Personnel Manager followed with another reason for not discussing the issue further: 'The whole policy on unpaid leave—or should I say 'authorized absence'— is currently being rewritten to try and improve and clarify the situation.'

At this stage, many of those present, including ourselves, began to push for wider discussion of the issue:

May: So what is the position now? If I want to stay off tonight—if I can't get in to work—do I have to take it as a holiday?

Eric: Um, that's a difficult one to answer. What do you think? The important thing is that we want people to tell us before they stay out, not after.

May: So you're saying I could stay out tonight so long as I tell you beforehand?

Eric: Well, not exactly …

Simon (*getting alarmed*): This is a difficult one. As I've said, Personnel are trying to write it up. We do want consistency.

May: I'm confused.

Eric: I think there has to be an element of flexibility.

May: I'm still confused.

Iain: I think what people want to know is what count as special circumstances in which unpaid leave will be granted. They're not asking for any more than they have got now, just some clarification of where they stand. The other issue is that, according to some people on the floor, the present policy encourages dishonesty. If you ring up and say you're ill, and can't get in, you don't lose any of your Alpen days. If you ask for time off for any other reasons, you stand to have the request turned down or have to lose a day of your holidays. Therefore the temptation, whenever you want time off, is just to make out you're ill. Apparently many do this and get away with it, whereas the more honest souls pay the price of their honesty.

Fred: That's one problem. The other is that the present policy causes difficulties for the supervision. We are not clear whether and in what circumstances unpaid leave can be granted, nor do we know whether people who stay away should lose their Alpen days.

Simon: Yes, this is a difficulty, but ...

Dick: And what happens if you have totally committed all your ten holiday days—if they're booked, or something—which we're quite entitled to do? If you then miss a day, how can you take it off your holidays?

Fred: All you can do is organize yourself. Put aside days from your holiday for those odd occasions when you need to take a day off.

Eric: If I can add a final word, you can go back and say that in the majority of cases, people should have no problem getting unpaid leave in special circumstances. I don't believe we shall ever reach a complete answer to this one. It's been a problem for a long time.

Simon: OK. I am grateful to you for raising this issue, but we're saying that it's a Personnel issue and one which should be resolved through Personnel and supervision.

The representatives were clearly disappointed by the management response, but elected to let the meeting run on to another issue—which unfortunately received similar treatment. Shirley, the chargehands' representative, asked whether shop floor personnel could have a shorter lunch break on Fridays and leave work earlier in the afternoon. The chairman replied that this was also a matter that required further discussion outside the group.

We were unhappy that these two items had been passed over before a proper clarification of them had taken place and decided to alert the managers to the possible dangers of doing this at the next Steering Group meeting.

March 1978—Steering Group meeting

At which we commented (to quote from the minutes): 'Too many issues had been referred outside the group, thereby limiting the group's opportunity to influence decisions.' One or two of those present suggested that one way to avoid this was to ensure that certain agenda items be filtered out before the meeting took place. Perhaps, it was suggested, the group was talking about the wrong things. We pointed out that it would not be wise at this stage to attempt to impose boundaries on the matters raised, since it had been explicitly stated that anything would be discussed.

It is important to place these events in perspective; the group was faring rather well on other items that had been raised, and members, although mildly

138

discontented, were not angry. The sticking points were still untypical and optimism was running fairly high. As we said in the earlier chapter, the Packaging group had begun well and we were not at this point particularly alarmed by the points of disagreement and lack of resolution. However, at the next meeting of the Participation Committee, it soon became evident that the unpaid leave issue was beginning to have an effect on the climate of the meeting in general.

Late March 1978—Packaging group meeting

Joan, the representative for the main Packaging floor, nervously raised the question of unpaid leave once more. She had reported the outcome of the last meeting to her group but they were now more confused than ever—as indeed she was herself. They had asked her to request clarification on the circumstances in which unpaid leave would be granted. It was at this point that Fred, the section head, delivered his first bombshell:

Fred: This all goes through Personnel now.
Joan: What do you mean?
Fred: We've been told that all applications for unpaid leave now need to go through the Central Personnel Department. We don't decide any longer.
Eric: Yes, unpaid leave is now a recognized category. We are now trying to firm up on the circumstances.
Mary (*ignoring Eric's point*): Fred, are you saying that we don't go through you now?
Eric (*jumping in*): Supervisors are still the focal point, but Personnel are the final arbiter. We are working on the whole policy at present, and there's no need to bother yourselves about this at present. In the time being, applications go through the supervisor who will then refer to Personnel.

It was interesting that the other representatives present elected not to join in, and that neither Joan nor Mary pushed the discussion any further. With hindsight, one can see that the management's message of 'Keep Away' had been received loud and clear by most of the people in the meeting, and that, not finding support from their colleagues, Joan and Mary had let the matter drop.

After the meeting, we tried to find out why the responsibility for giving time off had been transferred from departmental supervisor level to the Centre (and more precisely, to the Personnel Director, as we were to discover). The reasons given were fairly vague, but we were able to surmise that the Managing Director's insistence that there was a need for consistency in interpretation across the whole site and a need to retain control over the way the issue was handled had led to the change in procedure. The problem as he and his colleagues had defined it was that variations between departments and individuals had been largely to blame for shop floor dissatisfaction. The solution seemed to lie in ensuring equal treatment for everyone. However, whilst it was true that the representatives had complained about section heads having 'blue-eyed boys and girls' to whom they meted out special treatment, the main problems were not directly concerned with the supervisors' interpretation of the rules. Rather, the problems were that people were unclear as to their rights in the area of unpaid leave and resentful that it paid to be dishonest. Another problem—perhaps the most fundamental—was that many shop floor personnel objected strongly to the principles of the policy. To quote one of the representatives, 'If people feel they need unpaid leave, why can't they have it? After all, it's their loss of money. Why should they have to grovel for it—and sometimes have it refused, and why should they have to lose holidays when it's granted?'

If the managers' strategy had been to retain the initiative and close the issue off, then it was a strategy which did not work, and one which, in fact, gave rise to new problems. We discovered, in talking to the operators and representatives, that this action was construed as a decision to withdraw all entitlements to unpaid leave under all circumstances. The management's comments that there was no such thing as a policy for unpaid leave and their decision to stop the granting of unpaid leave by supervisors had both combined to form this impression. Furthermore, the confused state in which the representatives had been left had meant that *they* had been unwilling and, indeed, unable to correct these impressions.

May 1978—Participation meeting

Joan: I'm afraid I have to come back to the question of unpaid leave. Some of my girls are furious. We had a case the other week, someone wanted time off to take a relative to hospital for a fairly serious operation—and she was refused. Why was that? A lot of people said it was because the management had decided to stop all unpaid leave. Fred told us that he can no longer decide.

Michael (*department head*): I've been a critic of this system for a long time.

Eric: Look, one problem with a group like this is that we're looking for instant decisions when there aren't any.

Michael: I can't understand why the girls can't see our point of view. You can't take unpaid leave just like that. You wouldn't be able to plan the work or anything. Our headcount is tight, and if people could take unpaid leave whenever they wanted, nothing would get done.

May: But that's too extreme. People should have to provide a good excuse for having time off. It's not a matter of giving it just like that with no questions being asked.

Michael: OK, but what is a good excuse?

May: That's what I thought we were here to decide.

Eric: The problem in the past is that things have been decided arbitrarily. What we want to get is a policy which covers most of the issues. Until then, there will always be some dispute. In the interim, there have to be *ad hoc* decisions. At present, the Personnel Director is making the ultimate decisions.

Maggie: Well, aren't people going to be encouraged to be dishonest?—to say next time, blow-it, and then just go sick. There would be no argument then.

Eric: Yes, that is a risk we have to take.

Simon: I really feel we must draw this to a close. We could go on all day. We've discussed it a lot these last few meetings. We need to close up. Sorry it's still a bit loose. It's not really a permanent answer to the problem.

Paul: It seems to me that this issue is far from resolved. There are some fundamental differences about what is fair and equitable in the present situation. So long as these exist, you have a problem.

Eric: You're putting on your academic hat now. There will always be differences.

Paul: I don't disagree. What I am suggesting is that this group takes the opportunity—seeing that Personnel is now working on a new policy—to put forward its views. Let Personnel know what you consider to be fair.

Simon: But I don't believe you can list all of the situations when unpaid leave can or cannot be granted.

Fred: In answer to Paul, I hope that when Personnel get sorted out—when they get their proposals together—they will come back and discuss these proposals.

Iain: Can we not agree to go back to our respective groups and try to find out what circumstances people think would be fair to qualify for unpaid leave?

Simon: Yes, OK. But we need to get this in perspective. Over the past few months, there have only been a few occasions on which unpaid leave has been requested.

Eric: Some of you may be finding this frustrating. Possibly the impression all of you have got is that all we have done is jaw, jaw, jaw. But it is important that you don't switch off.

Many of the representatives had, in fact, 'switched off'. In conversation with our research student after the meeting, they made the following comments:

'I'm now running into difficulties with my people. They are saying that no concrete decisions are being made. I can't keep on saying, "Oh, that's being dealt with at the next meeting". The unpaid leave thing has been dragging on for ages. I know it's a difficult one to resolve—and I do feel that the discussion has been useful—but my people don't. Perhaps we need to get more aggressive and forceful.'

'I'm getting a bit sick talking about something and then Simon and Eric go off and do something about it. I would like to see the group actually tackling issues like unpaid leave, saying, "Look here, this is the type of thing where unpaid leave is OK". But instead it's a right mess. We're just bringing issues along and handing them over to management. We're not taking any responsibility for them. When they come back and announce what they have done, I can't really attack them on my own. They will just say that it's me having a go. Perhaps we should all be meeting on our own beforehand. I'm getting to the stage where I'm saying to myself, just let them get on with it.'

The supervision in particular were annoyed by the outcome of the unpaid leave issue:

Supervisor: It used to be Fred who said yes or no. He's done that for donkey's years. Now he's lost all that. They don't seem to want to put decisions where they belong—with people like Michael and Fred.

Researcher: So you feel you're losing your decision-making power?

Supervisor: Oh yes, definitely. I mean, in the past I could decide a lot more. I used to deputize for Fred. There used to be just me and Fred. Then Charles and Michael came over, and I no longer deputize for anyone. And then participation came about. ...

This supervisor also believed that participation had divided people in the department—managers from managers, and managers from shop floor:

'The managers are holding meetings in corners every other day. Nobody is telling me what is going on. The problem is that they're all busy trying to hold on to their jobs. They all see that participation is taking things away from them and they're all fighting to hold their position'. ... 'And now the shop floor are beginning to act like bloody shop stewards. Shirley won't discuss things with me. Like the other day, I questioned something she had done with the scheduling and she flew at me. "Don't you tell me how to do my job", she said. It's the same with the others. They all ignore me. I can't do anything now.'

Clearly, the pattern of relations within the Packaging department had begun to change since the introduction of the participation meetings. Some system of order had obviously been upset, and this had led to bitchiness, defensiveness, and a degree of disgruntlement. The unpaid leave issue had been singled out as the single most important factor in bringing this about. However, our view at the time was that the issue had precipitated rather than caused the problems that were now emerging. Relationships between management and the shop floor, as we have observed before, had not been particularly good, and the authority structure of the department had been upset two years previously when Charles and Michael had been drafted in. Somehow, participation had brought these matters to a head, had provided a forum within which problems had been exposed and the existing order challenged. The failure at this point to manage and resolve these problems had led people to express doubts as to the wisdom of proceeding along this path.

June 1978—Participation meeting

A decision was taken to review the structure and process of the group. The following points emerged and are worth recording for those who might wish to reflect on some of the problems associated with the implementation of participation:

(1) Issues that were raised were not being tackled successfully. This had resulted in frustration and a good deal of criticism of representatives. Moreover, the sheer volume of issues on the table at any one time had made it very difficult to get items recorded and discussed. This had led to further criticisms being levelled at representatives.

(2) Agenda. Complaints that it came out too late and did not allow for preparation (finding out what issues were all about and testing opinion back in the constituency groups). Some people also felt that it was tampered with by the chairman, and that certain things were deliberately left off. Request that agenda be more detailed. A line or a word was meaningless. A name against the item would also help.

(3) Minutes. Sometimes a bit vague, or did not capture the climate of opinion in the meeting at the time. Language often tortuous and involved. Suspicion that chairman

was editing out the more contentious comments and presenting the management in the best possible light.

(4) Chairman's role. Should exercise more control over the meetings and speed things up. Should provide more structure for the discussions, and try to provide space for everyone to contribute. Noisier people should be prevented from monopolizing meetings. Guidance should be given on the issues that could and could not be discussed in participation.

(5) Quality of the answers given by management. On unpaid leave, for example, where many of the arguments put forward had been incomplete or unconvincing. People more concerned about holding to their position rather than opening the issue up for discussion. Some issues declared finished when this in fact was not the case.

(6) Many trivial, but nevertheless important, items had been passed over too quickly in favour of the bigger issues.

(7) Committee overwhelmed with issues which could not be coped with in the time available.

(8) Too much 'dragging of the heels' and too little decisiveness. A need to speed up the process, specify the action, who is taking it, and then getting on with it. Some things left open-ended and not adequately followed up.

(9) Need for greater clarity and consistency in reporting back. Chairman should attempt to provide a summary of what has been agreed after discussion has taken place.

(10) Feeling that people holding back, either not prepared or afraid to say what was on their mind. Meeting felt tight, and far too much 'pussy-footing'. Also, consultants holding back on their opinions.

(11) Representatives split and disorganized, unable to provide support for each other. Need for a pre-meeting to work out a common approach.

(12) Some representatives having problems in pre-meetings with their constituents.

It is not our intention to provide details at this point on the steps taken at this meeting to resolve these problems. In fact, in some instances, the problems remained identified rather than resolved. In others, changes were made to the mechanics and procedures of the meetings in the hope of alleviating some of the problems (for example, in making agendas and minutes more precise and detailed; putting people's names by items so that people could seek them out beforehand and find out what the issue was all about; getting the chairman to summarize after completion of each item and representatives taking notes, and so on). Most of the process issues—'holding back', 'pussy-footing', 'indecisiveness', and so on—were demonstrated in that discussion was not forthcoming around them. We resolved at this point not to pressurize the committee into discussing these since we suspected (correctly, as later events proved) that two of the managers present—Simon, the chairman, and Eric, the Personnel Manager—were regarded as the source of the problem and that many of those present in that particular forum would be unwilling to discuss particular individuals.

Of particular relevance to the unpaid leave story it was agreed at the meeting that this, and the early finish on Fridays (which had been left hanging for the past three months), would be continued at the next meeting. Clearly, the chairman had been concerned to avoid this, but in the circumstances, had been unable so to do.

July 1978

Several of the representatives had alerted us to the problems they had encountered in reporting back to and managing the pre-meetings with their groups. On the unpaid leave issue, for example, some people had been highly aggressive towards the representative and had, wittingly or unwittingly, misinterpreted the messages that had gone back from the meetings. Some of the groups had threatened to withdraw their support for participation and the representative unless the situation improved, and two of the representatives had, in the face of these pressures, considered resigning from the committee. As an attempt at improving the process of reporting back, we decided to sit in on some of the pre-meetings when they were next held.

From the extract of a meeting we include below, it is not difficult to see why the unpaid leave issue had run into severe problems:

Scene: Main Packaging floor three days before Participation Meeting. Machines are switched off, thirty or forty girls sit in a circle round Joan, their representative. They are all talking amongst themselves.

Joan: Belt up, you lot, I can't hear myself think. What do you want to raise for the next meeting? (*They carry on talking.*) OK. Are you all satisfied with your rise? (*A loud 'yes'.*)

Operator: What about poor old Annie? She's not happy with her new scale.

Joan: Has she complained about it?

Operator: Yes. But you know they're all against her. (*Further pandemonium.*)

Joan (*loudly*): So you're still not satisfied, then. OK. I'll say something about it. Next, the half-hour lunch and half-day Friday. (*Various shouts of 'Yes', 'Yes'.*) I take it you're all in favour. (*People begin talking amongst themselves.*) Everybody, please, shush, shush! ... OK then, movements between bands and jobs.

Operator: This is never ending. They're still pushing us round.

Joan: I thought we had sorted it out. Where we are in the morning, we stay.

Operator: No, it's still happening. There's nothing we can do.

Joan: So you're not bothered, then?

Operator: 'Course we're bothered. There's nothing we can do. There's no point bothering.

Joan: You've got to keep banging away at it, you know.

Operator: But it's causing a rift betweeen us. (*Loud 'Yes'.*)

Joan: The other big thing is unpaid leave.

Operator: We're back to that again.

Joan: Have you got any suggestions, any reasonable suggestions?

Operator: No, there aren't any, really. (*Pandemonium.*)

Operator: If your face doesn't fit ...

Operator: You'll just have to tell them, don't employ married women.

Joan: So you're prepared to lose money? (*Loud 'Yes'.*) The next one is girls doing machine setting-up, and minor repairs. There would be less sitting around waiting for a fitter to arrive. So how do you feel about getting a little bag of tools on your bands? (*Loud laughter.*)

Operator: What about setting up slats?

Joan: Do you want to do it?

Operator: Some do, some don't. Those who are prepared to do it should get paid for it.

Joan: You don't think it would add more interest to your job? (*Loud 'No'.*)

Operator: What's interesting in getting oil up to your elbows? ...

Here, it can be seen that the operators' unconcern was bordering on anti-concern—an almost deliberate attempt to show that they were not in the least interested in or optimistic about participation. Understandably, Joan had found this negative response almost impossible to handle, and had simply gone through the motions of holding the meeting as quickly as possible. While her problems were the most extreme, her fellow representatives had met with a similar response. Maggie, the representative for the Label Room, had had to cope with a further problem: her group, much smaller, was a mixed one of men and women. The male porters, and one in particular, had always been the dominant members of the group, but being in a minority, had been outvoted in the elections to the Participation Committee. Since then, they had adopted the strategy of non-co-operation, and would turn up at the pre-meetings and snigger. Harry, their leader, would turn up regularly and sit with his back to the meeting and say nothing. The other representatives, Charlie, Alan, Shirley, and Mary, had fared a lot better in managing their groups.

Clearly, we had done little to help the representatives overcome these difficulties and had given far too much attention to the meetings themselves and too little to what was happening between the meetings. What we therefore resolved to do was to spend more time with the representatives and the group, helping them where we could to organize themselves into more effective units of action.

We mention this particular problem of reporting back because it does give the context in which discussion of the unpaid leave issue continued, and is central to the crisis which ensued.

July 1978—Participation meeting

One of us had agreed, in consultation with the chairman and subject to the agreement of the group, to chair the meeting for the discussion of unpaid leave. This was agreed and an attempt was made to identify instances, for the purpose of discussion, when the question of unpaid leave might arise. These were categorized as follows:

Half day and above
(a) What happens when the end of the year comes and holiday has been used up?
(b) Make up time

(c) Illness of immediate family
(d) Emergency in the home
(e) Shift situation—make up shift unpaid for full shift off
(f) Known home commitment
(g) Transport failure
(h) Hospital discharge
(i) Travel on Fridays
(j) Court attendance

Under half day

Doctors	School	Solicitors
Dentist	Court	Hospital
Optician	Transport	Bank

The ensuing discussion did much to clear the air. The management gave several reasons why unpaid leave could not be an automatic entitlement, and the worker representatives felt able to agree to setting aside a few days of their leave for unforeseen circumstances, and to limit applications for unpaid leave to problems of illness in the family and other major domestic upsets. Other applications could be made under the present compassionate leave policy. Spirits had been revived, people felt that some progress had been made, in that, although the issue was not resolved, they were clearer about the criteria for granting unpaid leave, and agreed with most of them. At this stage, it was therefore decided—with great relief—to take the item off the agenda.

Several learning points had emerged from this long and frustrating experience. Management had discovered that refusing to talk about a problem created more difficulties for them than actually talking about it. The representatives had experienced the difficulty of actually finding an acceptable solution to the problem, and had been exposed to some of the difficulties that management experienced in this area. They had also tried out a new approach to representation—persistence—and had discovered that they could gain from this without necessarily being punished.

Our learning, alas, was that lessons soon get forgotten and people soon lapse into their traditional patterns of operating. This was confirmed at the next meeting.

September 1978—Participation meeting

The chargehands' supervisor said that she wanted to revive the item on early finish on Fridays, and the chairman responded that this issue could not be explored at that time: 'It's a site-wide issue. To discuss it here would pre-empt discussions elsewhere.' Response—silence.

October–November 1978—two Participation meetings

'All Quiet on the Western Front'. No mention of unpaid leave or the early finish issues. A climate of brooding in the meetings. Chairman did most of the talking, and only one or two of the representatives made any substantial contribution. The department head arranged a private meeting with us: 'Fred's furious, you know. He was all for participation, but he's changed his mind now. He's lapsed back into his old autocratic style. People are annoyed with the chairman. He seems to be making out that all's going well—from his point of view, it might be—but people are getting sick of his monologues. As for me, I really don't know any longer. There's a lot more bitchiness between us and between the girls than there ever was before. We've really got to do something about all this.'

Ron, the supervisor, took a different view: 'Great, great. To begin with, I was very much against it, you know, seemed I was no longer able to decide anything on my own. All the girls were acting like shop stewards or at least refusing to talk to me without going through their representative. But I took them on. One day quite recently, something was wrong with one of the bands and I saw them approaching the representative who was working on the other band. She came over and I told her to get back to her machine, and leave me to sort out the problem. I won that one. Since then, she hasn't said a dicky bird. Yes, I'm well pleased. I'm now back in control.'

If the behaviour in the meetings and Ron's comments were anything to go by, it seemed that some of the representatives had given up. As one of them remarked to us at the time, 'We're knocking our heads against a brick wall. I don't know about you, but I don't like doing that. The management members are coming along with all the snap answers. They can do this because they meet as a group beforehand. We're all split and at their mercy.' The fact that, despite these complaints, the representatives did not withdraw needs some comment. Firstly, on other (mainly small) issues, the group was making some progress. Action had been taken successfully on problems with canteen queueing, canteen arrangements, the layout of new plant and facilities, banking facilities, lighting, heating, noise levels, ventilation, allergies, movement between bands, and so on. It was really only on two major points that the group had become dissatisfied—unpaid leave and early finishing. While being dissatisfied with these, it seems likely that the *representatives* perceived that participation was not a complete waste of time. Secondly, the decision taken by the director only to attend and chair alternate meetings and to let his immediate subordinate take over from him did lead to an improvement in the process of the meetings themselves. Representatives remarked that they felt more relaxed when Charles chaired the meetings, could be more open with him, and were given the opportunity to contribute more—'Yes, he's more one of us. Simon belongs to the top group and always takes their side. When you talk to him, you see a glazed look coming over his face. It's as though he's saying "OK, I hear you, now let's get on with implementing what I've already decided." ' Others said that they had actually felt intimidated by Simon—not because of his personality but by virtue of his status in the factory. Thirdly, members of the group had no doubt considered the consequences of withdrawing from the group, and had concluded that something, no matter how imperfect, was better than nothing; the prospect of returning to no participation at all was not very attractive. Finally, our comments about the long time-scale needed for change and the need for persistence had possibly been heeded. Few were expecting that the journey would be short and trouble-free. However, notwithstanding the decision to continue, the group was beginning to feel the effects of being caught in bad weather on the hills.

December 1978—Participation meeting

The group seized the opportunity of re-opening the early finishing issue with the new chairman. Fred, the section head, assumed the customary role of spokesman for the operator representatives:

Fred: Don't let us skip Item Five, Charles—the leaving early on Fridays. I can't see why we can't progress it further, do you? We thought that it might provide an opportunity to level off the hours across the site.

Charles: Eric, can you say something as the Personnel man?

Eric: I think Fred has a point. I'm happy to push for experiments in working arrangements, but mine is only one voice among many. Remember, too, that the question of shorter working hours is a national issue. What we have also got to be aware of is the knock-on effect this may have for other departments—we have to carefully weigh the politics of envy.

Fred: I wouldn't disagree, but it's not an argument for us not discussing this question. Frankly, no valid reason has been given why we can't.

Paul: So Fred is saying that he wants to re-open the three-thirty finish. What does the rest of the group think?

Joan: I don't see why we can't give it a try.

Charlie: I'm in complete agreement with Fred.

Eric: You might be better off asking for a four o'clock finish. There is a precedent for that on site. But the whole issue will have to be looked at in depth—the advantages and the disadvantages. We have to be careful how we present the issue. We have to get round the danger that it might be ruled out as a site-wide issue.

Charlie: Why all the delay? The majority of people want it, and that's all there is to it.

Paul: Be that as it may, Charlie, what Eric is saying is that we really need to get our facts and our case straight. Let's double-check. Go back to your people and find out what their attitude is. In the meantime, the management have to go back to their people and ascertain their views.

May: OK, but I know already what my people are going to say on the twilight shift. If the day people are going to have it, we want it. We should be able to work four longer shifts in the week and not come in at all on Friday nights.

And so the issue was re-opened. Had Simon been present, it is likely that it would not have been. The above extract also shows a change of position on the part of Eric, the Personnel Manager. What he wanted—and had in fact wanted from the beginning—was to be identified as the company's man for participation, the person responsible for steering the progress of the programme. His perception was that he was now being ignored, and that the programme was in danger of being abandoned because of the weight of 'ignorance and bureaucratic nonsense'. He had also asked us to speak with the Managing Director about his future role: 'I know it's a risk because they might tell me to go and take a running jump. But what have I got to lose? I'm only half-occupied now, and I might as well know where I stand.' Slightly ambivalent about what he was proposing (since whilst he had been indispensable as the insider with his ear to the ground, his presence had been somewhat counter-productive in the meetings), we left it that we would mention it 'when the time seemed right'. In the meantime, we suggested that he might try to help in preventing the senior management from closing down prematurely on issues, thereby putting the programme in jeopardy. However, to return to the story, his position and the conversation had led, we believed, to his adopting more of a helping role in the meetings.

January 1979—Packaging group

This view was to be qualified at the next meeting of the Participation Committee to read 'Eric may only be able to adopt the helping role when he basically agrees with the representatives and when he is not forced into having to defend a position'. Predictably, unpaid leave was the issue in contention. It seemed that it had flatly refused to lie down and die.

Joan: Can I get unpaid leave on the next agenda?

Eric: Come and see me after the meeting and we'll talk about it.

Fred: I want to hear what's being said about unpaid leave. Maybe we ought to have a special meeting.

Ethel: Can I come?

May: And me?

Michael: Fred's right. We can't let it get outside the meeting. Look what happened last time.

Eric: All I'm offering to do is help Joan get the communications clear with her group, perhaps have a word with them myself. But if that's what you want, I suggest the people who want to, stay behind after the meeting.

This was agreed and several of the representatives stayed.

Eric: Let's get one thing clear, we're not here to re-open the merits or otherwise of unpaid leave. The issue has been dealt with.

Joan: But my people don't think it has.

Eric: But the minutes state it all very clearly.

Fred: With respect, Eric, this isn't helping Joan. She is saying that her people are still confused about their entitlements, and that she is having a job persuading them to stop pressing the matter.

Eric: Christ! We're going round in circles again and again. All Joan has to do …

Fred: Why don't you give her some help? Go and speak to her group with her.

Eric: But I've already offered to do that.

Joan: What are you going to tell them—that unpaid leave no longer exists, and that Fred can no longer give time off?

Eric: But you have got it wrong. Unpaid leave can still be granted, the only difference being that Fred must consult Personnel before giving it ...

The follow-up was that Eric did in fact go and talk to the various shop floor groups, but this, in itself, did more harm than good. Our research student was told shortly after this had taken place that the shop floor were now clear as to the policy, but were now even clearer as to the points of contention. Eric's presence had also been interpreted as an attempt by the senior management to close the issue off once and for all. As one of the operators had remarked: 'That was the last straw. It proved that this participation thing is just a waste of time. From here on, I'm not interested.'

The early leaving issue also came up at the January meeting, chaired by Charles. The minutes of this meeting described in outline what happened:

It was reported that the majority of people were in favour of having half an hour lunch break and leaving at 3.30 on Fridays. The representatives considered the Pharmaceutical Services Group to be fairly self-contained and felt the proposal might be implemented for a trial period. In previous meetings, Dr Teffler had stressed that this topic needs to be considered as a site-wide issue and he still held the same view. He asked the representatives to try and put themselves in the position of employees working in other areas. How might they react in such a situation if they were not involved in the experiment? ... Charles undertook to summarise in some detail the points of view and he would elaborate on these outside the meeting with several of the participants. Dr Teffler would use this information to present the pros and cons to the Directors' Staff Group.

In the meeting itself, the representatives strongly resisted the definition of the 3.30 finish as a site-wide issue. They presented a case based on the argument that hours were not consistent across the site, that their unit was self-contained, and that management could have the right to restore the normal way of working after a trial period. However, they were not able to prevent the issue being taken to the Directors' Staff Group and away from their direct involvement.

February 1979—Participation meeting

Charles informed the group that Dr Teffler had communicated its views on 3.30 finishing to the Staff Group, whose members had agreed to conduct a similar consultative exercise in their own areas. This data would be assimilated and a decision taken shortly.

The representatives were understandably suspicious and pessimistic about the outcome: 'It's the same old story', one of them remarked to us outside the meeting, 'this Participation Group can't really do anything. We formulate the problem, we discuss it, we work out a proposal—but then it's taken out of our hands. We don't really decide, nor do our immediate management. Simon takes it away to his executive group—Staff Group or whatever—and they make a decision. They make it a site-wide issue. The excuse they can then use is that people in other departments would be envious if we had the scheme in our department. At the last meeting, all seemed to be going well. I think people on the shop floor probably got the feeling that it would go through. Now we have a complete turnabout. It's gone to the executive. We're immediately at a disadvantage because we rely on them to gauge the opinion of people in their departments. But we have no system for doing that—there's no way we can go around asking people elsewhere. They can always interpret the info to their advantage, say most people are anti-, and that is that. We really should have resisted them saying it was a site-wide issue. What annoys me is that they come this need for this consistency thing every time, but the fact is that there has never been consistency in many things across the site. They use the argument when it suits them, and forget it when it doesn't.'

March 1979

Simon, the chairman-director, arranges a meeting with us before the next Participation Meeting. He tells us that the Directors' Staff Group has rejected the request for an early finish on Fridays, and that he would be communicating that decision to the Participation Group the following week:

Simon: As I've said all along, I was easy one way or the other, but now the Staff Group have decided, I shall have to back them.
Paul: What stance did you take in the Staff Group?
Simon: I didn't attempt to sell the preference of the Participation Committee, if that's what you mean. I did inform them of the committee's feelings but did agree that consultations in their own departments was the best way of going about it. Actually, off the record, I was in favour of the early finish.
Paul: So how are you going to feed the decision back to the Participation Committee? As the bearer of bad news, you're likely to get a lot of flak.
Simon: Well, I shall run through the way we dealt with this, and tell them what we decided.
Paul: But do you intend saying you were in favour of the Participation Committee's proposal—personally, I mean?
Simon: Oh no. I don't see how I can open up the difference of opinion between myself and the Staff Group. I'm a member of that group and must present the issue as a decision of the total group.
Paul: You mean your personal feelings don't come into it?
Simon: At this stage, I'm not prepared to say what I think. I realize that this will be difficult for me and the committee ...
Paul: I think you have to watch this one. You're the one who has to deliver the bad news, and you're the one who will be blamed. What is wrong with you saying there were differences of opinion within the Staff Group and say where you stood?
Simon: No, it wouldn't be right.
Paul: What worries me is that it is assumed in this organization that management

have to present a common front—give no hint of disagreement between each other. How do you think people react to this 'one for all, all for one' image?

Simon: I see what you're getting at, but I'm still not prepared to separate myself from the Staff Group.

Paul: You mean, your loyalties are to them and not to the Participation Committee?

Simon: Absolutely.

Anticipating trouble at the Participation Meeting, we decided to make our own enquiries about the process the Staff Group had been through in coming to its decision. What we found was rather disturbing. While it had been agreed that each director would test the opinion of people within his own division, the way each had gone about doing this had varied widely. Some directors had consulted everyone down to the shop floor, whereas others had only consulted the supervision. There were also differences in the questions that had been asked: some had asked 'Do you want to have a shorter lunch break and an earlier finishing time?', whereas others had asked an entirely separate question, 'Would it create any problems for you if the Packaging people were allowed to finish early on Fridays?'. The entire process of consultation had been less than satisfactory, and care had not been taken to define beforehand who should have been consulted and what question should have been asked.

March 1979—Participation meeting

The 3.30 finish item had been placed last on the agenda, and it was not until twenty minutes from the end of the meeting that 'discussion' began. Simon began nervously, recapping on the procedure that had been agreed to, and then announced, 'We can't go ahead with the request at this time. I think I owe the group an explanation. Decisions of this type cannot be made in isolation. It's a question of being fair to all. There are some groups where it would be impractical to implement this. The majority on site weren't keen to do this anyway. Some employees expressed the wish to retain the three-quarter hour lunch break.'

May: But why does it have to involve everybody?

Shirley: And anyway, the present system is unfair. The office people finish at 4 o'clock every day. They are part of the factory. Surely we could do it once a week.

Simon: Well, there are historical reasons for this, and we've decided to preserve the *status quo*.

Shirley: The office always seem to get what they want, but the factory side never do.

Simon: Come off it, that's a bit of a general statement.

Charlie: What worries me is that it was us that was asking for it, but you said, Simon, that the majority on the site didn't want it themselves. That's not the point, surely?

Simon: No, my point is that we need consistency …

Shirley: Well, I've heard from people in other departments that they weren't even consulted on this one. So whose decision was it?

Simon: I really feel we must begin to close this one off...

Fred: We can't do that! Not just like that. We've been hanging around waiting for a decision for weeks now and you want to wrap it all up in a couple of minutes.

Simon: There's not a lot of point in going on. A decision has been made and there's nothing to be said.

Charlie: But what happens if we do not agree with the decision, and we don't. What happens now? You can't expect us to go back and say, 'Look what a great decision we've come to!'

Joan: No, you can't. I mean, if we don't accept it, we should say so.

Iain: Why don't we ask Simon to go through the reasons carefully and, one by one, we give our comments on each reason and suggest—in the light of these comments—that Simon goes back to the Staff Group.

Simon: I can't do that. A decision has been made.

Iain: And there is no going back?

Simon: No.

Iain: However good the reason? However badly and on whatever poor information it was made?

Simon: I do not think there is much purpose in taking this further.

Iain: I do. One of our ground rules was and is that reasons must be given for decisions or for refusals to discuss issues. It seems that a number of people here either do not know, do not understand, or cannot accept the reasons for this decision. I think we must spend time working this through.

Fred: There is no way we can just leave this. (*Loud chorus of agreement.*)

The discussion went on for several minutes before Simon insisted on closing it down once more:

Simon: Clearly, we are not going to get anywhere with all of this. A decision has been made, you have no choice at the moment but to accept it. (*Loud noises of dissent.*)

Iain: I think you will need to put the whole of this discussion in the minutes. I think it should be made clear that the group were not in agreement with the decision— quite the opposite, in fact. They can accept the decision but not necessarily the reasons.

One of the major difficulties now facing the representatives was how they were going to relay this information back to their constituents, who had been led to believe that the request would be granted. Our suggestion that the disagreements be recorded for all to see had been proposed as one way of helping them over their difficulties— helping them avoid having to defend a decision taken by the Staff Group.

However, at this point in the proceedings, Simon made a proposal which exacerbated the situation:

Simon: What about the twilight people? Most of the reasons for saying no to the day people do not apply to the night people.

Maggie: I don't follow. We're saying we need consistency between departments and now you're suggesting inconsistency within our department.

Charlie: I agree, but we must allow Simon's proposal to go forward. If we can grant it for the twilight girls in here and not have it go outside, then we should. At least it will mean we have achieved something for somebody within the group.

Sheila: But my people are going to be furious.

Joan: Mine too. This would make matters worse. How do I go back and tell them we haven't got it but the twilight girls have?

Paul: I appreciate your problem but you have to ask yourselves why you are wanting to turn down the twilight girls. I would guess that had you got your own way, you would have been quite happy for them to get theirs; that you believe it makes sense for them to work longer hours for four nights and take the fifth one off. Perhaps, then, the reason why you're against it is that it creates problems between you and your people. This is quite a testing point for the group. If you grant it, I agree with Charlie, the group will have achieved something for somebody, but you will have created personal problems for yourselves; if you turn it down, you may be denying the group a significant achievement for personal reasons. Be careful of sectionalism: the danger here is that you start fighting each other.

May (*twilight representative*): All of this puts me in an awkward position. All I know is that my people want this, and I'm here to fight for them. There's friction between the night and day girls anyway. My people could probably live with a bit more.

Maggie: But that's not a very nice attitude, is it?

Paul: Could I suggest that we see whether there is consensus in granting this to the twilights, despite the personal problems it may cause. (*Most agree, somewhat reluctantly.*)

Charlie: We can't do anything else. It must go through. We can also sell it back to our people on the basis that if one group has it, there is a better chance that in the long run we might get it too.

Having agreed, the group then spent what time remained considering ways in which some of the pressure could be taken off representatives when they met with hostility within their sections. This was quite successful, but did little to quell the strong feeling that they, as a committee, had just lost another important battle—a loss on the same scale as the unpaid leave battle that had been fought several months before.

To revert to our original metaphor: the weather was turning—the storm was about to break.

CHAPTER 9

Clearing the air

After the meeting, Simon informed us that he was extremely anxious about the prospects for participation in the future. If it did fail as a result of this crisis, he said, he did not want to be blamed for the failure. He and his colleagues were determined that the programme should continue, but the representatives would have to recognize the limitations on their ability to influence decisions. It was also necessary, he declared, to get the recent problems into some kind of perspective, since many issues had been dealt with since the group had been established. To 'prove' this, he would circulate a list of all the subjects which had received attention in the hope that the representatives might also get a realistic perspective. We pointed out that the list was unlikely to affect the attitudes which people had formed—they were concerned about the losses rather than the gains—and we added that any further losses might well lead to the group collapsing. Its future, as we saw it, was in jeopardy; unless the senior managers were prepared to consider making decisions in a less autocratic way, then the programme had no future. Participation was not just a matter of setting up another committee; what it involved was a fundamental reconsideration of how decisions were arrived at and who was involved in this process. It was, we reminded him, a process of *sharing* information and influence. We further reminded him of a conversation we had had with him some months before about the 'early finishing' issue, during which he had said that he could think of no solid reasons why the request could not be granted, and we asked him whether any 'solid reasons' had since occurred to him. This was a rhetorical question, we added, since we believed that such solid reasons did not exist, and that the staff group's decision to refuse the request was based on a good deal of personal whim and a shortage of canvassed opinion and information.

What lay behind this confrontation was a desire on our part to warn him that (in our view at least) the group could well be in danger of collapse, and to suggest that he and his colleagues would, in large part, be responsible for this should it actually happen. The time had come, we argued, when they would all have to think deeply about their actual level of commitment to participation.

We were not really surprised when, a few days later, the Personnel Manager telephoned us to say that we should come over to the factory as quickly as possible. He had heard that the representatives had met to discuss whether they should resign and that their constituents had threatened to withdraw all support for them. He requested that we meet the representatives privately and persuade them to continue. We agreed to meet them and turned up resigned to play, if not actually enthusiastic

154

about, our roles as entertainers, hired to jolly the travellers and to assure them that all would be well. From time to time since the early days of the programme, we had been urged by the Steering Group to do our bit for God and Country—sing 'em a good song; carry the message of hope—'There'll be Bluebirds over the White Cliffs of Dover'. ... More often than not, we had 'done our bit' and left the travellers, if not happy, at least willing still to travel on. As will be seen, this particular singsong caused us not only to reflect upon our role but to re-appraise it fundamentally.

The meeting took place the next day. The group had decided to include Fred, the section head, in their number:

Paul: We realize that feelings are running high about participation, and thought we ought to come and see you. It's true that we were asked to do so by Personnel after the last meeting but we had already decided we needed to get back to you.

Shirley: We're not happy. Whenever I go back to my group, I have to say we got nothing done, and they say 'Oh, we knew that before you went'. Actually, when they see you people coming down before the meeting, they feel you are feeding things to the management, and that the agenda is put together by you all.

Paul: Do the rest of you think we're management spies?

Charlie: No, not really, but we are unsure about the part you play. I suppose we would also like to see more of your opinions in the meetings. Often, we're not sure where you stand.

Fred: I think we need to alter the structure. The representatives need pre-meetings beforehand to work out their approach to questions. Can't you and Iain get this for us on the side? I mean, one of your jobs is to alter the structure when things are not going right. It's Bath's job to set up participation.

Paul: In consultation with all concerned.

Ron: The agreement is total here. You know our feelings. We want to change the structure. Can't you go back and say the representatives want this and that—act as go-betweens?

Paul: Could I just explain how we see our role? First, we need to stress that we are not management agents and do not intend being. If we think the management are wrong, we tell them so, Possibly a mistake we have made is to tend to do this outside the meetings, although you will have seen us taking a line against them in the meetings on such things as the 3.30 finish and unpaid leave. We try to provide a resource to all the parties including yourselves. If you want to see us privately at any time, one phone call is all we need to come down.

Joan: I didn't know we could do that—use you, I mean, to help us sort out our problems. You must give us your telephone number.

Paul: But the second point is that we would resist being seen as the people pulling the strings on structure. All of you are responsible for making sure that a system evolves which best suits your requirements. If you set us up as go-betweens, the whole thing could get fouled up. As we see it, an important part of the process is you taking responsibility for raising problems that you have and making any proposals for a change in the structure. But the rights you have vis-à-vis us are exactly the same as those the management has—you can contact us at any time, you can have a confidential meeting, you can use us in a consultation capacity, and so on.

It did come as something of a shock to us that the representatives had apparently seen us as management consultants working for the one side, and had suspected us of spying on them. On reflection, we could understand why they had regarded us as such: we had begun with an undertaking to spend considerable time with the representatives and their constituents, developing various skills and helping them overcome problems as they arose, but had in fact spent little time with them; when they had encountered problems with their groups, we had rarely been on hand to offer any help; most of our visits to the factory had been spent in the meetings themselves or in individual discussions with the managers. In the meetings, we had held back and had tended to avoid any open confrontations with the managers present. With the benefit of hindsight, it is fairly easy to see why this had come about: we were very hard-pressed for time—there were other groups to set up and maintain, there were new groups to plan, and there were continuous requests to attend managers' meetings. The fact was that two of us (even with the internal resources) could not hope to provide an adequate resource for maintaining and developing the programme. Fortunately, this encounter with the Packaging representatives brought this point home and, as noted earlier, we subsequently obtained agreement to bring in two colleagues from the University to help in setting up new groups. A shortage of time was not the only reason, however. We believed that change could only be implemented by working on the 'power points' of the organization—in this case, the managers—if they began to 'move', we argued, the effects would be felt elsewhere. We were thus drawn to the powerful rather than the relatively powerless. What we had failed to realize was that the success of the participation programme depended upon the co-operation and support of everyone, regardless of their personal influence—or, restated, that even the subordinates, the 'underdogs', possessed considerable power to negotiate order within the groups.

Arguably, our meeting with the representatives signalled the first step in a transition to a higher personal-risk strategy. We had originally gone to them in a 'Vera Lynn' capacity, to offer a few platitudes and to quell their restiveness, but as the meeting developed, we found ourselves working on a strategy which would obtain for them a greater degree of influence.

Paul: I agree that in the power stakes you are at a disadvantage. If they say 'No' to something, it's difficult for you to do much about that. But are there not things you could work on to give yourselves more influence? For example, you could always carry on with your threat to withdraw from the scheme, or even in the last analysis, actually pull out. You know that the managers are heavily invested in seeing it continue and may therefore be prepared to give some ground to avoid the scheme falling about their ears.

Fred: But that's pretty risky, isn't it? I mean, if we pulled out, we would be right back at Square One.

Charlie: Paul may have a point, though. Rather than just accept things as they are, we could let our dissatisfactions be known and also let them know that there is a possibility that we might pull out. Another thing we need to do is learn the game they are playing. When the chips are down, they close ranks on us—they all take the same view. What we need to do is act more as a total group, and in that group I would include Ron and Fred. I'm sure we could come to an arrangement beforehand that if you scratch my back, I'll scratch yours.

Paul: How might you bring this about?

Fred: Well, if the section heads got themselves better organized, they could bring pressure to bear at a higher level. At the moment, we're all isolated from each other.

Charlie: And we could have pre-meetings like this one and plan a common approach to problems. We need to get a good solid case together that they would find difficult to turn down. We could use Bath to help us get organized and present our case properly.

Paul: Perhaps it's a case of getting a lot sharper in the meetings.

Shirley: Yes, we need to follow the arguments better, and understand what's going on. See the red lights when they say they have to take something back to the staff group or try to say something or other has site-wide implications.

Charlie: So what about this pre-meeting? Could we hold it in Works time, and do we need to tell them we're holding it?

Joan: I don't see why we should have to tell them. They don't tell us when they are holding meetings.

Maggie: We could always hold the meetings in our own time. Anyway, we can tell them of our intentions at the next meeting—and not before.

Paul: Just re-calling the 3.30 issue, one of the problems was that the Managing Director made a decision without any contact with the group. Could you not invite him to attend some meetings before you get too far with a major item—you know, get it from the horse's mouth?

Charlie: Yes, I think we should do that more often.

Paul: Another important source of power available to you lies in the large numbers of people you represent. What could you do to use them more effectively?

Charlie: At the moment they're of little help to us—we have no credibility with them. Perhaps we should be working on this. It would be a great help if you could stir up a bit of enthusiasm. My group would benefit from a visit by you. With their backing, my job would be a lot easier. I would also be in a stronger position to push something at the meetings.

Joan: Me, too. With my lot, it's like flogging a dead horse.

Sheila: My people won't even listen. Participation is falling about all over the place. Actually, they've said they don't want me to continue. (*Most of the others agree.*)

Paul: OK. Why don't you go to the next meeting and make them aware of the urgency? Tell them that you're here representing yourselves. That's a pretty strong case for getting them to change the structure.

Ron: The risk is that they then decide to kill it stone dead. I mean, after all, participation does have some advantages. It's better than nothing.

Paul: Well, that's something you'll have to weigh up. Give some thought to how far you're prepared to push and how much you would stand to lose.

And so the conversation continued with the members of the group finally deciding that they needed more time to consider the issues that had arisen. We suggested to them, and they agreed, that they should continue the discussion at the next Packaging group meeting initially without the management side being present. Later, we put this proposal to Simon, the chairman, and he, somewhat apprehensively, agreed. We also asked him to come into the meeting after coffee and recap. on the 3.30 issue so that the entire group could see whether any points of learning arose from the way it had been handled.

May 1979—Participation meeting

Only representatives of operatives present, plus department head, section head, and supervisor. Consultant chairs the meeting. Much of the same ground is worked over but this time leads to action points. People said they felt inhibited by the presence of Simon, the director, and Eric from Personnel, and decided to ask them to withdraw from the meeting, leaving their immediate subordinates in their place. They rejected the idea of pre-meetings in the belief that the group might become more polarized, but agreed to a new procedure whereby an agenda with the names of people who had raised various items would be circulated 14 days prior to the meeting, and representatives would have the responsibility and the opportunity to contact each other to discuss the items. They also felt that minutes had been 'doctored' in the past and suggested that the new Personnel representative take and write up minutes, and thereby relieve the director's secretary of that duty. As a step towards bringing the process of participation closer to the shop floor, it was agreed that a limited number of observers be allowed to attend the meetings. Finally, considerable discussion took place on how 'management' might be prevented from closing issues off prematurely—being more persistent, marshalling the evidence beforehand, providing more support for each other, being more frank and questioning, presenting issues in a more acceptable way, and so on. In the event, all the proposals they made were acted upon.

Simon—now in his last meeting—came in and the group went back over the process by which the early closing decision appeared to have been made. The degree of frankness was overwhelming, and Simon was visibly shaken by this:

Michael: What went wrong, Simon, was that we didn't challenge the decision that was made. Either we didn't feel able or we felt you wouldn't be responsive.

Charlie: Yes, we didn't push you nearly enough. We just let it die.

Michael: In fact, we need not let it die. We should now send Simon back to the executive and tell them we're going to keep on pushing.

Joan: You see, my people don't accept that it needs to be a site-wide issue.

Michael: We talk about frankness and openness, but were you, Simon, either of these things on this issue? I think a way into this is for all of us to understand better what the hell is going on in these meetings.

Sheila: What I want to know is how the issue got passed over to the executive. Quite honestly, I haven't got a clue how things work around here.

Iain: Would you like to comment, Simon?

Simon (*nervously*): I went to the executive—I like to think with an open mind. I didn't expect our request to fall on deaf ears. I did have some optimism that they would agree and I did put your points to them. They decided to consult in their own areas, and they came back and convinced me that your request could not be implemented. In presenting this back to you, I probably did it too formally, perhaps because of my knowing you would be disappointed.

Charlie: The trouble was that the issue changed. They weren't considering how it would work here but in their own areas. That was not the point in question.

Iain: So the learning from this is that we get the message clear and make sure we get consulted if a new issue emerges.

Michael: Perhaps you're not getting a straight message at these meetings, Simon. People aren't going to take you seriously to task, because you are who you are. We can't take on someone of your level unless you invite us. You've got to help *us* to push you.

The meeting continued and we tried throughout and at the end to summarize points as they had emerged. It was agreed that, as a next stage, we should meet with the representatives' constituent groups and find out whether they wanted to continue. After the meeting had finished, we had a brief word with the representatives and later with Simon. Still shaken, he remarked that he did not wish to go through with that sort of experience again, but nonetheless wanted to push ahead with the programme.

It was reported to us later from a number of our contacts within the company that Simon's ambivalent feelings about this particular meeting had been made known to the Executive group; apparently he—and a number of others—were very concerned about our role and our activities and, once more, our competence was called into question. Perceiving the pressures we had been instrumental in putting on him, he had apparently said that we could have done a better job in handling the crisis, and should not have pushed the project along as quickly as we had done—that forcing the pace had left people muddled and unprepared. Clearly, at this point, we were seen by him—and some of his colleagues who had been 'exposed' in similar events—as more the foes than the friends. We were said to be 'running around the organization, acting as shop stewards'. In the culture of Alpen, there could be nothing more alarming.

Meetings with the constituent groups took place a week or so later, with us, this time, in the role of 'Vera Lynns' for the representatives as well as for the management. The response was predictable and, in fact, almost identical to that which we had encountered at our first meeting with them some eighteen months before:

– 'What's the use. Participation is a load of rubbish.'

– 'Simon Teffler has squashed everything we want.'

– 'The things that have been done could have been done without participation.'

– 'There's a lot of bitchiness now. Everyone is at everyone else's throats. It's all done secretly—Joan talks with her girls, not with her chargehands.'

– 'If we put anything forward, it's squashed. We're told before we start "You're not going to get anywhere with that".'

– 'The Friday thing really did it. It really got up my back. All we got was "You can't have it. That's it, bye ...".'

– 'We've got no chance. We try to change something like early finishing and unpaid leave and all we get is, "It's company policy", etc. Then they send somebody down like Eric Campbell to pacify us and we have to listen to him spouting a load of piffle. Frankly, this participation thing is not worth the bother.'

– 'What this has done for me is prove that the management are not really sympathetic to participation. They've been told to participate and now they're doing everything they can to slip out of it.'

– 'The management have ganged up against us.'

– 'There's still a complete lack of communication. As a matter of fact, communications have deteriorated. The management all meet together now and everything is cut and dried before our representatives go to the meetings. They now all work together against us.'

– 'There was a lot of disappointment and upset on the unpaid leave thing. They filled us up with yarns about attendance records, service ... and caused a lot of upset.'

– 'When it's company policy, we get a blank "No". Trouble is they can turn anything into a question of company policy.'

– 'Things have dragged on far too long. It's easy to see why people see this more as a case of being strung along.'

Although the anger and disappointment were unquestionably genuine, we did get the impression that a number of the people we spoke with were finding a perverse pleasure in running down the participation programme—a case of a triumphant 'we told you so', a confirmation of their initial opinions that management were uncommitted, selfish, and insensitive. The problem we had in these meetings was an instinctive desire to defend the progress of the project to date as we saw it, combined with a tendency to agree with them on many points.

They were also quick to understand that, through us, the management and representatives were asking a favour of them—to continue just a little longer to see whether things improved—and therefore that, possibly for the first time, they had some influence over the course of events. 'So what if we pull out now?', they asked, 'What happens if we say to our representatives "You no longer represent us"?' Our reply was that we believed withdrawal by them would lead to the collapse of participation in the department and possibly the division. However, as the conversation continued, we realized they were not ready actually to carry out their threat to withdraw, and would use an agreed three-month stay of execution as a period during which they might win a few battles. This was one reason for their continuing, but there were others. The first, of which we reminded them, was that to pull out at this point would be to return to a circumstance of no possible influence. The second, connected to this, is that they had conceded reluctantly that there had been some improvements since participation had begun. 'We would lose out. Ron and Fred are more approachable now than they were before. That's a bonus point for participation from our point of view.' The third, simply, was that no additional effort was being required on their part to continue with the programme.

Vera sings on other fronts

The 'concert party' was in heavy demand in other parts of the factory. Fighting had broken out on the Dry Products front over management's latest weapon, the microwave oven, and we were being called upon to quell the insurgents. This had first begun at the time when Eric, the Personnel Manager, had fed back the bad news that the group's request had been turned down. Before the meeting, he had said to us: 'Look, I'm expecting trouble today, especially from Steve, who I know feels pretty annoyed that, as a member of the sub-committee, he wasn't consulted before the final decision was taken. I want you to come in and say a few words to smooth things over, you know, tell them they can't win 'em all. They're more likely to listen to you than me. That's what we pay you for.' As the previous chapter shows, we did not succumb to the pressure to 'smooth things over', but chose instead to get people to open up their feelings about the way the issue had been handled in the hope that they would learn to avoid similar pitfalls.

A week or so later, Eric asked us to go in and meet the night shift workers from the Dry Products department, the people most affected by the microwave oven decision. The night shift supervisor, in particular, had complained to him about the new cooker. Apparently, removal of the old cooker posed a fundamental threat to his authority since previously only he could switch on the cooker at the designated time, and therefore plan when people would take their break. Now, however, the faster speed and smaller size of the microwave oven made it more desirable for individuals to put in their own food to warm through. Maurice (the supervisor in question) was furious with the Participation Committee and particularly Eric and ourselves, and requested that the two of us and Eric meet him and his crew. Arrangements were made and dates confirmed. At the appointed hour, we arrived, only to find that Eric had excused himself and Maurice had taken the evening off. Our audience for this late-night show was ten or fifteen people who had not requested a meeting with us, but who had been suitably stirred up by Maurice to 'have a go'. Needless to say, our songs did not go down particularly well that night, though in the circumstances, better than expected. Our suspicion at the time was that we had been set up—on the one hand by Eric so that he might avoid any personal confrontation, and on the other hand by Maurice who had wanted revenge on us (and particularly Eric, whom he had expected to be present) for upsetting the *status quo*.

A series of concerts in aid of the section heads and middle managers of the factory followed. Eric and some of his management colleagues had informed us that a number of these people had been speaking out against participation, saying that their authority position was being undermined, or was in danger of being undermined. Our job—as the management saw it—was to alleviate some of the anxieties and engender a more positive attitude towards participation. Our reasons for meeting them were somewhat different. We had seen how strongly resistant the senior management had been to genuine influence-sharing with the participation groups. By uniting the section heads across the site and, for the first time, giving them the opportunity to debate issues as a group, we and some of the section heads hoped that additional pressures could be brought to bear on the senior management to devolve some of their powers. We reasoned that if section heads—perhaps the most important climate-setters in the factory—were given more upwards participation, there would ultimately be more scope for participation by their subordinates.

Initial meetings with the section heads were lively affairs. A minority, mainly the older, longer-serving men, were extremely hostile about the programme, a typical comment being, 'I've done my job for forty years, and I know that this participation is a load of bloody rubbish. Why make something big out of all this? It's easy, just get the supervisor to do his job properly.' As some of these people admitted, not only were they against change, but they were also worried that they would be unable to cope with any change that did occur. The majority were curious about the participation notion, and used the sessions to explore some of the consequences for their level in the future. It soon became evident that here was a group of important people who were experiencing a number of problems, and who wanted to get them resolved as quickly as possible; some flavour of their attitudes may be had from the list they produced at the time:

1. On certain issues we are blatantly ignored. Mainly policy issues which are dealt with autocratically –
   –Writing of personnel manual (to include such things as unpaid leave policy), not even consulted.
   – Policy on wage structure, grading, evaluation, etc., excluded but expected to enforce.
   – Not consulted on manning levels/headcount policy.
   – No say in disciplinary policy.
   – Limited information on developments in the company.
   – Not allowed to influence capital expenditure.
   – Promotion opportunities limited. Many vacancies not advertised internally.
2. Does this company want to be inefficient? There are ways we could save money but no one seems to be bothered.
3. We are out on a limb if we take a hard line on inefficiency or, for that matter, anything else.
4. There is a fear of us being seen to be rocking the boat.
5. The Personnel Department does not provide us with a professional back-up service.
6. People are often unclear about their accountability and authority in decision-making.
7. We do not have enough 'professional managers'.

8. We tend to be measured by our failures rather than our successes.
9. Factory operates along 'country club' lines; it is, nonetheless, a very punishing place.

At the time, there was a good deal of uncertainty as to whether attempts should be made to resolve these issues. There was a danger, as the section heads saw it, that any such attempts would be construed by the senior management as acts of aggression which might require some form of retaliation. They believed there was a risk that their advancement and promotion prospects might be placed in jeopardy if they 'came out' into the open with their problems and criticisms.

After considerable debate, it was finally agreed that they would take a limited risk, and that we would orchestrate the event. The Managing Director and some of his colleagues would be asked to hold regular meetings with the section heads to discuss various issues. Initially, low key issues would be selected, and presented by one or two spokesmen who had planned and rehearsed their presentation. Everyone would be careful to avoid behaviour that might lead to recriminations. We left the section heads in no doubt that we would support such a proposal when it was next raised at the Participation Steering Group Meeting. However, we did emphasize that we were not empowered to make a decision about the proposed meetings, and therefore no guarantees of the proposal being accepted could be given. The mood at the end of this series of meetings was one of excitement and optimism. As one section head remarked, 'I smell change in the air, and you know, it smells good.'

The storm breaks

The air turned distinctly chilly when the Steering Group met a couple of weeks later—so chilly, in fact, that it nearly led to our being permanently frozen out. Word had gone back to the Managing Director about what the section heads were asking for, and he came to the meeting with a prepared answer: 'At present—no way. I'm not prepared to meet them as a group of thirty or forty people, and I'm not prepared to discuss items they raise. What I am prepared to do is meet them by department and talk to them about our trading prospects and budgets for the future.' The other directors present nodded in agreement and all seemed ready to move on to the next item on the agenda. We pointed out that the section heads were experiencing major difficulties in their jobs, many exacerbated by the participation programme. If a process could be evolved which permitted their involvement, one of the major resistances to shop floor participation would be removed. The Managing Director signalled that he appreciated the point we were making, but was clearly unwilling to allow a powerful group to be established which could directly challenge or even question the decisions of the management group.

Managing Director: And anyway, there's no reason why some of their difficulties can't be resolved through the normal channels on a one-to-one basis.
Iain: There is, you know. They're afraid of being seen to rock the boat. Complaining may be seen as treason.

Managing Director (Tony) (*in amazement*): You mean, you're telling me that people are afraid to speak up ...

Iain: Yes.

Tony: Don't give me that, I don't believe it. If there are people who hold to that view, they shouldn't be working here.

Iain: In making that last statement, you've just illustrated why people choose not to speak up—'if they don't agree with you, they can get out'. I would also guess that that feeling is not confined to the section heads. We know the shop floor feel the same, and, dare I suggest, there may be one or two people round this table who, for the same reasons, are not saying anything.

Tim: Of course, what you're saying is true in the main; it's common knowledge that you keep your nose clean with your bosses if you want to get anywhere. It's the same right through industry.

Eric (*Personnel Manager*): But we also know that this company is worse than most on that score. We really do have to ask ourselves whether this can continue if we are genuinely committed to participation at all levels ...

Tony: I am not clear what it is that is being said. Are you saying, Eric, that people *are* scared to speak out?

Eric: Yes, yes, I think they are. Quite honestly, I think quite a few are; it doesn't pay to say what you think sometimes.

Tony: It surprises me that you can say that. It really does—it must be a very individual thing, I am sure that hardly anyone else would say it. Quite sure.

Iain: You are doing it again, Tony.

Tony: What?

Iain: Making it difficult for anyone to disagree. I mean, do you want to know what they feel or do you want them to feel as you think they 'ought' to?

Tony: I'm not making anybody say anything, I'm just staggered that anyone can hold such peculiar views of the company and us, the way we try to run things.

Iain: It seems to me as though you would prefer to be told that everything is OK, everyone sees Alpen the way you see it.

Tony: Not the way I see it, the way it is! Ask anyone around here—they are as amazed as I am, aren't you?

Iain: If I were working for you, I'd find that question difficult to answer now.

Tony: Perhaps it's just as well you're not.

Later we heard that many of the people present had criticized us for pushing things too fast and too far. Relations between us and the management group were becoming soured. We were experiencing the same frustration that many of the shop floor people had experienced with the participation programme over recent months. In our perception, the management were unprepared to 'move' in any significant sense; their styles and attitudes seemed to be the same ones that had existed when the programme first began. In recent months, there had been a number of issues around which they had made a decision in isolation and then stuck to it. In previous chapters, we have discussed only three in some detail—the microwave, unpaid leave, and 3.30 finish—but there were others that had had the same hallmark. Added to our frustration was the perception that, if this situation continued, the participation groups would soon collapse; people would refuse to continue in a process which was providing so few benefits.

Although we held that the senior management were to be blamed for holding back on the introduction of more extensive participation—and recently for denying section heads the opportunity for influencing the factory policy making process—we could see a number of reasons why they should be adopting this position. Most important, they had up until this moment enjoyed considerable freedom in making major decisions without the need to consult the middle managers and operators. They had decided and then informed. Even after the participation groups had been established, they had been able to continue with this practice. In fact, the section heads had acted conveniently as the first line of resistance to the upward spread of participation. They were expected to travel along the rocky road to participation while many of the managers stayed at home. In short, all had been rather comfortable, participation was 'somewhere out there'.

Recently, however, their position had become less secure. The supervisors and section heads were now demanding to know who else was making the trip. Several of the directors, as chairmen of the departmental committees and somewhat reluctant voyagers, had already been manhandled and had given serious thought to retracing their steps. 'But retracing to where?' they had asked. No wonder they were alarmed and anxious about the participation programme—for the first time, they had been forced to accept that it could significantly affect their powers to decide, and meant, inevitably, that they would need to question the whole meaning of the concept of management. We had been used as the 'Vera Lynns'—the management's allies in keeping everyone happy—but had now signalled our unwillingness to continue in this role.

Spectre at the feast

To add to their distress, during the summer of 1979 came another problem, this time from the outside. A local, full-time official of a large trade union wrote to the management requesting permission to mount a recruitment campaign in the factory. Information would be provided on the goals of trade unions, and the kind of services they provided. If sufficient people chose to join, the trade union would subsequently seek recognition by the management. As we noted previously, the company was somewhat concerned about trade unions and had ruled that under no circumstance should they be allowed through the gate at Towcester. Some members of the Personnel Department held a different view; while they, too, preferred not to have to deal with unions, they felt that employees should at least be allowed to talk with their officials—'How can we defend a position where we say "We know what's good for you better than you do yourself"?', as someone put it. They also felt that, in allowing the union the opportunity to present its case, the management's position would be strengthened, not weakened: 'We know the majority is against joining the union, but until we give them a chance to vote one way or the other, they are going to continue saying things like, "You've only set up participation to keep the union out".

166

What we have got to do is remove the grounds they have for suspecting us of autocracy and manipulation.' Most of the members of the director's staff group, however, saw the situation somewhat differently. They saw the union approach being the 'thin end of the wedge', leading ultimately to 'a major erosion of managerial prerogatives'. We were consulted at the time, and could offer little comfort: 'Let them in and take the risk. If you don't, you're going to get more shit heaped on you for keeping them out.'

Perhaps for the first time since the programme began in 1975, the senior management were under considerable stress. Pressures were being brought to bear from all sides—the union, the participation groups, section heads, some members of the Personnel Department, a protesting shop floor, and ourselves—and this, like the proverbial execution, was having the effect of concentrating their minds wonderfully. A point had been reached where they had to do something—either seek to reassert their control, and restore the *status quo* by terminating the participation programme, or recognize that they, too, would have to take to the road.

Two or three of them decided that some reduction in the scale of participation was appropriate; as reported to us, at least one of the directors considered that we were expendable. He began to raise questions about the need for our involvement and reported to the management group that, based on his discussions with other companies, there was little or no need for external assistance in mounting such programmes. In fact, he added, the pressure of outsiders was likely to inhibit rather than facilitate progress. We were, he concluded, at best an irritant and at worst a focus for the troublemakers in the factory. We should be asked to withdraw.

We had come to a similar conclusion for very different reasons. We had been particularly annoyed by the dismissal of our proposal that the Managing Director should meet with the section heads and increasingly disturbed by the apparent reluctance of the management to allow the participation groups to influence any significant decision. We were very unwilling to continue in our roles as professional entertainers. On hearing of the above internal discussions, we resolved to meet with the Managing Director and state our position firmly—we wished to withdraw.

Clearing the air

Unexpectedly, the meeting proved (in our words at the time) 'wildly successful'. With us resolved to withdraw from the company, the meeting took on an unparalleled degree of frankness. We began by outlining each and every problem that we saw with the senior management group and the way that individual members and the collectivity had responded to demands for greater involvement. We said that we and many others within the organization saw the group as uncommitted to participation and very unwilling to surrender any part of their 'right to decide'. Our frustration was clearly evident but Tony, the Managing Director, pleaded innocent of the problems and crises that had befallen the programme:

Tony: After all, I have not been directly involved lately. I've left it to my team to get on with it.

Iain: But our belief is that you have had—and are having—considerably more influence than you think.

Tony: What do you mean? I don't follow you.

Iain: Well, they all look to you before they do anything.

Tony: That's not the case; as I've said, I've not been involved in the decisions around the participation groups. I've pulled back from them.

Iain: From where I sit, that's not been the case at all, Tony. All of the minutes, for example, come to you, and if you don't like what's on them, you speak to the managers about them.

Tony: That's true, but that's necessary. I mean, things were appearing on the minutes that ought not to be discussed. The managers should have had them stopped before they got onto the minutes.

Paul: That's precisely the point we are trying to make; as a result of your advice, help, interference, call it what you will, managers now don't know where they stand. They worry about what you are going to say about the meetings rather than about the meetings themselves. They allow no decisions, stifle discussion, because of what they anticipate you will say ...

Iain: Take the microwave issue, for example. Simon Teffler tells us that when the issue of canteen facilities first came up in the Dry Products area, it was you who suggested a microwave oven. After that, he says that he felt bound to push hard for it at the meetings. He wouldn't 'give' on any of the alternatives because he thought he knew your preferences.

Tony: But that's crazy. I mean, I can hardly remember it now. Perhaps it was me that suggested a microwave but I didn't feel strongly about it.

Iain: Simon took it to be what you wanted ...

Paul: ... which resulted in the men essentially being forced to accept what you suggested, rather than what they wanted.

Tony: But that's crazy. It was a suggestion, not an instruction.

Iain: Your style is such that the distinction is often difficult to make.

Tony: Obviously so, at times. What else—while you are at it, you may as well give me it all.

Iain: It's not a question of simply giving you a going over, much as though, at times, we might feel the urge to do just that—like at the last meeting of the Steering Group. No, there is something about your style which is so peremptory, it makes it difficult for anyone to challenge or disagree. Hats, for example. Can you remember the discussion about hats?

Tony: No.

Iain: Some time back we were in here talking to you about one of the groups. They had raised an item concerning the design of hats—not the wearing of them, they recognized the need to do that—and you said something to the effect—'Well, if they don't like the hats, they can go down the road and get another job'. Now that, as we hear you, is a typical off-the-cuff reaction. As other people hear you as well.

Tony: So?

Paul: It's pretty uninviting, isn't it? Doesn't exactly invite people to raise issues, does it?

Tony: But my intention is the opposite. At least, I think it is. I *think* I want people to feel free to say what they think.

Iain: Don't we all? But many of us end up shutting others out or indicating what it is we would prefer to hear. If participation is to succeed around here, it has to start from the top and be seen to be starting there.

Tony: OK. Point taken. But if I am to do anything about the tone I set, I am going to need your help and a lot more help than you have given in the past. And maybe you are to be criticized there—we need to do a lot more thinking—all of us.

Paul: You will need to give a bit more around some of these issues as well.

Tony: OK. Look, frankly, I don't give a damn about the bloody microwave. If they want something else, they can have it. I don't care. And the early finish, I don't feel strongly about that either. We've just set up a committee on flexible hours, we can get some reps from the groups on to that and then take it from there ...

The session continued at this level of frankness for some time with us all, at the end of it, feeling exhausted but quite pleased with ourselves. The strong expression of our thoughts, attitudes, and feelings had had a cathartic effect but, more importantly, had enabled us to break out from the rut of frustration and impotence within which we had been enmeshed. We had now negotiated a clear contract with Tony to be frank and open in our exchanges with him, to challenge him and to stay with the challenge as he sought to brush if off ('You've got to hang in there or I'll just shake you off and continue as before'). At his suggestion, a meeting of the Steering Group was convened and we made a presentation of the issues we had raised with him. It too was a very lively meeting, initially characterized by a welter of accusations flying back and forth across the table, but eventually marked by a sober consideration of the action that could be taken to demonstrate that the management was indeed prepared to travel with the rest, indeed prepared to stride out in front. Throughout the discussion we sought to adopt our new role and to encourage them to question and challenge:

Tony: OK. Well, that's been a very useful discussion. Thank you all. Now I see the 'Unpaid Leave' thing is surfacing once more. Simon, it's your lot, just tell them that it's all settled now and refer them to the new Personnel Manual.

Simon: But it's not all settled, Tony.

Tony: It is. It is. We have been through it time and time again. There's nothing left to discuss. What some members of these groups will have to understand is that, at times, the management is going to have to say 'No'; we are not saying it often enough nor, apparently, when we do, firmly enough since it keeps coming up.

Simon: It's not a question of 'No', it's a question of interpretation.

Tony: Look, it's perfectly clear. We've been through it often enough.

Simon: It's not clear to me, Tony.

Tony: What?

Simon: It's not clear to me. I was discussing it in the pub the other day with Charles and George here (*indicates two other directors*) and it turns out they were implementing it in a different fashion to me.

Tony: Oh Christ!

Simon: So if it's not clear to us, is there any wonder it keeps coming up?

Tony: But it is clear. Very clear, any fool can see it.

Iain: What are you doing now, Tony?

Tony: What? What do you mean?

Iain: Are you listening to what is being said or are you seeking to refute it, stifle it by beating the brains out of the one who brings the bad news? Sounds very much like the latter to me.

Tony: But, I mean. ... Oh well, I suppose we had better look at it again, but, I mean, it seems *clear* to me! God, this participation stuff is even more frustrating than I thought it would be!

Simon: Well, you did ask us to do it and if we can't do it here, what chance lower down?

Tony: I know, I know. Let's go through it. Simon, can you tell us the way you are interpreting it, then we'll follow with Charles, George, and the rest of us. ...

One consequence of this meeting, itself held as a result of our confrontation with Tony, was a commitment to bring a wider selection of managers together to consider the implications of the programme for themselves. The session was billed as 'Everything You've Always Wanted to Know About Participation At Alpen And Never Dared Ask' and after some initial timidity on the part of many of those present, turned out to be a very lively session.

We began by generating an agenda for the two days from the questions and concerns each manager had and throughout we concentrated on having the group address issues of consequence to themselves; not issues concerning some other group in some other company, or matter of national import such as the economic consequences of the implementation of the Bullock Committee report. Rather we used the meeting to encourage managers to ask questions of and comment upon the activities of ourselves and the senior management present. We presented an analysis of the results of the programme to date—very much as we have done in these pages—and a number of those present role-played the 'Great Microwave Disaster' from a script we had prepared, though no one took his own part. Together we attempted to draw out the lessons both from this case and what we had all been involved in over the past three years or so. The discussion was felt to be thoroughly worthwhile and strong support was promised for further explorations and forays along the path towards participation. There was, we all agreed, no going back; indeed, we were all surprised at the end of the two days that no one had even suggested such a course of action.

Subsequently, the Steering Group resolved to extend the activity to four more departments and looked to a site-wide participation committee by the end of 1980; but that, as they say, is another story.

CHAPTER 10

Still travelling ...

We began this book with an extended metaphor drawn from the idea of work as a voyage of discovery, an adventure into unknown lands, a journey undertaken with but the most indistinct of maps and the most vague of directions from those who had gone before us. Clearly we have not yet reached the Golden City of Participation—indeed we may never reach it. In our more depressed moments, we have been tempted to consider that our destination may be chimerical—a mere wild fancy, an unfounded conception. A traveller's tale, told by an idiot, signifying nothing. Nonetheless we continue to plod on, ever hopeful, ever striving for a glimpse of the promised land which *must* be just beyond the next line of hills. The time has come, however, to pause a while and examine our luggage, to consider once more the mental freight with which we set out, discard or repack it as now seems appropriate. Having considered each original piece, we will also spend some time considering the material which we have acquired en route before concluding with some comments on the effect of the journey upon ourselves.

Original equipment

It will be recalled that we began our journey with what we termed a 'relativistic' or 'particularistic' perspective on participation; a cautious, idiosyncratic, 'it-all-depends' approach to the design and implementation of participative systems. We noted, at the beginning of our journey, that although acknowledgement of the importance of contingency theory was becoming widespread, little or no effort had been made to answer questions relating to how a 'tailor-made' system of participation might be created. We were pointing out then—as now—that a wide gap remains between theory and practice, between prescription and implementation.

As can be seen throughout these pages, we attempted to operationalize 'contingency' in a number of ways. Primarily, even after some experience in parts of the plants, we sought to avoid the imposition of a blueprint for participation on other parts of the organization. In each case it was explained to prospective participants that, although the issue of greater involvement was under consideration and was indeed the reason for our presence, it would not necessarily prove to be either feasible or desirable in their particular circumstances; that which suited the Chemical Plant may not suit the Engineering Department, that which was appropriate to the Catering Unit may not fit at all with the Quality Control group. Despite our brave words and what we still consider to be our genuine commitment to a contingent

170

approach, significantly we did not discover a group whose circumstances ruled out further or greater involvement nor, perhaps even more significantly, did we encounter one which rejected *our* notions of evolution, *our* ideas about structure and process. More of this later. For the moment we wish to emphasize that whereas contingency theory had tended to stress the importance of considering the impact of the 'external environment' on organizational design and functioning (for example, with the constraining or facilitating effects of technology on levels of participation: Blauner, 1964; Indik, 1965; Rees, 1970), our work focused upon the needs, aspirations, and expectations of individual participants. Thus, whilst not denying the importance of external forces and not in any way seeking to ignore the influence of such forces upon consciousness and behaviour, we rejected the somewhat simplistic positivistic view that all behaviour is *determined* by 'social forces' and sought to give greater emphasis to the more personal and subjective determinants of behaviour. On the question of a system 'to fit what?', as can be seen throughout these pages, our overriding objective was to derive a process and structure of participation that was appropriate to the expressed needs of the people directly involved; one that was appropriate to the subjective contingencies of the situation.

We remain satisfied with the general notion of contingency and even in its somewhat shapeless form we are content to repack it for the remainder of our journey. While still not being able to reduce the concept to a neat, squared-off package, we have certainly acquired some better feel for it over the months and years we have sought to make use of it. We have come to recognize that the 'tailor-making' aspect of the concept—although very appealing—is misleading. A tailor works from careful measurement, often uses a pattern or template and, unless he takes an inordinate amount of time to make the suit, rarely finds that the shape of his client has changed radically when it comes to the fitting stage. In our case, as we have indicated, all too often our measurements were crude, our patterns non-existent and what is more, the situational contingencies we sought to determine changed as and when we intervened. Over the months and years we became less concerned with careful and assiduous checking out of each new group and its circumstances and became more prone to set up a form of structure which more or less met the needs of those concerned (as then expressed), knowing full well—and actually declaring— that the flow and process could be reviewed and if necessary changed at some point. Occasionally the review produced little more than adjustments of the stitching; more often it has meant some recutting, rearranging, and restitching of the entire suit.

We mentioned earlier that despite our attempts to give every new group a say in their particular structures and processes of participation, each group tended to accept *our* ideas and *our* procedures. Part of this is explained by the dependency we engendered in both management and workforce alike, part in the nature of the exploration—presumably they tended to reason that even if we declared we did not known where we were going, they sure as hell didn't, and needed some guide, however inept—part because of the powerful way our apparently 'open' style actually constrained them (of which more later in this chapter) and part because, in fact, circumstances were not as idiosyncratic as our theory led us to anticipate. For us, each new group manifested some of the needs expressed in previous groups and each new structure went through similar stages. The role of the section head, for example, and that of the supervisors came under question in each group and, within a week or two, we could predict when this would occur. Concerns about victimization—'black eyes'—was common to most of the operatives, followed by a period of relative indifference to the feelings and ideas of their supervisors and, in virtually every case, some tempering of their initial perceptions of those in authority—'He's human after all'. Each participation group appeared to go through some if not all of the stages of forming, norming, storming, and performing. As we have indicated throughout the text, initial stages were more often than not characterized by high energy, a great number of issues, considerable work on the rules—what can we discuss? what are the norms in this group?—followed in many instances by a crisis and in some by a resolution of the crisis leading, in turn, to a period of mutually satisfactory work. Clearly the progression is not linear, rather it is iterative, nor is it totally predictable but sufficiently so that we were able to approach each new group with some ideas about its likely development. Learning could be transferred and was. Contingency does not necessarily imply a new start each and every time.

Initially we considered contingent or particularistic approaches to be wholly good, entirely right, unquestionably proper. Essentially we found that what we were doing was paying attention to particular circumstances and seeking to *develop* participative structures and processes from the situation as it was defined for us—by operatives and managers. Again, as can be seen in many of the examples cited in the earlier chapters, we tended to accept the 'givens', to build on to existing meetings, for example, and to take current structures and hierarchies to be necessary. Our 'contingent' approach, therefore, could be—and no doubt was—seen to be essentially conservative; a cautious, all-depends, evolutionary movement rather than a radical challenge to the *status quo*.

By and large, however, we remain opposed to what we perceive as dogmatic, blueprint approaches to participation, whether they emanate from high powered government committees or are sold hard by professional consultants, and less certainly we remain opposed to radical attempts at restructuring. We will take up reservations on this point later in our discussion of models of change; for the moment, we wish to discuss another element of our original equipment: pluralism.

Antagonistic Co-operation

Unlike many of our colleagues working in Organization Development, we did not begin our journey with a strong commitment to integration nor with a belief in the possibility that all interest groups within the organization could be persuaded to adopt a united view on any particular issue. Our view then was—and is now—that organizations may be seen as 'congeries of hundreds of interest groups, with immediately overlapping memberships, widely differing power bases, and a multitude of techniques for exerting influence on decisions salient to them ...'. We believed then—as now—that the organization (any organization) may be depicted as cohering on the basis of 'antagonistic co-operation'. We attempted to operationalize these notions by, for example, establishing a steering group comprising as many of those people who had a stake in the project as possible. The main functions of this group were to negotiate mutually acceptable boundaries, to set time scales for the stages of the project and to approve or not the methods to be adopted. In our minds there is no doubt about the value of transferring the experimental initiative to such a group; as previous research has shown (Bernhardsen, 1969; Qvale, 1973; Mangham, 1975), the adoption of such a pluralist structure greatly aids the development of appropriate procedures which themselves increase the likelihood of people identifying with and ultimately 'owning' any substantive changes that may be agreed.

Despite our adoption of this perspective, however, two factors must be pointed out in regard to the steering group: first, the managers at Towcester were initially *instructed* to co-operate and thus, while given every opportunity to be antagonistic, they had no choice but to co-operate. There was little or no negotiation around this fundamental issue. We recognized this, of course, and invested considerable time and effort in establishing with the managers a base for the project and securing their commitment to it. That this time was well spent may be inferred from the fact that the project has outlived two managing directors and was extended by the local managers despite a lack of enthusiasm from a new team in the London headquarters. Second, it was noted earlier that only managers were involved in the steering group; nonetheless (as illustrated in much of what we have written) individual members of the workforce and interest groups were encouraged to comment at every stage. Subsequently, this intragroup negotiation was augmented by intergroup negotiation, occasionally with ourselves as intermediaries to secure agreement to particular courses of action. This was as true of our role *vis-à-vis* the Managing Director's executive committee with regard to the section heads as it was of our role within the departmental groups and across the divisions on the site.

The example of relations between the section heads and the Executive, however, alerts us to an aspect of pluralism which has tended to be overlooked. Naturally, having done our homework, we were aware of the criticisms of the perspective advanced by Fox, Eldridge, and others, but our experience in the field has significantly reinforced their structures. Many of those who advance a pluralistic perspective on behaviour in organizations assume some rough and ready balance of power and bargaining skill between the parties. A key assumption of 'interests' or pluralistic theories is that there exists an equality of skills and parity of power between the parties concerned such that the outcome of negotiation between them is a 'golden mean' between anarchy on the one hand and total domination by one party on the other (Eldridge, 1973). Given that the different parties will inevitably have divergent interests and goals, there will be a continuous process of negotiation between them to establish an order in which their separate interests can be accommodated. As Cohen (1968) sees it, this 'negotiated order' is the outcome of conflicts and compromises:

The argument, stated more fully, is this: each man preserves his own interests and conducts himself in a way best designed to do this; in so doing, he finds that this inevitably brings him into contact with others, that he must adjust to the conduct of others, and therefore take it into account. This may lead, at first, to clashes. But gradually, each individual will find that his interests are better served in the long run by avoiding such clashes with some men, and possibly, by cooperating with them; this leads to the establishment of certain mutual expectations of conduct and to the gradual modification of these until some balance is struck.

Relations between the section heads *as a group* and between the Executive Committee *as a group*, however, were marked by a profound asymmetry of power such that the latter, if it so wished (and as has been seen, it did so wish), had no occasion to meet with and interact with the former. The 'negotiated order' between groups was such that, for the most part, information, interaction, and influence was the prerogative of a small group of senior managers. Far from our activities seeking to reconcile the clash of varying interest groups, we spent time promoting pluralism, defining and stimulating coalitions; in effect, the involvement programme itself became the main vehicle for the renegotiation of order within the company. It can, of course, be argued that in attempting to set up a programme of this kind, we were disturbing a situation hitherto marked by relatively low conflict and high apparent integration. This is unquestionably true and there can be no doubt that our interest in pluralism led us to seek to identify interest groups and to create circumstances in which they could antagonistically co-operate. *We* decided that the prevailing conditions in which association was restricted and challenge to the senior management was anathema were not conducive to the health of the company. In this we were going considerably beyond Thomas' ideas concerning the need for an understanding of pluralism in the practice of Organization Development:

If OD is to significantly expand its application ... it will need to broaden its repertoire by incorporating pluralism into its mainstream—by taking conflict of interest seriously, empirically studying the interests of different groups in organizations, designing interventions which respect the integrity of those interest groups within an organization rather than restricting the change agents' formal accountability to management (Thomas, 1976).

Our activities—at times—went further than 'empirically studying the interests of different groups', inasmuch as without our intervention, there would have been no formally constituted groups to study. Further, in every instance our studies, our questions, and our interventions served to delineate more sharply than ever the informal groupings and coalitions that previously existed.

It's probably worth spending a paragraph or two more on this issue of pluralism, not only because it was and remains an essential part of our mental freight, but because much of what we have done at Alpen appears to run counter to notions cherished amongst OD practitioners, notions such as 'integration', 'collaboration', and 'co-operation'. Since its inception, the application of behavioural science to organizations has been biased towards the achievement of harmony, the stimulation of consensus, the reconciliation of the interests of the individual with 'the needs of the organization'. Indeed, one of the seminal texts in the field, much quoted, is entitled *Integrating the Individual and the Organization* (Argyris, 1964). We have commented elsewhere on this emphasis (Bate, 1978; Mangham, 1979, 1980) and have made a number of criticisms of it, some of which are probably worth repeating in the present context.

The perspective on organization advanced by those who work towards integration, consensus, collaboration, and the like is one which holds that, ultimately, there is no real conflict of interests. If only we can communicate more effectively with each other, if only we can express our needs clearly, we will be able to work towards an agreement that accommodates all points of view. The notion that harmony must prevail is taken to be the goal of all socialization, and of those responsible for development and training. As Fox (1974) remarks:

To the extent that they convince their employees their job is made easier; to the extent that they convince the public, they gain sympathy whenever their policies are challenged by their workers. Finally, the propagation of the idea that the interests of the rulers and the ruled are identical helps to confer legitimacy on the regime.

Our perspective tends to be less optimistic; we believe that organizations are essentially political arenas wherein individuals and groups struggle to have what they consider right and proper prevail. In some circumstances, perhaps even many, interests overlap and perceptions of that which is right and proper coincide; thus co-operation is possible and desirable. In other circumstances, interests do not overlap and perceptions do not coincide; thus antagonism is possible and inevitable. Behaviour in organizations—from either perspective—may be seen as a matter of tolerance *and* tension, conflict *and* co-operation, integration *and* division. Management is but one interest group in the arena but the one which takes upon itself the prerogative of setting the direction the company is to take consistent with the constraints within which it defines itself to be. One such constraint clearly is the amount of conflict its actions are likely to generate; thus management, beyond all other groups, has a clear and vested interest in notions such as tolerance, co-operation, and integration, and a marked animadversion towards tension, conflict, and division. If, as has been argued elsewhere (Salaman, 1980; Mangham, 1980), the energies of senior managers are largely devoted to controlling the activities of subordinates, and that of the subordinates are largely devoted to resisting such controls, any intervention which promises to enhance the control while simultaneously eliminating the resistance is likely to be welcomed by managers. We would argue that much of what purports to be Organization Development is of this ilk; indeed, we would go further and argue that virtually every application of behavioural or social science to organizations has had the effect of increasing managerial control, whatever its original intent.

The work of Thomas (which was not part of our original equipment, but which is now safely tucked into our knapsacks) contains a number of similar points. He roundly asserts that 'Organization Development serves in some very fundamental ways to conserve management interests'. Integration has a distinct pay-off for management in that 'effective team-work' is taken to mean that opposition to company goals is reduced, loyalty is enhanced, and authority is respected. Furthermore, as Thomas sees it, 'Preferred management doctrines coincide with some central features of mainstream OD theory—teamwork and commonality of interest, intrinsic motivation, voluntary power-sharing, minimizing disruption of the organization and an emphasis on trust and attitudinal change' (Thomas, 1976).

Despite our reservations about mainstream OD activities and our genuine intellectual commitment to pluralism, much of what we did at Alpen (and a great deal that we continue to do) had the effect of promoting management control of the enterprise. However assiduous we may have been in identifying, structuring, and developing potentially competing interest groups, we have for the most part stopped well short of giving them the skill or the support necessary to confront the senior group effectively. We have encouraged the notion that greater understanding will come from the opportunity of 'sitting down together and talking things through' and have ourselves colluded in the suppression of information as well as in the facilitation of it. We, like the management, have shown pleasure when 'awkward sods' have been excluded from participation and we, in association with the management, have been pleased when representatives have 'behaved responsibly' (i.e. done what we wanted them to do). We have taken it to be desirable that information has had the effect of converting doubters: 'I've found out a lot through sitting on the group. I now know a lot that I didn't know before and I can see why management has to do some of the things that it does ...'.

It could, of course, be argued that we have got the balance right; after all, we have been accused of being 'shop stewards' and of being 'management spies'. Such an interpretation would be reassuring but, we suspect, incorrect. Although we have often questioned the management, and our presence within the groups has affected their behaviour, our stance throughout has been to serve our own best interests which, by and large, have been coincident with those of the management. Occasionally, very occasionally and then somewhat dramatically, we have opposed their views and their interests at some risk to our own. Similarly, very occasionally but at no risk to ourselves, we have opposed the views of other interest groups within the organization. We, no less than any other interest group, are part of the pluralism of the organization; we, like other social scientists, have tended to operate pragmatically so as to survive. Despite our often expressed doubts, we have been unable to conceive of, let alone promote, an alternative to the concept of hierarchical control; our efforts have gone into reducing the impact of that control, in ameliorating the lot of some of those subject to it, but have done little to affect the essential nature of it. This outcome was perhaps inevitable given our commitment to one notion which legitimized the existing imbalance of power between management and the shopfloor (pluralism), and to another notion which clearly preferred evolution to revolution (contingency). Alpen at Towcester—as elsewhere—remains a management-dominated entity; for good or ill.

The process emphasis

One piece of mental freight with which we initially set forth was associated explicitly with our perspective on interaction and organization which, in turn, was derived from the symbolic and strategic interactionist tradition. This tradition has remained a central influence upon our work in the past four or five years and, indeed, has come to dominate it (Mangham, 1978, 1979, 1980; Bate, 1978). Ideas such as situational definition, impression management, and the negotiation of order have become the primary focus for many of our attempts to describe, conceptualize, and understand our experiences at Towcester and elsewhere. It will be recalled that such notions were but 'appurtenances' to our main freight at the beginning of our journey and 'as such, somewhat uncomfortable and but loosely tied to our other goods and chattels'. For the most part they are now firmly affixed to our backs clearly labelled 'essential equipment, needed on journey'. So important have they become to us that we intend to expend a few pages on their description beginning with a discussion of the concept of negotiated order and continuing with some examples of what we have come to term the dramaturgy of organizational politics (Mangham, 1978) which includes notions such as situational definition and impression management.

The theory of negotiated order is largely the product of the efforts of certain graduates of the University of Chicago's Department of Sociology, notably those working in association with Anselm Strauss. As can be seen by our previous brief reference to it in these pages, it calls into question the static, structural-functional, and rational bureaucratic explanations of complex organizations and suggests instead an interactional model with a heavy emphasis upon processes rather than structures (Strauss, 1963, 1978; Bucher and Stelling, 1969). Although the theory has roots in the sociology of occupations (Becker, 1963; Hughes, 1945, 1958, 1971) and in the wider field of symbolic interactionism (Blumer, 1969; Shibutani, 1961), its major development has occurred in the study of hospitals and psychiatric care. Strauss and his colleagues in their studies of medical institutions were much exercised by the problem of how order is maintained and sought inspiration from the work of G. H. Mead which led them to state:

... order is something at which members of any society, any organization, must work. For the shared agreements, the binding contracts—which constitute the grounds for an expectable, non-surprising, taken-for-granted, even ruled, orderliness—are not binding and shared for all time. Contracts, understandings, agreements, rules—all have appended to them a temporal clause. That clause may or may not be explicitly discussed by the contracting parties, and the terminal date of agreement may or may not be made specific; but none can be binding forever—even if the parties believe it so, unforeseen consequences of acting on the agreements would force eventual confrontation. Review is called for, whether the outcome of review be rejection or revision, or what not. *In short, the bases of concerted action (social order) must be reconstructed continually; or, as remarked above, 'worked out'* (Strauss, 1963; italics not in original).

Developing the original insights of Mead (and other interactionists such as Blumer) led Strauss and his colleagues to focus sharply upon the negotiating processes found in organizations. It has led us in the same direction.

Thus in Alpen we found directors, managers, section heads, supervisors, engineers, cleaners, security staff, sorters, moulders, machine operatives, clerical personnel, secretaries, cooks, safety specialists, etc., all on the same site, all—in the final analysis—there for a similar purpose—the manufacture and sale of drugs. As our conversations and investigations attest, however, these individuals and groups bring different experience, different education, different personal backgrounds, and different expectations with them to Towcester. They also occupy different hierarchical positions within the organization. As is implicit throughout these pages, they differ as to how the very general task of the manufacture of drugs should be accomplished, who should do what and what the relations between the various parties should be. They even differ within groups; some of the packaging operatives were happy, even enthusiastic, about the possibility of setting up machines for themselves, others regarded such activity as 'a job for the engineers'. Some senior managers believed that the control of absence without pay was best effected through the Personnel Department; others believed that the supervisors and section heads should be held responsible. Some operatives working shifts believed that the catering staff should prepare meals for them at night, others disagreed, and so on.

According to the rational-bureaucratic theory of organizations (and according to many at Alpen), the organization should formulate and apply rules and regulations to resolve these kinds of internal conflicts and problems. But, as we observed time and time again within the organization, many people did not know all of the rules and regulations or how and when to apply them. Even where they are aware of a rule, the context often made it difficult to apply sensibly or the vested interests of a particular person or group caused some bending or fudging of the rules. Thus Tom had some rules or guidelines for the assignment of personnel to various shifts, but—previous to worker involvement—adapted them to his own ends. The long running discussion concerning 'unpaid leave' indicated forcibly to all concerned that no rule could be devised that covered all contingencies. Thus Alpen (like all organizations) could, in part, be characterized as consisting of a series of informal and tacit agreements as to how to get the work done. Groups, individuals, and levels of the organization relate to each other through a more or less temporary, tacitly negotiated order; nothing is fixed, nothing continues forever. The worker involvement groups simply highlighted and made obvious that which occurred on a day to day basis within the organization. More significantly, the creation of the groups affected the nature of the power relationships within the organization. From the negotiated order perspective, power and power relationships may be depicted as varying according to the specific set of events or actions that are in focus. Power is then seen to be situational or contingent in nature; thus on a simple matter such as the supply of food at night, without the platform provided by the group meeting, shift workers had no impact upon the management around this issue; with the group, their public refusal to accept the micro-wave oven caused consternation and considerable activity by very senior managers. Thus the 'underling'—the worker—winds up controlling a particular incident or event. It will be recalled that in our discussions with the shop floor of the Packaging Department, it became obvious to them and to us that although technically without power, in the circumstance in which the management desired a continuation of the Participation project, their agreement was essential.

Thus the perspective emphasizes that power and power relationships are situationally contingent and subject to change as, indeed, it holds are all agreements. Towcester, like any location, can be seen as a locale where each and every day, myriad, tacit agreements are being created, sustained, or terminated. The order which has been attained in the past is therefore always *potentially* subject to change (Strauss, 1963, 1978).

We have become firmly attached to the perspective for a number of reasons. Primarily because it fits squarely with the assumptions we make about the nature of man and the nature of social and organizational reality. The theory implies that individuals within an organization play an active and often self-conscious role in the shaping of the social order to which they then subject themselves. Rather than depicting the individual as a victim of the 'social forces' which surround him, or a cog in the gear wheel of society, negotiated order theory holds out the possibility of influence and active self-direction; it stresses the micropolitical aspects of day to day interaction, emphasizes the importance of idiosyncratic situational definition, and highlights the essentially fragile nature of accommodation. The view of organizational reality propounded by Strauss and his colleagues accords with our experience of organizations since it moves sharply away from the idea of fixed, rigid systems of offices, rules, and regulations. Close association with many organizations and in particular with Alpen has led us to be sympathetic to a perspective which emphasizes the changing quality of interactions between members and the fluid nature of order. As we have argued elsewhere (Mangham, 1978, 1979), conflict and change are just as much part of organizational life as are consensus and stability. Negotiated order theory provides such a perspective and enables us to depict organizations as 'complex and highly fragile social constructions of reality which are subject to the numerous temporal, spatial and situational events occurring both internally and externally' (Day and Day, 1976). It also provides us with the beginnings of a theory of change since it treats power not as an absolute but as situational contingent, thus the 'followers' or 'underlings' may by refusing to go along with particular definitions modify not only the balance of power, but the formal structure of the organization. Thus, as Day and Day note, there is an implied dialectical relationship 'in which the informal structure of the organization acts upon the formal structure which leads to social change'.

We will have more to say about change later in this chapter; for the moment we wish to comment upon the 'negotiated order' of participation at Alpen. Given that different individuals representing various groups coming from varying backgrounds and with different expectations (articulated or not) came together to 'participate', what emerged, what meaning was negotiated for the activity, and what were the factors which affected this negotiation?

Negotiating meaning at Alpen

In a sense, of course, this entire book is about the processes of negotiating a meaning for participation at Alpen, a process which continues beyond these pages. In this particular passage, however, we will spell out some of the micropolitical processes which appeared to us to be important. A somewhat fuller discussion of these processes in different contexts occurs elsewhere (Mangham, 1978, 1979; Hall, 1972; Merelman, 1969; Allison, 1971). Much of what follows below benefits from the observations and comments of Bob Westwood, a graduate research student who worked with us at Alpen for some fifteen months or so.

Let us restate our organizing question: how is it that certain meanings come to be associated with participation at Alpen? Theoretically, 'participation' could be defined in a great many ways; what definition was negotiated and whose views (if anyone's) prevailed?

Clearly there were differences in the preliminary definitions individuals and groups attached to the notion of involvement and participation. Such differences may have been a function of cognitive capacity or of experience. They may also have been occasioned by differences in awareness. From our discussions with the shop floor representatives at Alpen it was clear that few had any preconceived notions relating to participation; they frequently asked us what it was all about. It appeared that they were generally unaware of the media and academic debate concerning its function and nature. Senior management, on the other hand, were generally more familiar with the issues and were pretty well versed in the jargon. They were even reasonably clear as to what—for them—it was not about: wages, conditions of service, and company-wide decisions. Thus, at the outset, the shop floor representatives existed in a kind of definitional vacuum. The notion of participation was as unknown as a yogi fruit; unless someone told them its shape, size, general configuration, and taste they were unable to comprehend it. The management, on the other hand, had some idea, some definition which they wished to see attached to the notion (even preferring to call it involvement rather than participation). Both parties, however, looked to us for a definition and it was our definition that, initially, tended to prevail. We shaped the definition through our introductory meetings in which we stressed the gradual, evolutionary nature of the process, the openness of the agenda, the right to demand reasons for decisions, and so on. We also shaped it through our notes and presentations to the management, through our training sessions with all concerned, and through our interventions at meetings.

Initial definitions were undoubtedly influenced—and continue to be influenced—by issues concerning the self-presentations of the various parties to the meetings. Defining a situation includes defining one's own position in that situation, indeed it may involve defining for oneself and others a particular 'situated identity' (Scheff, 1966). For a number of people, problems of 'who I am to be in this circumstance' manifested themselves. The section heads, such as Tom and Fred, for example, had considerable problems in early meetings as they struggled to find an identity. Tom's initial self-presentation as the 'man in charge', the 'wise uncle' ('Leave it to me, lads') was challenged and deemed to be inappropriate by other members of the group. His presentation had to be brought in line with the expectations of other members who demanded that he should be a participant not a detached and apparently somewhat cynical observer of the process. Simon Teffler's identity has never been fully accepted by the group; he presents himself as a representative of management rather than a group member and is treated accordingly, although his occasional attempts to be one of them serves only to confuse them and himself.

The position is complicated, however, since there can be no guarantee that everyone or anyone in the group will accept the claims to identity put forward by anyone else. The fragility of claims to identity is occasioned by the fact that each of us is aware that the presentations of others are part of the situation and may be manipulated. Thus, for some, Fred's self-presentation as concerned spokesman for the workers as well as himself, and his determined pursuit of management evasions, was accepted by some at face value; for others it was Fred 'up to something', behaviour that was not to be trusted and thus an element in the definition of participation which produced very different interpretations from individual to individual, interpretations which affected the development and process of interaction within the group.

For an episode to proceed at all, individuals need to convey to others some definition of what they take to be appropriate to the circumstance. As Perinbanayagam (1974) reminds us:

the actor becomes aware of the other, as well as the other's subjective experiences, only to the extent that those experiences are dramaturgically available ... interaction proceeds on the basis of whatever it is one takes to be the other's subjective experience, and to the extent that neither the other, nor 'brute facts' challenge what one takes to be the case, an ongoing definition of the situation has been negotiated.

Some behaviour must be offered, some presentation made but—and it is an important 'but'—there is no imperative to display one's real intention, one's actual definition of the situation. Participation meetings for Fred may have been important vehicles for furthering the cause of his subordinates or he may have been working other issues. ('He's just trying to impress top management because he thinks they are in favour of all this stuff. He hasn't changed really.') Either way, his self-presentation was, for some, sufficiently ambiguous to become an issue in the way they in turn defined the meaning of participation and, consequently, behaved in relation to it.

Thus it is clear that one person's self-presentation is another person's data and, simultaneously, any self-presentation is an attempt to structure the response of others. It is a pre-emptive strike in the game of interaction. By expressing one's own role, one is at the same time articulating a response for others present. Tom's 'wise uncle' implies dutiful and respectful nephews and nieces, Fred's crusader role implies grateful followers, and so on. The managers at Alpen, in adopting a presentation which stressed a serious-minded, responsible, task-orientated, for-the-good-of-all approach cast the others present into complementary roles. Some of the representatives, in adopting a persistent, questioning but no less 'responsible' behaviour, effectively forced the managers to respond. They refused to be 'put off' by management's expressions of good intent, they were not deflected by the presentations of various managers which implied that 'they, the representatives' should defer. Some have gradually built identities that are resistant to the flattery and vague threat. Their 'situated identities' as representatives have radically affected initial notions of participation and involvement. As they have elaborated their situated identities, so the management has seen the need to change its identity within the groups.

Staging the event

The overall definition of participation has undoubtedly been shaped by the physical setting (Bate, 1976; Emerson, 1970; Carlen, 1976; Rosengren and DeVault, 1964).

Aspects of the physical setting can be interpreted by individuals as symbolically meaningful. To neglect the physical setting is to neglect the whole realm of socially significant symbols, symbols that can be employed in staging a particular presentation; symbols that can be displayed as part of the rhetoric marshalled to profess and maintain particular definitions of the situation.

It will be recalled that the initial participation meeting took place in the office of the Managing Director, a vast place complete with expensive furnishings and fittings. 'Big enough for band practice', as one put it. The location was chosen to emphasize the 'importance we attach to the project', but its utilization may have conveyed all sorts of other signals to those summoned there. It is away from the main production areas and, of course, entirely dissimilar to the areas in which they spent their working lives and with which they were familiar. To use yet another analogy, the management representatives were 'playing at home' whereas the shop floor people were 'away'. Arguably the setting (and others like it currently used for the meetings) had some symbolic if only half appreciated significance for all concerned; the place settings, the table, the secretary hovering in attendance, notebook at the ready, serve to shape the form, if not the content, of discussions. 'Just like Parliament', declared one operative on being ushered into the room. All concerned, including us, appeared to accept the rhetoric of the situation—this was to be a civilized, clean, sanitized, reasonable discussion. We were to comply with certain standards of behaviour and decorum; those who inadvertently swore felt constrained to apologize, those in overalls felt the need to place pieces of paper on their seats (and thereafter to come suitably dressed for the meetings). Thus many turned up at the meetings with some vague ideas of how to behave which in association with the physical clues inspired them to politeness, task orientation, generally interested demeanour, and low expressions of affect. The kind of sober, serious, and responsible behaviour that is widely taken to be the norm at management meetings. The setting, though quite intimidating, did not in and of itself have this effect. Initial discussions with the Chemical Plant operatives were far from polite and were marked by personal comment and a high level of feelings. Gradually, however, our counsel, combined with the surroundings, served to 'civilize' proceedings. The general climate and styles of behaviour at the meetings seemed particular to the setting and, in a number of cases, bore little resemblance to the behaviour of representatives in other settings. Thus, the setting and the props, coupled with the expectations of meeting behaviour which the participants brought to the sessions and with the actual behaviour of experienced meeting attenders, subtly shaped and formed the practice and the meaning of participation.

In other areas and on other occasions, props and features of the setting implied further elements of the definition. At a number of the meetings, for example, overhead projectors were used, blackboards were covered in figures, printed circulars were handed around, and illustrated specifications were produced. Occasionally, others were called to the meetings and they made a 'presentation' by film or slide. Such activities have certain symbolic features in that they help to define circumstances and shape discussions. They also function as powerful tools of differentiation; they help the manager present himself as an 'expert'. Perhaps more pertinently, they help him to display his 'managerialness'. They are part of his attempt to present himself as a legitimate, reasonable, well-organized leader. The props help to give him authority, just as do his clothes and the overall setting. The props are not readily available to the other representatives, nor is access to the 'staff' who prepare the presentations; physical location, props, and access to staff define what it is to be a manager, and their utilization may significantly, if somewhat invisibly, affect the definition of 'participation'.

We are not suggesting that the managers at Alpen consciously manipulated these devices to have their views prevail; such manipulation is, of course, possible and is the stock in trade of confidence tricksters, salesmen, prelates, judges, and the like. What we are suggesting is that a number of factors may influence the definition of reality adopted by a particular individual or group and that one such factor which is manipulable is physical setting, another is props.

A further factor is time; control of which represents another potentially powerful tool. Those who are able to manage the sequencing of episodes, the duration of discussion within and between episodes, those in control of start and finish times can manipulate these features strategically if so inclined. In many circumstances, the chairman as timekeeper exercises considerable influence on the course of events. Within the participation groups at Alpen, however, the chair has not been always taken by management representatives nor, where it has, have other representatives necessarily felt constrained by the chairman's attempts at time management. Management, on the other hand, has exercised general control of the development of the project as a whole and has been largely responsible for the timing of new projects. Only when members of management felt 'comfortable' with activities has the Steering Group recommended progress and, on a number of occasions, movement to other parts of the organization has been held up since it was declared that 'the time is not ripe'. Thus, participation has come to be associated with a slow, cautious, evolutionary approach to change and many comments have been made about it being a five or even ten year process.

Knowledge is Power

By far one of the most important factors influencing situational definition is information. 'Knowledge is Power'. Information and its control are key aspects shaping the meaning social actors attach to an event or piece of behaviour. The more an individual knows about a particular situation, the more effectively he can deploy his resources. Pertinent and credible information relating to an issue that one party has and others do not have can be used to add weight to any definition proposed by the first party. It may, of course, also be used to counteract the claims these actors are advancing. Clearly certain types of information may be of such value and importance to a situation and those in it that its disclosure may lead to a redefinition of the situation.

On the other hand, the withholding of information can be an equally powerful tool. If the management at Alpen, for example, suspects that telling the workers of an approach from the union may lead them to redefine their attitudes such that they would wish to listen to an official, they may deliberately withhold the information (as they did). Similarly, withholding information temporarily may seem beneficial until events have run a particular course—'allow them to discuss it, we know the answer anyway but it will make them feel good.'

At Alpen, as elsewhere, the management had greater access to and control over relevant information. Initially they had a greater awareness of the general development of the programme and its relation to the organization as a whole. At the more specific level they had greater control over the formation of the agenda and information relating to it. Knowing the answers to the various questions being raised they could—and did—plan their tactics for the meetings. Again, initially and perhaps crucially, they had control over the production and distribution of the published minutes of meetings. Since the minutes were edited versions of events, there was scope to control the form and content of the information provided. The minutes can be seen as only one of many possible interpretations of the events which occur during a meeting and it is more than likely that some of the minutes reflected management perspectives to the detriment or exclusion of others. Not surprisingly, control of the agenda and of minutes became an issue in more than one group and, in some, remains so.

In the meetings, notably in the early stages, management were provided with the definitional initiative by the other representatives in that they were constantly asked to respond to problems or to provide information. In shaping how they responded and what they chose to provide by way of information, inevitably and inexorably the management shaped and moulded the essence of participation. We sought to reduce the impact of this by insisting that all questions be answered, that all decisions be justified but since we, like the other representatives, did not know what information was being withheld (if any), we were in a relatively weak position to challenge and provoke those who chose to play their cards 'close to their chests'.

The rhetoric of participation

Language is far the most powerful tool in situational definition. Human beings manipulate and direct themselves and each other largely through the medium of language. Language is not just a means of expressing thoughts, categories, and concepts; it is also a vehicle for achieving practical effects. In our preliminary talks to the representatives and to the shop floor as well as in our conversations with the management, we shaped the notion of participation by our use of language. Throughout we kept it ambiguous and relatively ill-defined; we used words to prevent the concept becoming too specific. We sought to prevent any of the parties from unilaterally declaring this or that subject to be in or out. We also expressed our view that 'it' would be marked by problems and reverses and, in so describing it, we contributed very strongly to 'its' definition. Participation to managers, workforce, and ourselves remains a shapeless term, a process which is evolving slowly into something recognizably different from a state of non-participation, but as yet not tightly defined in and of itself.

The management, like us, had a rhetoric as well. Its rhetoric may be seen in its attempts to define issues on its terms and to respond accordingly. Unpaid leave, which in the language of the operatives was concerned with individual circumstance, was translated by the management into the language of equity. Thus rules were suggested for the benefit of all, questions of fairness were urged upon the workforce, the company's overall 'package of benefits' was stressed and management's need to have everyone at work was emphasized. To the individual worker, the rhetoric was of little consequence since his language was concerned with one-off, personal circumstances which, to him, had little or no connection with the symbols he saw as being manipulated by management. The rhetoric of reasonableness and equity was powerful but, as we have seen, not necessarily overwhelming.

Throughout our time at Alpen, those of us involved in the exercise have been concerned with a struggle for control of the 'script' (Mangham, 1978). In making speeches, questioning others, seeking clarification, disagreeing, refuting, or whatever, we have, each and every one of us, sought to legitimize our own interpretation whilst—to a greater or lesser extent—simultaneously seeking to delegitimize the position adopted by others. Whenever one side or the other has made an attempt to declare such and such to be the nature of participation, we have either challenged it or sought to encourage others to challenge. Of course such action creates problems since in and of itself it creates circumstances in which many of the fundamental issues relating to what others may define as 'participation' do not surface. Questions of the redistribution of power, for example, are discouraged when we are around, not that we are not interested in them, just that *given the present balance of power* we deem it inappropriate to discuss such issues at this stage. And say so. Thus our words, our rhetoric as well as those of all others to a greater or lesser extent, contributed to the negotiated order of participation at Alpen. How we present ourselves, the roles we cast others into, the influence we seek to exercise, constitute the dramaturgy of organizational politics which we have sought to illustrate in these few paragraphs. The major illustrations, of course, are embedded in the text, which is why we have chosen to illustrate our work so profusely. In each and every conversation, in each and every note, and in each intervention, there is an attempt to give shape of direction to the emergent notion of participation. Every page of this book reflects the negotiation of meaning which has taken place at Towcester and which continues to take place as we write.

Two final points need to be made before we turn to some comments upon another piece of our original equipment—the notion of planned change. The first refers back to the discussion of language we embarked upon some paragraphs back. One of our original concerns was that the language used within organizations, particularly between groups, was marked by the absence of a bridge-building or constructive vocabulary. As Allen (1968) points out, industrial relations in the United Kingdom may be characterized by the language of conflict; there are dozens of words signifying hostility, aggression, force, and the like, and few acceptable ones designating compromise and agreement. Similarly, much of the language of American-influenced behavioural science has a distinctly one-sided emphasis although, in this case, the stress is upon consensus, empathy, warmth. Whatever else we may have been doing at Alpen (and there have been times when we did not know what we were doing), we have sought consistently to build a vocabulary for the development of relationships at the plant; a lexicon for interaction which would enable clear messages to be passed from one member of the organization to another without recourse to the clichés of either United Kingdom industrial relations or American management philosophy.

The second point refers to the concept of negotiated order and the associated idea of organizational politics. And again it is a matter of language. Without wishing in any way to detract from anything we have written above, we believe that the concepts we have used are, at best, about half right. Both 'negotiation' and 'politics' imply conscious, manipulative behaviour, both demand rational, self-aware social actors who know where they are going and who take steps to get there. In some cases, perhaps many, this may be the case; in others, interactions occur and adjustments are made in a much less conscious fashion. Our experience at Alpen was not characterized totally (or even largely) by manipulation and negotiation; rather many of our relations were *improvized*, elaborated from half remembered performances in other settings for other purposes, or constructed in a somewhat vague fashion to accommodate some other social actor, to save his face or our embarrassment. It could be that order in Alpen, as elsewhere, is quite frequently improvized, cobbled together rather than planned and strategically informed. It is an idea which we will develop as we continue our journey (Mangham, 1980).

Such a thought brings us to a major problem with the concept of negotiated order. Like so many others working in this tradition our adoption of the perspective effectively narrowed our vision; the idea of improvized order forces us to look up from our concern with individuals and groups and to ask the question: improvized within what kind of framework. Negotiated order theory has enabled us to describe accurately and with considerable detail the interaction between individuals and groups where what was at stake were relatively minor adjustments of day to day working relationships. In so doing it has tended both in theory and in practice to divert our attention away from the structural limits within which negotiations always occur, the macro-sociological order within which order is improvized. Thus our initial concern with the meetings of the groups did not lead us to question the overall structure of the company with its plethora of managers and its intense bureaucratization of procedures. To switch metaphors for a moment, a concern with what happens on the stage—the focus on subjective realities, multiple interpretations, self-presentation, and the like—may have led us not to ask whose theatre is it anyway, what is its function, how is it staffed, how does it relate to the broader society, and so on. Our comments with regard to our own role and other points we make throughout these pages relating to the general relationship between levels in the organization reflect our incipient concern with the narrowness the perspective produced in us. As the months and the years went by, we came to recognize that our interest in the daily give and take of behaviour was not a sufficient base for the effecting of change in the larger system. We needed to understand—and still need to understand—the larger structures and features of social life that constrain the range of improvization open to the actors at Alpen.

Lewin, Dalton, and all that ...

We began our journey with some notions of the stages of planned change deriving from Lewin, Dalton, and a number of other writers and practitioners. Like many, we were much taken with Lewin's simple three-phase model of change: unfreezing, moving, and refreezing. As a brief outline to students and colleagues of what we took to be occurring at Alpen, it served its purpose; as a guide to our practice, it was considerably less useful, as indeed were most of the other models. Throughout, we operated with but the sketchiest of maps and although we began with the equivalent of Michelin guides to good practice derived from intensive reading of the founding fathers in Organization Development, we soon discovered that their nostrums and wise saws provided us with little more than entertainment value. For the most part, other explorers appeared to have been infinitely wise and far-sighted and, perhaps more significantly, to have operated in much less hostile territory. With very few exceptions, they appear to have suffered few setbacks and even fewer major reverses; their projects unfold as neatly as a bed-roll and as tidily as a kit-inspection. Our progress was slow, our steps halting and blind, our gait often lame and stumbling, and our path-finding haphazard and frequently marked by disappointment; we found little help or solace in reading the wise words of our masters; their journeys had clearly been on other planets at other times.

The work of Gene Dalton (1969), although of a different order, was an exception. His essay we found useful in understanding some of the processes with which we found ourselves surrounded, although our experience suggests some modifications to his overall model of the process of change. Where change did occur at Alpen, it may be seen to have been characterized by the subprocesses Dalton identifies: in the Chemical Plant, for example, the move was from generalized goals concerned with better communication and the like to very specific objectives such as achieving a change in the manning levels; relationships between the operatives and the supervisors and between one shift and another were redefined to support agreed changes in practice; initial self-doubt and lowered self-esteem was replaced by confidence and pride as the 'pioneers' carried the message of greater involvement to the rest of the company and as they experienced success within their own plant; change clearly became something to be initiated by them—of all the groups, they have been and continue to be the most active, the most innovative, and the most challenging. Such processes, as noted by Dalton, we found to be occurring simultaneously; as changes occurred in relationships within and across groups, so changes were occurring in self-esteem and in the objectives that were being pursued. Our modification to Dalton's schema is not therefore in those ideas with which, as we have indicated, we have much sympathy.

Our reservations concern his overall model of induced change; like so many before him, he accepts an order of events which was not that which obtained. Specifically, he proposes that tension is experienced within the system *before* the intervention of an influencing agent. Our experience elsewhere, as well as in the particular case of Alpen, is that tension is often the consequence of the intervention of an influencing agent and not, therefore, a preliminary to his or her intervention. There was little overt, acknowledged, or even experienced tension evident at Towcester before we arrived; nor was there any at the London headquarters. We created the tension which we then—together with those who were experiencing it—sought to resolve. Clearly in some reports of organizational change and development, the steps are similar to those recounted by Dalton—there is a sense of crisis and someone is called in to help resolve it. Equally clearly there are other accounts—and we are not alone in this—where the influencing agents are not called in but rather sidle in, or worm their way in, and reveal to the astonishment and chagrin of everyone else concerned that there is a problem to which they ought to be responding. This would appear to be particularly true of OD practitioners since, in many cases, their 'clients' do not know what to expect of them; if your machinery breaks down, you need an engineer; if your accounts are in a mess, you need an accountant; but when do you need an applied behavioural scientist? Frequently, we submit, when he diagnoses that you need him. He appears to be called in rather like a surveyor; you do not necessarily suspect dry rot, but his report not only points out that you have it, he also warns that unless you do what he suggests, your entire building may fall down around you. The applied behavioural scientist sniffs out the dry rot, the patches of damp, and the structural weaknesses that perhaps you never suspected were there; his probing, his analyses, and his diagnoses may create the tension; his comments may actually lower self-esteem rather than simply report it.

In summary, we are arguing that the Dalton model does not accord with the activities of change agents as we see them operating nor, as in the case of Alpen and elsewhere, as *we* operate. Dalton tends to underestimate the impact of the external influencing agent and to underemphasize the power of the new schema, the external motive that such an agent may provide. The managers of Alpen were not aware that they had a problem of involvement until we—using our ideas as to how a healthy organization should operate—defined the issue for them. Our intervention created the problem and the tension just as, we would argue, in many of the texts we have read and the practices we have observed, the intervention of other change agents serves primarily to define the problems and to create the tensions to which they *then* help the members of the organization respond. Lest we be considered cynical in this statement (an accusation which springs readily to the lips of some of our professional colleagues), let us attempt to be very clear as to what it is we are saying. Just as in an annual medical check up the individual may be experiencing no tension and, as far as he is concerned, manifest no symptoms, so with an organization. It may appear to be healthy and functioning well, but the applied behavioural scientist may, in running his stethoscope over it, reveal latent disease. We are *not* saying that the disease is imaginary or invented for the advantage of the practitioner; we are saying that the definition of it is closely related to his expert view of health. Some doctors say (or used to say) that to prevent sore throats occurring, children's tonsils should be removed; we were saying that to prevent organizational deterioration, Alpen needed a programme of involvement. As with doctors, the dependency relationship created by the intervention of a prestigious influencing agent is dangerous, but essential.

Plus ça change

We began our journey as optimists; we considered change to be desirable and possible. Like so many before us, we considered adaptation to change to be relatively easy; 'radical change is possible and ... any reasonably intelligent and able manager *can* attain it in his organization' (Skibbins, 1974). Our failure to stimulate anything faintly resembling radical change at Alpen led us both to reflect upon why members of organizations tend to persist in their practices (Bate, 1978; Mangham, 1978, 1980).

Skibbins (1974) serves as a convenient starting point for the discussion. Although less well known than many OD practitioners, his views are, we believe, shared by many. Like them and us he holds that 'A specific goal of the advanced, organic organizations will be to make life inside them one of man's most exciting adventures instead of the insufferable boredom that afflicts most of us today'. Whatever the aspirations of change agents, whatever their aims and however noble their practices, the results have been very mixed indeed. Consequently for some, the original optimism of the late 1960s and early 1970s has been somewhat tempered. Bennis, for example, an early prophet whose optimism did not survive his responsibility for the direction of a large organization, has reconsidered his original ideas about consensus and collaboration:

'There was a time when I believed that consensus was a valid operating procedure. I no longer think this is realistic, given the scale and diversity of organizations. In fact, I have come to think that the quest for consensus, except for some microsystems where it may be feasible, is a misplaced nostalgia for a folk society ...'.

Such recantations, however, are few and far between. For the majority, the optimism is not misplaced; the mixed results, the setbacks, and the failures serve only to refocus their energies and renew their faith in the brave new world. For them, an understanding of these failures is to be sought in order to explain how 'a manager can radically change his own organization starting Monday morning'. Such faith, maintained in the face of the facts, derives at least in part from the assumptions that are made by those who hold to them about the nature of man and organization. Most, if not all, of the optimists have an image of man as 'basically good' (Tannenbaum and Davis, 1969), as caring, even loving, toward his fellow men, and as motivated not to take advantage of them. Although careful to stress the importance of emotions and feelings, many OD practitioners appear to hold to a rational action or classical model of organization. They appear to hold that consensus is reached through the rational actions of reasonable men; that collaboration is 'natural' and but temporarily inhibited by particular structures and processes. For those of this persuasion there need be no conflict between members nor between individuals and the organization (whatever that term may mean). As Winn (1971) notes: 'Most of the OD practitioners rely almost exclusively on ... the "truth–love" model, based on the assumption that man is reasonable and caring and that once trust is achieved, the desired social change within the organization will take place ...'

Our position was different as we began our journey and is markedly so now. We have more recently come to believe and increasingly sought to put into practice the view that the outsider can (and, perhaps, should) act as a radical (Bate, 1978); should, that is, seek to clarify and strengthen 'expression of the conflicting interests of the diverse groups'; should exercise his influence in order radically to redistribute 'decision-making prerogatives so that lower-power groups can have more influence over an organization's fate' (Schmuck and Miles, 1971). Our experience at Towcester has given meaning to the views of people such as Schmuck and Miles, Pages (1974), and Herman (1971), who takes a similar line:

If we in OD indeed believe in a wider distribution of power it would be well for us to stop trying to deny power's existence, muffle it, wish it away, or disguise it under velvet wrappings. Rather we can encourage as many people as possible at *all* levels of the organization from the highest manager to the lowest subordinate to discover his own power and use it.

Increasingly we have found ourselves in the position of urging groups and individuals to recognize their interests and to fight for them. Our activities have become more and more directed towards building new organizational power structures, new roles, new norms, and new procedures through negotiation rather than through a procedure of bringing people together, sitting back, and waiting for the magic consensus to arise. Our journey has helped us to understand that the political perspective in social and organizational life, the notion of 'negotiated order', leads to, or *ought* to lead to, quite different practices within organization development than have hitherto been the norm. That in this particular case it has not always done so is more a reflection of our timidity and incompetence than an invalidation of the approach. Our theory indicated what was necessary, our practice all too often failed to reflect it. To be fair to ourselves, we did not begin with this view. Our views some years ago, as reflected in the earlier chapters of this book, were much 'softer'. We understood intellectually the notion of 'negotiated order' and we appreciated the magnitude of the task facing us.

The interactionist perspective highlights the different definitions and world-pictures of participants and implies that joint change acts can only be brought about by a sharing of meaning, an understanding of (though not necessarily a sympathy for) other participants' definitions and interpretations of values, people, events, acts and situation, and a negotiation of new contingent meanings.

There was no mention of training people and groups to fight for their rights, indeed we saw ourselves then as nice men in white coats dedicated to helping our fellow men: 'From this perspective, Organizational Development becomes less a matter of values, feelings and styles of management and much more a process of helping individuals and groups examine their definitions and processes of interaction in order to accelerate or facilitate changes' (Mangham, 1975).

Somewhere along the route we picked up the strong feeling that the idea of negotiation implied something very different. Actions and decisions, we decided, were the outcome of political processes. In this process, individuals can and do oppose each other, can and do fight and can and do win or lose. Occasionally the friction of one group against another produces a result different from that which any of the individuals involved may have initially desired. Whatever the process, the resultant action arises not simply from the 'reasons that support the course of action, or the virtues of the organization' but from 'the power and the skill of proponents and opponents of the action in question' (Allison, 1971).

Lacking such a perspective and such assumptions, it is not surprising that our initial influence upon the management of Alpen at Towcester was not as great as we would have liked. Not only had they—and everyone else for that matter—evolved a way of handling each other, a series of habits and routines, a set of situational scripts to which they more or less adhered (Mangham, 1979), they also had a vested interest in maintaining these practices *and* the processes which brought them about. In effect they wrote the scripts for a great number of others (terms of employment, roles, patterns of interaction, styles of address) and, understandably, were not about to give up their 'power to determine decisive socialization processes and, therefore, the power to produce reality' (Berger and Luckman, 1966). Their resistance to change and their success in preventing us from 'helping' was and is based upon a recognition of their own best interests. Our attempts to engender more openness, different patterns of interaction, a wider negotiation of reality definition, and a sharing of influence were seen to be and reacted to for what they were—political demands. We failed to recognize them as such, but one or two managers did not and took action effectively to block any action which threatened their positions.

The problem with such conclusions is that they rest upon an assumption that some one individual or some group of people *consciously* sought to prevent change. Only rarely at Towcester could we perceive this to be the case. In many cases we believe the managers were not acting politically but were simply unable to see either the advantages or disadvantages of wider participation. As Goodwin Watson (1966) in his article on resistance to change notes, 'once an attitude has been set up, a person responds to other suggestions within the framework of his established outlook'. Alpen employees, managers, and shopfloor, were convinced that Alpen was a good employer, that relations between individuals and groups were good and that the style of supervision was 'open'. It was considered that you were 'lucky' to secure a job at Alpen, it was 'a good place to work' and people 'knew how they would be treated' in the plant. Thus the norms and patterns of behaviour to be expected of potential employees were known beyond the factory gates and the initial steps of socializing people to the company took place even before the employees were inducted into the organization. Few 'trouble-makers', ardent union organizers, or 'awkward sods' bothered to apply. Once through the gates, Alpen—as every other employer—took steps methodically to shape the values and perceptions of new members into the 'Alpen way of doing things'. Not surprisingly (although somewhat disturbingly for those of us who expected to be received with open arms, at least by the employees), by the time the member had been with Alpen some years, he or she had internalized its folk ways, objectives, procedures, and outlooks. The result of such socialization at Towcester as elsewhere is to produce a trained incapacity to see things in a way that may appear dramatically obvious to those not so conditioned—or to those of us who march to a different drummer. Let us be clear what we are saying: it is not that the members of Alpen were wanting in intelligence, humanity, or good intentions, it is simply that after some years of socialization, their ways of going about their business were considered by them to be the natural and automatic way of behaving. Time and time again we were told that such and such a practice persisted because 'It's only right', or because 'That's the way things are', 'That's what management's there for, isn't it?', 'Our job is to do what we are told, that's what's right, isn't it?' Even the 'moaning and groaning script' that we experienced was delivered to us as an inevitable concomitant to working at Alpen: 'Sure we are dissatisfied, but nothing can change that.' As Kaufman (1972) puts it, in such circumstances 'Not only are they (the members of the organization) *disturbed* by suggestions that change is required; they are *astounded* because any other pattern is unimaginable.'

Our process orientation, of course, gave us an insight into how to tackle such persistent routine and pervasive definitions. We sought to alienate the participants from their worlds-taken-for-granted, to put the 'frighteners on naturalness' (Mangham, 1980) such that 'givenness became possibility', but we constantly underestimated the difficulty of doing so.

Even where we did bring about the necessary awareness, little was gained unless appropriate and timely solutions were formulated. Insight in and of itself, however stimulating and disturbing, was not enough. It was recognized, for example, that the role of the personnel representatives constituted a barrier to change; whilst they continued to function as 'spokesmen for the management', there could be little change in the handling of problems experienced by the workforce who wanted 'personnel to act for us, not against us'. Some members of the function recognized the issue and wanted to change their role, but were unable to do so either through lack of support or lack of personal expertise. Others recognized the issue and yet sought to perpetuate the *status quo*; it was far easier organizationally and personally for some of the personnel representatives to 'take the company line' than to act in any other way. Even where the 'naturalness' of such a course was challenged, the challenge was brushed aside by those with a vested interest in having things remain as they were. Such reactions are, of course, frequently noted in the literature. Watson (1966) remarks that the most obvious source of resistance 'is some threat to the economic or prestige interests of individuals'. Shephard (1967) comments that change is likely to run counter to 'certain vested interests', as does Judson (1966). The range of rewards that induce people to contribute to organizations is so broad and so complex that it is impossible to conceive of a change that does not avoid reducing some of those rewards. As Kaufman (1972) notes, since people work for salary, for influence, for pride, fear, loyalty, moral obligation, intellectual challenge, and 'every other sentiment known to man', it is seldom that any change can 'avoid impinging negatively on some interests'. Occasionally at Towcester, such a threat to interests was obvious and the response clear and unequivocal; the potential alliance of section heads across the site brought about by our training event and their request to 'meet the management' was such a threat. The response—to deny them any such meeting and a resolution to deal with them 'through the normal channels' (the hierarchical divisions)—was designed to maintain the present lack of interaction between them *as a group* and management *as a group*. Since we had not anticipated this refusal to 'negotiate', we had no response and those with the power won the day. Worse still, our intervention and our lack of success significantly reduced our credibility with the section heads.

Even where we were able to promote a different awareness and where we were able to overcome resistance to change, there was no guarantee that any subsequent change in behaviour would persist. Indeed one of the barriers to change most prevalent at Towcester was and is the tendency of behaviour changes to be temporary, induced by training and counselling and stillborn in the 'real' worth of actual working practices. Watson (1966) and Skibbins (1974) use the concept of homeostasis to explain the 'reversion to complacency' which they both see as a characteristic of organizations faced with a demand for change. Time and time again after group meetings, individual talks with managers and representatives or training sessions, we emerged optimistic and even delighted with the progress made only to discover subsequently that little that had been so enthusiastically discussed and agreed had been translated into action. The pressure of day to day events, it was claimed, often left little time to 'put this new method into operation'. Only where strong support for change and individual vested interest could be allied (as in the Chemical Plant and, interestingly enough, as with many of the individual section heads within the participation groups) did changes in attitude and behaviour persist.

By far the most devastating barrier to widespread change was the simple and manifest indifference of a large number of employees to what was being attempted. It would be true to say, we believe, that a few members of Alpen came to understand what it was we were trying to do and supported us, a few understood and opposed us, but by far the majority neither understood nor cared. Their indifference was neither studied nor spectacular. It was simply heavily there beyond each participation group, out there in the offices and on the shop floor. Those involved in the meetings, the planning sessions, the training groups, and the Steering Group were often enthusiastic, occasionally negative, but never indifferent. Those not so involved rarely showed any interest at all after our initial discussions with them all. The logic of collective life is deeply conservative; what is and has been has been derived from and has stood the test of experience, even if that experience has not been particularly rewarding. 'No point in bothering with all this participation stuff. It will be a waste of bloody time like everything else we've had in here.' Anyone who proposes a change in the *status quo* must demonstrate that the benefits of change will outweigh the imperfections of that which currently obtains. Kaufman (1972), who makes a similar point, quotes the Declaration of Independence in support of collective conservatism: 'All experience hath shown that mankind are more disposed to suffer, while evils are sufferable, than to right themselves by abolishing the forms to which they are accustomed.' The vast majority of employees at Alpen prefer to suffer; customs and practice, habit and experience are powerful barriers to change.

Lack of awareness, lack of appropriate and timely solutions, prevalence of vested interests, tendency of changes not to persist in the face of the pressures of work, inertia, and indifference are among the principal causes of our relatively slow progress at Towcester. Lack of skill is another contributory factor. Many who wished to become more participative openly admitted to not knowing how to behave differently; our advice and help was sought by a large number of managers and representatives and training has become a central feature of our present activities as a direct consequence of this expressed need. By far the most powerful single factor to inhibit progress, however, has been our lack of appreciation of our own power and, consequently, our failure to exploit this position. Latterly we have begun to realize, along with John Stuart Mill, that 'no great improvements in the lot of mankind are possible until a great change takes place in the fundamental constitution of their modes of thought'. More importantly, we have come to recognize that such changes in modes of thought are unlikely to come about by a process of gradual adjustment lasting over several years, particularly in an organization such as Alpen, with a sophisticated, apparently open, yet actually quite punitive, culture. Fear of 'black eyes', of 'blotting your copy book', and 'rocking the boat' is by no means confined to the shop floor employees. Indeed, over the months and years we have found ourselves being quietly and effectively brainwashed into doing things so 'as not to upset people'. We, like many of the full time employees, have convinced ourselves that particular courses of action were not worth the 'aggro', not worth the disfavour we would be in if we were to proceed with them. Rarely is this culture made manifest, rarely has anyone said 'Do not suggest that, do not follow that course of action', rather a subtle disapproval of 'going too far' permeates the organization. Everything is open to discussion but, oddly, we all seem to know the boundaries and voluntarily remain within them. Step out of line and disapproval *is* made clear, as with our meeting with the Executive concerning the section heads. The meeting was followed almost immediately by moves to expel us from the organization; we were, at last, arousing someone to action. Our stance, since that encounter, has been to challenge the culture, to recognize our strength, and to exploit our position as radicals and outsiders. Since both professionally and personally we can afford to give up our connection with Alpen, since neither of us needs the organization (as a research site or, for that matter, as a source of income), we can act more independently than in the early days when our commitment and action was influenced by other personal and professional goals. Since we are clearer as to how we see organizations operating—essentially as political entities—and since we have come to see companies in general and Alpen in particular as marked in fact by processes of control and resistance (see below), our own actions have become more premeditated and explicit. The change in the fundamental constitution of mode of thought envisaged by Mill has been in *our* mode of thought not yet in the client's. We have learned that we are important, that the members of the organization depend upon us to provide alternative ways of seeing their world and depend upon us to suggest ways forward and, ultimately, to stimulate, challenge, or force them to take some action. Not only have we discovered that we must train the disadvantaged to recognize their disadvantage and fight for redress, we have recognized much more fundamentally that we must fight for our perspective and exploit our advantage to the full. Recently, therefore, we have put aside our white coats and friendly bedside manner and taken to wearing gloves and adopting a more challenging demeanour as we pass through the gates. No longer the seven stone weaklings with sand in our eyes, we have begun to thumb our noses at authority, begun to flout the control that, earlier, we had been happy to place upon ourselves like all good Alpen employees.

Healthy organizations?

It will be recalled that underlying much of what we undertook to do at Alpen was informed by a vague notion of organizational health or effectiveness deriving, ultimately, from biological analogies. At the beginning of the work we were strongly influenced by the ideas of Fordyce and Weil with respect to 'healthy' and 'unhealthy' systems; we took it to be self-evident that 'good' organizations would be characterized by factors such as widely shared objectives, pragmatic problem-solving, extensive delegation of decision-making, collaborative structures and processes, open discussion of differences, honest relationships, flexible leadership, and a sense of optimism. True, we were a little uneasy with this transatlantic millennialism but, by and large, we took these features to be desirable and attainable and their absence to mean that even if the organization was not actually doomed, its growth was inhibited.

Alpen had few of these characteristics. Indeed it manifested many of the opposite 'unhealthy' features which were roundly condemned by Fordyce, Weil, and others of their ilk: there was little personal commitment to organizational objectives, status was more important than competence in problem-solving, decision-making was highly centralized, competitive behaviour was the norm, feedback was avoided, leadership for the most part stiff-necked and dogmatic, and many took refuge in policies and procedures, playing games within the organization structure to protect themselves and minimize risk-taking.

As we indicated above, Alpen—in our opinion—has not changed radically; it remains 'unhealthy' and 'immature', yet it continues to be highly profitable. By all the measurements of business, it is and looks like continuing to be a most successful company; anyone would be well advised to sink his or her nest egg into its stocks. Even in terms of less 'economic' measures, Alpen may be seen as successful; its turnover of employees is low, their wages and satisfaction relatively high, their productivity enviable. Close association with it and with its internal processes has had a considerable effect upon us and it has led us to be more explicit about our views on the nature of organizations.

A question of tension and tolerance

As we have indicated several times throughout this book, the balance of power is of central importance to the negotiation of order and the reaching of mutual accommodations. Work, at Alpen or elsewhere, is designed in accordance with certain principles and priorities which tend to concentrate power within the organization in the hands of the management. Work at Alpen varies in its degree of differentiation and in its complexity; the job of a section head is somewhat more complex than that of a packer or a fork lift truck driver, that of a manager more than that of a canteen hand. Most, but not all, of the shop floor work is simple, repetitive, and highly controlled; the logic of the division of labour dictates that it should be so.

Most, but not all, of the non-shop floor work is more complex, less repetitive, and less controlled. Thus the division of labour (and the philosophy of management that accompanies it) creates conditions in which the amount of 'freedom' permitted to the employee varies. Schrank (1978) terms this 'schmoozing time':

> But compared to the repetitive work of the furniture factory, I preferred the machine shop, though many men I worked with did not. A day in the machine shop would go fast, and at least some work was a challenge. ... However I found that one of the best things about being a machinist or a toolmaker was the freedom to move around, to schmooze. Often when a machine tool has been set up for an operation, there can be considerable time to schmooze with the guys around you—go get coffee, a Coke, or a smoke. ...'

The relative differences in freedom from control and specification, and the freedom to schmooze, to figure out your *own* task, or just to take time out are significant distinctions between and within organizations (Mangham, 1980).

Fox (1974) and others have argued that this schmooze factor is, indeed, the most significant distinction to be found within the workplace. He distinguishes three levels of discretion (freedom to schmooze)—high, medium, and low—and discusses them in some detail. At Alpen low discretion jobs are the lot of many of the shop floor employees, the type of job that in the words of F. W. Taylor (1911) requires these workers 'do what they are told promptly and without asking questions or making suggestions ... it is absolutely necessary for every man in an organization to become one of a train of gear wheels'. Work in the Chemical Plant, in the Packaging, Blow Moulding, Labelling Room, and Capsule departments is prescribed, controlled, and supervised to such a degree that negotiation appears to be impossible. In this respect, Alpen is a model of 'scientific management'; the managers design, schedule, and control the work, the workers execute it. Taylor argued that not only should the management specify what was to be done but 'how it is to be done and the exact time for doing it'. Alpen does not go in for crude methods of work study, but in the careful design of machinery and processes and its constant pressure on productivity, it achieves very much the same consequence—high output—without the reaction that time study frequently engenders. Taylor, the founding father of scientific management, proposed that the test of his method should be that not only should productivity increase but the worker should willingly do the task; his man, Schmidt, was to move 47 tons of pig iron per day and 'be glad of it'. At Alpen as we have indicated, the employees worked hard and were indeed apparently 'glad of it'.

Theoretically, as Fox (1974) notes, the person subjected to heavy prescription of his work and tight supervision is likely to react: 'The role occupant perceives superordinates as behaving as if they believe he cannot be trusted, of his own volition, to deliver a work performance which fully accords to the goals they wish to see pursued, or the values they wish to see observed.' In response, the employee is likely to trust his employer less.

Trust, we would argue, is an important if little understood variable at work. It is perhaps too easy to look back nostalgically to the time when the small scale of operations and the minimal division of labour that accompanied it made possible a personalized set of relations between master and men. It would certainly be foolish to conclude that such circumstances constituted 'the good old days' for all concerned, but it is arguable that relations were marked by greater trust, greater mutual reciprocity, more give and take than the present circumstance of impersonal and contractual obligations manifests. In many circumstances the imposition of low discretion tasks and the enforcement of contractual obligations upon workers has resulted in the employees working without enthusiasm, to 'rule' with little or no personal commitment, indulging in restrictive practices and generally behaving in a 'bloody-minded' fashion. Resistance, we would argue, is an inevitable concomitant of control. If so, why, we asked ourselves, was resistance less obvious at Alpen than in many other organizations; less so, in fact, than in the other Alpen plants in the UK? Why are the Towcester employees moving 47 tons and being glad of it?

We have indicated some of our answers elsewhere in this text; discontent and potential resistance was certainly evident when we gained access to the workers. Many resented and continue to resent the relentless pressure to produce and the tight supervision to which they are subjected. A great deal of energy in early meetings was expended upon challenging supervisory prerogatives and upon the discussion of hours and conditions of work. Much of this discussion and most of the displayed resentment was a surprise to the management; previously the expression of discontent had been discouraged and resistance had no focus. By design or otherwise, the structure of Alpen at Towcester and the practice of rotating people across groups and shifts significantly inhibited the power of informal groupings. As a number of studies have shown, membership of a group serves to redress to some extent the power imbalance created by extreme differentiation and simplification. Relations at work are often characterized by a strong desire to be part of a group or a team. Not necessarily or even primarily for the friendship it affords—in one study, for example, fewer than ten per cent of the respondents claimed particular friends at work—but more for the protection it provides from the attempts at control imposed by the management (Mangham, 1980). As Roy (1954) graphically states it: 'You can't "make out" if you do things the way management wants them done.' He goes on to explain—as do so many other studies—that attempts at control by the management led to workers on 'the drill line' co-operating with

each other as fellow members of a combat team at war with management. ... This network effectively modified certain formally established shop routines, a too close attachment to which would handicap the operators. The 'syndicate' also proved adequate in circumventing each of a series of 'new rules' and 'new systems' introduced by management to expurgate all modifications and improvizations and force a strict adherence to the rules.

Our intervention at Alpen significantly affected the balance of power inasmuch as it provided a focus for the expression of resistance. The structures and processes we advocated and established provided a forum and a means for the expression of discontent that hitherto a number of *individuals* had felt. The discussions and disagreements that we prompted by the project served to bring together people who had previously been divided and ruled. It promoted the 'network' that is so much part of any organization and encouraged individuals to question and even challenge the rules and the policies. Not surprisingly, for many of the shop floor representatives it is regarded as being of great value—for the first time they have a legitimate opportunity to voice their opinions and an audience which is required by the rules of the game to respond. Not surprisingly, for these very reasons, for many of the managers it is regarded as being of little value; for some it is a direct threat.

Attitudes and responses to the participation programme

The initial reason for setting out on this journey was to collect data to add to the existing body of knowledge on worker and managerial attitudes to participation. In particular we were interested in 'the propensity to participate and its correlates' (Bate, 1976)—people's aspirations to influence various kinds of decision at various levels of the organization, and the factors which affected these aspirations. The methods and instruments we used in the Chemical Plant experiment were designed to permit comparisons to be drawn between our findings and those of the existing body of 'quantitative' research. In the event, as we have already recounted in some detail, our attempts to apply these methods turned into a farce, and to avoid further embarrassment to everyone—but mainly to ourselves—they were given a quiet but decent burial. As we now cast our eyes back over the journey, however, it does occur to us that, although the traditional methods of data-collecting were abandoned early on, we continued to gather 'qualitative', impressionistic data on the original issue of people's attitudes to participation. It is a summary of this which will be the concern of the present section of this chapter. We may add that we have (with some difficulty) attempted to meet the original aim of drawing some comparisons with the literature (if only to criticize some of the foundations upon which that literature is based).

Initial responses to participation: a minority taste

The level of interest in participation when we first arrived was generally low; indeed it might be said that *before* we arrived it was pretty well non-existent. If any real interest was being shown early on, it was largely a product of us implanting notions of information- and influence-sharing in people's minds and suggesting to them that many of the present difficulties they were having in their jobs might be solved by the adoption of some kind of participation scheme. While references have been made to 'a substantial minority' (Wall and Lischeron, 1977) or 'a considerable minority' (Marchington, 1980) who, like the employees at Alpen, showed little interest in having more say in decisions, the overall conclusion to be drawn from the literature is that there exists a fairly strong and widespread desire for participation, particularly at the level of 'own job' (Holter 1965; Hespe and Warr, 1971; Ramsay, 1976). For example, in reviewing the literature and the wide research carried out by the MRC Applied Psychology Unit of the University of Sheffield, Hespe and Wall (1976) state: 'In general terms, therefore, we may reach the conclusion that some degree of involvement is desired by most people at all levels within organizations. Such a fact is unsurprising in a society which endorses democratic values.'

Our experience, by contrast, is that most people (initially at least) had a take-it-or-leave-it attitude to the question of greater involvement. Participation for participation's sake stirred few emotions. It was only when participation was suggested as a possible way of redressing any grievances that existed (about which there were strong feelings) that the notion began to acquire any value for the people concerned.

While this serves as a brief summary of Alpen employees' responses to participation, there are important variations of attitude within this general pattern which should be noted. We think it is possible to identify at least four:

(1) *The non-plussed*   These were the many people who really had little idea what we were talking about—even after we had struggled to break the term participation down into simple phrases such as 'having more say' and 'knowing more about what goes on round here'—and who either tried very hard to smile dutifully and go along with that 'something' which *we* were obviously enthusiastic about, or who opted to sit it out, eyes firmly fixed to a spot on the floor a few feet in front of them. Perhaps some did understand and did have a view, but were caught unawares by the novel situation in which they found themselves, where they were actually being consulted about something, were being asked to give their views. Nevertheless, in all cases the notion of participation was new; in some cases, as we have noted before, it was as unknown as a yogi fruit—a kind of 'definitional vacuum' existed; cognitions of the term were either very simple or non-existent.

We now look back with a mixture of humour and horror on the way people must have felt about our initial interview schedule in the Chemical Plant. Fortunately only a few were exposed to it and the schedule was dropped before the programme had been extended into the Packaging Department where most of the non-plussed were to be found. It should be borne in mind, however, that similar scales and instruments to the ones we abandoned have been widely used and in fact form the backbone of most of the available attitudinal research on participation. Whilst they come in many shapes and sizes, they all have one thing in common: they assume that respondents actually have a formed attitude to participation, and assume that there exist relatively complex and sophisticated cognitive notions about it. For example, take the general question, 'Do you feel that the employees in general participate sufficiently in decisions that concern the management of the establishment as a whole?' (Holter, 1965): respondents were presumably expected to know the meaning of 'participate', 'decisions', and 'management', to have an attitude to the subject, to be able to know and take into account how 'employees in general' felt about the subject, and finally to condense such a complex reasoning process into the unequivocal 'Yes' or 'No' reply! In the event, ninety-five per cent of the respondents did actually reach the stage of replying 'Yes' or 'No'. This is not really surprising for, in our own case, we would guess that, confronted with a similar question, most of the non-plussed would have done the same, if only to avoid betraying their ignorance about the meaning of the question, or to 'help these nice boys as best we can'. What does surprise us is that such highly questionable evidence continues to be quoted some fifteen years later.

By way of contrast, the instruments designed in recent years have been more sophisticated: in reply to the question 'how much influence do you feel you and your workmates have in this firm over ...?', respondents have had the luxury of giving their ratings on a five-point scale ('a great deal', 'quite a lot', 'some', 'very little', 'none') on at least ten separate decision items (Lischeron and Wall, 1975*a*, *b*; Ramsay, 1976). Even here, however, the assumption is still the same—that people do have a clear and fairly sophisticated view about participation; the stimuli are complex, and the response (in contrast to the earlier general question) is expected to reflect subtle differences in attitude. Again we feel that confronted with such questions, the non-plussed would be overwhelmed by what was expected of them, and might be tempted to 'play the game' by filling them out as best they could, or would fall on their knees and beg to be returned to the authoritarian world from which they came!

(2) *The indifferent*   Whereas most of the people in the Packaging Department were non-plussed about the notion of participation, the majority of those in the Dry Products Department were indifferent towards it. They had a fair notion of what it was all about, and asked for details about the degree and kind of participation envisaged. Knowledge, unfortunately, did not mean interest. Many made it quite clear that they 'didn't give a damn about participation ... we've seen all this before ... it's a load of crap ... another two-day wonder ... the current flavour-of-the-month'. This indifference (as distinct from hostility) was, we believed, a product of what Garson (1977) calls regressive expectations: people said that there were long-standing and unresolved problems in the factory; at various points in time new ideas like participation had appeared and promises had been made that the problems would be resolved, that things would be different; this had not happened and understandably people had come to expect that few things would ever change and that the problems would persist; thus a vicious circle was set up—as long as people expected that problems would never be resolved, they made few attempts actively to resolve them. Underpinning this take-it-or-leave-it attitude was the perception that what was being proposed was not in the least 'radical'. Even when we argued that to us, at least, genuine participation was a radical notion and could if properly translated into practice have major effects on the factory, the 'indifferents' quietly pointed out that in *their* factory, genuine participation of the kind we described would be given no place.

Here was another group, then, that had little enthusiasm for participation, and again we wonder how they would have responded to the participation researcher's stock-in-trade questions such as 'How much influence would you ideally like to have in this firm over ...?' To these people, ideals had no part to play in their attitudes to work and participation. The question was irrelevant; the reality was that they had little or no participation and stood little chance of getting more. The challenge to us was, 'You try. Go on, prove us wrong'. Such, for example, was the attitude to rates of pay at Towcester: obviously people would have liked more influence in setting the annual salary increase, but to them such a thing was inconceivable in practice, and there was no point in making out a serious case for it.

(3) *The hostile*   A few of those we spoke with were so embittered that they seemed virtually anti-everything and anti-everybody to do with work. In their eyes, participation was another management ploy, a way not of increasing employee

influence but of taking it away, an alternative to effective trade unionism and collective bargaining. Their refusal to participate was thus part of a wider refusal to co-operate with anyone outside their immediate work group. 'B' shift in the Chemical Plant adopted this attitude in refusing initially to meet with us, and later in seeking to cause a major upset by withdrawing from the participation experiment. What they shared with the indifferents was a belief that participation had been designed by the management for the management, that there was absolutely nothing in it for them.

This group, like the previous ones, has not been adequately described in the literature, and it is not surprising. Where people were given the opportunity of deciding whether to take part in or opt out of an investigation (Holter, 1965; Sadler, 1970; Bate, 1976; and presumably most of the investigations conducted by the MRC, University of Sheffield), it is most likely that 'the hostiles' would have been the first to opt out and their views would simply not have been recorded. For them, co-operation in the research investigation may have been seen as a compromise of principles, a 'sell-out', similar to co-operating with the company in general. Even those persuaded to take part might have given responses which later would have been open to misinterpretation. For example, confronted with a five-point scale for rating 'desired influence', they may well have chosen the 'very little' to 'none' range, not necessarily because they were against having more influence, but that they were against the company and against a scheme which in their view would be non-participative. Ironically, we suspect that, in a different circumstance, members of this group might express the greatest desire for genuine participation.

(4) *The pros: the minority exception* Only a small number of people we spoke with initially were actually in favour of 'more' participation. These were the few who had a good idea what the term meant and what it might mean in their own case. Nevertheless, even these were heterogeneous in that they seemed to have very different motives for supporting it: some saw it as a way of 'hitting' the management—exposing the malpractices of the immediate supervision or getting direct access to senior managers; others saw it as a way of short-circuiting supervision, getting their personal problems and difficulties sorted out; still others saw it as a way of making a name for themselves in the factory.

To summarize, the flavour of our findings about people's desires for participation is very different from that which can be found in the literature. Initially, only a small minority of people had a positive attitude to participation in any shape or form. The remainder had negative, non-existent, or indifferent views about it. In explaining this difference, we acknowledge that Alpen may be very different from other research sites in terms of size, technology, degree of unionization, culture, market, and so on, and together these may have been responsible for this difference. However, it is equally or more plausible to suggest that the difference in results may be attributed to a difference in methodology. As we have tried to show, conventional, quantitative approaches to the study of attitudes to participation are in many ways exclusive of the non-plussed, indifferent, or negative attitude, and may exaggerate the strength of the desire for participation. Support for this latter interpretation comes from a re-examination of the limited 'quantitative' data produced in our initial Chemical Plant survey using the conventional approach of rating scales and a list of 'relevant' decision-making items. Analysis of this did not 'pick up' the first three groups described above and gave a misleading impression (to quote from our 1976 paper) of a 'moderate and generalized desire for participation'—an impression which, as we pointed out at the time, accorded closely with the published research. That the groups were not picked up is not surprising since 'B' shift (the 'hostiles') had already withdrawn, and the non-plussed and the indifferents had been strongly encouraged to give some kind of response, positive or negative. There is often, it seems, more to the final write-up of an investigation than meets the eye, and in this, our work, and undoubtedly the work of many others, is no exception.

Later responses to participation: the notion begins to acquire value

The story of our journey clearly underlines the considerable effects that the *experience* of participation has on attitudes and feelings. While the views of the non-participating constituents are little changed—and many people continue to ignore, decry, or chip away at the scheme—the views of many of the participants have gone through a remarkable transformation. Most now take it for granted that participation is a 'good' thing, and that more participation would be a 'better' thing. Criticisms of the scheme continue to be made not on the grounds that participation does not 'work' but that it is not working as well as it should be. Expectations and aspirations for participation are high and still rising.

The cross-sectional nature of most research has obviously had the effect of ignoring the question of whether attitudes to participation change over time: in the overwhelming majority of cases, a 'snapshot' had been taken of employee attitudes in one or more companies, followed by processing and rapid display of the picture. Perhaps a longitudinal view of the same subject, particularly over a period of time when the extent of participation was being increased, would reveal—as in our case—great changes. Many of our 'hostiles' and 'indifferents' have now joined the 'pros' camp. Judging by what they have said to us, there appear to be two reasons for the change: the first is that, contrary to original expectations, the participation scheme has, they concede, yielded tangible benefits for employees—hard fought but still worth fighting for. Relationships with supervision in particular have been eased, and the way has been opened for wider influence outside the department. The second reason is more personal—that the act of participation has been (not their words) 'ego-enhancing'; they admit to having enjoyed time away from their jobs to rub shoulders with the powerful, have liked the recognition and esteem membership of the committees has sometimes brought them, and have enjoyed the variety afforded by the meetings and by various training sessions that they have attended. The same people have also been keen to point out that this has in no way required them to 'go soft' or to 'sell out' to the management side; on the contrary, much of their personal pride derives from being seen as a good representative, accurately presenting views to the meeting, and challenging the reasoning behind managerial decisions.

While cross-sectional research is not equipped to deal with the issue of change in attitudes to participation over time and is arguably only valid for the day on which the data was collected, there is another aspect of this research which is disquieting. Our own finding has been that people who don't have much participation won't want much participation: what you want is closely connected with what you have or see yourself as having. Such a finding, in fact, finds confirmation in the literature, with a noted high correlation between the perceived opportunity for participation and the aspiration for participation. One therefore wonders whether, despite the sophisticated design of the instruments of research, one is really measuring aspirations for participation or simply the perceived levels of existing participation. Clearly there is a possibility that research which has revealed high aspirations did so because it took place in a company with (unlike Alpen) an already high level of perceived or actual participation. We examine this further and in a different context below.

The kind of participation preferred

An almost universal conclusion of the literature is that the desire for participation will vary according to the kind of issue under discussion (e.g. Globerson, 1970). The customary way of dealing with this subject has been to distinguish between 'immediate' and 'distant' participation (Strauss and Rosenstein, 1970; Pateman, 1970; Hespe and Wall, 1976; Wall and Lischeron, 1977): immediate participation refers to employee involvement in decisions normally made at lower levels within the organizational hierarchy, typically involving supervisors and first-line managers; such decisions are normally specific to a department or section and are usually task- or job-related. Wall and Lischeron (1977) define 'distant participation' as follows: '[it] refers to employee involvement in higher levels of organizational decision-making, often, for practical reasons, through varying forms of representation. The decisions involved are typically less directly relevant to workers' own job activities but of greater concern to the organisation as a whole.'

Most of the evidence points to a strong and widespread desire for immediate participation and a weaker, more limited desire for distant participation. The question here is how far does this accord with our own observations? Firstly, we need to admit to some definitional difficulties: at Alpen, many 'distant' decisions did have a direct relevance to the workers' jobs—all the more so since decision-making was highly centralized; we also noted many decisions which although of concern to the organization as a whole (e.g. the 3.30 finish, unpaid leave), were at the same time directly relevant to the workers' jobs. It does seem that the separate questions of 'level' and 'relevance' have got rather mixed up in the definitions. However, our experience is that level of decision, of itself, had little effect on workers' desires for participation, the attitude being, 'if it is of direct relevance to us then we want to talk about it—regardless of how near or far it is and how widely it affects other people in the company or on the site.' For example, discussions about BUPA and fringe benefits in general (in the case of the Engineering Department, leading to enquiries being made about the fringe benefits offered to company employees in Puerto Rico) often took place in participation meetings since, although being distant they were considered to be directly relevant to the workers' lives.

However, we can agree that initially at least, most discussion did take place around 'immediate' issues. In this story we have referred to them as the hygiene issues—physical working conditions, machinery, manning, etc.—and have indicated that most of the groups moved into discussion of these in the early stages of their establishment. The reasons are many but fairly comprehensible: the issues were 'tangible' and readily understood by those concerned, they were judged to be important, and they did not appear to be insoluble; they afforded the opportunity for the new committee to 'cut its teeth' on things that were manageable and not too threatening. We too, it must be remembered, encouraged this, as did the management who felt less threatened by discussion of immediate issues. However, with time, interest in the 'distant' issues has grown—a consequence, we believe, of the experience of participation, and of the successful resolution of 'immediate' issues—and this, as we have recounted, has often led the groups into crises where management have attempted to restrict them to issues of a less distant, less far-reaching kind. It must be remembered that much of the impetus to move from departmental to divisional to site-wide participation committees has come from pressure from the groups to move from influencing departmental (immediate) to divisional to site-wide issues (irrespective of the strong managerial resistance encountered *en route*).

Clearly the *experience* of participation is again important—desires for participation will move upwards together. Initial desires for immediate participation are not fixed; part of the evolution process, it seems, is a raising of the sights. Such a process has been referred to as 'the taste of the good life' (Morse, 1953), 'the salted nut paradox' (i.e. the more you eat the more you want) (Ullrich, 1968), and the 'give them an inch and they'll take a mile' (Lischeron and Wall, 1975b).

Here a cautionary note must be sounded for those who, having seen the findings of the literature, claim that 'distant' participation through such things as worker-director schemes should be dismissed in favour of 'immediate' participation through autonomous work groups and various job enrichment schemes. It is our view that a low degree of interest in distant participation schemes is mainly a product of a lack of direct experience of such schemes, and that this present low degree of interest should not be used as a justification for not extending participation to the higher level. On the contrary, since it seems that people value what they have, it is not inconceivable that they would also, given time, feel the same way about participation at the highest level. Clearly the experience of the worker-director scheme in the BSC confirms this possibility (Bank and Jones, 1977). We do, however, agree with those who suggest that the way to arrive at this kind of participation is through evolution from lower levels of participation.

Factors affecting desires for participation

Here we will briefly consider some of the factors which may, or which previous studies have suggested may, have affected attitudes towards participation.

Present level of participation

This was discussed above and it was suggested that attitudes to participation were affected to a great extent by how much participation people currently enjoyed.

Age/length of service

In reviewing previous research, as Marchington (1980) observes, 'a totally confusing picture emerges'. Some say that older, longer-serving employees will feel sufficiently confident to express their views, while others say that these people will be more settled and more socialized to the company's values, such that they feel no need for participation. Others (cf. Wall and Lischeron, 1977) argue that younger people will demand a greater say, owing to changing social and educational standards. Our impression is that while younger people did tend to show greater interest, there were notable exceptions in both the older and younger groups.

Occupation

Wall and Lischeron (1977) found a correlation between higher skill levels and desire to participate, and these observations roughly accord with our own. Notable amongst our 'high aspiration' groups were the engineers and male chargehands; the lowest aspiration group was the female operators' group in the Packaging Department. The engineers in particular tended to be the better educated and less parochial of the other groups—they got round the factory, saw the place 'in the round', and tended to work at a number of levels—manual, staff, and managerial.

Sex

As Marchington (1980) confirms, 'the final variable that has been regularly tested is the effect of sex on the desire to participate, and here the findings are uniform and relatively strong, in that men show a much greater interest than women'. In our case, the same applies. Not only have women shown the lesser interest, women participants have had the greatest difficulty coming to terms with the participation process. This could be because it is male-dominated, but we also feel that the women have shown greater timidity in bringing issues forward, and have had greater difficulty freeing themselves from the 'moaning and groaning' script. Perhaps it is no coincidence that the group which continues to encounter the most problems is the Packaging group, where a sizeable proportion of the members are women. It should be borne in mind, however, that most of the female employees occupied the lowest skill jobs, and it may have been this which accounted for our findings.

Supervisory and managerial attitudes to participation

Comparatively less has been written about managerial attitudes to employee participation and, despite work by Hespe and Wall (1976), Guest and Fatchett

(1974), Brannen *et al.* (1976), and Clegg *et al.* (1978), 'We still know relatively little in detail about management attitudes to participation' (Marchington, 1980). The weakness of these works is that attitudes have been inferred solely from what management have said, and not from observation of what they have actually done—which may, as we have discovered, be a very different issue. As Hespe and Wall (1976) have pointed out, 'a manager may show a clear orientation in favour of participation when filling in a questionnaire but may follow a different course of action when faced with the reality of increased decision-sharing'.

Our experience at Alpen would confirm this. From the outset managers agreed that participation was a good thing, that one could no longer manage effectively without involving the workforce, etc. Undoubtedly, had they been asked at the time to fill in a questionnaire, their responses would have been very positive and supportive. Unfortunately, in practice, this was not always the case, and it soon became clear that the managers only supported a particular kind of participation. Put rather simply, this definition had the following components: (a) workers should be involved and should be consulted but managers retain the right to decide; (b) the exercise of influence is permissible so long as it is not in my own job (for example, recall the early responses of the Personnel Department during the preparations for the Chemical Plant experiment); (c) priority should always be given to the 'normal' channels—these should not be upset in any way, supervisors should not be by-passed, and participation committee members should never have *more* influence or information than supervisors; (d) limits should be placed on the subject matter of participation—wages and other things decided centrally will not be discussed.

Hespe and Wall (1976) point to a 'degree of congruence' between worker and managerial attitudes to and definitions of participation. Our findings do not accord with theirs. As we have said elsewhere, the whole participation process revolved around the 'negotiation' between divergent and competing definitions of participation in *practice*. Management were consistently trying to concede less than the workers wanted both in terms of degree of influence and breadth of subject matter for discussion. Also, understandably, they were preoccupied with issues which either helped 'the company' (i.e. issues on which they were judged by their superiors!)—variances, absenteeism, flexibility—or which offered no challenge to their own territorial autonomy.

Whereas in the case of middle and senior managers, attempts were made to impose a restrictive definition which suited them, many of the supervisors and section heads chose outright resistance to participation in any shape or form. Their attitude, at least initially, was negative and hostile. Participation, to them, offered few direct benefits and a good deal of threat to their own jobs—a fairly accurate perception, we believe, particularly in the early stages of the participation programme.

It is our view that this divergence of attitudes, and attitudes of resistance on the part of management, have not been clearly identified in the literature, possibly for the reason suggested above—that what a manager says he will or would like to do in terms of sharing information and influence may not be what he will do in practice.

By way of conclusion to this section we would point out, as have others, that in spite of considerable research activity stretching back several decades, evidence about people's attitudes to participation is incomplete, inconclusive, and frequently contradictory. The proposed solution has usually taken the form of a plea for more 'data', more of the same kind of research, more standardization of research instruments and approaches. As we have indicated at various points of this section, we do not believe that further replication and corroboration hold the key to a solution. In our view, the scientific, quantitative approach most favoured in research of this kind has inherent weaknesses which will be magnified rather than minimized by 'more of the same'. Recent adoption of the 'case study' approach by Buckingham et al. (1975), Bank and Jones (1977), Blackler and Brown (1978), Mumford and Henshall (1978), Knight and Guest (1979), and Marchington (1980) seems to confirm our view that such an approach potentially offers a better and more realistic way of describing managerial and worker attitudes to participation.

As conclusion to both chapter and book we should perhaps offer some general comments upon how we now feel about what has happened, and how we may have changed over the five years in terms of our values and beliefs. Such comments may offer one or two signposts to those about to embark on a similar journey, and may conceivably deter one or two.

No doubt, like the reader we are at this point suffering from a degree of mental and physical fatigue—five years of 'dawn patrols' to Towcester and five years of meetings, plans, and crises have taken their toll. What idealism and Messianic zeal we originally had has been tempered by the realities of participation and an appreciation of the enormity of the task that has and will continue to face us and all concerned. We began the journey with a spring in our step and scrambled up hills and over obstacles with little effort and a great deal of boyish enthusiasm. The sprint has now become a slow plod, more cautionary, more the pacing of a long distance runner. We are now more aware of potential obstacles, particularly political ones erected by supervisors and managers, and try to circumnavigate them before it is too late to do so. We are now more politically astute, better able to survive in all winds and weathers. We now look more carefully for the short-cuts, using previous experiences or additional manpower to reduce the 'start-up' times for new participation groups. Such an economy of effort has only been made possible by what we have learnt about participation and organizational change en route.

Arguably we have adjusted our pace to the rest of the field in which we have found ourselves. With one or two exceptions, most of the people at Alpen have also been prepared to plod on rather than sprint. They too, it seems, have noted the length of the course and the need to conserve energy. The shared philosophy is not one of conservatism but evolution. The programme continues on its inevitable course; it is not, we believe, being absorbed into the conventional organizational culture and patterns. Significantly, no one has been lost on the way, and it is our belief that adjusting our pace to that of the slowest has accounted for this. Surprisingly, the impatient 'flyers'—mainly the younger, male representatives—have also checked their step to enable the others to catch up.

Some might argue that all this signifies that we have been 'taken over' by Alpen's culture. While this might sometimes have appeared to be the case, we do reject it.

The pace, to some extent, is the one we have set; the direction and route have also largely been set by us. If anything we are more controlling than ever, more concerned with achieving our ends than being 'client-centred'. We are unaware of ever having done anything against our will or having 'lost' an argument about the direction the route should take. All this, we would argue, has been possible because we have been highly influential and have been able to provide a kind of expertise and leadership of which the participants have approved. They have depended upon us for advice, protection, and direction and we have willingly provided these things as best we could—not because altruism has ever had a great part to play in our value systems, but because the power accorded to us has enabled us to be exploitative and follow our self-interest. Like all politicians, we have also been careful to cultivate allies, people who wanted to gain some personal advantage out of the participation programme.

Having preserved our own self-interest, we have been quite happy to help others advance theirs. Initially we had high-minded notions about 'multi-client' systems—a reaction against the management consultancy orientation of Organization Development, a concern of being available to all, the mediators, the Men from the Ministry, the men on the fence. Such views have been tempered by experience. Not surprisingly, we soon found we had views and prejudices, and had allegiances to some groups rather than others (although these allegiances frequently changed) and soon discovered that we were working to advance the interests of some groups to the disadvantage of others. In the early days, for example, we sympathized with workers who recounted horrific tales about their supervisors, and paid little attention to the needs and views of the supervisors themselves. Later on, having got to know the supervisors better, we began to appreciate the dilemma in which they found themselves, and began to act as their agents in their dealings with the senior managment (not with much success, we might add). True to the maxim 'Don't bite the hand of the feeder', we clearly colluded with the senior managers (at many different points of the programme), and continue to collude with them. While it is true that we chastised or poked fun at them from time to time, we were always cautious not to upset the applecart. However, as the story of our journey shows, over time we began to work less and less for them alone; sometimes we even worked against them—not only because they were, in our view, being unreasonable in their attitudes to participation, but also because they were forcing us into a role that we were not prepared to occupy. Over time, our sympathies have (although not exclusively) moved to the lower levels of the Alpen hierarchy—the supervisors and the operatives—and surreptitiously we have worked to 'get something' for them in the form of various changes or concessions.

Although politically more astute, we are less cautious than before. We do not depend on Alpen for our salaries or research, and could put up with (or rationalize) the ignominy of ultimate rejection by them. We maintain a strong commitment to our consciences and individuality, and, unlike many of the people at Alpen (at even the most senior level), we continue to enjoy the luxury of being our 'own men'. Recent notions about fundamentally changing our approach to participation and our own role are a direct consequence of our being able to sit down and consider what we would like to see, and of not depending exclusively on Alpen as the testing ground.

As we said at the beginning of the final chapter, the Golden City of Participation remains a long way off. We are still firmly of the belief that, properly translated into action, that city holds the key to a solution of many of our present industrial relations and organizational problems. The notion of participation is sound. We shall continue to search for the city. Whether or not we—or far more important, the employees—find it at Alpen remains uncertain. We remain hopeful.

APPENDIX I

The design and implementation of processes of worker participation

S. P. Bate and I. L. Mangham (1975)

Part 1 of this paper gives a brief account of the current state of the participation debate in Britain. Part 2 suggests ways in which a range of appropriate strategies for participation might be identified and conceptualized. Part 3 focuses on the immediate need for national and industry-wide initiatives in change programmes relating to participation, and also considers some of the additional functions that national associations and institutions might have to assume as the programmes unfold. Finally, Part 4 looks at change programmes at the level of the enterprise, and discusses ways in which these might be related to national and industry-wide programmes.

1. Recent developments in the participation debate in Britain

Much of the impetus behind present discussions on the future status of worker participation can be traced to sources outside Britain. Nearly ten years ago the Governing Body of the International Labour Office was requested by its General Conference to 'undertake a study of the various methods currently used throughout the world to enable workers to participate in decisions within undertakings' (ILO, 1969, 1970). Several 'technical meetings' followed during the period 1967–69, and were attended by representatives from Britain and most other countries. Experiences were shared and information exchanged, albeit on a fairly superficial level. In 1967, the International Institute for Labour Studies, a specialist agency within ILO, was invited to establish an international comparative research project on participation at national, industrial and enterprise levels, and once again Britain was closely involved (IILS Bulletin nos 2, 5, 6, 7, 10, 12). By the early 1970s, the Technical Assistance Sector of the United Nations and the Organization for Economic Co-operation and Development (OECD) had also joined in the debate (OECD, 1972).

One cannot judge accurately the extent to which British thinking on participation has been influenced by these international developments, but there are some grounds for assuming that a good deal of present research and opinion has been prompted by them.

Certainly more recent developments on the European, or more precisely, the EEC front have had a considerable impact. On accession to the EEC in January 1973, Britain was asked to comment on proposals that had been put forward by the European Commission in September 1972 relating to the harmonization of participative practices and company law in member countries. A European joint stock company statute, containing 47 articles and running up to a length of 100 pages, had been proposed. In particular, views were sought on the 'Draft Fifth Directive' which referred to representative systems of participation at company board level being made obligatory in public limited liability companies with more than 500 employees. Alternatively, certain multinational and international companies opting voluntarily for status under new European law might be required to establish European works councils with powers of veto over a wide range of personnel and social issues (TUC, 1973, 1974; Balfour, 1973; IPM, 1971; Crighton, 1974).

Political parties, trade unions, and employers reacted immediately to these 'radical' proposals. British company law had always given supremacy to the annual shareholders' meeting, and there was no provision for separate supervisory and management boards, with employees represented on the former and exercising considerable influence on the latter. Britain was the only Western European country where works councils were not mandatory either by statute or by national agreement. British trade union structure and function, particularly at workplace level, differed greatly from the European model. In contrast with Europe, little previous attention had been given to the practicalities of introducing systems of worker participation into British industry. Whilst it was unlikely that the EEC 'blueprint' would take a precise obligatory legal form, the British commitment to harmonization had to be accepted, and the proposals carefully sifted and evaluated.

Some of the reactions and counter-proposals of various associations and agencies have been examined below (Industrial Society, 1974).

(1) *Conservative Party*   The Conservative Government reacted by asking the Commission on Industrial Relations to investigate participative practices of EEC member countries (CIR, 1974). It also promised a Green Paper on participation after consultation with the TUC and CBI. In fact, the Green Paper never saw the light of day and the CIR report appeared only after the Government had resigned in 1974.

Although the Conservative Party's proposals have never been definitive, there are clues as to the ways in which it might deal with the participation issue in future. Sections 56 and 57 of its 1971 Industrial Relations Act imposed a duty on the employer to disclose information for purposes of effective collective bargaining, and, in undertakings with more than 350 persons, to circularize annually a written financial statement to all employees. These particular sections were not to be enacted until the CIR had examined the question of information disclosure more fully, and, in the meantime, employers were urged to follow certain related principles that had been set out in the non-statutory Code of Industrial Relations Practice (Industrial Relations Act, 1971; CIR Practice, 1971). In September 1973, a Conservative Research Department paper reiterated the earlier proposals. A consistency of attitude over the past five years adds weight to the suggestion that a future Conservative

Government would give serious attention to questions of compulsory information disclosure.

On the question of joint supervisory boards, neither the research paper nor the 1974 Conservative Party Manifesto suggested that they be given a legal identity. Possibly, consultative employee councils would be made mandatory instead in large and medium sized firms, although considerable discretion would be maintained under the law: 'It is much too soon to be dogmatic about the exact form of participation in management. ... We want to leave the precise methods and procedures as flexible as possible' (Conservative Party Manifesto, 1974).

(2) *Labour Party* The present Labour Government has undertaken to introduce an Industrial Democracy Bill during 1975 or 1976. Its contents are not known, but again, certain clues have been given in various speeches and reports as to the form it might take. Perhaps, prior to the 1974 TUC Annual Congress, the Government had intended to introduce statutory supervisory and management boards on the lines proposed by the EEC. In a Green Paper on company law reform (May 1974) it had supported the principle of the two-tier boards and subsequently had incorporated this into plans for the extension of public ownership. However, in the light of a resolution at the 1974 TUC Congress in favour of voluntary two-tier boards it is now possible that a similar approach may be adopted by the Government. Generally it accepts the need for a 'legislative push' (Prentice, 1973) toward greater participation, but whether this takes a coercive or enabling form remains to be seen. What is certain is that any policy adopted on board level participation will conveniently disregard the warning of its 1967 working party on industrial democracy that 'it gives rise to a number of difficult problems and we cannot see it as a suitable starting point for the extension of industrial democracy' (Labour Party, 1967).

It does not support the Conservative Party proposal for statutory works councils on the grounds that these would infringe the principle of single-channel trade union representation.

To what other aspects of participation might the legislation apply? Firstly, it seems certain that employers will be obliged to disclose information on a wider range of issues than envisaged by the Conservatives. The Government has admitted that 'the wider question of disclosure of information about the company to individual employees is being considered as part of the Government's legislation on industrial democracy' (Employment Protection Bill, 1974), and its Industry Bill and the 1974 Health and Safety at Work Act already provide for compulsory information disclosure. Secondly, the concept of a 'national capital sharing scheme'—a workers' capital fund which would hold workers' shares in private firms and which would be financed by private employers—has been endorsed by the Executive of the Labour Party (*Guardian*, 1973). In fact, the scheme was conceived in the late 1960s as a possible means of enforcing a prices and incomes policy. It was argued that, if workers were given a share in industrial wealth, they might choose to co-operate in a policy of wage restraint. In view of the present economic situation and despite criticisms from the Left that such a scheme would shore up capitalism, capital sharing could well become mandatory in the near future.

(3) *Liberal Party* The Party has concurred with the TUC on the question of two-

tier boards. It has advocated fifty per cent employee representation on supervisory boards of firms employing more than 200 people, in place of the one-third in firms of more than 500 employees as recommended by the EEC Commission. Like the Conservative Party, it has also supported the idea of statutory works councils which would be obligatory in all firms regardless of size, and which would give employees rights of co-regulation with the management. Furthermore, the Liberals have long-established plans for a variety of profit-sharing and co-partnership schemes.

(4) *Trades Union Congress*   In the two years since its initial reactions to the EEC proposals, the TUC has apparently adopted a more flexible pragmatic attitude to participation. At the outset, the General Council had argued contrary to the EEC that representatives on supervisory boards should be nominated not by works councils but by local union and/or joint shop stewards' committees; that half of the seats on the boards should be allocated to union representatives and the other half to shareholder nominees and that the boards should become the supreme bodies of the enterprise having veto rights on appointments to management boards and decision-making powers on investments, mergers, takeovers, closures, redeployment issues, etc. This kind of representation would also be extended to nationalized boards, local government, and the hospital service. In the first instance, a two-tier board system would apply to all companies with more than 2000 workers but later the Minister would be able to extend its application to enterprises employing over 200 workers (TUC, 1973, 1974).

When a second report of the General Council was discussed at the 1974 Congress, divisions soon became clear. The 'moderate' General and Municipal Workers Union and the 'right-wing' Electricians and Plumbers Union petitioned for workers to have a choice on whether they wanted trade union elected worker-directors or some other form of industrial democracy. Certain 'left-wing' unions, notably the constructional section of the engineers, also argued against the Council Report—but for different reasons. They pointed out that supervisory board representation would divide loyalties, compromise unions' abilities to negotiate wages, and blur the lines of class conflict. Ultimately, a compromise resolution was adopted for the TUC to press for legislation that still gave workers some choice of participative system (*Times*, 1974; *Daily Telegraph*, 1974; *Financial Times*, 1974).

(5) *Confederation of British Industry*   In a 1973 report, the CBI made clear its opposition to the introduction of two-tier boards. Its central arguments were that conditions in European countries were very different from our own, and the position of shareholders would seriously be weakened. If harmonization with European industrial relations systems was considered worthwhile, it would have to be achieved through evolution not by legal coercion (CBI, 1973). Perhaps governments could take a lead in furthering workers' participation by drafting a code of practice and model rules for joint consultation. It offered support for the principle of extended participation particularly at workplace level, but opposed all forms of legal 'coercion', especially when this involved giving workers more than advisory powers in decision-making. The law could possibly play a supportive role in establishing company consultative councils, but the discretion of management as to the forms these would take should be retained.

Several recurrent themes emerge from this brief review. First, all parties and interests seem to be united in their support for 'more' participation. Second, a strong, reactive attitude to participation at board level has tended to exclude workplace practices from the debate. Third, everyone has agreed that collective bargaining should be retained in its present form. Fourth, each interest has stated *a priori* what system it wants or, at least, has stipulated a range of acceptable alternatives, of which most include a degree of legal intervention. Fifth, and somewhat paradoxically, everyone has advocated experimentation with different forms of participation at different levels, but no one has yet stipulated what form this experimentation should take, who should take it, and how its outcome might be related to changes already recommended. And sixth, although at an ideological level there is consensus on the need for participation, at a practical policy level there is, to say the least, considerable divergence of view.

Perhaps the most disturbing feature of these attitudes is their 'unitary' orientation, or, an assumption that a predetermined, semi-universalistic approach to change can be made from a national standpoint. In other words, a substantive framework for participation is likely to be imposed upon companies and, although there will be scope for variance in practice, this variance will be contained by prescribed and discernible boundaries. Legislation or national agreements for participation will therefore be based upon prior judgement, prejudices, or vested interests of influential parties and not upon the results of widespread experimentation and knowledge of the needs, aspirations, values, and expectations of people and groups within the British industrial relations system; nor, it seems, will there be any planned attempt to make change programmes contingent with the different needs of people or with the different environments in which they work. Evidence for this view is provided by the fact that, even before research has been undertaken, national associations and agencies hold strong beliefs concerning the direction of change, and assume that they are in a position both to set a course and to legitimately impose it upon the people they represent.

The implication here is not that national bodies should have no role in participation programmes or that all initiatives should come unprompted from enterprises. On the contrary, as we argue below, evidence of national concern is essential to the introduction and diffusion of change. It is not a question *whether* but of *how* they can be given a useful role to play for if national bodies were excluded then joint regulation would most likely remain fragmented both horizontally and vertically. However, if they were allowed to dictate the direction of change on substantive issues, their proposals could well fall upon barren ground or prove hopelessly inappropriate.

As a first step towards formation of alternative change strategies in the area of workers' participation we must seek to conceptualize some of the relevant issues.

2. Conceptualization of a change strategy for workers' participation

The strategic complexities involved in the initiation and implementation of effective participative systems have been noted but mainly avoided by politicians and practitioners. Dronkers (1973) has described the inertia often created by these complexities: 'A lull has been reached. We have got ourselves into a vicious circle: the need for participation comes up against the wall of complexity and collapses into a sense of powerlessness. This strengthens bureaucracy which in turn further reduces the possibility of participation.'

If we are talking about the design and implementation of *systems* of participation it does seem logical, as a first step, to examine whether the general concept is useful in the particular context of participation. We have tried below to illustrate how the concept might be used to make people aware of the major pitfalls of change strategies for participation, and to focus attention on ways of reducing the complexities to a manageable state. Some of the main properties of 'the systems approach' have been identified and their relevance to participation discussed.

(a) Openness

Although a system consists of interdependent parts operating as a recognizable bounded unit, it is always 'open' to influences lying outside it. If these influences are ignored—for example, when participation is being considered at plant level—then future stability and effectiveness may be placed in jeopardy. Unfortunately the initiators of change programmes often react to the difficulty of evaluating between and interpreting these influences by adopting a closed view of the programme's requirements (Baker, 1973). Many of the failed experiments on participation have also been attributed to the same view:

These experiments look at the micro level as if it is a closed system, but leave out the influence of the meso and macro level. ... However, it should be acknowledged that situational variables play a major role in the process of change. A model that does not explicitly recognise these factors undoubtedly will lead to disappointments (van Gils, 1973).

In Britain, for example, most of the informal procedures of joint regulation at workplace level came into existence in response to the needs of people *within* the plant, but totally disregarded situational influences and other needs in the wider context. For some time they were functional and stable, but later became increasingly 'out of joint' with national practices and procedures. Disintegration and fragmentation led to a dramatic increase in the number of unofficial disputes and serious wage drift and ultimately to external legal intervention.

This situation arose because few people acknowledged that rule-making systems could only be stable and effective if they were congruent with the needs of the people they were directly intended to serve *and* with the environment within which they operated: 'Any attempt to optimise for one without due regard to the other will lead to sub-optimal overall performance' (Emery, 1967). Because systems are interrelated and interdependent, there is always the danger (as the example shows) that one system may benefit at the expense of other systems, and create a 'zero-sum game' situation (Emery and Trist, 1965).

This first property of openness serves as a reminder that future policies for participation must take account of a wider range of needs and mediating influences.

In other words, the conception should be 'a multi-level one, involving industrial, regional, and national participation as well as local and firm-based participation' (Labour Party, 1967). It requires a holistic, wider view of the participation phenomenon.

(b) Congruency

Brief reference has already been made to the property of 'congruency' or 'fit' between participative systems and their 'environments'. To enlarge on this, it is necessary to distinguish between internal and external environments. Internal environments can be defined as the immediate, subjective conditions for effectiveness. For instance, at plant level, participation will only be 'effective' if it is congruent with the functional needs of individuals and groups within the plant ('needs' being used in the broadest sense to include personal values, expectations, orientations, aspirations, etc.). At the same time—and using the same example to define external environments—plant level processes of participation must seek congruence with norms, values, and interests in the wider context. If they do not achieve this, external forces may constrain or undermine their successful operation. Equally, the stability and effectiveness of industry-wide systems will be threatened if they are not congruent with the functional needs of the employers and trade unions (internal conditions), and with the needs, values, and interests of individuals and groups within companies and plants (the external conditions).

It follows that an 'optimal' system of participation will be one that, in fact, maximizes fulfilments of the many needs operating in the industrial relations arena. However, although in this pluralistic situation it may be possible to synchronize or accommodate some needs in a single participative system, it can be expected that certain other needs will actually be frustrated by it. Thus, to some extent, pluralism and integration must always be irreconcilable.

Generally speaking, people have tended to overlook the relevance of the two properties described to future participation programmes, and have instead adopted a so-called 'unitary', 'universalistic', or 'blueprint' approach to change. This has been founded on a belief that people and situations are 'constants' and that a single formula for participation would suffice. This belief has been prevalent among governments, employers, and trade unions in Britain and has been reflected in their support for 'one of the other' forms of worker participation. It has contrasted sharply with the 'pluralistic', 'relativistic', 'contingentistic', or 'particularistic' approach recommended by academics which assumes that people and situations are 'variables' and that an effective participative system must be one that is tailor-made to fit divergent requirements and situations.

Certainly, the evidence collected by ourselves and others (Bate, 1975) supports the second view that there is no single, consistently effective form of participation. And yet, belief in the universal panacea dies hard. Perhaps the reason for this lies in the close association between the first approach and the 'participation ideology'. Advocacy of a panacea can be a useful means of legitimizing one's actions and beliefs to oneself and to others, and a convenient way of avoiding the complexities and confusions of the issues involved.

What are the strategic implications of a contingency approach to workers' participation? Perhaps some brief extracts from its advocates' writings may well furnish an answer.

The theme of the first extract is that legal promotion of participation will only be successful in situations where legal intervention is accepted, expected, and valued. Drawing on the Indonesian failure with legislation on participation in the 1960s, a national observer has pointed out (somewhat prosaically) the need for a contingency approach. Promotion of participation can

be compared with the planting of—say—an apple or mango tree, two kinds of trees with very nice fruits; but if the apple tree is planted in a soil which is not responsive, then of course it cannot bear fruits as expected, and even if it is planted in a responsive and fertile soil, if the timing is not good—say for instance to plant an apple tree in a soil covered with snow—then again it will not grow properly as expected (Panggabean, 1969).

Commenting on international experiences with participation, the ILO has also warned against the imposition of a 'universal' programme: '... clearly no one formula or approach could satisfy the widest variety of conditions and customs at workshop level which are prevalent in various parts of the world' (ILO, 1969).

Empirical support for this view has been provided by Heller's investigations of managerial attitudes to participation in South American countries:

Clearly, it seemed that global advocacy of participatory methods was in conflict in some countries with prevailing values concerning interpersonal relations, the roles of older people, the role of the church, the father in his family, and so on. If they were to be effective, therefore, participatory techniques would have to be modified to meet the particular needs of different groups of managers (Heller, 1973).

Focusing attention on internal-environment contingency at plant level, M. R. van Gils has argued that it is essential to

acknowledge that people have different sources of orientations to work and different kinds of involvement in the organization. Participation experiments should explicitly recognise this and accordingly deal with it in the change strategy. Unfortunately many experiments are too exclusively based on preconceived ideas of how things ought to be, instead of recognising how things actually are (van Gils, 1973).

In Britain, criticisms have already been made of the unitary, semi-universalistic prescriptions of national associations and agencies. For example, Foy (1974) has warned that 'Participation must be planned, but not packaged. Each company is different. Each department is different. Each product is different. Each job is different. The form which participation takes must be tailored to suit all these facets of the organisation.'

Unfortunately, some critics have also implied that participation must come exclusively from the enterprise, and that national bodies should have little part to play in the overall plan (Rogaly, 1973). The critics have warned against two possible dangers of the unitary approach. Either it can lead to vague, unhelpful recommendations for change which are not 'tempered to the realities of the limitations and difficulties of participative methods' (Cowton, 1974), or to the imposition of precise, pre-conceived, and doctrinaire programmes which would give little scope for subsequent interpretation by others. For example, statutory provision for specific kinds of works council, supervisory board, or profit-sharing scheme would inevitably narrow the range of choice available to practitioners at the level of the enterprise.

The need to adopt a contingency/systems view of participation strategies has been expounded by M. P. Fogarty (1972):

'Each manager, union leader, and government official faces a unique set of problems of negotiation and co-operation in his own time and place. To match it he needs a system tailor-made to fit his case and to cover all aspects of it, each in its proper relationship to the system as a whole. It has to be a system, because joint relationships are a seamless web in which each part influences the rest and none can safely be taken in isolation from the rest. But it cannot be a system made up by simply plugging in standard components irrespective of their national and industrial environment, for the components available. ... are multi-purpose, and the service to be expected from each varies according to the context in which it is used. ... All levels of the network are important; one must never depart from the concept of the seamless web or leave a foothold for the hellish words either/or.'

Now, piecing together these extracts into a set of overall guide-lines for strategy formation in participation programmes, we are led to prescribe the following: participative systems must evolve from the needs, expectations, values, etc. of the prospective participants; because these are pluralistic and divergent, there will need to be many varieties of system; at the same time, because their effectiveness will be contingent upon external environments, some attempt will have to be made for integration and synchronization within the overall industrial relations framework; on the one hand, there must be a unitary commitment to the construction and maintenance of systems of participation, but, on the other hand, there must be adequate provision for working through conflicts and negotiating a basis for further co-operation.

(c) Equifinality

This principle asserts that there is no single, 'right' way of introducing participation, but that a 'right' way can be found in a variety of different approaches. This is, of course, closely related to the contingency principle which also stresses that different combinations of variables can lead to similar or different outcomes, and to the openness principle which prescribes that we take a wider, multi-dimensional view of possible change programmes.

(d) Entropy

This last principle is more relevant to participative systems once they have been established. Katz and Kahn (1969) have defined the 'entropic process':

To survive, open systems must move to arrest the entropic process; they must acquire negative entropy. The entropic process is a universal law of nature in which all forms of organization move toward disorganization or death. ... The open system ... by importing more energy from its environment than it expends, can store energy and can acquire negative entropy.

Social systems and sub-systems are never stable simply because their internal and external environments are always changing. If a participative process has been arrived at by negotiation, the parties involved will in varying degrees have compromised their original aspirations, and sub-optimized their potential rewards. Thus, for example, where there is variance in the locus and distribution of power between the bargaining parties subsequent to a collective agreement, or when a firm's technology or national and local product and labour markets change, there will be a tendency for the agreement to be seen as increasingly inappropriate, irrelevant, or 'inequitable' by certain of the parties, and become the focus for 'restorative' actions.

Systems theorists argue that the process of 'dynamic equilbrium' must be built into a change programme, with various adaptive mechanisms being used to review and up-date structures, thereby ensuring congruency with wider systems' changes. In introducing participative processes, one would therefore reject attempts to create a 'once-for-all-times' structure (for example, on the basis of a permanent, 'comprehensive' body of legislation) and instead focus on the construction of specialist mechanisms for monitoring and implementing required changes and for maintaining a degree of stability and continuity.

Unfortunately, as van Gils (1973) has noted, 'in many [participation] experiments even with good results one sees that the original situation is restored.' Below, we have outlined several steps that might be taken to reduce the risk of this happening. For example, resources for systems maintenance might be differentiated so that certain bodies would manifestly concern themselves with reviewing effectiveness and facilitating change. At a national level, a review body might integrate enterprisal and industrial systems of participation (by providing information, education, and training, and by initiating and diffusing experimental findings) and might recommend changes in the law and in the roles of interested bodies. At plant level, a 'steering committee' might initiate action experiments, deliberating on and feeding back their findings and implications. Although these review/maintenance bodies might be permanent, they, too, might be expected to modify and elaborate their own functions over time. However, their overall manifest function would remain constant—namely to divert their energies to the servicing of participative systems in order to stave off entropic forces.

Before looking at action on the national level let us look at the problems of effecting change at both the national and at the level of the enterprise since the two aspects are inextricably interrelated. The model of change is illustrated in Figure I.1 and described in the remaining sections of this paper.

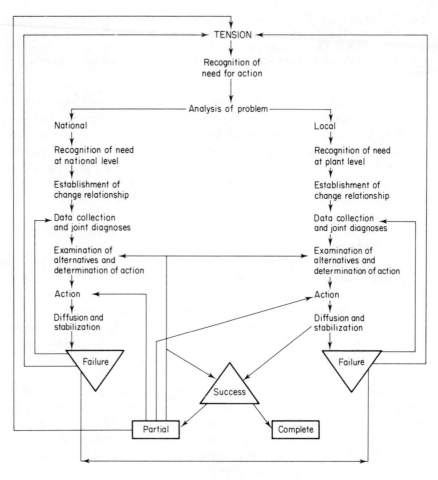

Figure I.1

3. Towards a national change strategy for workers' participation

This section deals with the roles that might be played by government agencies, legal institutions, labour market organizations, and other specialist bodies at national, industrial, and regional levels of the British industrial relations system regarding initiation, integration, and diffusion of change programmes for workers' participation. Additionally, it considers some of the ways in which these roles and functions might, themselves, have to change as the various programmes proceed.

Our discussion is based upon two assumptions. Firstly, it is assumed that all parties to the participation debate genuinely acknowledge that there is a problem to which participation is or may be an answer (partial or otherwise); in the jargon of the organization development experts, that there is a 'felt need'. The second assumption is that each of the parties is willing to negotiate change with neither seeing such negotiations as a negation of its positions. In other words, that each is willing to work within a co-operative framework rather than seeking to destroy the basis of co-operation.

With these two assumptions as background we can return to Figure I.1 and consider the national level (to the left of the diagram) in more detail. We suggest that intervention on the national level would look something like Figure I.2.

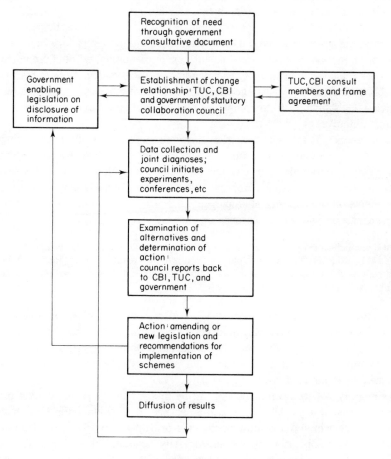

Figure I.2

(a) A consultative document on worker participation

This document would aim to reiterate government commitment to exploring the potentialities of workers' participation in Britain. It would be informative regarding definition of issues and practices and would contain draft procedures relating to various change programmes. It would warn against over-hasty political approaches to participation, and would, therefore, set aside any predisposition towards recommending particular institutional forms. It would emphasize the need for further experimentation with alternatives, and point out that, although pressure for change would come from a national level, the real initiatives on the nature and direction of change would come from an enterprisal level. Finally, in accordance with the policy of 'bounded flexibility', it would invite comments from interested parties.

In effect, we are suggesting that political parties put to one side their proposals for supervisory boards, capital-sharing schemes, statutory works councils and the like and admit to the need for more experimentation with a range of participative forms. However, the government would make clear its intention to introduce framework or enabling legislation in order to facilitate this experimentation, without prejudicing its outcomes. This would also apply to amending or ancillary legislation which would possibly be enacted at a later stage either to establish or diffuse successful changes, or to give a 'legislative push' to companies that had not responded in the spirit of the original initiative.

Experiences of foreign countries have supported this flexible/contingency approach to worker participation. For example, the Norwegian Industrial Democracy Programme which began in the 1960s with statutory provision for employee representation on company boards was a failure largely because it had little impact on the majority of employees, and provided no impetus for diffusion of experimentation with other participatory forms:

From the conclusions we note that it is difficult to see how real sharing of influence can be started at board level. If democratic participation is to be a reality, it seems inevitable that this must start at a level where most of the employees are both apt and willing to take part (Bernhardsen, 1969).

Perhaps the EEC Commission, TUC, and present Labour Government could usefully pay heed to the Norwegian experiences. At the same time, the Conservative Party would do well to note from the Finnish and Danish experience that statutory works councils imposed from 'above' can be entirely inappropriate to workplace industrial relations systems (SAF, 1972).

As Fogarty (1972) has pointed out, in the first instance a country must use the ideologies that it has. All of the parties in Britain (including the CBI) have an expressed belief in and a commitment to the principle of worker participation, but this basis for co-operation would immediately be undermined if the EEC Fifth Directive on certain other blueprints were adopted (e.g. a Conservative Government would alienate the TUC if it were to establish statutory works councils).

Furthermore, a preconceived unitary approach to participation at a national level would hardly be congruent with the 'external' environment of the British industrial relations system with its emphasis on voluntarism, industrial and workplace autonomy, and decentralized power. It will be recalled that the 1971 Industrial Relations Act foundered as a result of departure from these very same values, norms, and practices.

However, what we advocate should not be equated with national *laissez faire* policies for, as is shown below, governments and labour market organizations do have an important part to play in the overall participation programme.

(b) Government consultations with the TUC and CBI

From the outset, it is important that any 'contract' on worker participation should involve both employers and trade unions. If it does not, its fate could be the same as the recent TUC social contract on collective bargaining. Here, the government could play an important mediating role in bringing the two bodies together to negotiate a 'mutually acceptable basis for cooperation' (Fogarty, 1972). Possibly, as with Norway and Sweden, existing policy documents could form such a basis for discussion; and hopefully, agreement could be reached that, at the moment, precise participatory forms could not be prescribed.

(1) *A TUC–CBI collaborative agreement*   This too would be necessarily imprecise but would serve to consolidate the basis for co-operation. The overriding purpose of the agreement would be to identify the mutual objectives of the participative programme. This is important because, as K. C. Sethi (1973) has noted: 'Plurality of objective leads to plurality of interpretations which in turn lead to plurality of mechanics. Workable method of participation is directly dependent on what we conceive as the objectives of workers' participation.'

We envisage that three classes of objective could be identified and agreed upon: Firstly, the ethical objective to increase the freedom and dignity of working men (e.g. 'All human beings are born free and equal in dignity and rights. They are endowed with reason and conscience and should act towards one another in a spirit of brotherhood.'). Heller (1973) has called this the 'human relations' objective. Secondly, the politico-social objective to give the worker exactly the same political rights as any other citizen: 'The plain fact is that factories and concerns are not 'private only' institutions but social ones. It is no longer possible for the conduct of their business to be determined exclusively in the interests of an individual, or even of the grouping immediately affected' (Haferkamp, 1969). Thirdly, the economic objective would be to use participative methods to make the undertaking more efficient. This 'human resources' objective has been stated as follows: 'The approach to collaboration questions ... builds upon the principle that firms shall earn profits and carry on their business with maximum efficiency. The object is to create and maintain a competitive economy and thereby also contribute to good working conditions for the employees' (Graftström and Moreau, 1972).

Collaboration agreements are common practice in Scandinavian countries, and do seem to have been effective in the area of participation. However, they are only a start and do rely on other factors for their effectiveness. Parties to the agreements must also decide on a set of procedures and priorities for implementing participatory systems. For example, one hopes that the following statement would be included: 'The development of co-operation in [British] enterprises should be based on practical experiments of the type carried out by a Development Council which would provide the only way in which to shed light on the complicated processes involved in new forms of co-determination' (SAF, 1971). There is no reason why it should not be since all interested parties have advocated experimentation.

(2) *A statutory Collaboration Council*   This would comprise a Council of

employers', trade union, government, and academic representatives, a permanent secretariat, and a body of direct- and sub-contract research staff. It would be empowered to establish experiments in participation where it thought fit, to intervene with complete discretion or on request from any involved parties, and to administer education and training programmes for worker participation. It would be designated the permanent 'change agent' for participation and would be obliged to furnish their regular reports on its activities. If, for example, in the first instance the Council were required to make a general survey of practices and research needs, it would be required to report by a pre-arranged date.

The success of specialized committees and councils in mobilizing interest in and commitment to participation has been well proven. The Whitley Reconstruction Committee in Britain, the Masselin and Mathey Committee in France, the Aspengren Committee in Norway, the Verdam Committee in the Netherlands, and various other committees in Denmark, Finland, Sweden, Austria, and Ceylon have all played key roles in the development of programmes for participation.

However, their existence *per se* is no guarantee of success. In Finland, for example, the committee comprised only scientists and took three years to make an initial report. Consequently, its labour market organizations submitted their own reports and ultimately nullified the official committee report. Other committees have faltered as a result of their impermanence and unrepresentative/non-specialist members. Perhaps the Swedish Council for Collaboration Questions, the Norwegian Samarbeidsradet, and Danish Samarbejdsnaevnet have been comparatively more successful because of their permanence, representativeness, *and* specialist expertise (IPM, 1971; ILO, 1969; Bernhardsen, 1969; SAF, 1972).

The problem with temporary committees is that they are not in a position to monitor the results of experiments, and to diffuse them to a wider audience. They can play an important part in initiating research experiments but will be unable to prevent their being a one-off affair. Moreover, unless committees are pluralistic and representative there is certainly no guarantee that non-participants will comply with their recommendations. Although it is too early to be categorical, much of the recent success of the new Advisory Conciliation and Arbitration Service (ACAS) in Britain can possibly be attributed to the fact that its council includes government, employer, academic, and trade union representatives. Finally, if committees comprise solely political representatives, there is a danger that they will not be fully conversant with academic research on participation and with organizational development techniques. In Norway, for example, there seem to have been no regrets that the Oslo Work Research Institute has been involved in the Industrial Democracy Programme from the outset. (See also Qvale, 1970, 1973; Emery and Thorsrud, 1969; Thorsrud, 1974; Trist, 1974.)

The Council's initial functions might include: definition of the terms and issues of participation; a review of participative practices, formal and informal, in Britain and elsewhere; a report on desirable research priorities and procedures; and initiation of a small number of experiments on participation. In Sweden the Development Council reached the last stage three years after its inception, and acknowledged this with a statement entitled: 'The need for trial programmes experimenting with new forms for more profound industrial democracy'. This was subsequently detailed and agreed by TCO, LO, and SAF, and the Stockholm Institute for Social Research was commissioned to establish several experiments (Development Council, 1969).

Later, the Council might extend its functions to providing training courses in participation for managers, shop stewards, and employees, and arranging conferences, publicity, and publications. Most important, it would seek to co-ordinate and integrate national, industrial, regional, and enterprisal participative programmes. As a result of the Council's work orientations to participation would hopefully become less ideological and more practical although the ideological aspect would still be nurtured as the basis for 'co-operative negotiation'.

(3) *Enabling legislation for disclosure of information*   Undoubtedly, experiments on participation will fail unless essential information is given to participants. For example a local 'steering committee' on participation (similar to the one described below) could only function effectively if it were given details of company finance and social and personnel policies. Legislation similar to that proposed by the Conservatives could give a factual basis to negotiations for change and could still stipulate certain confidentiality rules: alternatively, the TUC's recommendations to the 1974 Congress could provide a similar basis for negotiation, and a means of involving the Advisory Conciliation and Arbitration Service in any disputes arising over information disclosure. The importance of information disclosure has been stressed at various international conferences of the ILO:

A number of participants stressed that information to workers was an indispensable prerequisite for the success of any system of workers' participation in decisions within undertakings. It was pointed out that it was not enough simply to transmit this information, which was sometimes of a very complex nature and—particularly as regards annual reports and balance sheets—might not always be easily understood by the workers concerned but that when transmitting the information management should be prepared to discuss the information with the workers or their representatives and the latter should be entitled to receive explanations or additional information (ILO, 1969).

(c) Experimentation programme for participation

Initially, the Council might commission only four or five experiments involving academic 'action' researchers. Target review dates would be set, and once the experiments were underway the Council would devote its attention to opinion formation and promotion of discussions on participation generally (Drenth, 1969). Choice of field sites would have been agreed by the Council in consultation with the enterprises involved (unions and employers). A good 'mix' of firms with different technologies and of different sizes might usefully have been aimed for.

Later, reports would be submitted to the Council for its consideration. Perhaps, at this stage, it would decide to recommend new legislation and further experimentation with different participative forms. Again, this would have to be agreed by the TUC, CBI, Government, trade unions, and employers. Roles of the programme's participants would also be reviewed, modified, and changed if necessary.

We believe that the programme outlined above is consonant with the conceptual principles enunciated in the previous section, and congruent with the 'internal' and 'external' requirements of the British system of industrial relations. Its intention is to evolve from an ideological basepoint of co-operation to a firmer basepoint of 'proven practice' by involving from the outset all parties with possibly divergent views and thus providing a system whereby cumulative agreements can be negotiated with government, academics, and a Joint Council acting as mediators. Essentially, this involves the national programme moving from a reactive to a proactive base.

4. Towards an enterprisal change strategy for worker participation

This final section examines the internal aspects of Figure I.1 and looks more closely at some of the substantive and procedural aspects of workplace experiments with participation (see right-hand side of the diagram). As with the previous section, its emphasis is on the roles that participants might usefully play, and on the ways their related activities might be logically associated with industrial and national developments.

In the first instance, only a small number of experiments would be undertaken. Their effectiveness would then be reviewed, and certain strategic changes made in the light of experience gained. This course of action was successfully followed by the Norwegians in the mid-1960s and, in a period of a few years, led to a diffusion of experimentation from four to more than thirty enterprises (Qvale, 1973).

What form would these experiments take, and how would one ensure congruence between them and their internal and external environments? Engelstad (1970) has noted that:

There is not yet any standard pattern as to how far a project can develop within a single company. In all cases there have been periods of conflict and stagnation lasting for as long as up to a few years. In some cases periods of bargaining, negotiations, information activities, etc., have led to the establishment of conditions to continue. ... In other cases resistance ... has been strong or top management's commitment and/or ability to handle the problems have been insufficient and all development has stopped.

However, although no precise experimental procedures can as yet be prescribed, there are certain lessons on general strategy to be drawn from the experiences of others. By way of a perspective, P. L. Dronkers (1972) has distinguished three possible strategies for change in relation to participation. The first involves the so-called 'missionary approach': a person is sent by his company to lectures, conferences, teach-ins, etc., on participation in the expectation that on his return he will use his experiences to make various organizational changes. Generally speaking, this approach has enjoyed little success because 'a person returning from a lecture or course is influenced for a time by what he has heard or learnt, but since nothing has changed "at home" he soon feels isolated with his new ideas.' The second alternative has been called the 'formal approach' and refers to the imposition from above of structural measures designed to change the organization through a series of 'response changes' (simply translated to mean the introduction of participation by non-participatory methods). This too, says Dronkers, has met with little success in the absence of negotiated consensus.

The third approach—the 'cybernetic' or 'process' approach—has been favoured by action researchers and organization development experts, and has been used with some success in participation experiments in Norway and the Netherlands:

By means of a process guidance system the process of change is closely followed and continuously adjusted. A kind of experiential situation emerges, in which various ways and means are used in an attempt to start a change process, which is kept under continuous supervision to see whether it is on the right lines. This again implies continuous adjustment, making it undesirable to formalise and fix matters too quickly (Dronkers, 1972).

Let us return to Figure I.1 and follow through the seven-stage process outlined with respect to change at the level of the enterprise. The process very clearly is the mirror image of that which would occur nationally (see Figure I.3).

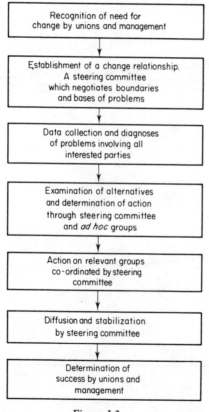

Figure I.3

The strategy illustrated above seeks to build upon the processes of change outlined by a number of experts who have effected organizational change. Much of the model has been tested and validated in fieldwork settings (Mangham, 1975).

Before analysing in detail the separate elements of the process outlined, it is perhaps in order to say a brief word about the role of the outsider, the researcher-consultant, who would act as a facilitator for the process. His presence is neither necessary nor sufficient, but many programmes in the implementation of change have found the use of someone external to the system to be of considerable benefit. This should be particularly the case with regard to participation and the negotiation of co-operation since, by its very history and evolution, the notion is fraught with insecurity, special pleading, and emotion.

The researcher-consultant can serve a number of roles, varying his behaviour and his input with each stage of the process (see Figure I.4).

	Role of consultant			
Steps in change process	Catalyst	Resource	Expert	Process
Recognitions of need	×			×
Establishment of change relationship		×		
Data collection and joint diagnosis			×	×
Examination of alternatives and determination of action				×
Action				×
Diffusion and stabilization				×
Evaluation—success or failure		×		

Figure I.4

In the early stages he can and, indeed, may need to act as a catalyst focusing the pressure for change; still later he may adopt an expert stance notably in methods of data collection and data processing. In his resource role he will use his skill to bring to bear relevant knowledge from within or without the system. His greatest utility, however, will probably be in his role as process consultant. Process consultancy is a method of consultancy which is designed to help the members of an organization perceive, understand, and take action to influence the way things happen in their organizations. It is concerned with style rather than content, music rather than words. Its focus is on individual, interpersonal, and intergroup levels of interaction and the events it takes as its concern occur at the level of human actions in the normal flow of work. In the change situation, for example, process consultancy would seek to make the members aware of how they diagnose problems, how they arrive at alternatives and plans for action. It seeks primarily to provide the client with some degree of 'insight' into what is happening beyond the content of a particular event. In building this capability for the members to do their own process analysis and consultancy, the researcher-consultant aims to work himself out of a job. The change process, utilizing as it does people who not only learn what to do but the consequences of certain styles of operation and who develop skills of handling this latter area, will become auto-catalytic (self-generating and capable of self-reinforcement). The need for external assistance is thus considerably reduced.

To return to our overall model. The overall aim of the programme at enterprise level is the negotiation of change, not the imposition of a formula. It is, therefore, important that throughout the process careful monitoring takes place of the extent that needs are being met and actions are being taken that are congruent both with the needs and the demands of the environment. This is best achieved by the provision of a formal monitoring process clearly and explicitly sanctioned by both unions and management. This implies that the process itself must be a joint union/management initiative. It is, indeed, important that the initiation of the programme at plant level is seen to be approved of by relevant, prestigious, and authoritative figures. As Dalton (1973) puts it: 'The persons being influenced need confidence that the change can, in fact, be effected, and a large part of the confidence comes initially from their confidence in the power and judgement of the influencing agent.'

A large part of this power and influence must rest with the Steering Committee. This group, charged with initiating, co-ordinating, and monitoring the change programme *must* include all who have the power to defend or destroy the project. Qvale (1973) reinforces this point when he indicates that the 'choice of partner for co-operation' should be determined by consideration of who would immediately harm the project (see also Mangham, 1975).

The Steering Committee is critical to the success of the venture and considerable time should be invested in helping it to work effectively (Mangham, 1975), particularly at the process level. That the time is well spent is evident. Much of the success of the second Norwegian experiment at Hunsfor Fabrikker (a paper mill) has been attributed to transfer of 'the experimental initiative to a local action committee inside the company' (Bernhardsen, 1969; Thorsrud and Emery, 1970). And in Great Britain, the incorporation of a 'Main Joint Working Party' for initiating change at the Mitcheldean plant of Rank Xerox was seen to have contributed significantly to the evolution of effective participatory systems (Peacock, 1972).

The Steering Group is primarily responsible for the transmission of information about the nature and state of the exercise in participation, the change project. One of the most effective communication devices is the briefing group where members of particular groups can be addressed by members of the Steering Group (workers, managers, and externals). At such meetings, the programme could be outlined and modified in the light of comments from those likely to be subjected to the procedures.

It could, for example, be explained that data about how the members perceived their roles, rights, and obligations were to be considered and that subsequently, working from these descriptions, participants would have the opportunity of declaring—with regard to specific work issues—where they saw themselves in terms of aspiration to participate, perceived ability to participate, and opportunity to do so.

This would represent the data-collection stage of the change process and would be complemented by a joint diagnosis by the Steering Committee working from profiles based on the data constructed by the researcher (Bate, 1975).

At a series of subsequent meetings, discussions would broaden out to consideration of potential participatory issues beyond those concerned with the immediate task and task environment. Further profiles summarizing the responses pictorially could be constructed and linked with qualitative data.

Depending upon the scope of the experiment, interviews would be held with all or a sample of personnel from the shop floor to senior management. For discussion purposes the data collection would be analysed against such variables as age, length of service, grade, work satisfaction, etc., and summarized in a report which would be submitted to the Steering Committee. It is anticipated that, by this stage, the project would have broadened out to include matters not directly associated with the issue of worker and employee participation.

Having considered the report, the committee would possibly request that additional information be collected before moving on to the next stage of the programme. Once satisfied, the committee would convene 'mixed' groups to consider some of the issues raised by the investigation and to generate alternative actions. Here, the consultants would feed in selected information as a stimulus to discussion rather than as statements of fact. One would expect to find changes of individual opinion at a different time and in a group situation.

The purpose of the groups would be to identify and clarify some of the problems relating to 'action' for participation (Heller, 1973; Dalkey and Helmer, 1963; Mandanis, 1968). With the profiles as an aid, they would, for example, consider some of the incongruencies between aspirations, perceived abilities, and perceived opportunities for participation, and would seek to locate the sources of these incongruencies (including both 'people' and 'things'). Throughout, the Steering Committee and consultants would provide additional information as and when required, seeking consensus on problems and priorities, and evaluating any conclusions that might have been reached. Once this stage of consensus had been reached, the consultants would summarize its bases, and circularize a report to the groups and Steering Committee. Even at this stage, they would have to be prepared to collect and analyse further data.

The groups would be encouraged to focus on and to be precise about the methods for implementing a change programme for participation. Again, consultants and the

Steering Committee would provide information and would be empowered to reject proposals (giving reasons).

As a basis for action, a report summarizing agreed recommendations would be circularized.

Action could be taken by the same groups, but perhaps it would be more desirable to change membership before implementing the proposals. At this stage the external researcher-consultant would be much less in evidence, having fulfilled his major purpose of facilitating the change. He may still, however, be called upon to help the action groups or advise on specific problems of implementation.

The final stages of evaluation, replication, and diffusion are part of the continuing process. To the extent that participation has been brought about successfully, the demand for participation may increase. If an organization's technical, political, economic, or cultural systems are changed to fulfil their participative aspirations it is more than likely that these many aspirations will become greater and 'the deficiency gap' thus wider. The cycle will thus need to continue.

For this reason, it is crucial that the Steering Committee be a permanent committee committed to regular review of the change programme. Perhaps, after a period of one or two years, it may choose, once again, to recall the consultants—or better still, to draw on its own resources—to repeat the experiment. If it does not, then it is likely that entropic forces may become the victors. Qvale (1973) has observed: '... initial changes in job design coupled with some training usually generate expectations and pressures for further changes. The hypothesis that it will be possible to start a continuous learning and change process departing from changes in the immediate job, has generally found confirmation.'

We have chosen to conclude this paper with a quotation from the same author which takes us back to a national level of analysis, and which emphasizes the mutual dependency between macro- and micro-change strategies. Change, he says:

will most likely not occur unless supported by parallel changes in other sectors of society, and they may still lead to considerable conflicts in society. Whether or not these conflicts may be resolved will to a large extent depend upon how employees and the two labour market organizations arrange their relations and use their political influence (Qvale, 1973).

It is only to be hoped that these bodies will choose to exercise political influence on the basis of informed opinion and research, and recognize that in the context of the design and implementation of participative processes, pluralistic and unitary frames of reference are not either/or but complementary and relevant constructs.

APPENDIX II

Employee participation and organizational change: a field experiment

S. P. Bate and I. L. Mangham (1976)

This paper is a report of a field experiment on the design and implementation of a system of participative decision-making in one of the chemical plants of a multinational pharmaceutical company, located on a site in the Midlands. The experiment, which began eighteen months ago and which is still continuing, forms part of a larger body of research currently being undertaken by some members of the Centre for Organizational Change and Development at the University of Bath, England. The paper examines the way in which a change in the level of employee participation was planned and executed. To this end, it has two related emphases, the first being the participation phenomenon itself, and the second the phenomenon of change.

The participation aspect of the project aims to provide information on two general issues which we feel have been inadequately covered by previous research and which are of academic and practical importance: firstly, the nature, extent, and variance of employee aspirations, perceived abilities, and perceived opportunities for personal participation in specific industrial decision-making processes, and the relationships and discrepancies between them; and, secondly, the factors which may mediate and account for such variance. The central purpose of the change aspect of the project is to develop, test, and refine a model of change for the implementation of processes/systems of participation. The relationship between these two aspects of the study has been symbiotic, with much of the participation data proving useful at different stages of the change process and, in fact, being treated as an implicit part of the change model. At the same time, useful data on the participation variables under study have been provided at several stages of the change process.

The chemical plant where this experiment is taking place occupies an isolated position on the site, away from the main factory comprising the capsule plant and such other departments as filling and finishing, laboratory and technical services, store and warehouses, and administration. Within the plant several kinds of chemical are manufactured in reaction vessels situated on each of the three floors of the modern building, and are dried, sieved, and packed on the ground floor. Although the process is highly automated, working conditions are unpleasant and dangerous. There are sixteen process operators working in four shift groups. Each of these has a supervisor and, during the day, three indirect service workers, a section head, and plant manager. Each group works four consecutive daytime shifts of twelve hours, followed by four days off, and then works four twelve-hour night shifts, and so on. Basic wages of the process operators are very high compared with other workers on the site and in the local labour market.

In addition to the twenty-five employees in the plant itself, a number of other people have also been involved in or affected by the experiment, namely the factory managing director, production director and personnel director, production manager, area manager, personnel manager, employee services manager, and a personnel manager. Even with these people included, it is obvious that this has been a very small-scale experiment and we make no claims as to its general application. However, as we shall describe, the implications have been a good deal larger and wider than the numbers involved might suggest, as indeed have been the problems.

The purpose of this paper is to trace in some detail the different stages of the project in which these people were involved, and to place our findings in the context of the literature on change and participation. To this end, Part 1 describes the conceptual perspectives and underlying value premises of the experiment, and Part 2 outlines the planned model of change that developed from these perspectives. In Part 3 we describe more fully the experimental procedures and the data-collection methods that were used. Part 4 discusses the main findings on the participation aspect of the project, and compares them with the results of previous research by the authors and others. Part 5 focuses on the change process itself, and describes the form and consequences of the data feedback, and the ways in which changes were negotiated. In the final section, we examine some of the theoretical and empirical issues raised by the experiment.

1. Conceptualization of a change strategy for participation

A pervasive theme in the organization change and development literature is the call for improved paradigms or models of the change process, and for a more explicit recognition of the value premises underlying these models (Golembiewski, 1972; Thomas and Bennis, 1972; Kochan and Dyer, 1976). The purposes of the first section of this paper are to develop this theme in the context of the design and implementation of systems of participative decision-making (PDM), and to outline the conceptual perspectives that formed the basis of the planned model of change (PMC) for the particular PDM experiment reported here.

The strategic complexities involved in the design and implementation of processes of employee participation might largely explain why, despite the popularity of the idea, there has been a paucity of genuine experimentation (Blumberg, 1968), a preference for alterations rather than alternatives (Bate, 1975), generally disappointing levels of accomplishment (Derber, 1970), and frequent restoration of the original situation (van Gils, 1973). As Dronkers (1973) has noted: 'A lull has been reached. We have got ourselves into a vicious circle. The need for participation comes up against a wall of complexity and collapses into a sense of powerlessness.

This strengthens bureaucracy which in turn further reduces the possibility of participation.'

Clearly, one way of breaking out of this circle might be to conceptualize, represent, and, to some extent, idealize the complexities in a model of the structure, function, and process of change. Such a model might conceivably aid the development of an overall perspective, and contribute to the organization and systematization of data, and to the generation of relevant questions and hypotheses (Ackoff, 1960, 1962; Fox, 1971).

With certain notable exceptions (e.g. Jaques, 1951; van Gorkum et al., 1969; Bragg and Andrews, 1973; Donaldson, 1975; Frank and Hackman, 1975), the literature on PDM—either because of reporting omissions or because explicit models were not used by the researchers—makes little specific reference to the various frameworks within which levels of participation were adjusted. Consequently, while there exists a good deal of valuable (and contradictory) evidence concerning the effects of increasing levels of involvement in a variety of organizational settings, there is little way either of identifying the distinguishing features of the successful and less successful experiments, or of evaluating the change models. In short, implementation of predictably effective systems (however defined) remains a hit-or-miss affair (Bate and Mangham, 1975).

This point is well illustrated in studies of the individual effects of participation. Some researchers have drawn attention to its positive effects in increasing employee satisfaction and creating favourable work attitudes (Shister and Reynolds, 1949; Wickert, 1951; Weschler et al., 1952; Morse and Reimer, 1956; Aiken and Hage, 1966; Lowin, 1968; Obradowicz et al., 1970; Scontrino, 1972; Siegel and Ruh, 1973; Waters and Roach, 1973; Lischeron and Wall, 1975a), while the results of other research have either shown the opposite to be true or have suggested that PDM has no measurable effect on participants' feelings towards their job (Pelz, 1952; Morse, 1953; Bennett, 1955; Patchen, 1965; Rus, 1970; Lischeron and Wall, 1975b). The dilemma here—and one which cannot be resolved by close scrutiny of the literature—is that by not being able to determine the direct and indirect mediating effects of the various models of change, one cannot identify the conditions in which they might be appropriate in future experiments.

The task, then, for researchers on participation should be explicitly to delineate the models that guide their work and thus open them to continual analysis and evaluation. It is with this objective in mind that we begin by describing our own value premises about organizational change and participation, followed by an account of how these were operationalized in a model of the various stages of a PDM experiment.

(1) Functional perspective

Our approach to both participation and planned change may be defined as 'contingentistic', 'relativistic', or 'particularistic'. It derives from what has become, during the past decade, an important strand of conventional wisdom on the subject of organizational design and behaviour, and goes by such names as open systems theory or contingency theory (e.g. Woodward, 1965; Katz and Kahn, 1966; Lawrence and Lorsch, 1967, 1969; Emery and Thorsrud, 1969; Lupton, 1971; Child, 1972, 1973; Baker, 1973; Dessler, 1976). Such theories advise a cautious, idiosyncratic, 'it-all-depends' approach to organizational design, and reject the view held by early 'classical' theorists and human relations writers that there are universal principles of good practice, and standard formulae of effectiveness which can be identified and applied in any situation. They are grounded in the assumption that people, things, events, and situations are neither independent nor constant, but interact and vary in a complexity of different ways to produce outcomes that are difficult to predict. Unlike the 'Lego-logic' (Mangham, 1974) which characterized early views on the management of organizations, the logic of contingency is 'its acknowledgement that the process of designing organization involves the selection of a configuration that will best suit that particular situation which prevails' (Child, 1973, p. 237), and not the mere plugging in of standard components.

The slow transition from the universal to the particularistic perspective has also been witnessed in the participation literature during recent years, although it cannot be said with any degree of certainty that it has yet gained a wide measure of acceptance. In an analytical sense, this has been reflected in a rejection of simple cause–effect relationships between participation and satisfaction and productivity, and a focus upon such conditioning variables as personality needs and value systems (Vroom, 1960; French et al., 1966; Tosi, 1970; White and Ruh, 1973; DeVries and Snyder, 1974), culture and demography (French et al., 1960; Cascio, 1974; Juralewicz, 1974), technology and organizational structure (Heller and Yukl, 1969; Thorsrud and Emery, 1969; Rus, 1970; Heller, 1971, 1973), and the nature and form of the PDM system itself (Patchen, 1970; Ritchie and Miles, 1970; Lischeron and Wall, 1975b).

Our own assumptions underlying the PDM experiment reported here can best be summarized in a quotation from M. P. Fogarty:

Each manager, union leader, and government official faces a unique set of problems in his own time and place. To match it he needs a system tailor-made to fit his case and to cover all aspects of it, each in its proper relationship to the system as a whole. It has to be a system because joint relationships are a seamless web in which each part influences the rest and none can be safely taken in isolation from the rest. But it cannot be a system made up simply by plugging in standard components irrespective of their national and industrial environment, for the components available ... are multi-purpose, and the service to be expected from each varies according to the context in which it is used. ... All levels of the network are important; one must never depart from the concept of the seamless web or leave a foothold for the hellish words either/or (Fogarty, 1972).

Unfortunately, acknowledgement of the importance of this perspective has not, of itself, generated much interest in questions relating to how a 'tailor-made' system might be created, and how it might affect the value premises, structure, and process of the change programme. Consequently, a wide gap has remained between prescription and operationalization of the contingency approach. With this in mind, we can outline briefly some of the levels and ways in which the approach affected our own model of change and the PDM experiment itself. Firstly, it was explained to the prospective participants that, although the issue of greater participation was under consideration, it would not necessarily prove to be either feasible or desirable in their circumstances. Indeed, an appropriate tailor-made system might be one that provided little or no participation for some groups of employees. Nevertheless—and this is a point dealt with more fully in the section dealing with the structural perspective—we emphasized that the *potential* for increasing organizational effectiveness and individual satisfaction was possibly greater under PDM conditions, and that it was therefore worth making a feasibility study.

Secondly, it was necessary once the experiment had been established to collect data that was relevant to the diagnosis and design stages of the change programme. In other words, in order to answer the central question, 'tailor-made to fit what?', certain information on the situational contingencies of the experiment needed to be collected. Here, the main emphasis of our research differed in important ways from traditional contingency approaches. Whereas these have dealt, by and large, with the 'external environment' (for example, with the constraining or facilitating effects of technology on levels of participation (Blauner, 1964; Indik, 1965; Rus, 1970)), our experiment turned to the individual level and focused upon participants' needs, aspirations, and expectations for greater personal influence in decision-making. Thus, whilst not denying the importance of broad environmental influence on consciousness and behaviour, we rejected the popular positivistic view that behaviour is determined by 'social forces', and gave greater stress to the subjective dimensions of behaviour. On the question of 'to fit what?', as later sections on the research methodology and change process will show, the overriding objective of the experiment was to derive a PDM system that was appropriate to the expressed needs of the people directly or indirectly involved; one that was appropriate to the subjective contingencies of the situation. This was our criterion of functional effectiveness.

(2) Structural perspective

Another strand of conventional wisdom which influenced our approach has appeared in a great deal of contemporary discussion and analysis of industrial relations. This has been referred to as the pluralist framework (Cyert and March, 1959; Clegg, 1960, 1975; Kornhauser, 1960; Polsby, 1963; Kerr, 1964; Fox, 1966, 1971, 1973). Its starting point is that organizations are, using Polsby's words, 'fractured into a congeries of hundreds of small interest groups, with incompletely overlapping memberships, widely differing power bases, and a multitude of techniques for exercising influence on decisions salient to them ...' (Polsby, 1963, p. 118). In this respect, it differs from a unitarist perspective such as that held by early human relations workers who described and prescribed a unified authority and loyalty structure for the enterprise, who assumed that managerial prerogative was willingly legitimized by its members, and asserted that common objectives and common values united and bound people together in a co-operative system. Pluralists, in contrast, stress that opposition is both natural and legitimate; that the stake-holders in the enterprise do hold divergent perspectives and aspirations; that 'management's power superiority is no longer sufficient to permit the luxury of imposed solutions' (Fox, 1973, p. 194); and, finally, that a mutually acceptable basis for collaboration—'antagonistic co-operation' (Simmel, 1955)—has to be arrived at and maintained by coalition-type bargaining and compromise.

At this stage some examples might usefully be given of the ways in which our approach was affected by the pluralist perspective. Perhaps most important was the decision to establish, from the outset, a steering group comprising those people who had a stake in the experiment, and who had the power to defend or destroy it. The main functions of this group were to negotiate mutually acceptable boundaries, stages, and methods of the project, and later jointly to diagnose and consider ways of working through changes on the basis of various data fed back by ourselves. The value of transferring the experimental initiative to such a group soon became evident. As previous research has shown (e.g. Bernhardsen, 1969; Qvale, 1973; Mangham, 1975), this pluralist structure aided the development of appropriate procedures, which themselves increase the likelihood of people identifying with and ultimately 'owning' any substantive changes that follow.

However, two important points must be stressed: firstly, the managers in the plant where the experiment took place were initially instructed by their head office to co-operate, and they had little choice in the matter. However, recognizing the dangers inherent in this unitary approach, we invested considerable time and effort in establishing with these managers a new pluralist base for the project, and in isolating it from outside interference. That this time was well spent became evident later when, despite a lack of support from the American parent company and some opposition from members of the board in London, unanimous if tentative support was given by the participants to continue and to extend the project to other parts of the plant. A second point is that only managers were involved in steering group meetings. In view of what has already been said about pluralism, this may appear somewhat surprising. However, had it been possible to establish a 'mixed' steering group of employee and management representatives from the outset, there would have been little need for either an experiment or a planned programme of change. In fact, the opinions of the workforce were taken into account at every stage of the project, the equivalent of the steering group being frequent group meetings with members of each of the four shifts, and individual meetings with operators and supervisors. Indeed, one could argue that there was less unitarism in the case of the workforce since, unlike that of management, its members were given (and some invoked) the right not to take part in the experiment. In effect, then, pluralism was operationalized in two sets of meetings, at which agreements on the procedures and, later, on the meanings of the data, were negotiated between group members. Subsequently, this intra-group negotiation was augmented by inter-group negotiation through ourselves as intermediaries, to secure agreement on a *basis* for face-to-face collaboration. This entailed securing agreement on an agenda and a general procedure, and deciding upon a time and place for the first joint meeting between representatives of the two groups. Obviously, once the PDM system had begun to operate, a pluralism of a different kind—no longer based simply on the original groupings—began to emerge.

Generally speaking, we believe that adoption of a pluralist perspective did enable us to plan a model of change that was congruent with the perceptions and felt needs of the stakeholders in the experiment. Both the substantive and procedural 'rules of the game' were arrived at by negotiation, and not unilaterally imposed either by ourselves or by anyone else. However, as we shall describe more fully later, we did make the mistake of failing to appreciate that a pluralistic situation comprised more than a 'management' and an 'operative' group, and that a somewhat different structure providing for the legitimate involvement of such 'men-in-the-middle' as foremen and section heads was needed.

(3) Process perspective

Much of the theory of pluralism reflects some of the disadvantages of beginning and ending with this perspective alone. The root of the problem lies in the pluralist assumption of bargaining parity between the parties, and a rough equality of skills between them, such that the outcome of the process is a 'golden mean' (Eldridge, 1973) or satisfactory compromise. As several writers (Pen, 1966; Miliband, 1969; Eldridge, 1973) have recently reminded us, industrial relations systems are characterized by an asymmetry of power and authority, where dominant individuals or coalitions enjoy a decisive and permanent advantage in the process of competition. To establish a pluralistic structure, such as the one described above, might be merely to institutionalize and reflect the inequalities of a situation in a process of pseudo-participation. As Allen has tersely observed, in collective bargaining 'employees with no power may get nothing. There is no automatic distribution based on a sense of fairness of equity. Shares have to be fought for, sometimes bitterly' (Allen, 1971). Furthermore, because collective bargaining is founded essentially upon power struggles and not on these 'consensus' criteria of equity, dignity, and fairness, or even upon understanding each other's point of view, and because its agreements rarely serve as principles of precedent for subsequent negotiations, any shift in the balance of power between the parties will mean that one or other of them may mobilize to improve on its previous gains or to minimize its previous losses. In brief, the pluralistic perspective may well become a self-fulfilling prophecy since the processes it may give rise to, while containing short term conflict, may perpetuate longer term conflicts. More seriously, there is a danger that participants in these processes may begin to perceive (and thus make) them permanently oppositional and meaningless. Cole has written that

this has led to the viewpoint that the best course is simply to mobilize for the inevitable economic struggles. Such an attitude cannot be concealed. It manifests itself plainly and is contagious; the result is that the difficult and delicate problems to which the parties must address themselves are approached in a spirit of futility and belligerence (Cole, 1963).

In this part of the paper we would like to develop the argument that in accepting the *structural* implications of the pluralist perspective, one does not have to embrace the inevitability of *processes* of competition, mistrust, and disjuncture. The processes that occur between parties in a pluralistic structure, we believe, are negotiated and, given certain conditions, negotiable. To illustrate this point, we need to outline, very briefly, our perspective on interaction and organization.

The perspective we are proposing is derived from a number of sources but its heaviest debt is to writers in the symbolic and strategic interactionist tradition (Mead, 1964; Blumer, 1965, 1969; Goffman, 1970; Eldridge, 1973; Mangham, 1975, 1977, 1978). From this perspective man is seen as uniquely self-aware, someone who defines, designates, evaluates, plans, and organizes his actions by way of a process of self-interaction. In other words, he is an object to himself, has conceptions of himself, and acts towards himself. As Blumer has noted, man's actions are not contingent upon the 'objective world' but determinant of it: 'The process of self-interaction puts the human being over against his world instead of merely in it, requires him to meet and handle his world through a defining process instead of merely responding to it and forces him to construct his action instead of merely releasing it' (Blumer, 1965, p. 536). Thus, put into a situation which he perceives requires some line of action from him, man will identify what he wants, establish an objective or goal, map out a prospective line of behaviour, note and interpret the actions and intentions of others, size up the situation, and so on—in short, he will construct his act.

An important point to be made here, and one which we will return to in discussion of the prescriptive implications of the perspective for PDM change programmes, is that these constructions will be based upon selective perceptions and experiences, and will not be right or wrong in any absolute sense. In fact, to the observer, and sometimes even to the person himself, these constructions might appear highly prejudiced and one-sided, lacking in balanced appraisal, and highly inappropriate to the situation. In other cases the person may be unaware of the nature, origins, and consequence of his perceptions since, over a period of time, and as a consequence of replication and repetition, they may move beyond the realm of introspection to become what Mangham (1974) has called 'world-taken-for-granted-perspectives'.

From this interactionist viewpoint, 'joint action' such as one might encounter in many PDM situations, can be characterized as a series of moves 'made in the light of one's thoughts about the other's thoughts about oneself' (Goffman, 1970), which are in some way fitted together. Each participant necessarily occupies a different position, ascribes meaning by interpreting and defining a web of symbols which surrounds him, and conveys indications to other participants as to how they should act. Blumer has traced how different individual acts come to fit together:

Their alignment does not occur through sheer mechanical juggling, as in the shaking of walnuts in a jar or through unwitting adaptation. Instead, the participants fit their acts together, first, by identifying the social act in which they are about to engage, and, second, by identifying each other's acts in forming the joint act. By identifying the social act or joint action the participant is able to orient himself. But even though this identification be made, the participants in the joint action that is being formed still find it necessary to interpret and define one another's ongoing data. They have to ascertain what the others are doing and plan to do and make indications to one another of what they do (Blumer, 1965).

The result of such interpretations, definitions, and acts is collective structure; cycles of behaviour are established between actors (or groups of actors). In Allport's terms:

there is a pluralistic situation in which in order for an individual (or class of individuals) to perform some act (or have some experience) that he 'desires' to perform (or for which he is 'set') it is necessary that *another* person (or persons) perform certain acts (either similar or different and complementary to his own). In this we have what can be called a fact of collective structure (Allport, 1962).

A series of cycles or patterns of behaviour are built up which gradually assume an automatic, taken-for-granted nature (Weick, 1969; Mangham, 1978). In the words of Strauss (1963) this is the 'negotiated order' and, as such, it can be an order which exists between individuals, between groups, or between large collectivities. It is a tacit temporary agreement about the 'meaning' of a situation or set of circumstances and the appropriate, complementary behaviour to be enacted within that situation or circumstance.

Meaning, as we noted above, does not reside outside the actor(s) in any situation, it is imported by the actor(s). Crucial to our model is the view that the participants in PDM will bring with them definitions and interpretations, predispositions and repertoires to create the environment to which they can respond. The PDM situation will constitute a flow of experience all of which will be *potentially* available for attention to all participants, but most of which will go unnoticed as the parties to the interaction seek to bring into play patterns, or cycles of behaviour with which they are familiar. In so doing, the workforce will ascribe 'meaning' to certain management actions, and the management will ascribe 'meaning' to the actions of the workers. The range of ascribed meaning may be wide and—since ascription is retrospective and influenced by attitudes in the here and now—variable (Weick, 1969). Seen in one light an action may be termed 'co-operative', in another 'antagonistic'. Not only therefore will the situation not be one of simple co-operation or conflict, as the unitarists and pluralists would have us believe, but it could be one marked by co-operation *and* conflict, domination, exploitation, consensus, indifference at different times.

For the remainder of this section we consider some of the implications of this perspective for the change process of PDM programmes. Firstly, it should be noted that pluralistic structures provide an arena for the negotiation of meaning between as many different definitions-of-the-situation as there are participants, but no guarantee that these can be fitted together to form a joint act nor that such acts will be stable. Secondly, in view of the fact that PDM may involve people who have not previously been required to define and interpret each other's 'symbolic communications' in a face-to-face situation, it might be expected that there will be difficulty in achieving any joint acts in the early stages, and considerable discomfort may be felt by these people. For example, in the present case the person appointed as Chairman of the Joint Participation Committee was the Site Managing Director, an American who had spent most of his working life in his native country. None of the worker representatives had spoken to him before, or knew very much about him. Their background and past experience were very different, as were their present circumstances. The interactionist perspective highlights the different definitions and world-pictures of these participants, and implies that joint change acts can only be brought about by a sharing of meaning, an understanding of (although not necessarily a sympathy for) other participants' definitions and interpretations of various people, events, acts, and situations, and the negotiation of new contingent meanings. In brief, this perspective suggests what the primary objective of the PDM change programme should be, and draws attention to the magnitude of the problem of achieving it. Furthermore, in doing these things, it also begins to define the role of the OD consultant, and to suggest how might facilitate the process of change:

If we want to know how order is sustained within an organization we must consider the organization as seen by its members; if we want to effect change, we must influence their definitions and bring about a re-construing, a re-negotiation of the world-taken-for-granted by the actors concerned. From this perspective, Organization Development becomes less a matter of values, feelings, and styles of management and much more a process of helping individuals and groups examine their definitions and processes of interaction in order to accelerate or facilitate changes (Mangham, 1975).

An important feature of the perspective adopted by the authors in the present study was to create circumstances in which the parties to the joint action could not only talk about substantive issues concerning their work and decision-making but also could become aware of the nature and processes of their interlocked behaviour and, once aware, choose either to change it or persist in it. Such an approach is built upon the premise that since order is socially constructed and socially sustained it must be capable of being socially transferred. 'Awareness is the key' (Mangham, 1970). As Berger (1963) notes: 'all revolutions begin in transformations of consciousness'. Once the social actor knows what he is doing and what is happening to him he is in a position to change things. In order to know what he is doing, to understand more fully the nature of the collective structure in which he is engaged, the actor must achieve some form of role-distance (Stebbins, 1969), disengagement (Mangham, 1977), or alienation (Mangham, 1970). Alienation in the sense that it is used theatrically by Brechtians illustrates clearly the concept we are addressing. Brecht's purpose in the theatre was to prevent the actors and audience getting carried away on a wave of emotionalism and was expressed very simply in his rejection of the word 'einbilden' (to imagine) in favour of the term 'abbilden' (to portray). The former implies involvement and lack of consciousness, the latter relative detachment and a degree of critical appraisal. The act of alienation creates conditions for portrayal by making the familiar strange:

We make something natural incomprehensible in a certain way, but only in order to make it all the more comprehensible afterwards. In order for something known to become perceived, it must cease to be ordinary: one must break with the habitual notion that the thing in question requires no elucidation (Brecht, 1940).

Alienation—the art of stepping or standing outside oneself—transforms one's awareness of own and other's behaviour in such a way that 'givenness becomes possibility' (Berger, 1963).

The *process* emphasis of the change programme, therefore, became one of helping the parties involved in the PDM situation become alienated, gain insight into the nature of their interaction—what was going on around individuals/groups, within them, and between them. In short, we sought at regular intervals to focus upon the processes of interaction, the cycles and patterns of behaviour, to enable the participants to question their own definitions, interpretations, and behaviours and to give them opportunity to re-define, consensually to validate alternative meanings and actions. In this way, we sought to bring about an understanding of patterns of conflict, aggression, and co-operation, and feelings of confusion and satisfaction as they occurred within the PDM arena. In short, we paid attention not only to *what* they participated in but also to *how* they participated and how they conceptualized their experiences.

In a later section on the change process, we shall examine the implications of this perspective in greater detail, and give some illustrations of the ways in which it impacted on the PDM experiment. However, by way of a conclusion to this particular section, it must be said that the process interactionist perspective differs from the one implied by pluralism, and suggests an important alternative approach to organizational change. As with the pluralist and contingency perspectives it is not new to itself, but integrated with these in a model of the process, structure, and function of PDM and change, it can arguably provide a view of OD and participation which is somewhat different from others currently available.

2. The change model

There have been many attempts to define a multi-stage model of planned change. Perhaps the earliest and the most succinct was that of Kurt Lewin (1946) who characterized change as occurring in three phases: unfreezing, moving, and refreezing. This three-step process, simple, clear, and bordering on the naive, has formed the basis for many subsequent models of change. Schein (1969), for example, later developed considerably many of Lewin's original ideas, examining more carefully the sub-processes involved within the three broad stages. Lippitt, Watson, and Westley (1958) also elaborated some of these ideas in a five-step process of organizational consultancy: development of a need for change, establishment of a change relationship, working towards change, generalization and stabilization of change, and achieving a terminal relationship.

More recent models of planned change, whilst still clearly influenced by the Lewin criteria, use the language of organization development and action research (French and Bell, 1973; Clark, 1972). Lawrence and Lorsch (1969) suggest a four-stage model: diagnosis, action planning, action implementation, and evaluation. Schein (1969) outlines seven stages: contact with the client, defining the relationship, selecting a setting and method of work, data gathering and diagnosis, intervention, reducing involvement, and termination.

Other writers have developed both descriptive and prescriptive models of change. Greiner (1966), for example, from a survey of several case studies of planned change, arrives at a model characterized by a strong emphasis upon pressure and intervention at the top: 'Until the ground under the top managers begins to shift, it seems unlikely that they will be sufficiently concerned to see the need for change both in themselves and in the rest of the organization' (Greiner, 1966). This emphasis is present in almost all available models of planned change (Argyris, 1970; Blake and Mouton, 1969; Golembiewski, 1972; Fink, Taddeo, and Beak, 1971). Also present is an emphasis upon participation within the change process, not only between the consultant and the client—an emphasis within the literature and practice of Organization Development which stresses that the consultant will do little *to* or *for* the members of the organization but a great deal *with* their active collaboration—but also a sharing of decision-making within the client system. In the cases studied by Greiner (1966), successful change attempts were marked by *shared* approaches where authority figures sought the participation of subordinates in making decisions about changes. Less successful cases were characterized by either a unilateral approach—order, decree, or re-structuring—or by a delegated approach.

The model we developed for use in this project drew upon the literature and the experience of the authors (see Figure II.1 below). Like many others, it was prescriptive and normative and, of course, was originally based on our view of the change process, but unlike them it was explicitly derived from a theoretical approach to the implementation of PDM (as outlined in the first part of the paper). The contingency aspect, for instance, was explicit in the data-collection stage, which focused on issues relevant to the participants and specific to their situation. The emphasis upon a pluralistic structure was evidenced in the bringing together of several groups with different perspectives and (in contrast with many change models) in the lesser emphasis on bringing about change exclusively from the top. The process orientation is less immediately obvious since Figure II.1 implies a rigidity and fixity which in practice was not the case. In fact, each stage was *negotiated* with the result that the parties concerned were not only involved in the change process, but also part-creators of it. The result was clearly a framework for the intervention process (i.e. implementing changes) and not one which sought to predict and explain the process of change itself. (The latter is currently the subject of an extensive research within the Centre for the Study of Organizational Change and Development and this experiment is a contribution in that direction.)

For the remainder of the section we shall briefly sketch in the first two stages in the model as they refer to the present experiment and in the later sections of the paper shall describe in some detail the remaining stages.

The model begins with the almost classic organization development stage: the recognition of the need for change—the theoretical rationale being that without the recognition of the need for change on the part of the client, planned change will not be forthcoming (Benne, Bennis, and Chin, 1969). The bald statement contains and obscures a number of issues: Who is the client? What are his expectations? How does he define the problem? When does he recognize the 'need'? In the present case the need to do something was determined for the factory by the headquarters management group in London. The factory management was informed that it had been 'selected' for the experiment and was 'invited' to co-operate with the action-researchers—an offer that was difficult for them to refuse. Our process orientation

244

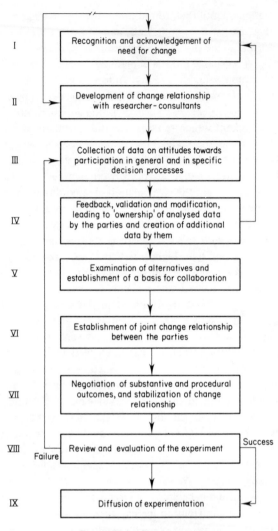

Figure II.1   The change model.

led us to examine this aspect of the problem with them but not to resolve it. The recognition of a need to do something on the part of the factory management came only after the data was collected, at which point they invested more in their relationship with ourselves and more in the collection of data. Again, in terms of our general theoretical perspective this is to be expected. Meaning is formed after behaviour, not before. The concepts around participation arose and were formulated as the project unfolded and could only make sense in the context of the project. There can be no 'felt need' for 'participation' in the abstract; the concept only takes on meaning in the concrete situation and becomes more meaningful as the participants experience it.

We identified our client as being the chemical plant and negotiated entry with management and men separately. Similarly, the development of the change relationship was a matter of separate negotiation with the interested parties, men, management, and supervision (although, as will be noted later, we tended to underestimate the importance of this group). This approach was in line with our views on pluralism and a recognition that for both management and men the issue of building different relationships was likely to be difficult. The relations that existed, the world-taken-for-granted view of each group, the automatic patterns of behaviour that subsisted between the groups would, we felt, be brought into play immediately if they were brought together too soon to discuss the proposed study and would thus prejudice any work. The change relationship, therefore, was explicitly built around ourselves coming between the parties. Our aim was (and is) to build trust not only between the management and men but also between ourselves and each of the groups. Many writers have claimed that trust is a key variable (Golembiewski and McConkie, 1975; Deutsch, 1973; Zand, 1972) and we invested considerable time in talking with each person at his place of work and at a time convenient to him (in some cases during the night shift) in order to develop trusting relationships. The purpose of so doing was not solely a desire to establish warm relationships with our clients; our theory of personal and organizational change, particularly in its process emphasis, stresses the importance of both confrontation and support (Mangham, 1978). In brief, we believe that changes in relationships are attempted when the parties concerned feel sufficient mutual support, sufficient mutual empathy to take some risks, to face some issues realistically and sharply. 'The burgeoning literature pounds home one major point: trust acts as a salient factor in determining the character of a huge range of relationships' (Golembiewski and McConkie, 1975).

Trust implies some degree of uncertainty, but also some degree of optimism; something is to be risked in the expectancy of gain. Our role was, and is, to be seen as non-partisan by all sides, to facilitate the development of more trusting relationships between the various parties by encouraging an exploration of the risks, real and fantasized, and the possible benefits of increasingly participative decisions.

The development of such a role formed a major part of the initial stages of the work. We actively sought to develop multiplex relationships with our clients, eating and drinking with them, talking about personal and social issues as well as about the project. Occasionally, as we shall discuss later, our role has been very academic and obscure to the other participants, but even at these times we have sought to be very aware of our own primary duty of facilitators and confidantes.

3. The Data-collection Methods

The data-collection stage of the experiment was designed to provide information which could be fed back to the parties and used as an aid in change negotiation (see Part 5), but which could also improve our understanding of the PDM phenomenon in a wider academic sense (see Part 4). Our main concern in designing the methods themselves was that they should be both relevant and specific to the chemical plant and to the employees involved, and not merely a repeat of previous research formats. As Lischeron and Wall (1975a) have rightly pointed out, employees will often have difficulty in expressing their views towards participation since it is a concept with which they are likely to be unfamiliar. Their task will be even more difficult if the decisions chosen for inclusion are not clearly relevant to the organization studied or are stated in general or abstract terms.

Our other concern was to avoid the assumptions either that people necessarily had an attitude towards participation or that it was fixed and relatively enduring. A two-stage procedure was designed to take account of these points:

(1) The derivation of items for an interview schedule

Firstly, the operators, supervisors, section head, and plant manager were given a preliminary interview and asked to describe in detail their rights and obligations with regard to what they did or could do, and what decisions they made or could make. The interviews were held with each person in turn and lasted from one to two hours. They began with an introduction along the following lines: 'As you know already, we are interested in your attitudes towards your job and various aspects of it. However, before we can decide which issues to focus upon, we need to know more about the job itself. We hope that while we are familiarizing ourselves with you and your job, you will also be able to familiarize yourself with us. Before we start, may we stress that we are particularly interested in the responsibility aspects of your job—that is, the discretion, judgement, decision-making power, or influence that you do or do not have—and the more detail you can give us on this the better it will be.' Initial discussions then took place around each person's job description, which had been made available to us by the Personnel Department. The aim was to discover whether the duties comprising the formal job description were, in fact, being performed by the designated person—if they were, then their precise nature was ascertained; if they were not, attempts were made to discover who was performing them and why. This was followed by a wider questioning on people's work rights and obligations, such as those pertaining to training, discipline and grievance procedures, remuneration, hours of work, holidays, sickness benefits, and so on.

As a result of this first stage, it was possible to build up a perceptual ('as I see it') and normative ('as it should be') map of activities and substantive and procedural decisions, reflecting various attributes of the roles of different levels of employees in the chemical plant. This map, as we explained later to members of the Steering Group, contained information on the potential sources, areas, and varieties of involvement. Firstly, with regard to the sources, employees might be involved in a number of duties: those which were part of their formal role description but which were, in fact, being performed by a superior or subordinate; those performed by their superiors as part of their formal roles; those which should have been but which were not being carried out by anyone; and those carried out by people in other departments but which directly concerned the Chemical Plant. Secondly, this involvement might take place in three areas of decision-making: the task performance (e.g. work speeds and methods); task environment (e.g. the physical conditions of the job); and task conditions (e.g. determining the contractual aspects of employment). Thirdly, that this involvement might take two forms: enlargement, where a person's job duties were extended with regard to doing rather than deciding, and participation, where a person's job duties were not necessarily extended, but where his personal influence on determining what they should be were increased.

Two other consequences of this introductory stage are worth mentioning briefly. In addition to identifying items for an interview schedule, we were also able to acquire a working knowledge of relevant technical and chemical processes, and to establish a working relationship with the plant personnel. Both of these proved valuable to the carrying out of our role of researcher-consultant at subsequent meetings of the Steering Committee and joint working party, since we were better able to understand the issues that were being discussed, and, thus, the behaviour and feelings of the people involved.

(2) The creation of data by interview

During the week that followed the familiarization period, a list of separate activity and decision items was drawn up by us and subdivided into twelve role 'zones' (mainly corresponding with the subheadings of people's job descriptions): *production and ancillary issues* included such activity items as 'drive fork-lift truck as and when required', 'check stock levels and stock records for variance', and 'take corrective action in the event of breakdown', and such decision items as 'the decision as to who shall drive fork-lift truck when required', 'the decision on procedures for handling solvents', and 'the decision on methods of labelling and coding drums and vessels'; *scheduling and manning* included both activity items (e.g. 'produce, review, and modify annual schedule in line with plant capacity'; 'prepare weekly production schedule and output targets'; 'prepare daily work schedule') and decision items (e.g. 'decision on moving men to another department'; 'decision on shift and manning levels'; 'decision on nature and extent of promotion opportunities'); *plant and equipment* referred to 'checking and identifying faulty equipment', 'raising capital requests for new or replacement items' and other activity items, and to decision items such as 'deciding on new plant or equipment; *quality* issues included 'establishing annual re-work targets', 'carrying out in-process analytical checks', and 'liaising with quality control' (all activity items), and such decision items as 'deciding on quality levels and criteria'; with the exception of the 'decision as to where budget cuts should be made', all of the other items under the heading *costs* related to activities (e.g. 'draw up raw materials budget for forthcoming year' and 'take action generally to reduce waste of time, material, and plant services'); the *safety* issues were also mainly activity related (e.g. 'review plant safety procedures', 'carry out daily safety checks', and 'read, publicise, and ensure compliance with statutory safety requirements') with one or two exceptions relating to decisions such as 'decision on and implementation of new safety procedures' and 'decision to purchase safety equipment for particular jobs'; activity items subsumed under *personnel and training* included 'test and select senior operators' and 'conduct appraisals', whereas decision items referred to 'decide when operator ready to take operator's test' and 'decide on implementation of disciplinary code'; *documentation* issues were all activity related (e.g. 'write manufacturing ticket', and 'keep effluent treatment log'; the remaining five areas, *remuneration* (e.g. 'decision on changes in pay methods', 'decision on pay grade for plant employees'), *hours of work* ('length of working week', 'shift starting times', 'length of rest periods', etc.), *holidays and leave, sickness and injury, pensions and life assurance benefits*, and *discipline and grievance procedures*—the personnel or contractual areas—referred exclusively to decision items.

There were, in total, sixty-three activity items and fifty-six decision items finally included in an interview schedule for the next stage, and although the distinction between them was sometimes slight, people were later asked to provide different kinds of information on each. However, before carrying out the interviews, we showed a draft of the schedule to members of the Steering Group and asked them for their opinions. What followed were some constructive comments on the phrasing and technical content of some of the items, and some less constructive comments on the dangers and illegitimacy of asking certain questions. Ironically, most anxieties were expressed at this time by members of the Personnel Department who, until then, had not been directly affected by the experiment but by virtue of their now being implicated by certain items became very protective towards their own traditional prerogatives. However, by adopting a position which required them to make a rational case for *not* including the item and by relying on the pressures wilfully brought to bear on them by the production managers, we were able to keep the original list intact.

Within the space of a few weeks we were able to return to the operators, supervisors, and section head, and begin the confidential interviews. Although these interviews followed a rigid procedure and mainly involved attitude scales, they did not exclude people from enlarging upon their answers or dealing with related issues in their conversations with us. However, in retrospect, we believe that much useful 'soft' data on people's attitudes to and perceptions of involvement was sacrificed to the more artificial 'hard' data yielded by the rating scales, and therefore in future we will give greater attention to designing interview schedules better suited to respondents' own response categories.

The following instruction and scale was given for the activity items:

Here is a card with a one to five scale on it which corresponds to various attitudes you may have towards different aspects of your work. What I shall do is read out and describe to you a list of work activities which you may or may not be performing at present, and I would like you to choose a number on the scale which corresponds to the way you feel about either continuing with or performing each activity in the future. Your choice should be determined as far as possible by consideration of your ideal and should not be limited by feelings of inability or lack of opportunity to carry it out. Is that clear? For example, how much would you like to be able to drive or continue driving the fork-lift truck ...?

1	2	3	4	5
Would not like to at all	Would not much like to	Not bothered one way or the other	Would quite like to	Would like to very much indeed

The penultimate sentence, asking that the rating be based as far as possible on consideration of the ideal situation, was included to minimize the so-called anchoring effects of perceived 'givens' such as ability and opportunity. Obviously, as change agents, we were assuming that perceptions of personal capability nor environmental opportunity were not given and unchangeable but could conceivably be affected by training and organizational re-structuring schemes of various kinds, but we had to be sure that the respondents also recognized this. Although we realized that it was impossible for people to wholly disregard their present situation, we were still concerned to gain some measure of the ways in which aspects of the organizational structure might be better accommodated with people's desires, and not they to it. From this part of the interview information was collected on the level and variance of respondents' desires for job enlargement or contraction. For example, Table II.1 below provides an illustration of the analysis of responses on activity items in just one of the twelve role zones (i.e. production and ancillary, chemical operators only), which in fact comprises part of the portfolio of statistics that was fed back to the Steering Committee. The vertical lines in the centre of each box denote the mean ratings given for each activity item on the five-point scale, and the boxes themselves indicate the spread of responses: the vertical lines at each end are situated at a distance of one standard deviation away from the mean, so that for each factor approximately two-thirds of the total response lie within the box. More will be said about the results themselves in the next section.

Three separate aspects of the *decision* items were investigated, namely the respondents' aspiration, perceived ability, and perceived opportunity for participation. For these the following instructions were given:

Here is a different card with a one to five scale on it which corresponds to differing degrees of influence that employees can have on various decisions associated with their jobs and work in general. Again, what I shall do is read out and, if necessary, describe to you a list of decisions which you personally may or may not be making at the moment, and using the scale I would like you for each decision to

(i) choose a number which corresponds to the amount of influence you would *ideally* like to have—regardless of your present abilities and opportunities—upon the making of this decision in future;

(ii) (having done this) choose a number which corresponds to the amount of influence you *think* your present personal abilities might limit you to with regard to the making of this decision;

(iii) (having done this) choose a number which corresponds to the amount of personal influence you are presently allowed to have on the making of this decision.

1	2	3	4	5
No influence at all	A little influence, i.e. complaining, advising, or making suggestions	As much influence as the person who makes this decision at the moment	A little more influence than the present decision-maker	Absolute personal control over making the decision

Similar profiles were also constructed from the data to depict the level and

Table II.1 Activity items, production and ancillary (chemical operators $N=11$)

'How much would you like to be able to . . . ?'

	1	2	3	4	5

Drive fork-lift truck as and when required

Unload lorries, and receive goods and raw materials

Transport finished goods to chemical store

Check stock levels and stock records for variance

Arrange purchase of raw materials and supplies, and ensure availability

Control effluent treatment

Control demin. water plant

Maintain the quality of cooling brine and check daily

Be involved in the cleaning up and good housekeeping in Chemical Plant and yard area

Sign and check 'key points' on manufacturing ticket

Check accuracy of manufacturing ticket and sign before job started

Check that manufacturing ticket has been signed by operator after completion of task

Experiment with different settings on new machinery

Take corrective action in event of breakdown, departures from schedule/ticket, etc.

Liaise with members of other shifts

Take samples for intermediate product checks

Establish and monitor research projects/experiments

All production and ancillary items

1 = Would not like to at all;   3 = Not bothered one way or the other;   5 = Would like to very much indeed.
2 = Would not much like to;   4 = Would quite like to;

variance of people's desires, perceived abilities, and perceived opportunities for participation. More will be said about the results themselves and the variables in question in the next part of this paper. However, it might be useful to mention at this stage that that two additional kinds of profile were constructed from data on the decision variables: firstly an 'intellectual deficiency' profile based upon the discrepancy between aspirations and perceived abilities for participation in particular decisions or decision zones, and secondly an 'environmental deficiency' profile based upon the discrepancies between aspirations and perceived opportunities for participation. Unlike previous research with deficiency scores the present scores were equated not with satisfaction levels but with a concept which we called 'potential satisfaction', which we defined as the extent to which increased capabilities and opportunities for participation in decision-making could lead to possibly already satisfied people being more satisfied. This concept is examined in detail in Part 4.

The interviews with the section head, supervisors, and operators lasted approximately one and a half hours per person, but during this time additional questions were asked about levels of job satisfaction and other measures of group cohesion and tolerance for ambiguity were taken. At the end of each interview, we explained that we would return in approximately two months with a summary of each individual's responses.

4. Some preliminary data on participation and its correlates

It was mentioned in the introduction to this paper that although the chemical plant experiment was primarily concerned with the design and implementation of a PDM system, it was also undertaken as part of a wider programme of research into other aspects of the participation phenomenon. They include (1) the nature, extent, and variance of employee aspirations, perceived abilities, and perceived opportunities for personal participation in specific decision-making areas and processes; (2) the role of differences between individuals (biographic and psychological) and structural differences within the PDM situation itself in mediating the effects of participation; (3) the relationship between attitudes towards participation and job satisfaction. The aim of this section is to present some preliminary findings from the experiment concerning these three areas. Discussion will be confined to the eleven process operators who took part in the interviews, and, because of the small numbers involved, will not concern itself with arguments about the generalizability of the findings or with demonstrations of their statistical significance. However, we intend to examine the responses of both operators and supervisors in more detail in a future paper, and to compare them with the findings of other research currently being conducted within the Centre. For the moment, we shall confine ourselves to an illustration of one approach to the study of the nature, correlates, and effects of PDM.

(1) Attitudes towards participation

Because of either a paucity of research or inconsistencies between findings, the present state of knowledge does not give a definitive answer to the fundamental

Table II.2 Operators' desires to participate in certain decision-making areas*

'How much influence you would ideally like to have?'

		1	2	3	4	5

Decision zone

Production and ancillary (9) †

Scheduling and manning (7)

Plant and equipment (1)

Cost (1)

Safety (2)

Personnel and training (4)

Remuneration (7)

Discipline and grievance (5)

Hours of work (7)

Sickness benefits, etc. (5)

Holidays and leave (8)

1 = No influence at all;

2 = A little influence, i.e. complaining, advising, or making suggestions;

3 = As much influence as the person who makes this decision at the moment;

4 = A little more influence than the present decision-maker;

5 = Absolute personal control over making the decision.

* N=11.

† Figures in brackets indicate number of items within each decision zone.

Table II.3 Operators' perceived abilites to participate in certain decision-making areas*

'How much influence your personal abilities might limit you to?'

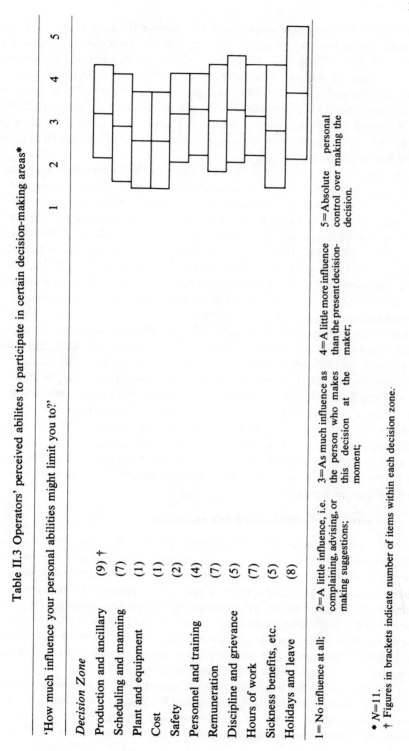

Decision Zone		1	2	3	4	5
Production and ancillary	(9) †					
Scheduling and manning	(7)					
Plant and equipment	(1)					
Cost	(1)					
Safety	(2)					
Personnel and training	(4)					
Remuneration	(7)					
Discipline and grievance	(5)					
Hours of work	(7)					
Sickness benefits, etc.	(5)					
Holidays and leave	(8)					

1 = No influence at all;

2 = A little influence, i.e. complaining, advising, or making suggestions;

3 = As much influence as the person who makes this decision at the moment;

4 = A little more influence than the present decision-maker;

5 = Absolute personal control over making the decision.

* N=11.
† Figures in brackets indicate number of items within each decision zone.

questions of to what extent employees want, perceive themselves capable of, and consider themselves as having the opportunity for participation (Strauss and Rosenstein, 1970; Clarke *et al.*, 1972; Bate, 1975). Tables II.1, II.2, and II.3 consider these questions in relation to the nature of the chemical plant operators' attitudes towards participation in eleven different areas of decison-making. Mean ratings on each results profile are represented by the vertical lines in the centre of each box, while vertical lines at each end are situated at a distance of one standard deviation from the mean (so that for each factor approximately two-thirds of the total response lie within the box).

As Table II.2 shows, in all of the decision-making areas the operators express only a moderate desire for participation ('as much influence as the person who makes this decision at the moment'), and although their responses vary by up to two points on the scale, none reflects a wish for 'workers control'. Similar evidence of a moderate and generalized desire for participation has been presented by Whitehill and Takezawa (1968), Rus (1970), Hespe and Warr (1971), and Lischeron and Wall (1975*a*, *b*); but the findings differ from those presented by Bate (1975, 1976), which suggested somewhat higher aspirations among another sample of manual workers.

Table II.3 shows that levels of perceived ability are of a similar magnitude to desires for participation. However, the degree of variance between respondents is less while the variance between average ratings on different decision areas is slightly greater in this profile. This table (and a correlation shown on Table II.5) suggest that perceptions of self-ability might be important determinants of desires for participation, but unfortunately little evidence exists elsewhere to support this.

As Table II.4 shows, most of the operators feel that they have no influence at all on any area of decision-making—even on such immediate task-environment and task-performance issues as production, scheduling, and manning. The consensus is particularly striking on the personal issues, and clearly highlights the fact that the 'human relations' orientation that one might expect to be prevalent among many personnel specialists in no way commits them to actually involving employees in their own decision-making activities.

(2) Some correlates of attitudes towards participation

Table II.5 presents the correlations between attitudes to participation and certain other measures taken. Contrary to our expectations, desires for participation were not found to be any higher among the younger, shorter-serving employees, or among those with a higher school leaving age. Age and school leaving age were also found to be unrelated to perceived abilities for participation, although there was some evidence that higher self-competence ratings were given by the longer serving employees. However, age and length of service are related to perceived participation, the first negatively, the second positively. Furthermore, those who left school later also tend to have higher levels of perceived participation.

A negative relationship was found between desired influence and job satisfaction, and in this respect is identical to Lischeron and Wall's conclusion that 'those who express the strongest desire for participation are also the least satisfied. The implication is that the relative dissatisfaction of those who desire greater involvement

Table II.4 Operators' perceived opportunities to participate in certain decision-making areas*

'How much influence your personal abilities might limit you to?'

Decision Zone		1	2	3	4	5
Production and ancillary	(9) †					
Scheduling and manning	(7)					
Plant and equipment	(1)					
Cost	(1)					
Safety	(2)					
Personnel and training	(4)					
Remuneration	(7)					
Discipline and grievance	(5)					
Hours of work	(7)					
Sickness benefits, etc.	(5)					
Holidays and leave	(8)					

1 = No influence at all;

2 = A little influence, i.e. complaining, advising, or making suggestions;

3 = As much influence as the person who makes this decision at the moment;

4 = A little more influence than the present decision-maker;

5 = Absolute personal control over making the decision.

* N=11.

† Figures in brackets indicate number of items within each decision zone.

Table II.5 Product-moment correlations between measures of participation and job satisfaction, tolerance of ambiguity, and biographic factors*

Aspirations of participation	
Perceived abilities for participation	+0·82
Perceived Opportunities for participation	−0·19
Overall job satisfaction	−0·46
Tolerance of ambiguity	+0·26
Age	−0·08
Length of service	−0·05
School leaving age	+0·02
Perceived abilities for participation	
Perceived opportunities for participation	+0·13
Overall job satisfaction	−0·32
Tolerance of ambiguity	+0·16
Age	+0·01
Length of service	+0·36
School leaving age	+0·15
Perceived opportunities for participation	
Overall job satisfaction	+0·40
Tolerance of ambiguity	+0·20
Age	−0·44
Length of service	+0·70
School leaving age	+0·30

* $N=11$

is in part a function of the lack of fulfilment of their participatory desires' (Lischeron and Wall, 1975a). Similarly, perceived abilities and perceived opportunities for participation are related to job satisfaction, the first negatively and the second positively. Taken together, the preliminary findings of this confirm the view expressed elsewhere by one of the authors that perceived opportunities and abilities, and desired participation, may be relevant and important dimensions of job satisfaction (Bate, 1975, 1976). Whilst the high correlation between aspirations and perceived abilities suggests that they could be related to job satisfaction through each other, the low correlations with perceived opportunities suggest that this latter variable is a separate determinant of job satisfaction.

Previous research by Vroom (1960), French, Kay, and Meyer (1966), Tosi (1970), and DeVries and Snyder (1974) shows that personality factors can have an important mediating effect on employee attitudes to participation. The results in Table II.5 refer to one such factor, 'tolerance of ambiguity' (defined by Budner (1962) as the tendency to perceive ambiguous situations as desirable). It has been suggested by Juralewicz (1974) that persons with a high tolerance for ambiguity might be more satisfied with situations that permit PDM than persons with a low tolerance for ambiguity. Although his research failed to confirm the hypothesis, we decided to investigate whether this trait could affect desires, perceived opportunities, and perceived abilities for participation. The results do in fact confirm that people with a high tolerance of ambiguity express greater desires for participation, and to a lesser extent perceive a greater ability and opportunity for participating.

In conclusion to this subsection it can be noted that each of the three main study variables relates to job satisfaction and in every case the relationships are mediated by one or a combination of the biographic or personality characteristics of the respondents.

(3) Participation and satisfaction potential

A more contentious area of the present research deals with a measure of the 'satisfaction potential' of PDM situations. The aim in developing this measure has been to provide something of greater practical utility than the traditional measures of satisfaction—something which, by being indirect and stressing the 'ideal' response, minimizes the contaminating effect of the 'socially desirable response', provides information on the scope and areas for increasing satisfactions (and therefore clues as to the priorities of the change programme), and evokes responses that are initially based upon the assumption made by the respondents that a situation is not necessarily given and unchangeable.

The concept of 'potential' or 'latent' satisfaction has its origins in a proposition forwarded by expectancy theorists (e.g. Tolman, 1932; Lewin, 1938; Porter, 1961, 1962, 1963; Porter and Lawler 1965, 1968; Haire *et al.*, 1966; Lawler and Hall, 1970; Carpenter, 1971; Shepard, 1973) that satisfaction is a product of cognitive comparisons between expectations and perceived existing fulfilment $(E - PF)$, and that dissatisfaction can therefore be represented as the 'deficiency' between these two factors. Although the measure used for this piece of participation research incorporates the idea of deficiency, it differs from expectancy theory in two fundamental respects. Firstly, deficiency is in no way equated with dissatisfaction. Secondly, it is defined somewhat differently, to take into account the discrepancy between what a person would ideally like (as opposed to what he thinks should be) and what he thinks he has at present, *and* in addition, the discrepancy between what he would ideally like and what he thinks he is personally capable of achieving. A more detailed outline of the reasoning behind this can be presented as follows: that a state of 'optimal' satisfaction will be experienced when personal aspirations (A) are perceived to be completely fulfilled. (Although the individual's aspirations are unfulfilled he will not necessarily be dissatisfied since, if his needs and expectations are to some extent fulfilled, he may derive satisfactions of a lower order.) The term 'deficiency' can be used to represent the difference between aspirations and perceived existing levels of fulfilment. It may be equated with 'latent', 'potential', or 'suboptimal' satisfaction but in no way whatever should it be regarded as synonymous with dissatisfaction. Two different kinds of obstacle may prevent fulfilment of a person's needs, expectations, and/or aspirations: the first may emanate from a conception and assessment of his own abilities and skills ('perceived abilities' = PA); and the second—logically separable from the first—may be derived from a conception and assessment of the potential of the 'external' environment to fulfil his needs/expectations/aspirations ('perceived opportunities' = PO). If these variables are shown to be independent of one another (as indeed is the case of the present study where the correlation between PA and PO is only $+0.13$—see Table II.5) they can be treated as two separate dimensions of 'potential satisfaction'. The same two sources of constraints may give rise to two independent deficiencies— firstly the 'intellectual deficiency' (ID) defined as the difference between perceived abilities and aspirations (PA–A), and secondly the 'environmental deficiency' (ED) defined as the difference between perceived opportunities and aspirations (PO–A). The final aspect of the argument has a practical implication for experiments such as the one reported here: by removing constraints and thus making good the deficiencies, we have reasoned that it should be possible to increase satisfaction.

Table II.6 below presents the results of applying the measure in the Chemical Plant experiment, and shows how such data as these were presented to members of the Management Steering Group. Working from left to right, columns one, two, and three are merely the numerical equivalents of the profiles already included in this section. Columns four and five show the intellectual and environmental deficiencies, and these are also presented in the profiles on the right-hand side of the table. The results clearly show that the scope for increasing satisfaction levels is considerably greater with regard to the environmental (rather than intellectual) aspects of the environmental situation. Perhaps it therefore has greater implications for the production and design functions of the organization than for the education and training functions provided by a personnel department. However, in so far as the environmental satisfaction potential is greatest in the personnel issues, it could be argued that the personnel department might be very much involved in increasing satisfaction levels by permitting greater worker participation in its own decision-making activities.

In the next section we shall describe the ways in which data of the kind presented here were fed back to the parties in the change experiment. We shall in fact illustrate how it achieved the objective of providing information on the participation phenomenon, but did not achieve its other objective of facilitating the implementation of an effective PDM system.

5. Data feedback and the negotiation of change

An important question to be addressed in any programme of planned change is: 'Who's problem is this anyway?' A secondary but important question is: 'Who wants to do anything about the issue?' (Schein, 1969; Beckhard, 1969; Bennis, 1969; Argyris, 1970; Golembiewski, 1972). Put in other terms, no change will be forthcoming if there is no ownership of the problem and no commitment to do anything about it *within* the system (Greiner, 1966; Dalton, 1969).

In the present study the pressure to experiment initially came from outside the system and whatever tension occurred was a result of this pressure rather than a factor associated with participation or lack of it. Participation was not an issue in the plant, nor the factory; internal pressure to change practices and procedures was minimal. In this circumstance, our intervention by way of meetings with both the management and the men and our data collection was catalytic. We served to focus

Table II.6 Attitudes towards participation and 'intellectual and environmental' deficiencies in 'satisfaction' levels (as defined)*

Decision zone	1 × Perceived ability (PA)	2 × Aspirations (A)	3 × Perceived opportunities (PO)	4 × Intellectual deficiencies (PA–A)	5 × Environmental deficiencies (PO–A)
Production and ancillary	3·04	3·01	1·47	+0·03	−1·54
Scheduling and manning	2·87	2·96	1·27	−0·09	−1·69
Plant and equipment	2·63	3·09	1·09	−0·46	−2·00
Cost	2·63	2·90	1·18	−0·27	−1·72
Safety	3·00	3·13	1·27	−0·13	−1·86
Personnel and training	3·04	3·09	1·04	−0·05	−2·05
Remuneration	2·94	3·36	1·02	−0·42	−2·34
Discipline and grievance	3·09	3·23	1·00	−0·14	−2·23
Hours of work	3·03	3·09	1·07	−0·06	−2·02
Sickness benefits, etc.	2·78	3·16	1·00	−0·38	−2·16
Holidays and leave	3·31	3·59	1·04	−0·28	−2·55

Environmental deficiencies: 1 2 3

Intellectual deficiencies: 4 // (1)

Area of congruence

1 = No influence at all;

2 = A little influence, i.e. complaining, advising, or making suggestions;

3 = As much influence as the person who makes this decision at the moment;

4 = A little more influence than the present decision-maker;

5 = Absolute personal control over making the decision.

* N=11.

Area of congruence

an issue which, at best, had been somewhat diffuse and ill-defined. A less generous observer could argue that our intervention created the issue. If change were to be effected it was necessary that we did not remain alone in the ownership of the problem and the commitment to the data. Thus the crucial stage of the process of planned change was to feed back the data and to provide an opportunity for the participants to choose whether or not they wished to proceed with the experiment. In Argyris' (1970) terms we were providing valid information in order to facilitate choice and internal commitment to any change which may be agreed. We recognized that several pressures were operating against a free and informed choice. Firstly, the experiment had the blessing and interest of the London Management Group and even though we had agreed that the local plant was our client and its needs were to be paramount, the pressure of attention was very real. Secondly, we noted that we, ourselves, were interested in pushing the experiment to its next stage. Our needs, as experimenters, were to learn more and not to suffer the research equivalent of arrested development. Thirdly, we recognized that our intervention had produced some form of tired inevitability expressed as 'well we can't stop now' on the part of the management, an equally tired 'they won't do anything about it' on the part of the workers, and, more importantly, an awareness of the workers' attitudes on the part of the management. Thus the pressure to 'do something', if only to prove the workforce mistaken in their views of management, was strong.

In feeding back the results of the interview to the management we consciously attempted to take a neutral, quasi-scientific stance: 'Here are the data, let the facts speak for themselves; the diagnosis, the attribution of meaning, the determination of action is yours.' Unfortunately, the facts did not speak for themselves and it soon became obvious that they were not as clear to the management as they were to us. As our theory should have led us to predict, there was a great deal of questioning as to the meaning, not primarily of the data, but of terms such as 'deficiency scores'. To the management, 'deficient' was an evaluative term and a non-positive one at that. The ensuing discussion of the charts and figures we provided was made more difficult by our refusal to lead the group to solutions. Several comments were made about 'woolly-minded academics' and 'people who don't have to work for a living'. The obvious confusion of the group and the pressure upon us to justify how we had 'been spending the last few weeks' led us to abandon our neutral position and to move towards a more active role of explaining and offering alternative courses of action. Our intervention remained slight and was qualified by drawing the attention of the management to the process dynamics of the situation; that, for example, they were pressing us into doing the diagnosis for them and making minimal effort themselves. The point was taken and the management group resolved to take the material away, decide what it may mean to them and consider what they may do next. They also decided that we would be of no use to them in that process—thus moving rapidly from dependence to counterdependence. We pointed out to them the pressures to do something and said that these should be acknowledged and considered as overt factors rather than allowed to operate covertly. We sought to be very clear with the group that a commitment to meet with the workforce around any of the issues was, in fact, a first step along the road to PDM and as such would be difficult to retrace. No longer would there be talk about participation, but participation through talk about participation.

At a subsequent meeting we were confronted with a number of points written on a blackboard by the management:

Objectives
1. Agree specific topics for further involvement of Chemical Plant staff.
2. Agree methods and broad lines of communication.
3. Agree methods of processing topics.

Suggested topics
Safety; Suggestions; Allocation of holidays; Shift changeover arrangements; Immediate task enlargement; Job descriptions.

Considerations
1. External (company) considerations may force you to choose some topics
2. Are we certain that supervisors' attitudes are compatible with some of the suggested topics?
3. Consider selecting a topic, carefully observe, and evaluate the changes that are occurring.
4. In selecting a topic, make sure that it is one where action can be implemented fully

During the meeting that followed we assumed a process consultant's role in order to help the group members become more aware of how they perceived and arrived at their list of alternatives and plans for action.

By the end of that meeting the following substantive and procedural conditions for collaboration had been agreed: a working party should be established to consider the issues described above; to avoid awkward questions from the London Office Management Group, it should be known simply as the 'working party' and not (as suggested by the researchers) as the 'joint working party'; communications should take place as follows:

1. A note should be sent to the operators outlining the agreed topics and asking for nominations for their representatives; 2. The site managers should be kept informed of the progress of the project by a statement at their next Group meeting; 3. The employee representatives should be paid for attendance at the meetings; ...

the first meeting could possibly be held in March 1976; we ourselves should meet separately with all of the groups prior to the first full meeting of the Working Party; the first meeting should deal with only one or two of the agreed issues; and, finally, management representatives of the Working Party should give serious thought to any background information they needed to action issues, to the time that should be allocated to each item, and to the nature of the meeting itself (e.g. 'who addresses the meetings, the role of the outsider, how meetings should be recorded, how and to whom the minutes should be circulated, frequency of meetings, and evaluation criteria').

We agreed to feed back the results of the interviews, shift by shift, for the supervisors and section head individually, and to ask the workforce for their views about the issues and about the idea of sitting down with the management to discuss some of them.

The reaction to the data from the workforce was mixed, some accepting it with an apathetic attitude, some considering it irrelevant, some becoming excited and wanting to do something about it. By this stage, we had abandoned our quasi-scientific neutral stance and were explaining the data and interpreting it. We were also advocating that the workers 'sit down' with the management, although occasionally, catching ourselves in this role, we backed off and returned to our commitment to a 'free and informed choice'. There was considerable ambivalence around any move towards a joint meeting marked by a strong desire 'to get something done' and an anxiety about the consequences expressed in references to firings and collecting redundancy money. The result was a high level of anxiety.

The level of anxiety also rose amongst the management, who reacted sharply to the fact that one of the workforce had walked out of a feedback session with ourselves and had complained about us to his supervisor. The supervisor had involved the section head and within hours the plant was alive with rumour and the Managing Director was on the 'phone to us. The incident was quickly resolved but, at this stage, we missed its significance in terms of the supervisor and the section head. Although we involved the supervisors and the section head we did not devote a great deal of effort *with them* considering the implications of a joint meeting with management. The working party was to contain the section head and one representative of the supervisors and we considered this sufficient safeguard for their views.

Additionally, the working party involved one worker from each shift, the Plant Manager, Personnel Services Manager and the Managing Director. The worker representatives and the supervisor representatives were elected by their respective colleagues (by shift in the case of the workers). The management representatives consisted of those with a direct interest in the operation of the plant and those with the power to effect changes on a broader front should they be necessary. Imperceptibly and unconsciously the emphasis shifted from meeting to talk without commitment, to meeting with a commitment to effect agreed changes (the saving clause, 'wherever appropriate' being occasionally added).

The first session was to be chaired by one of the researchers and was to agree the basis for future joint meetings—if there were to be future meetings. Our commitment to a contingent approach left even this issue open and certainly left the form of all possible meetings open to the expressed desires of the participants. The question of the roles, the conduct, the reporting relationships were all discussed at the first joint meeting with ourselves seeking clarification and commitment from the participants. We spent some time with both management and workforce representatives (separately) before the meeting, attempting to help them identify forms of behaviour which would inhibit open discussion and those which would facilitate it. Throughout the meeting we operated to keep communication as clear and unequivocal as possible and encouraged the participants to do the same.

The outcome of the meeting and the meaning attached to the experience by both the managers and the workforce was one of cautious optimism. 'Certainly something worth talking about and some possibility that changes could be brought about to mutual advantage.' Not so from the supervisors, nor from the section head, the grouping which in our eagerness to bring together management and men we had largely ignored. Occasionally we had recognized the importance of the section head, but had excluded him from the Steering Committee because, in terms of personality, we considered him so authoritarian as to prejudice any study—within *our* pluralistic framework some groups were apparently more equal than others! Our role between the management and the men had resulted in some degree of power equalization (Bennis, 1966) because both groups considered what we were doing had some validity and legitimacy. We had no such role with the supervisors and section head, who saw their interests being ignored or downgraded in the working party. Accordingly, this group brought strong pressure to bear to have the working party's terms of reference clearly set down in such a way that it could be seen to be no challenge to their prerogatives as supervisory personnel. In this they were unsuccessful as they were in their attempts to attack our activities in the period immediately preceding the first meeting.

In the second or third meeting, however, the process orientation was vindicated when one of the workforce representatives suggested that we suspend substantive business and discuss the 'difficult situation' the supervisors had been placed in by the workings of the group. It is difficult to reproduce or recapture the essence of the discussion and it would be foolish to pretend that it resolved the difficulties. The important fact is that it was explicitly recognized and openly considered with all parties to the difficulty present. Issues such as 'undermining authority', 'using the meeting to express personal grievances' or 'to get back at the supervisor' were looked at in detail and often with considerable expression of feeling. No one pretended that the issue did not exist nor that it should not. The outcome was that the workforce representatives offered to be circumspect in their roles, referring issues to the supervisors whenever possible and not acting as channels for grievance. In return the supervisors acknowledged that the workforce had an important contribution to make to the running of the plant and that they, the supervisors, occasionally acted capriciously and without full knowledge. It remains an issue, but is not a dominant one nor one that is ignored. It is expressed as a concern for who gets what out of the experiment, and pressures to extend participation have come from the supervisory group, who see themselves as deriving benefit from greater participation in the affairs of the factory as a whole.

A short example of the operation of the joint working party will indicate its evolving structure and process. An issue identified as one for joint resolution was that of holiday arrangements. The plant closes down completely for two weeks for maintenance and cleaning and all members other than the management had to take their holidays in this period irrespective of personal needs and desires. Very occasionally a person, sometimes two, would be allowed to work during the shutdown and to take their holidays at a time more convenient to them, but the occasions were few and far between and appeared to be subject to arbitrary decision by the section head. In tackling this issue, the Plant Manager was invited to explain the process for determining the shutdown date and for granting the right to work during it. The workforce representatives fed into the meeting the views of their constituents on the holiday arrangements. From a study of the figures it was determined that it would be possible to allow four or five people to take holidays outside the shutdown period without having to have recourse to overtime. The management representatives outlined in detail the case against overtime in the context of the chemical plant and, with qualification, it was recognized that their case was reasonable. The workforce returned to their constituents to check whether or not four people could be given time off (it required a commitment from each of them not to further weaken the manning by also taking time off without pay outside the holiday period) and, if agreed, what would be an appropriate means of selecting the four to benefit each year. The management agreed to check whether or not there was work available for the four during shutdown, what would be the nature of such work and the rate of payment for it. The supervisory representative undertook to check his colleagues' attitudes towards the holiday situation and their feelings about operating with reduced shifts to enable holidays to be taken outside the shutdown period.

The issue was eventually resolved to mutual satisfaction: four people allowed to work as unskilled labour with the Engineering Department at reduced rates of pay during shutdown. Selection to be by shift and out of the hat (not to be given another opportunity for four years unless no one else wanted to work). The resolution of the issue highlighted a number of the features mentioned earlier. For example, the supervisory group claimed special status and demanded, in the first instance, the right to work during the shutdown irrespective of the claims of the workers. When this was resisted they claimed the right to first choice amongst their shifts and, when this failed, the right to full rates of pay if they were successful in the ballot and they worked during the shutdown. Eventually, it was agreed that whatever the job and whoever was doing it the same rate of pay should persist. As one worker put it: 'if I'm cleaning out the vessels and you're cleaning out the vessels we're both getting the same for it.' Nonetheless it was acknowledged that if the supervisors were undergoing training or acting as supervisor elsewhere then normal rates of pay would prevail.

The discussions were often heated and marked by open declarations of position: 'If that's your attitude we may as well pack up and go home'. 'We've got to have some rights left to us'. The confrontation with the section head was equally sharp and stark. In seeking to determine the criteria for selection of the people for work during the shutdown he was addressed as the guardian of the old practices. 'Don't you worry yourselves about that', he said in as an avuncular a manner as he could manage, 'I'll do the selecting'. He took resistance to this to be an attack on his managerial prerogative and a personal affront, all the more so when he was asked to reveal his selection criteria: 'Look, first of all it's none of your business, secondly, I know what I'm doing. With some people you can tell ... it all depends on the bloke, what you know about it ... it's a management decision ... nothing for you to worry your heads about.' Pressed by both senior management and the worker representatives he could offer no clear criteria and admitted that it was an arbitrary decision. It was a situation he disliked and one which he remembers. The lesson he learned was that in such meetings arbitrary rules and prerogatives can be challenged, and he has been active since that time in raising issues of promotion, career development, pay, and training which affect him directly. He is vociferous in his desire to extend the scheme so that 'I can get something out of it'.

At the time of writing, the group has met six times and has begun to evaluate the work. The worker representatives have run into problems of apathy amongst their constituents and the management has met some resistance from the London management consequent upon a change of personnel. The supervisory group now appear to be the group with fewest problems and the keenest desire to continue and extend the experiment. The process orientation has enabled issues such as the management's motivation and commitment to be considered—'Is this just a device to prevent a union getting in?' (although not very fully considered), and issues such as lack of progress and low commitment to be addressed. The outcome is uncertain. Few express a desire to let the experiment die, most want it to succeed, but no one knows what to do to raise the energy level of representatives and those represented. The atmosphere currently is very much one of several characters in search of an issue. In this case we can take what little solace there may be from Engelstad (1970) who, in a review of a number of Norwegian projects in the 1960s, has noted

There is not yet any standard pattern as to how far a project can develop within a single company. In all cases there have been periods of conflict and stagnation lasting as long as up to a few years. In some cases periods of bargaining, negotiation, information activities, etc., have led to the establishment of conditions to continue ... in other cases resistance ... has been strong or top management's commitment and/or ability to handle the problems has been insufficient and all development has stopped.

Conclusions

It will be recalled that this paper has two purposes: to provide data on employee aspirations, abilities, and opportunities in decision-making, and to contribute towards the development and testing of a model of change. The numbers involved are such that we make no claims for the generalization of findings with respect to the former. Similarly, the model of planned change utilized in this experiment may be regarded as no more than a sample of one and, as such, not readily transferable to other PDM situations. Nonetheless, the experiment has raised a number of issues which, we feel, either provide a stimulus to discussion and/or point to the need for further research.

Since a summary of the preliminary findings of the participation aspect of the research can be found in a previous section of the paper (see Part 4), we have confined our concluding remarks to the change aspect of the experiment. However, we would like to make one general observation concerning the former: that both the present and previous research by the authors suggests that desires, abilities, and opportunities for involvement—all current knowledge lacunae—are factors which must be taken into account to a far greater extent if we are to gain better understanding of the participation phenomenon, and that it should therefore be a prime task of future research to determine, more precisely and more comprehensively, their nature, correlation, and effects.

From the standpoint of planned intervention, however, the data and presentation format proved to be of little value, that is—if one accepts Friedlander's comment that 'a mutual learning should emerge from the research situation' (Friedlander, 1966)— little *mutual* learning was actually involved. After the feedback of the data neither it nor the interviews which preceded it were referred to by workers, supervisors, or managers in subsequent discussions.

In retrospect it is clear why the data were ignored; indeed, in terms of our earlier theoretical discussion it is understandable that they should have been. We have argued that there are cultural differences in the cognitive and inferential structure with which people perceive and explain the world, differences in the ways in which people define and judge situations and build their philosophies and theories about man, organizations, and change. In effect, we are arguing here that there are phenomenological and epistemological differences between cultures, sub-cultures, groups, and individuals. Yet in our procedure for research and, to a lesser extent, for experimentation we have attempted to reduce these differences by the application of one epistemology, namely that of the researcher/experimenter. *Our* system of classification was imposed upon the subjects and apparently rejected by them as being meaningless *to them* and of no use *to them*. In Maruyama's (1969) terms: 'Interpretation of one epistemological universe by a researcher from outside may produce a theory which is self-consistent and is therefore satisfactory to the researcher, but nevertheless is incorrect and irrelevant from the point of view of the universe being interpreted.'

This difficulty highlights once more the issue of the researcher/consultant/client interface and the effects of socio-psychological research (Argyris, 1970; Friedlander, 1966). One way to overcome the barrier might be to have the cultures conceptualized and analysed by those people who are subject to these cultures, rather than by outsiders. This is a stance adopted by many in the field of planned change who see the outsider's role as essentially that of helping and advising in the design of instruments and methods for diagnosing problems and issues. Similarly, the task of collecting data and deciding what data is relevant is seen to lie primarily with the participants. There is a definite attraction in such a method applied to participation since what could be more participative than participation in the design of the study itself.

The problem of such an approach, however, is that the issues may become meaningful to the participants, those within the culture but not necessarily so to those outside the culture. In effect, we may be exchanging one epistemology for several with no guarantee that the researcher/consultant can understand the social situation sufficiently well to be able to generate meaningful data (in his terms) or to be able to intervene. In the present circumstance the data collection was important to us both as researchers and consultants; it helped *us* to understand the situation and it helped *us* recognize and work on issues as they arose in the working party. In so far as it did not help the other participants, this reflects our failure to negotiate meaning for our data. The problem thus remains: good research data, valid, reliable, comparable, capable of replication, rarely leads to application.

The experiment has also called into question the models of planned change adopted throughout the literature. As stated earlier, most models emphasize intervention from outside as a consequence of tension or 'felt need', and many stress that without a strong, initial desire to change, little change will be forthcoming. This experiment, and other related work upon which we are engaged, suggests that change may not necessarily be preceded by a strong expressed desire to change. In this experiment there was no recognition of a need until the data had been collected. Indeed, the need to change only became apparent after the working party had met and begun to develop its procedures. The postulation of initial recognition or need implies a conceptualization of a situation in advance of experiencing that situation: the need to participate implies a conceptualization of a situation in advance of experiencing that situation: the need to participate implies a cognition of participation. Our emphasis would be that the need for participation cannot properly be conceptualized until the participation issue has been raised and, arguably, until participation has actually been experienced. Clearly new definitions of the concept will arise from the experience of the activity and will be contingent upon that experience. In the present case, only after the parties were brought together was there the recognition and desire to *do* something about participation.

In attempting to summarize what we have learned from the experiment about the process of change itself, we can usefully refer to the model of change which has been developed by Dalton (1969). The research that we have done is largely in accord with Dalton's model in that we have certainly experienced the growing specificity of objectives, the interruption of social ties and the formation of new relationships, the rise in levels of self-esteem and the internalization of motives for change. The experiment, however, does not confirm the simple linear development implied in Dalton's models. The process is not smooth nor parallel nor horizontal. It is probably best characterized by a series of loops and spirals, a movement from general to specific, specific to general, new ties taken up and old ones resuscitated, esteem and motives for change fluctuating continuously.

It reminds us once more that a model, however good, is by its very nature an abstraction from and a simplification of reality. In this experiment, as in so many others, the postulate that simplicity is anterior to complexity has been demonstrated to be ill-founded and, as a guide to action, dangerous.

APPENDIX III

Employee briefing

TO: DIRECTORS/MANAGERS   From: Personnel Department

Date: 18th October 1977

BRIEFING GUIDELINE

Brief down to: ALL EMPLOYEES

URGENT – Commence 09.00 hrs. 20.10.77 end Friday 21.10.77 plus shift a.s.a.p.

NOTE This text is issued as a guide to Directors and Managers involved in briefing staff under their control.

It should not be read out to staff, but used as a quick guide (a) prior to the briefing meeting, and (b) during the meeting as a discreet check.

As far as possible brief the matter in your own words with normal style and phraseology so that your discussion is natural, EXCEPT that certain words and phrases in the written text are italicized; these should be retained in your own version intact, since they are more critical in retaining the correct emphasis or interpretation in the matter.

SUBJECT: WORKER PARTICIPATION

An experiment in worker participation has been taking place in the Chemical Plant for the past eighteen months. Its purpose has been to *enable employees to take a more active part in influencing decisions which affect their day to day working in the Company. In addition, the aim has been to improve communications and to achieve a better understanding between all levels within the plant of each other's problems.*

An important part of the project has been the continuing assistance of Professor Iain Mangham and Dr Paul Bate, both of the Centre for the Study of Organizational Change and Development, at Bath University. They are acknowledged authorities in this field.

Column for (i) personal notes prior to meeting, if any – (ii) questions raised during meeting—whether answered or referred back for clarification.

The results of the experiment to date have been encouraging and a decision has been made *to extend the scope of the experiment. Because it offers some important differences in work population and environment to that of the Chemical Plant*, the Packaging Area has been chosen for this extension of the experiment. As you know, the Chemical Plant is an area where we have continuous shift operations and this has given us good experience with solving problems particular to that environment. With the Packaging Area, its larger number of employees and the nature of the work, we can gain experience in an environment which is more typical of some of our other factory operations.

It is hoped that the benefits which have occurred in the Chemical Plant will be repeated here and every effort will be made to accelerate this new phase of the project *whilst bearing in mind the need to evolve a participation system suited to this different group*. If the results prove favourable it is the intention to extend participation to *all parts of the Company within the next twelve months*.

Iain Mangham will be on site within the next week and will be spending some time with us to discuss the principles and ways and means to participation.

With the broader and continuing successful introduction of worker participation we will be in the forefront in adopting the best of current practice in industry.

It will also provide an opportunity to re-emphasise, in practical terms, *the Company's belief that the solving of any individual employee or work problems is best done in a climate of frank, open and informal discussion.*

In many areas we are already adopting varying forms of participation. Naturally such activity should continue and be encouraged by all of us.

APPENDIX IV

Company and departmental organization

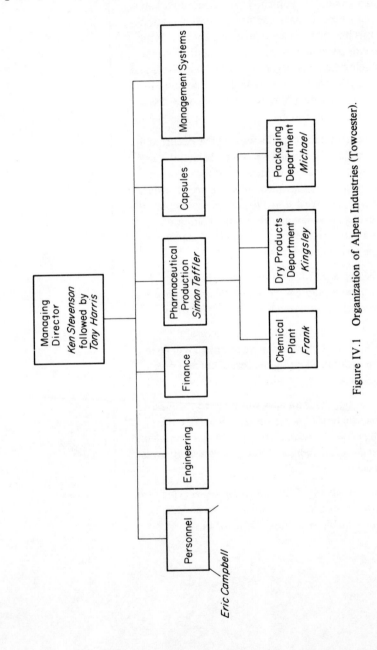

Figure IV.1 Organization of Alpen Industries (Towcester).

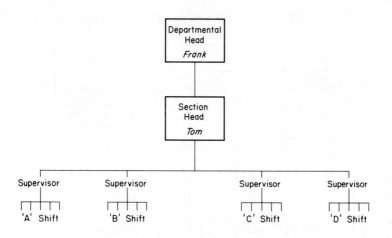

Figure IV.2 Organization of Chemical Plant.

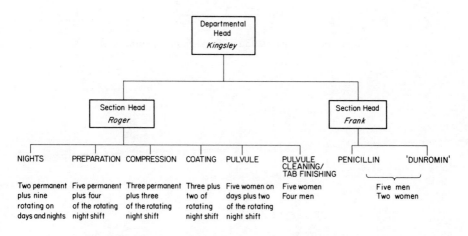

Figure IV.3 Organization of Dry Products Department.

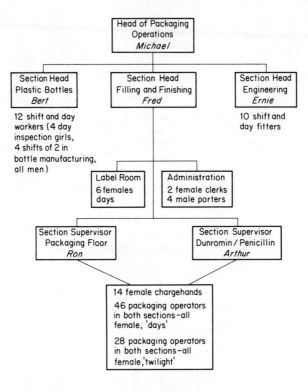

Figure IV.4   Organization of Packaging Department.

APPENDIX V

A manager's view of participation

In February 1980, Simon spoke to a mixed audience of employees and outsiders and made the following points:

(1) He saw great merit in an evolved rather than a blueprint approach.

(2) There was also great merit, he argued, in establishing and maintaining a pilot project.

(3) He noted that, for managers, it was often difficult for them to appreciate the problems of the shopfloor representatives in being representatives and urged all thinking of going along these lines to consider carefully how to provide training and support for the representatives.

(4) He particularly urged the use of other employee representatives in the training of new ones.

(5) Although he personally experienced anxiety with the open agendas, he could see the value of them.

(6) He was particularly impressed by the success of periodic reviews of process issues.

(7) He urged that all such projects should have the active public support of senior management.

(8) He stressed the need for multiple and, indeed, for over-communication after meetings so that the constituents were sure of receiving the message.

(9) He elaborated on the time that it may take for meetings to become productive.

(10) Finally he stressed the need for training and development for all, but particularly for senior managers.

He concluded by listing what he, and his colleagues, took to be the strengths and weaknesses of the entire programme:

Strengths
(1) Improved two way communications
(2) Better appreciation of company policies
(3) More consistency in implementing policies
(4) Departmental issues dealt with at the appropriate level
(5) Position of some section heads and supervisors has been strengthened
(6) Planning, purchasing, and installation of new equipment has become more effective

(7) Better quality decisions in certain instances

(8) Provides an opportunity to make the most of individuals' abilities

(9) Some change of attitude at all levels

(10) Favourable impact on group identity

(11) Encouragement to | management to get some
     Pressure on | issues resolved

(12) Encouragement to | representatives to clarify issues
     Pressure on | and eliminate trivia

(13) We will be better prepared to meet any statutory requirements

(14) Improved performance?

Weaknesses (?)

(1) Needs a heavy commitment of time

(2) Expectations are sometimes too high

(3) Needs considerable training effort

(4) Danger that representatives become divorced from their constituents

(5) Meetings can be taken to be the only arena for participation

(6) Some individuals at all levels have difficulty in adapting

(7) Problems can arise if conflict cannot be handled constructively

(8) Some section heads and supervisors perceive their position has been weakened

(9) Perceptions of influence and progress vary considerably between individuals (Can be demotivating)

(10) Difficulties resulting from the time taken to expand site wide

References

Ackoff, R. L. (1960). 'Systems, organizations and interdisciplinary research', *General Systems Yearbook*, **5,** 1–8.

Ackoff, R. L. (1962). *Scientific Method: Optimizing Applied and Research Decisions*, John Wiley, New York.

Aiken, M. and Hage, J. (1966). 'Organization alienation: a comparative analysis', *American Sociological Review*, **4,** 497–507.

Allen, W. (1968). 'The consequences of games playing in the British political economy', Occasional Paper No. 3, Industrial Educational and Research Foundation.

Allen, V. L. (1971). *The Sociology of Industrial Relations: Studies in Method*, Longman, London.

Allison, G. T. (1971). *Essence of Decision*, Little Brown, Boston.

Allport, F. H. (1962). 'A structural conception of behaviour: individual and collective', *Journal of Abnormal and Social Psychology*, **64,** 3–30.

Argyris, C. (1964). *Integrating the Individual in the Organization*, John Wiley, New York.

Argyris, C. (1970). *Intervention Theory and Method*, Addison-Wesley, Reading, Mass.

Baker, F. (ed.) (1973). *Organizational Systems. General Systems Approach to Complex Organizations*, Irwin, Homewood, Ill.

Balfour, C. (ed.) (1973). 'Participation in Industry', Industrial Democracy Report to EEC Congress.

Bank, J. and Jones, K. (1977). *Worker Directors Speak*, Gower Press, London.

Bate, S. P. (1975). 'Theory and practice of workers' participation in industrial rule-making processes: a field study of manual workers in the Port Transport Industry', PhD thesis, London School of Economics.

Bate, S. P. (1976). 'Workers' aspirations to participate: a field study of its nature and correlates', unpublished paper, University of Bath.

Bate, S. P. (1978). 'Cultural analysis, confrontation and counter-culture as strategies for organization development', paper presented to the 19th International Congress of Applied Psychology, Munich.

Bate, S. P. and Mangham, I. L. (1975). 'The design and implementation of processes of workers' participation', Working Paper No. 75/01, Centre for the Study of Organizational Change and Development, University of Bath.

Bateson, G. (1972). *Steps to an Ecology of Mind: Collected Essays in Anthropology, Psychiatry, Evolution and Epistemology*, Ballantine Books, New York.

Becker, H. S. (1963). *Outsiders: Studies in the Sociology of Deviance*, The Free Press, Chicago, Ill.

Beckhard, R. (1969). *Organization Development: Strategies and Models*, Addison-Wesley, New York.

Benne, K. D., Bennis, W. G., and Chin, R. (1969). *The Planning of Change*, Holt, Rinehart and Winston, New York.

Bennett, E. B. (1955). 'Discussion, decision and commitment', *Human Relations*, **8,** 258–273.

Bennis, W. G. (1966). *Changing Organizations*, McGraw-Hill, New York.

Bennis, W. G. (1969). *Organization Development, Its Nature, Origins and Prospects*, Addison-Wesley, New York.

275

276

Berger, P. (1963). *Invitation to Sociology*, Penguin, London.

Berger, P. and Luckman, T. (1966). *The Social Construction of Reality*, Doubleday and Co., New York.

Bernhardsen, B. (1969). 'The Norwegian approach to the development of worker participation and democracy at the workplace', ILO International Seminar in Workers' Participation in Decision within Undertakings, Belgrade.

Blackler, F. H. M. and Brown, C. A. (1978). *Job Re-design and Management Control: Studies in British Leyland and Volvo*, Saxon House, London.

Blake, R. R. and Mouton, J. S. (1969). *Grid Organization Development*, Addison-Wesley, New York.

Blauner, R. (1964). *Alienation and Freedom: The Factory Worker and His Industry*, University of Chicago Press, Chicago.

Blumberg, P. (1968). *Industrial Democracy: The Sociology of Participation*, Constable, London.

Blumer, H. (1965). 'Sociological implications of the thought of George Herbert Mead', *American Journal of Sociology*, **71**, 535–548.

Blumer, H. (1969). *Symbolic Interactionism*, Prentice-Hall, Englewood Cliffs, N.J.

Bragg, J. E. and Andrews, I. R. (1973). 'Participative decision making: an experimental study in a hospital', *Journal of Applied Behavioural Science*, **9**, 727–736.

Brannen, P., Batstone, E., Fatchett, D., and White, P. (1976). *The Worker Directors: A Sociology of Participation*, Hutchinson, London.

Brecht, B. (1940). *Kurze Beschriebung einer neuen Technik der Schausspielkunst, die einen Verfremdungseffekt Hervorbringt*, Versuche, Frankfurt.

Bucher, R. and Stelling, J. (1969). 'Characteristics of professional organizations', *Journal of Health and Social Behaviour*, **10**, 3–15.

Buckingham, J. L., Jeffery, R. G. and Thorne, B. A. (1975). *Job Enrichment and Organizational Change*, Gower Press, London.

Budner, S. (1962). 'Intolerance of ambiguity as a personality variable', *Journal of Personality*, **30**, 29–50.

Carlen, P. (1976). 'The staging of magistrates' justice', *British Journal of Criminology*, **16**, 48–55.

Carpenter, H. H. (1971). 'Formal organizational structural factors and perceived job satisfaction of classroom teachers', *Administrative Science Quarterly*, **16**, 460–465.

Cascio, W. F. (1974). 'Functional specialization, culture and preference for participative management', *Personnel Psychology*, **27**, 593–603.

CBI (1973). 'The responsibilities of the British public company', CBI Report, September 1973.

Child, J. (1972). 'Organizational structure, environment and performance—the role of strategic choice', *Sociology*, **6**, 1–22.

Child, J. (1973). *Man and Organization*, George Allen and Unwin, London.

CIR (1974). 'Worker participation and collective bargaining in Europe', CIR Study No. 4, HMSO, London.

CIR Practice (1971). Code of Industrial Relations Practice.

Clark, P. (1972). *Action Research*, Prentice-Hall, London.

Clarke, R. O. Fatchett, D. J., and Roberts, B. C. (1972). *Workers' Participation in Management in Britain*, Heinemann, London.

Clegg, H. A. (1960). *A New Approach to Industrial Democracy*, Blackwell, Oxford.

Clegg, H. A. (1975). 'Pluralism in industrial relations', *British Journal of Industrial Relations*, **13**, 309–316.

Clegg, C., Nicholson, N., Ursell, G., Blyton, P., and Wall, T. (1978). 'Managers' attitudes towards industrial democracy', *Industrial Relations Journal*, **9**(3), 4–17.

Cohen, P. S. (1968). *Modern Social Theory*, Heinemann, London.

Cole, D. L. (1963). *The Quest for Industrial Peace*, Meyer Kestenbaum Lectures, Harvard University, McGraw-Hill, New York.

Conservative Party (1974). Conservative Party Manifesto.

Cowton, R. (1974). 'Fruitful participation in industry', *The Times*, 12 August 1974.

Crighton, S. (1974). 'The proposed 5th Directive of the EEC Commission and its effects on member states, notably the UK', MSc thesis, University of Aston in Birmingham.

Cyert, R. M. and March, J. G. (1959). *A Behavioural Theory of the Firm*, Prentice-Hall, Englewood Cliffs, N.J.

Daily Telegraph (1974). 20 August 1974.

Dalkey, N. and Helmer, O. (1963). 'An experimental application of the Delphi method to the use of experts', *Management Science*, **9**.

Dalton, G. W. (1969). 'Influence and organizational change', paper presented to Conference on Organizational Behaviour Models, Kent State University.

Dalton, G. W. (1973). 'Influence in organizational change', in *Modern Organization Theory: Contextual, Environmental and Socio-Cultural Variables* (Ed. A. R. Neghandi), Nijhoff, The Hague.

Day, R. A. and Day, J. V. (1976). 'A review of the current state of Negotiated Order Theory', paper presented to 40th Annual Meeting of the Midwest Sociological Society, St Louis, Missouri, 22 April.

Derber, M. (1970). 'Crosscurrents in workers' participation', *Industrial Relations*, **9**, 123–136.

Dessler, G. (1976). *Organization and Management: A Contingency Approach*, Prentice-Hall, Englewood Cliffs, N.J.

Deutsch, M. (1973). *The Resolution of Conflict*, Yale University Press, New Haven, Conn.

Development Council Statement of 24 September, 1969.

DeVries, D. L. and Snyder, J. P. (1974). 'Faculty participation in departmental decision-making', *Organizational Behaviour and Human Performance*, **11**, 235–249.

Donaldson, L. D. (1975). 'Job enlargement: a multidimensional process', *Human Relations*, **28**(3), 1–19.

Drenth, P. J. D. (1969). In van Gorkum, P. H., Drenth, P. J. D., de Wolff, C. J., Ramondt, J. J., van Gils, M. R., and Jonker, H. W. *Industrial Democracy in the Netherlands: A Seminar*, Boom en Zoon, Netherlands.

Dronkers, P. L. (1972). 'Labour/Management cooperation for productivity and satisfaction', OECD Regional Joint Seminar, October, Paris.

Dronkers, P. (1973). Quoted by D. F. Wilson in 'Facelift for the shop floor', *Business Observer*, 9 September 1973.

Eldridge, J. E. T. (1973). 'Industrial conflict: some problems of theory and method', in *Man and Organization* (Ed. J. Child), George Allen and Unwin, London.

Emerson, R. M. (1970). *Judging Delinquents*, Aldine Publications, Chicago.

Emery, F. E. (1967). 'Democratisation of the workplace', *Manpower and Applied Psychology*, **1**(3).

Emery, F. E. and Thorsrud, E. (1969). *Form and Content of Industrial Democracy*, Work Research Institute, Oslo.

Emery, F. E. and Trist, E. (1965). 'The causal texture of organizational environment', *Human Relations*, **18**, 21–33.

Employment Protection Bill, (1974). Consultative Document, paragraph 92.

Engelstad, P. M. (1970). *Teknologi og Sosial Forandring pa Arbeids plassen*, Oslo.

Financial Times (1974). 3 September 1974.

Fink, S. L., Taddeo, J., and Beak, K. (1971). 'Crisis model of organizational change', *Journal of Applied Behavioural Science*, **7**(1).

Fogarty, M. P. (1972). 'Labour/Management cooperation on the enterprise: its development and prospects', OECD Regional Joint Seminar, October, Paris.

Fordyce, J. K. and Weil, R. (1971). *Managing with People*, Addison-Wesley, Reading, Mass.

Fox, A. (1966). 'Industrial sociology and industrial relations', Royal Commission on Trade Unions and Employers' Associations 1965–8, Research Paper No. 3.

Fox, A. (1971). *A Sociology of Work in Industry*, Collier-Macmillan, London.

Fox, A. (1973). 'Industrial relations: a social critique of pluralist ideology', in *Man and*

Organization (Ed. J. Child), George Allen and Unwin, London.

Fox, A. (1974). *Man Mismanagement*, Hutchinson, London.

Foy, N. (1974). 'Pathways to participation', *Management Today*, January 1974.

Frank, L. L. and Hackman, J. R. (1975). 'A failure of job enrichment: the case of the change that wasn't', *Journal of Applied Behavioural Science*, **11**, 413–436.

French, W. and Bell, C. (1973). *Organization Development*, Prentice-Hall, Englewood Cliffs, N.J.

French, J. R. P., Jr, Israel, J., and Ås, D. (1960). 'An experiment on participation in a Norwegian factory', *Human Relations*, **13**, 3–19.

French, J. R. P., Kay, E., and Meyer, A. H. (1966). 'Participation and the appraisal system', *Human Relations*, **19**, 3–30.

Friedlander, F. (1966). 'Performance and interactional dimensions of organizational work groups', *Journal of Applied Behavioural Science*, **50**, 257–265.

Garson, G. D. (1977). *Worker Self-management in Industry*, Praeger Special Studies, New York.

Globerson, A. (1970). 'Spheres and levels of employee participation in organizations', *British Journal of Industrial Relations*, **8**, 256–262.

Goffman, E. (1970). *Strategic Interaction*, Blackwell, Oxford.

Golembiewski, R. (1972). *Renewing Organizations*, F. E. Peacock, New York.

Golembiewski, R. and McConkie, M. (1975). 'The centrality of interpersonal trust in group processes', in *Theories of Group Processes*, (Ed. C. Cooper), John Wiley, London.

Graftström, L. and Moreau, J. E. (1972). National Report: Sweden, OECD Regional Joint Seminar, October.

Greiner, L. (1966). 'Patterns of organization change', in *Organization Change and Development* (Ed. G. Dalton and P. Lawrence), Irwin, Homewood, Ill.

Guardian (1973). 'Labour clears open road to workers' control', 12 June 1973.

Guest, D. and Fatchett, D. (1974). *Worker Participation: Individual Control and Practice*, Institute of Personnel Management, London.

Haferkamp, W. (1969). 'Codetermination in the basic programmes of the German Trade Unions', ILO Report No. 33, p. 9, Geneva.

Haire, M., Ghiselli, E. E., and Porter, L. W. (1966). *Managerial Thinking: An International Study*, John Wiley, New York.

Hall, P. M. (1972). 'A symbolic interactionist analysis of politics', *Sociological Inquiry*, **42**, 35–75.

Heller, F. A. (1971). *Managerial Decision-making: A Study of Leadership Styles and Power-sharing among Senior Managers*, Tavistock, London.

Heller, F. A. (1973). 'Leadership, decision-making and contingency theory', *Industrial Relations*, **12**, 185.

Heller, F. A. and Yukl, G. (1969). 'Participation and managerial decision-making as a function of situational variables', *Organizational Behaviour and Human Performance*, **4**, 227–241.

Herman, S. N. (1971). 'Gestalt orientation to Organization Development', conference paper.

Hespe, G. W. A. and Warr, P. B. (1971). 'Do employees want to participate?', paper presented to International Congress of Applied Psychology, Liège.

Hespe, G. W. A. and Wall, T. (1976). 'The demand for participation among employees', *Human Relations*, **29**, 411–428.

Holter, H. (1965). 'Attitudes towards employee participation in company decision making processes', *Human Relations*, **18**, 297–321.

Hughes, E. C. (1945). 'Dilemmas and contradictions of status', *American Journal of Scoiology*, **50**, 353–359.

Hughes, E. C. (1958). *Men and Their Work*, The Free Press, Glencoe, Ill.

Hughes, E. C. (1971). *The Sociological Eye: Selected Papers*, Aldine/Atherton, Inc., Chicago.

IILS (1972). 'Workers' participation in management in Britain', *IILS Bulletin*, No. 9, 175–208.

ILO (1969). 'Participation of workers in decisions within undertakings', Labour-Management Series No. 33, ILO, Geneva.

ILO (1970). 'Report on the international seminar on workers' participation in decisions within undertakings, Belgrade', ILO, Geneva.

Indik, B. P. (1965). 'Organizational size and member participation', *Human Relations*, **18**, 339–350.

Industrial Relations Act (1971). Code of Industrial Relations Practice, HMSO, London.

Industrial Society (1974). 'Practical policies for participation'.

IPM (1971). 'Workers' participation in Western Europe', *IPM Report*, No. 10, 71–73.

Jaques, E. (1951). *The Changing Culture of a Factory*, Tavistock, London.

Johnson, J. M. (1975). *Doing Field Research*, The Free Press, Glencoe, Ill.

Judson, A. S. (1966). *A Manager's Guide to Making Changes*, John Wiley, London.

Juralewicz, R. S. (1974). 'An experiment on participation in a Latin American factory', *Human Relations*, **27**, 627–637.

Katz, D. and Kahn, R. L. (1966). *The Social Psychology of Organizations*, John Wiley, New York.

Katz, D. and Kahn, R. L. (1969). 'Common characteristics of open systems', in *Systems Thinking* (Ed. F. E. Emery), Penguin, London.

Kaufman, H. (1972). *The Limits of Organizational Change*, University of Alabama Press, Birmingham, Ala.

Kerr, C. (1964). *Labor and Management in Industrial Society*, Doubleday, New York.

Knight, K. W. and Guest, D. (1979). *Putting Participation into Practice*, Gower Press, London.

Kochan, T. A. and Dyer, L. D. (1976). 'A model of organizational change in the context of union-management relations', *Journal of Applied Behavioural Science*, **12**, 59–78.

Kornhauser, A. W. (1960). *The Politics of Mass Society*, Routledge and Kegan Paul, London.

Labour Party (1967). Report on Industrial Democracy, June 1967.

Lawler, E. E. and Hall, D. T. (1970). 'Relationship of job characteristics to job involvement, satisfaction and intrinsic motivation', *Journal of Applied Psychology*, **54**, 305–312.

Lawrence, P. R. and Lorsch, J. E. (1967). *Organization and Environment*, Harvard Business School, Boston.

Lawrence, P. R. and Lorsch, J. W. (1969). *Developing Organizations: Diagnosis and Action*, Addison-Wesley, Reading, Mass.

Lewin, K. (1938). *The Conceptual Representation and Measurement of Psychological Forces*, Duke University Press, Durham, N.C.

Lewin, K. (1946). 'Frontiers in group dynamics', *Human Relations*, **1**(1).

Lippitt, R., Watson, J., and Westley, B. (1958). *The Planning of Change*, Harcourt Brace, New York.

Lischeron, J. A. and Wall, T. D. (1975a). 'Attitudes towards participation among local authority employees', *Human Relations*, **28**, 499–517.

Lischeron, J. A. and Wall, T. D. (1975b). 'Employee participation: an experimental field study', *Human Relations*, **28**, 863–884.

Lowin, A. (1968). 'Participative decision-making: a model, literature critique and prescription for research', *Organizational Behaviour and Human Performance*, **13**, 68–106.

Lupton, T. (1971). *Management and the Social Sciences*, 2nd edn, Penguin, London.

Mandanis, G. P. (1968). 'The future of the Delphi technique', paper presented to the European Conference on Technological Forecasting, Glasgow.

Mangham, I. L. (1970). 'Interpersonal styles and group development', PhD thesis, University of Leeds.

Mangham, I. L. (1974). 'Conflict, change and management', *Industrial Training International*, **10**(7).

Mangham, I. L. (1975). 'Negotiating reality: notes towards a model of order and change within organizations', Working Paper No. 75/04, Centre for the Study of Organizational Change and Development, University of Bath.

Mangham, I. L. (1977). 'Definitions, interactions and disengagement', *Small Group Behaviour*, **8**, 487–510.

Mangham, I. L. (1978). *Interactions and Interventions in Organizations*, John Wiley, London.

Mangham, I. L. (1979). *The Politics of Organizational Change*, Associated Business Press, London.

Mangham, I. L. (1981). 'Relations at work: a matter of tension and tolerance', in *Personal Relationships* (Ed. S. Duck and R. Gilmour), Academic Press, London.

Marchington, M. (1980). *Responses to Participation at Work*, Gower Press, Farnborough, Hants.

Maruyama, M. (1969). 'The epistemology of social science research', *Dialectica*, **23**, 229–280.

Mead, G. H. (1964). In *Selected Writings* (Ed. A. J. Peck), Bobbs-Merrill, New York.

Merelman, R. M. (1969). 'The dramaturgy of politics', *Sociological Quarterly*, **10**, 216–241.

Miliband, R. (1969). *The State in a Capitalist Society*, Weidenfeld and Nicholson, London.

Morse, N. C. (1953). *Satisfactions in a White Collar Job*, Survey Research Centre, University of Michigan, Ann Arbor, Mich.

Morse, N. C. and Reimer, E. (1956). 'The experimental change of a major organizational variable', *Journal of Abnormal and Social Psychology*, **52**, 120–129.

Mumford, E. and Henshall, D. (1978). *A Participative Approach to Computer Systems Design*, Prentice-Hall, London.

Obradowicz, J., French, J. R. P., Jr, and Rodgers, W. L. (1970). 'Workers' Councils in Yugoslavia: effects of perceived participation and satisfaction of workers', *Human Relations*, **23**, 459–471.

OECD (1972). Regional Joint Seminar on prospects for labour/management cooperation in the enterprise, October 1972.

Pages, M. (1973). 'An interview with Max Pages—N. Tichy', *Journal of Applied Behavioural Science*, **10**, 8–26.

Panggabean, D. (1969). Report to ILO United Nations Development Programme Technical Assistance Sector, Belgrade, December.

Patchen, M. (1965). 'Labor-management consultation at TVA: its impact on employees', *Administrative Science Quarterly*, **10**, 149–174.

Patchen, M. (1970). *Participation, Achievement and Involvement on the Job*, Prentice-Hall, Englewood Cliffs, N.J.

Pateman, C. (1970). *Participation and Democratic Theory*, Cambridge University Press, London.

Peacock, L. (1972). 'Participation pays', *Industrial Society*, September 1972.

Pelz, D. C. (1952). 'Influence: a key to effective leadership in the first-line supervisor', *Personnel*, **28**, 209–217.

Pen, J. (1966). *Harmony and Conflict in Modern Society*, McGraw-Hill, New York.

Perinbanayagam, R. S. (1974). 'The definition of the situation: an analysis of the ethnomethodological and dramaturgical views', *Sociological Quarterly*, **15**, 521–541.

Perrow, C. (1972). *Complex Organizations*, Scott Foresman, Glenview, Ill.

Polsby, N. W. (1963). *Community Power and Political Theory*, Yale University Press, New Haven, Conn.

Porter, L. W. (1961). 'A study of perceived need satisfaction in bottom and middle management jobs', *Journal of Applied Psychology*, **45**, 1–10.

Porter, L. W. (1962). 'Job attitudes in management, 1. Perceived deficiencies in need fulfilment as a function of job level', *Journal of Applied Psychology*, **46**, 375–384.

Porter, L. W. (1963). 'Job attitudes in management, 2' *Journal of Applied Psychology*, **47**, 141–148.

Porter, L. W. and Lawler, E. E. (1965). 'Properties of organization structure in relation to job attitudes and job behaviour', *Psychological Bulletin*, **65**, 23–51.

Porter, L. W. and Lawler, E. E. (1968). *Managerial Attitudes and Performance*, Irwin-Dorsey, Homewood, Ill.

Prentice, R. (1973). Conference on Participation in British Industry, *Financial Times*, 29 November 1973.

Qvale, T. U. (1970). 'The industrial democracy project in Norway', IIRA Second World Congress, Geneva.

Qvale, T. U. (1973). 'Participation and conflict: some experiences from the Norwegian Industrial Democracy Programme', IIRA Third World Congress, London.

Ramsay, H. (1976). 'Participation ... the shop floor views', *British Journal of Industrial Relations*, **14**, 128–141.

Rees, A. (1970). *Workers and Wages in an Urban Labor Market*, University of Chicago Press, Chicago.

Ritchie, J. B. and Miles, R. E. (1970). 'An analysis of quantity and quality of participation as mediating variables in the participative decision making process', *Personnel Psychology*, **23**, 347–359.

Rogaly, J. (1973). 'The plant, not the boardroom, is the key', *Financial Times*, 3 July 1973.

Rosengren, W. R. and DeVault, S. (1964). 'The sociology of time and space in an Obstetrical Hospital', in *The Hospital in Modern Society* (Ed. E. Friedson), The Free Press, New York.

Roy, D. (1954). 'Efficiency and "The Fix": informal group relations in a piecework machine shop', in *Sociology: Progress of a Decade* (Ed. S. Lipset and N. Smelser), Prentice-Hall, New York.

Rus, V. (1970). 'Influence structure in Yugoslav enterprises', *Industrial Relations*, **9**, 148–160.

Sadler, P. J. (1970). 'Leadership style, confidence in management and job satisfaction', *Journal of Applied Behavioural Science*, **6**, 3–19.

SAF (1971). 'On collaboration in firms', Svenska ArbetsgivareForeningen.

SAF (1972). 'The development of industrial democracy in Denmark, Finland, Norway and Sweden', Svenska ArbetsgivareForeningen.

Salaman, G. (1980). *Work Organizations: Resistance and Control*, Longman, London.

Scheff, T. J. (1966). *Being Mentally Ill*, Aldine, Chicago.

Schein, E. (1969). *Process Consultation: Its Role in Organization Development*, Addison-Wesley, New York.

Schmuck, R. I. and Miles, M. B. (1971). *Organization Development in Schools*, National Press, Palo Alto, Calif.

Schrank, R. (1978). *Ten Thousand Working Days*, MIT Press, Cambridge, Mass.

Scontrino, M. P. (1972). 'The effects of fulfilling and violating group members' expectations about leadership style', *Organizational Behaviour and Human Performance*, **8**, 118–138.

Sethi, K. C. (1973). 'Workers' participation in management conflicts in concept', *Economic Times, Bombay*, **13**, 14 August 1973.

Shepard, J. M. (1973). 'Specialization, autonomy and job satisfaction', *Industrial Relations*, **12**, 274–281.

Shephard, H. (1967). 'Changing interpersonal and intergroup relationships in organizations', in *Handbook of Organizations* (Ed. J. G. March), Rand McNally and Co., New York.

Sherwood, J. (1971). *An Introduction to Organization Development*, Experimental Publication System.

Shibutani, T. (1961). *Society and Personality*, Prentice-Hall, New York.

Shister, J. and Reynolds, L. G. (1949). *Job Horizons: A Study of Job and Labor Mobility*, Harper, New York.

Siegel, A. L. and Ruh, R. A. (1973). 'Job involvement, participation in decision making, personal background and job behaviour', *Organizational Behaviour and Human Performance*, **9**, 318–327.

Simmel, G. (1955). *Conflict*, The Free Press, New York.

Skibbins, G. J. (1974). *Organizational Evolution*, AMACOM, New York.

Stebbins, R. A. (1969). 'Role distance, role distance behaviour and jazz musicians', *British Journal of Sociology*, **20**.

Strauss, A. (1963). 'The hospital and its negotiated order', in *The Hospital in Modern Society* (Ed. E. Friedson), The Free Press, New York.

Strauss, A. (1978). *Negotiations*, The Free Press, San Francisco.

Strauss, G. and Rosenstein, E. (1970). 'Workers' participation: a critical view', *Industrial Relations*, **9**, 197–214.

Tannenbaum, R. and Davis, S. A. (1969). 'Values, man and organizations, *Industrial Management Review*, **10**, 67–86.

Taylor, F. W. (1911). *The Principles of Scientific Management*, Harper and Brothers, New York.

Thomas, K. W. (1976). 'Workers interests and managerial interests—the need for pluralism in organization development', Proceedings of IRRA, 1976.

Thomas, J. and Bennis, W. (1972). *Management of Change and Conflict*, Penguin, London.

Thorsrud, E. (1974). 'Democratization of work and the process of organizational change', paper presented at the Conference on Work Organization, Technical Development and the Individual, Brussels, November 1974.

Thorsrud, E. and Emery, F. E. (1969). *Form and Content in Industrial Democracy*, Tavistock Publications, London.

Thorsrud, E. and Emery, F. E. (1970). 'Industrial democracy in Norway', *Industrial Relations*, **9**, February 1970.

Times (1974). 2 August 1974.

Tolman, E. C. (1932). *Purposive Behaviour in Animals and Men*, Appleton-Century, New York.

Tosi, H. (1970). 'A re-examination of personality as a determinant of the effects of participation', *Personnel Psychology*, **23**, 91–99.

Trist, E. L. (1974). 'Work improvement and industrial democracy', paper presented at the Conference on Work Organization, Brussels, September 1974.

TUC (1973). TUC Industrial Democracy Report to Congress, TUC, London.

TUC (1974). TUC Industrial Democracy Report to Congress, TUC, London.

Ullrich, R. A. (1968). 'A theoretical model of human behaviour in organizations', unpublished paper, London School of Economics and Political Science.

van Gils, M. R. (1973). 'Shop floor participation', paper presented at the IIRA Third World Congress, London.

van Gorkum, P. H., Drenth, P. J. D., de Wolff, Ch. J., Ramondt, J. J., van Gils, M. R. and Jonker, H. W. (1969). 'Industrial democracy in The Netherlands: a seminar', J. A. BoomenZoon, Netherlands.

Vroom, V. (1960). *Some Personality Determinants of the Effects of Participation*, Prentice-Hall, Englewood Cliffs, N.J.

Wall, T. D. and Lischeron, J. A. (1977). *Worker Participation*, McGraw-Hill, London.

Waters, L. K. and Roach, D. (1973). 'A factor analysis of need-fulfilment items designed to measure Maslow need categories', *Personnel Psychology*, **26**, 185–190.

Watson, G. (1966). *Concepts for Social Change*, NTL Institute, Washington, D.C.

Weick, K. (1969). *The Social Psychology of Organizing*, Addison-Wesley, New York.

Weinstein, E. A. and Deutschberger, P. (1963). 'Tasks, bargains and identities in social interaction', *Social Forces*, **42**, 451–456.

Weschler, I. R., Hahane, M., and Tannenbaum, R. (1952). 'Job satisfaction, productivity and morale: a case study', *Occupational Psychology*, **26**, 1–114.

White, J. K. and Ruh, R. A. (1973). 'Effects of personal values on the relationship between participation and job attitudes', *Administrative Science Quarterly*, **18**, 506–514.

Whitehill, A. M. and Takezawa, S. (1968). *The Other Worker: A Comparative Study of Industrial Relations in the US and Japan*, East-West Center Publishing, Honolulu.

Wickert, F. R. (1951). 'Turnover and employees' feelings of ego involvement in the day-to-day operation of a company', *Personnel Psychology*, **4**, 185–197.

Winn, A. (1971). 'Reflexions sur la strategie du T-Group et le role d'agent de changement dans le development organizationnel', *Bulletin de Psychologie*, **25**, 250–256.

Woodward, J. (1965). *Industrial Organization: Theory and Practice*, Oxford University Press, London.

Zand, D. E. (1972). 'Trust and managerial problem solving', *Administrative Science Quarterly*, **17**.

Author Index

Rogaly, J., 217
Rosengren, W. R., 182
Rosenstein, E., 203, 254
Roy, D., 196
Ruh, R. A., 234, 235
Rus, V., 2, 234, 235, 236, 254

Sadler, P. J., 201
SAF, 222, 223, 224
Salaman, G., 175
Scheff, T. J., 180
Schein, E., 6, 28, 242, 258
Schmuck, R. I., 190
Schrank, R., 196
Scontrino, M. P., 234
Sethi, K. C., 223
Shepard, J. M., 257
Shephard, H., 192
Sherwood, J., 74
Shibutani, T., 177
Shister, J., 234
Siegel, A. L., 234
Simmel, G., 3, 237
Skibbins, G. J., 189, 193
Snyder, J. P., 2, 235, 256
Stebbins, R. A., 5, 241
Stelling, J., 177
Strauss, A., 4, 177, 179, 240
Strauss, G., 203, 254

Taddeo, J., 7, 243
Takezawa, S., 254
Tannenbaum, R., 189, 234
Taylor, F. W., 196

Thomas, J., 233
Thomas, K. W., 174, 175, 176
Thorsrud, E., 2, 19, 224, 229, 235
Tolman, E. C., 257
Tosi, H., 2, 235, 256
Trist, E. L., 215, 224
TUC, 211, 213

Van Gils, M. R., 215, 217, 219, 233, 234
Van Gorkum, P. H., 234
Vroom, V., 2, 235, 256

Wall, T., 198, 203, 205, 206
Wall, T. D., 2, 198, 200, 203, 204, 205, 234,
    235, 245, 254, 256
Warr, P. B., 198, 254
Waters, J. K., 234
Watson, G., 191, 192, 193
Watson, J., 6, 242
Weick, K., 4, 240
Weil, R., 10–12, 195
Weinstein, E. A., 68
Weschler, I. R., 234
Westley, B., 6, 242
White, J. K., 2, 235
Whitehill, A. M., 254
Wickert, F. R., 234
Winn, A., 189
Wolff, Ch. J. de, 234
Woodward, J., 2, 235

Yukl, G., 2, 235

Zand, D. E., 245

Subject Index

Action research, 16, 72
Alienation, 5–6, 241
Antagonistic cooperation, 3, 172–176
Anti-concern, 144
Apathy, 95, 119, 200–201, 262

Briefing system, 69, 71–72, 83–84, 115, 268–269
Bullock Report, 14, 48, 51, 169

Collaboration agreement, 223
Confrontation, 154, 169, 176, 194
Consensus, 52, 55, 65, 68, 186, 189, 190
Conservatism, 192–193, 207
Constitution-building, 102–103, 124
Contingency, 2, 6, 8, 14, 69, 116, 170–172, 176, 178, 216–218, 222, 234–236, 262

Deficiency scores, 28–29, 230, 251, 257–259
Definitional initiative, 180
Definitional vacuum, 184, 199
Demonstration effect, 51
Disengagement, 5, 241
Dramaturgy, 177, 181

Energy level, 44, 45, 57, 133
Entropy, 218
Equifinality, 218

Felt need, 7, 47, 66, 71, 72, 220, 243–244, 267
Free and informed choice, 28, 54, 78–79, 116, 260

Homeostasis, 193
'Hygiene' issues, 103, 105, 106, 107, 108–109, 124, 204

Impression management, 177
Integration, 172, 174, 175
Interactionism, 3–6, 176–186, 190, 239–242
Internal change agent, 44, 49, 51, 148

Interpersonal goals, 116
Interventionist
  perceptions of, 155–156, 176
  role, 6, 66, 73–74, 85, 100, 161, 166, 168, 187–188, 208, 228–229, 242, 245
  self interest, 15–16, 28, 208
  values, 9–13, 207–209

Management style, 17, 56, 64, 67, 68, 100, 164
Managerial prerogative, 12, 79–80, 107, 166
Meaning attribution, 28, 36, 52, 68, 89–90, 116, 179–186, 240, 260, 266
'Moaning and groaning' script, 74, 85, 96, 99, 109, 119, 192, 205
Mutual learning, 31, 266

Negotiated order, 4, 5, 65, 69, 173–174, 177–186, 190, 229, 240–241
Neutrality, 28, 30, 73
Normal channels, 92, 104, 106, 192

Open system, 2, 214–219
Openness, 120, 142, 158, 161, 168
Organization Development, 5, 6, 7, 16, 174–176, 189–190
Organizational change
  criteria of successful, 8, 71–74
  evolutionary approaches to, 12–13, 53, 61, 66, 69, 112, 172, 207
  models of planned, 6–8, 13, 28, 31, 52, 187–188, 219–231, 242–245, 267
  nature of, 38, 44, 61, 135
Organizational culture, 14, 19–20, 159, 191, 194, 201, 207
Organizational health, 9–13, 174, 195
Ownership, 28, 74, 75, 135, 258

Participation
  approaches, 2–6, 102
  attitudes, 17, 20–22, 33, 45, 50, 72, 85–91, 94–97, 100–102, 107–108, 116–118,

289